W9-DDL-205

Kishwaukee College Library
21193 Malta Road
Malta, IL 60150-9699

Sister

Sylvia Bell White at the Fond du Lac Avenue Farmers' Market in Milwaukee, June 1999. (photo by Robert LePage)

Sister

*An African American Life
in Search of Justice*

Sylvia Bell White and Jody LePage

The University of Wisconsin Press

Half of the royalties for this book will go to Sylvia.

Jody's half will fund
the Sylvia Bell White Scholarship for African American students
at the University of Wisconsin–Milwaukee.

The University of Wisconsin Press
1930 Monroe Street, 3rd Floor
Madison, Wisconsin 53711-2059
uwpress.wisc.edu

3 Henrietta Street
London WC2E 8LU, England
eurospanbookstore.com

Copyright © 2013
The Board of Regents of the University of Wisconsin System
All rights reserved. No part of this publication may be reproduced, stored in a retrieval system, or transmitted, in any format or by any means, digital, electronic, mechanical, photocopying, recording, or otherwise, or conveyed via the Internet or a website without written permission of the University of Wisconsin Press, except in the case of brief quotations embedded in critical articles and reviews.

Printed in the United States of America

Library of Congress Cataloging-in-Publication Data
White, Sylvia Bell, 1930–
Sister: an African American life in search of justice /
Sylvia Bell White and Jody LePage.
        p.   cm.—(Wisconsin studies in autobiography)
Includes bibliographical references and index.
ISBN 978-0-299-29434-2 (cloth: alk. paper)
ISBN 978-0-299-29433-5 (e-book)
1. White, Sylvia Bell, 1930–
2. African American women—Wisconsin—Milwaukee—Biography.
3. Milwaukee (Wis.)—Biography.
4. Milwaukee (Wis.)—Race relations—History—20th century.
I. LePage, Jody.   II. Title.   III. Series: Wisconsin studies in autobiography.
F589.M653W47 2012
977.5'043092—dc23
[B]
2012032691

Contents

Contents

Acknowledgments

Sylvia and I would like to thank everyone who has contributed to bringing this project to fruition, including many more individuals than we can mention here. First and foremost, we are grateful to our acquisitions editor at the University of Wisconsin Press, Gwen Walker. From the start, Gwen recognized the quality and importance of Sylvia's narrative. She has guided us with thoughtful insight through the publication process.

We also wish to express our appreciation to individuals whose lives touched Sylvia's and whose later interviews enhanced the framing of her narrative. Walt Kelly and Curry First top Sylvia's list here, for their work with the Bell family in the 1980s civil rights lawsuit and for the time they generously shared with me later. Another important landmark on the way to this autobiography was the 1987 Milwaukee Repertory Theater production about the Daniel Bell case. We would like to thank John Dillon, the director of *An American Journey*, as well as playwrights Kermit Frazier and John Leicht, for recalling Sylvia's presence and consulting role in the creation of that play. Many thanks also to Reuben Harpole, affectionately known as Milwaukee's "unofficial mayor," for sharing memories of the black community that Sylvia joined in the late 1940s.

We owe a debt of gratitude to the scholars whose research, thought, and writing in the field of African American studies provided the basis for contextualizing Sylvia's story. A few have touched our work directly. Before her passing, Nellie Y. McKay made time repeatedly to talk with me about the project and to nurture perseverance. Patrick D. Jones, whose feedback on our 2002 edition helped orient me to a new field, has remained a friend to the project. More recently, William P. Jones contributed significantly with suggestions as a reviewer for UW Press. William L. Andrews grounded the final revision process with his unequivocal approbation.

I must also acknowledge the ever present influence of my graduate advisors: Martine D. Meyer at the University of Wisconsin–Milwaukee, as well as Suzanne M. Desan and the late Edward T. Gargan at the University of Wisconsin–Madison.

Many individuals and institutions have assisted with practical matters. We received gracious help from librarians and archivists at the Milwaukee Public Library, the Milwaukee County Historical Society, the University of Wisconsin–Milwaukee Archives / Milwaukee Area Research Center, the Wisconsin Historical Society Library and Archives. Gina Barton, Alan King, Michael Sears, and Elizabeth Brenner at the *Milwaukee Journal Sentinel* all had a hand in finding and providing photos from the newspaper archives.

Thanks also to everyone at my workplace who has helped and supported this effort over the years.

Of course, we wish to express gratitude to family members and friends. With her parents and her brothers now many years gone, Sylvia's first thought went to "my Douglas," her son, Douglas Lamont Bell. Sylvia and I both thank her niece, Lorraine Bell Botelho, for her efforts to find and hand-deliver family photos. Heartfelt thanks to Lisa Goodrich and all those whose care has made a real home for Sylvia at Highland House in Watertown.

My personal acknowledgments must begin with dear friends. A vital presence in my life since we met as graduate students in the History Department at University of Wisconsin–Madison, Franca Barricelli helped sustain me with her certainty that the project would one day materialize in print. A distinguished professor and literary scholar, friend, and intellectual mentor, Martine Meyer enthusiastically read and critiqued version after version of the manuscript. Our friendship has intersected with this project in multiple, sometimes inexplicable, ways. It was in Martine's kitchen that I happened to see my friend Sylvia on TV and learn that she was Daniel Bell's sister. A regular shopper at Milwaukee's Fond du Lac Avenue Farmers' Market, Martine had invited me along the day that Sylvia asked me to help write her life story.

I want to thank everyone in my family who encouraged this effort over the years, particularly my sister, Mary Pat Muirhead, for her wholehearted support and critical reading.

Finally, my partner Robert LePage has contributed immeasurably. This project has exemplified the shared intellectual life and mutual support that gives our marriage its amazing depth. Bob has helped in so many ways, from the meals he prepared for us the day that Sylvia and I began taping her story, to his skill at negotiating a fourteen-year succession of word-processing programs. He spent days with me going through boxes of court records from the Bell family's civil rights lawsuit at the federal courthouse in Milwaukee; worked with me in libraries and archives; sat in on interviews. No one has read the product of these labors more times, nor offered so many useful insights. I can never thank Bob enough.

Sister

Introduction

That evening of February 2, 1958, Sylvia Bell White and her friend Stella were driving down Center Street in Milwaukee. The two women, then in their twenties, had gone to pick up the cake pans, punch bowl, and cups that Sylvia had left at her younger brother Dan's birthday party the night before. Now they were hurrying back to Sylvia's house, so that she could get ready for her night shift at a nursing home. As they crossed Sixth Street, flashing police lights caught Sylvia's eye. "That looks like Dan's car down there," she remarked without stopping.

Further down Sixth Street, Daniel Bell lay dead in the snow, shot by the police during a traffic stop. Unable to justify the killing, the shooter planted a knife on Dan's body. He and the officer with him devised a cover-up story. Without notifying the family, the police department gave the officers' account to the media.

"Mama, they killed Dan!" Sylvia was getting dressed for work, when her son cried out the news. Stunned, she struggled to make sense of the television newscast. One detail rang false. The police said that Dan had jumped out of the car with an open knife in his right hand. Anyone close to Dan knew that he was left-handed. When she and her brothers, Lawrence and Patrick, raised the issue at the police station that night, they received only racial insults in response. Twelve days later, on Valentine's Day, an all-white inquest jury declared the killing "justifiable homicide."

Sylvia lost more than a brother to this incident, because she had always been more than a sister. More than that fun-loving little girl who braved playing in the Louisiana swamps with the boys. More than the beautiful young woman the Bell brothers could be proud to dance with at nightclubs; the cool jazz/blues enthusiast who married Milwaukee's first black deejay,

3

O.C. White. The only girl of thirteen children, Sylvia had shouldered responsibility at an early age for mothering her siblings. Later, when younger ones came North, she and the older brothers acted as parents. Now the shooting of Daniel would destroy two additional lives. When Jimmy and Ernest, the two closest to Dan, went to identify his body, the trauma did irreparable psychological damage to both.

A wrongful death lawsuit filed in 1960 only brought the Bells greater sorrow. Their father collapsed in court and never regained his health. He died a broken man, crushed by what seemed a cruel irony. He had raised his thirteen children in a Deep South state notorious for violent racism. Yet Dan had been killed up North—where this father had sent his children as if to the Promised Land. Dock Bell lived his last years in inconsolable grief. Just before dying, he predicted that what had really happened that night would one day come to light. Remarkably, it did.

∞

Twenty years after the death of Daniel Bell, one of the officers involved, Louis Krause, decided to reveal how the killing had occurred. Hearing Krause's narrative, Milwaukee District Attorney E. Michael McCann and Assistant DA Thomas P. Schneider decided not to reopen the case unless they could get the shooter, Thomas Grady, to confirm the allegations. Krause had credibility problems. When the story broke a year later, the *Milwaukee Sentinel* headlined his ten convictions for offenses such as check fraud in an article that cast him as an opportunistic alcoholic.[1] By then, however, the DA had wiretap tapes of Grady confirming much of Krause's account.

Further corroboration came from an unimpeachable witness, former Milwaukee Police Detective Russell Vorpagel. Vorpagel had always felt that "justice had not been done" in the Daniel Bell case. Disturbed about his own involvement, he had consulted his pastor in 1958, requested a transfer, and then left Milwaukee for a career with the FBI. When the Bell case reopened, he revealed aspects of the cover-up that Krause and Grady were still trying to hide. Grady said on the tapped phone that telling the truth would cause "problems for everybody way down the line . . . hundreds, hundreds of people that'd be in the soup." In court, he claimed that this referred only to family and friends. Krause gave contradictory testimony about his superiors' involvement. Vorpagel implicated three higher-ranking detectives, the former chief of police, and district attorney. Equally important, his testimony helped expose an underlying culture of racism.[2]

Daniel Bell's family had mixed emotions about the reopened case. A *Milwaukee Sentinel* article entitled "Confession Ends Family's 21 Years of Pain"

4

made clear that no such closure had occurred. Patrick Bell told the interviewer that some brothers would not even want to hear this news, since "they wanted to get as far away from the memory of the incident as possible." Lawrence spoke of a family formerly "always together on things," until the pain of Dan's death "tore us apart."[3] Sylvia angrily recalled the courtroom bullying of her late father. By the time Grady confessed, Jimmy Bell had spent twenty years institutionalized for mental illness too severe to permit any statement. Ernest lived in and out of institutions. His 1980 deposition alternated between moments of lucidity and fantastic ramblings about the killing. Other siblings struggled with depression and nightmares. The toll already taken tempered their expectations, as they filed a civil rights lawsuit. During the family's depositions, Patrick was asked whether he would feel any better if he learned that the killing was accidental. "I never feel right about that, about the killing of my brother," he declared. "Never."[4] Rough handling of the unhealed wounds came with this new possibility of vindication.

The courtroom/media battle did not end, even after a jury agreed in December 1981 that a racially motivated conspiracy had violated the civil rights of Daniel Bell and his family. Unwilling to pay the $1,795,000 awarded, city officials appealed and repeatedly refused the family's offers to settle for smaller sums. In an editorial for the *Milwaukee Journal*, City Attorney James Brennan accused the Bells of treating Daniel's death as "a legal gold mine to be exploited for maximum profit."[5] Few heard the deposition where Lawrence Bell answered such questioning of the family's motivation. "We want justice when we come in here," he said. "Understand? If you're wrong, you're wrong. If you're right, you're right. It's no more than anybody else wants."[6]

Cutting remarks proliferated, as local politicians used public discussion of the case to score points with constituents. Sylvia and her brothers felt particularly stung to hear their family stereotyped as welfare-dependent in the media buzz following the county's demand of reimbursement from any eventual settlement. Other than what the county paid for the institutionalization of Jimmy and Ernest, the Bells had made limited use of welfare. They persevered through hurtful experiences of racial discrimination, found jobs and stayed working. Eddie had put in twenty-five years at American Motors; Patrick thirty-one years and Lawrence twenty years at A. O. Smith. "My brothers and I have worked," said Sylvia in tears to a county board meeting, "We have paid taxes."[7] After nearly three years, the city finally made serious settlement offers—but only in the last hours before the federal appeals court ruled. Now the Bell family, with Sylvia in the lead, chose to await the verdict.

In September 1984, the U.S. Court of Appeals in Chicago ruled largely in their favor. The award of $1.6 million was twice the amount the Bells had offered to settle for earlier. Approximately $1 million remained after attorneys' fees. Milwaukee County received more than $70,000 in reimbursement. The rest did not go far when divided by twelve. Sylvia used most of her portion to restore the family homestead in Louisiana. To her, the real compensation lay in winning a measure of justice.

The Daniel Bell case matters to history because it exposes abuses that African Americans have all too commonly endured in a society that proclaims its commitments to equality before the law. What happened to Dan and his family exemplifies the experiences behind divergent black/white views of race and policing. Rarely does police testimony so clearly show that minority communities have reasons to mistrust the law enforcement system. In Milwaukee, the Daniel Bell case re-enters public discussion with each new questionable incident. Historically, the case also holds interest because the unusually long period between Dan's death and the final disposition falls across key decades of civil rights activism and changing attitudes. The years since have shown the rarity—and thus heightened the importance in the history of civil rights law—of the Bells' legal victory. In another frame of reference, the Daniel Bell case has significance because Sylvia's involvement stimulated her desire to tell the kind of life story that history seldom has occasion to record. From outside the privileged sectors of society comes a woman's story. An African American story. Or, as Sylvia would prefer, a "plain American" story.

᷍

"What so proudly we hail," answered Sylvia, when I wished her an especially happy Fourth of July 2009. I had phoned thinking about the first African American president of the United States. Her response seemed to sweep past that historical moment to a larger picture: of a nation whose words promising freedom, equal justice, and brotherhood many African Americans have made deeply their own, despite a history that has often contradicted those ideals. Sylvia's poetic leap to the national anthem "came straight from the heart," she told me later. Of course, she intended specifically to hail the presidency of Barack Obama. The morning after the election, she told me she had stayed up all night watching TV, "trying to take it in"—and keenly aware that the history she had lived through had everything to do with the emotion she felt.

Sylvia's autobiography does indeed wind through much history. She mentions grandparents born in slavery and lore about black Southerners voting during Reconstruction. She details what the New Deal meant to her family, her brothers' experiences as black soldiers in World War II, her own participation in the massive African American migration from the South. She talks about the Civil Rights Movement and the frustrated attempts to protest the Daniel Bell killing that ultimately helped spur civil rights activism in Milwaukee. In the early 1960s, Sylvia left the city for the nearby countryside, an unusual step for twentieth-century African Americans in the North. She bought land and worked out relationships in an all-white farm community where many inhabitants had never had contact with black people. She moved to Los Angeles for five years beginning in 1968, a high point in the youth countercultural movement of the Sixties and, more important for Sylvia, the popularization of Black Power culture. Returning to rural Wisconsin, she found signs there, too, of the "different world" that would frame the reopening of her brother's case. Sylvia harbors no illusions, however, about the persistence of racism. Entering the twenty-first century with incisive observations about the harm done by decades of backlash, she lived to witness the historic 2008 election and the unprecedented incivility in opposition to the first African American president. Her story says all the more about how far we have come—and still have to go—as a nation, because it connects with our history in a wide geographical sweep.

The first half of Sylvia's narrative takes place near Springfield, Louisiana, forty miles north of New Orleans, in a long-established African American community called Haynes Settlement. These chapters develop a vivid sense of place. Sylvia's words transport the reader to the dreaded yet beloved swamps where she and her twelve brothers played, the strawberry fields they worked, the house her father built. She shows us a nurturing space that family and community created for children, despite the economic deprivation and cruel racial traditions that necessarily touched their lives. At the center of this picture stands a powerful father. The chapter about him opens with the kind of Louisiana tropical storm that once "blew away" the nearby church. In a house battered by rain and wind, a man with arms outstretched stands praying aloud over the children assembled at his feet. The father who shaped Sylvia's childhood remains a presence throughout her life. She proudly tells how the community honored his work and integrity by naming a road for him. Dock Bell left his children a rich legacy of values and showed them how an African American could maintain dignity in the 1930s and '40s South.

Until age seventeen, Sylvia knew no other world than this region where officials brazenly maintained racial disparity in services such as public schooling; where electoral systems kept blacks from voting; where laws segregated public and private spaces. These official forms of discrimination encouraged an undisguised regional version of the racism that African

Americans faced nationwide. Louisiana resembled the rest of the South in much of this, yet maintained its distinctive character.

During slavery, African captives in North America feared sale to Louisiana more than anywhere else. The swampy land around New Orleans proved exceptionally lethal for both slaves and slaveholders. Poisonous snakes, alligators, malaria-bearing mosquitoes, and waterborne micro-organisms accompanied the area's intense heat, high humidity, hurricanes, and tropical storms. Sugar production—a Louisiana particularity—added to higher slave mortality rates. After the 1793 invention of the cotton gin, cotton growers settled the Deep South, bringing more than a million slaves—most of them forced to journey from East Coast states on foot. These newcomers to Louisiana joined an unusual population. On the one hand, New Orleans slave-importing brought in many first-generation Africans. On the other, the area's early French and Spanish settlers married and freed slaves more readily than whites along the East Coast. A relatively large number of African Americans lived free in Louisiana during slavery, some wealthy and highly educated. After emancipation, however, white reaction placed the state among the worst for deadly violence against people of African descent.[8]

Sylvia's birth in 1930 coincided with the beginning of the Great Depression, when racial violence had decreased some and making a living demanded more attention than anything else. Planters still grew sugar cane just south and west of her home. Cotton dominated the northern part of the state, reaching southwards near Springfield. In rural Louisiana, most African Americans worked as sharecroppers or agricultural wage workers. Earning next to nothing, they commonly fell ever deeper into debt. During the Depression, many could find no work. At a time when land ownership was relatively rare among Southern blacks, Sylvia's father cultivated his own five-acre plot. He and other local truck farmers grew vegetables for market, but specialized in strawberries. In the late 1860s, the Illinois Central Railroad had initiated strawberry growing in the area by distributing plants. By 1900, the "Strawberry Express" was carrying trainloads of berries to Chicago. Dock Bell began berry growing as he cleared his land in the 1920s. He bought the farm—and continued supplementing his income—through a job at one of Louisiana's many small sawmills. After logging the land, the sawmill owner had sold parcels of it to her workers because, Sylvia explains, "she wanted to keep 'em there."

More than a million African Americans left the South in the Great Migration that began in 1914 and lasted until the Depression. Later, as lumbering declined and agriculture mechanized, African Americans in the rural South saw their jobs disappear. Many followed the lead of an earlier generation. In

1947, Sylvia joined a second wave of migration that would include some five million people by 1970. Like other migrants, Sylvia had noticed the dignified demeanor of visiting relatives from up North. She imagined the North as a place where black people found the equal opportunity promised by America, but denied them in the South. In Sylvia's narrative, a teenager's idealized expectations and indignant response to the disappointments bring migrant experiences into sharp focus. Her daring constantly tested the limits imposed by Northern racism.

Sylvia migrated to Milwaukee, then a city of about 620,000 people, located ninety miles north of Chicago on Lake Michigan.[9] Lake breezes chilled her June arrival. In January that year, sixty-mile-an-hour winds had turned eighteen inches of snow into drifts that reached first-floor eaves. Wisconsin's cold contrasted strikingly with Louisiana's sub-tropical weather. Yet Sylvia found the city's racial climate far more shocking. On her first day there, she learned that the bread-baking factory across the street hired only whites. The news left Sylvia "almost ready to 'bout face and go back." Instead, she applied for a job at the bakery and received one of many racially motivated refusals. Taking what work she could get, Sylvia would continue seeking, but never obtain, that good Milwaukee factory job.

Many black Southerners came to Milwaukee in these years expecting to find work. Among the most industrialized cities in the nation, Milwaukee employed about 56 percent of its workforce in manufacturing in the late 1940s and early '50s. The city's well-known brewers, tanners, and meat-packers remained significant employers, although no longer as important to the local economy as industries manufacturing metal goods, precision instruments, machinery, and heavy equipment such as cranes. Birthplace of Harley-Davidson, Milwaukee also produced automobiles. Companies there had begun hiring blacks during World War II, pressed by a labor shortage and government oversight of defense industries. When large numbers of workers returned after the war, many employers resumed their prewar practice of hiring only whites.

In Milwaukee, as in other Northern cities, undercurrents of racism surfaced as the African American population increased. Growing from 7,501 in 1930 to 12,400 when Sylvia arrived in 1947, the number of blacks in the city reached 63,458 by 1960. Between 1940 and 1970, the African American portion of the population went from 1.5 percent to 14.7 percent. Residential segregation increased. Divisions intensified within the city's black community. Long-established black Milwaukeeans felt their situation worsening as whites reacted to the influx.

Earlier waves of immigration had given Milwaukee its size and character. In the nineteenth century, Germans came to dominate the ethnic mix that also included large Polish, Irish, and Italian sectors and smaller numbers from the Balkans and Eastern Europe. The percentage of immigrants and their children peaked at 86.4 percent in 1890 and remained among the nation's highest for decades. As elsewhere, different nationalities formed enclaves and developed rivalries. Milwaukee had less turf violence among ethnic youth gangs, however, than large cities such as nearby Chicago. The city took pride in its lower crime rates, cleanliness, and work ethic. A conservative culture respected authority, enforced rules, and curbed individual behavior. Yet Milwaukee also had a fun-loving side. When Prohibition ended in 1933, some twenty thousand citizens attended a gigantic beer party that the city had sponsored—but postponed for eleven days until Lent ended. Bound up with ethnicity, religion pervaded everyday life in this predominantly Catholic city.

Milwaukee history features a striking combination of cultural conservatism and leftist politics. The city's voters kept a Socialist mayor, Daniel Hoan, in office from 1916 until 1940—twenty years after the collapse of the Socialist Party nationwide. Although Hoan made speeches comparing profiteers to democracy-hating kings, he also improved municipal services with a conservative thrift that impressed non-socialists. In 1936, *Time* magazine put Hoan's picture on the cover and praised him for running "perhaps the best-governed city in the U.S." Later, as Cold War rhetoric prevailed elsewhere, Milwaukee put socialist Frank Zeidler in the mayor's office in 1948 and reelected him until he quit running in 1960. Before the 1956 election, his opponent instigated a rumor campaign saying Zeidler so favored blacks that he had billboards down South inviting them to Milwaukee.[10] Although Zeidler did show some concern for this growing part of the city's population, and conservatives cast the left as giving preferential treatment to blacks, socialism certainly did not translate into any less racial prejudice and discrimination in Milwaukee than black people faced in other Northern cities.

Media-highlighted moments reveal a contradictory mix of racial attitudes during Sylvia's Milwaukee years. In 1949, when a black World War II veteran moved his family into a county-operated trailer park, a white mob forced them to leave. Immediately, leaders of the city's Urban League and NAACP chapters, the mayor's Human Rights Commission, and local newspapers mobilized support for the black family's rights. Squeezing an apology from mob ringleaders, Milwaukee congratulated itself. A few years later, however, well-meaning liberal members of a mayoral commission blamed inner-city poverty and substandard housing not on job and housing discrimination or slumlords, but on black residents described with racist stereotypes. This report differed little from one issued under Zeidler's more conservative successor, Henry Maier, whose commission on race asserted in 1963 that black migrants "lack a sense of family intimacy and interdependence."[11] By then, Sylvia wished that she and her family had stayed in the segregated South.

Sylvia's account of her life has historical importance beyond its intersection with events in national and local history. She speaks from a social position shared by most African Americans of her generation, but one underrepresented in the historical record. Her autobiography complements the fine array of Civil Rights leaders' memoirs, for example, with the perspective of those African Americans who watched the movement on television, heard about it on the radio and by word of mouth. Born outside the small circle of the black middle class, Sylvia did not receive the education usually prerequisite to having one's say. On one level, she recounts experiences shared by the multitude of African Americans eking out a living by menial labor. Yet what she has to say takes unpredictable, non-representative turns. A woman, she has a relationship to gender shaped by growing up with twelve brothers. Raised a Southern Baptist, she emerged deeply religious, but in an unconventional way. Her views, her moves, and the unfolding of her life make an improvisational jazz on the theme of human possibilities.

Sylvia's story exemplifies the complexities of an issue that arose when history turned its attention to oppressed groups. Debate has raged over where to focus. Do we risk downplaying the harm of oppression if we also celebrate what oppressed people have managed to do with their situation? Sylvia stands among those indomitable individuals who press the limits and make everything they can of their lives, no matter what. Despite the deprivations of a black childhood in the rural South and rampant discrimination in the North, she found jobs and eventually owned property, obtained a GED, played a key role in seeking justice for the killing of her brother, and influenced the Milwaukee Repertory Theater to address larger issues of racial injustice in its play about the Daniel Bell case. Honored in her rural home community, she also had a large and enthusiastic following at Milwaukee's Fond du Lac Avenue Farmers' Market where, until 2004, she sold produce. Or, as one observer put it, she "held court." People gathered around her vegetable stand for the pleasure of a moment's conversation. Finally, she succeeded in getting her story told and taped years before feeling the symptoms of Alzheimer's disease. Yet Sylvia remains painfully aware that racial injustice prevented her from realizing her dreams of getting a good education, becoming a nurse—or even getting a job that would have allowed her to retire. "What happens to a dream deferred?" asked Langston Hughes in one of his most famous poems.[12] Sylvia's story answers with both clarity and nuance.

∞

When Sylvia and I met in 1973, we were both selling vegetables at the farmers' market in Madison, Wisconsin. She had just returned from her sojourn in California and looked the very image of "Black Is Beautiful." Her large Afro harmonized with a face deep in color and glowing from within. I had never met a person so quick to love. Or so easy to love back—for her energy, her intelligence, and the inexhaustible wellspring of fun that accompanies her quest for racial justice. We talked earnestly about changing the world. We joked about boyfriends and such. Sylvia's sparkling youthfulness dissolved the eighteen-year age difference between us. I imagined that she, too, was in her twenties. What pleasure conversing with this witty, hip, joyous woman! Never would I have guessed what she suffered. I hadn't heard of the Daniel Bell case and would not connect her with it when I did. I knew her by her married name, Sylvia White. She said nothing to me about Daniel in those first years. "Trying to forget," she later explained.

By 1987, Sylvia's desire to remember and speak had rekindled. That summer, she asked me to help write her story. We agreed to start when I finished school, neither of us imagining how long that would take.

As we began making tapes in 1998, we had multiple reasons for envisioning a nonscholarly book. Sylvia wanted to reach readers who had not gone to college—thinking particularly of her nieces and nephews then in their teens. I had university students very much in mind. That impatient intelligence ever ready to click away or read past. The bravado to declare history "a bunch of lies"—fair warning to historians against telling the stories without mentioning the debates. I certainly did not imagine entering into those debates among experts in African American studies. My area of specialization was in European history. The question of objectivity hovered as well, although academic discipline also discourages claims of neutrality. Required to consider differing views, we speak from our positions—and produce more reliable work when we make clear where we stand. I have loved Sylvia for years and stand with her among all who seek to eradicate racism. In that respect, we do not differ from most scholars in this field.[13]

Our work did seem to overstep academic bounds in other ways, however. Contrary to guidelines, I did not insist on controlling the length of taping sessions. Nor did the quality of Sylvia's narration diminish, even when she kept us going for five hours on the first day. Every session, we interrupted taping with off-the-record remarks and playful gab. Perhaps this helped Sylvia speak more freely than she would have in an impersonal setting. Yet experts could argue that such procedures create as many problems as they solve. Our relationship bridges racial and social differences that some oral historians see as insurmountable obstacles.[14] I had second thoughts myself. Three weeks into the project, I told Sylvia I thought a black person should really do this work for her. "Yeah," she answered, "but who?"

Increasingly popular in the early 1980s, oral history faced questions about reliability. How could we believe the stories captured by tape recorders? Defenders countered by noting the bias and inaccuracy in standard historical evidence such as newspapers, letters, or written memoirs.[15] Indeed, under relentless scrutiny in the last decades of the twentieth century, no sources proved able to offer more than versions of what happened. Where possible, historians corroborate—comparing Sylvia's words to court records, for example. Yet such strategies cannot provide access to an actual past. Written or oral, memoirs have the added problem of depending on long-term memory, a notorious function not even reliably unreliable.[16] That Sylvia developed Alzheimer's disease raises the issue of pathological conditions entailing memory loss. "Normal" memory, too, gives plenty of reasons for doubt. Historians took note decades ago of findings in neurophysiology and psychology that memory works not by storing and retrieving remembered material, but rather by constructing memories—and updating them to fit the rememberer's present views. Individuals "reshape, omit, distort, combine and reorganize details from the past," in a memory construction process that resembles historians' work with documents.[17] Standing on ground this shaky, many historians have abandoned traditional claims of factuality and turned to complementing standard methods with greater transparency about viewpoints, procedures, and debates.[18] Meanwhile, interest in a wider world has reshaped history departments and heightened appreciation of oral testimony.

Vital to documenting the point of view of oppressed groups, oral history has helped restore credibility to a field of study long distorted by one-sidedness. Before scholarly questioning of Western Civilization went deep, majorities of people worldwide knew an untold other side to stories of Enlightenment, democratization, and humane values.[19] For African Americans, the other side held horrors glossed over in most histories of slavery and Reconstruction until the mid-1950s. Once resolved to draw forth these neglected viewpoints, historians grappled with problematic documentation. For example, whites gathered most North American slave testimony—and under questionable circumstances.[20] Better-documented periods present problems such as a "culture of dissemblance" among early-twentieth-century black women, who responded to racist oppression by choosing not to speak about important gender issues.[21] Although oral history permits us to hear from people who cannot or would not write their stories, practitioners have recognized that interviewing/taping procedures can reproduce unequal power relationships.[22] We must qualify any claims, then, of hearing the oppressed speak "freely."

Complicating the picture here, Sylvia initiated and drove this project. She sat down at the tape recorder with a story she had been preparing to tell for years, a narrative partly shaped by courtroom experiences. Of course, the telling affected what she had to say. Yet Sylvia remained firmly at the wheel, even as my questioning expanded her initial story. She also participated to an unusual extent in the work that followed taping. In addition to reading version after version, she contributed perspectives throughout the initial research phase. Enthusiastic about framing her chapters with historical information, she regularly made the fifty-mile round trip to meet and discuss what I was reading.

During such untaped sessions, I noted remarks of particular interest and added them to the text. It didn't work well to ask Sylvia to retell something. Using these notes and ten tapes made over three years, I cut and reorganized the narrative—guided by her comments and my commitment to the integrity of her words.

Her own words. That imperative seemed less complicated before I began transcribing the tapes. At the time, Sylvia was reading Ernest Gaines's *A Gathering of Old Men* and Zora Neale Hurston's *Their Eyes Were Watching God*. Since she found it difficult to read phonetic renditions of dialogue, I tried removing nonstandard spellings—such as the initial *th-* that Sylvia pronounces *d-* about half the time. The text retained the cadence of her speech. Later, a more difficult issue arose. Denied a basic education in childhood, Sylvia has strong feelings about how this injustice affects her words—no matter how articulate she seems to others. When we first met, I took for granted that she spoke Black English and easily imagined that she, like me, had a year or so of college. In fact, Sylvia has taken adult education courses since her teens. She corrected grammar here and there in the transcribed text. When she wanted me to "correct" her narrative further, however, I balked. Arguments for an "authentic" voice did not impress Sylvia. I had already cut and rearranged her words—and elicited whole chapters by questioning her on topics she had not emphasized or mentioned. We moved beyond this impasse only after several memorable discussions.

"Grasp," Sylvia suggested. I had stopped midsentence, looking for a better word than "register" to describe how we can't see—can't "grasp" what we're seeing—without using language. Sylvia had jumped ahead, already responding to my point that language affects not only how we communicate, but also how we perceive and think. Now her facial expression said, "Okay. But so what?"

Why would this matter here? To start, because European languages such as English carry racist threads that reach back hundreds of years. You grow up using a language saturated with fear and hatred of the "other"—even if you yourself are targeted. Maybe you throw out the most blatantly offensive words and expressions. But what about less obvious words and grammar rules that hold your mind in certain patterns: subject/object, superior/inferior, superordinate/subordinate? Underlying messages in language can easily go unrecognized and warp our thinking in ways we might not choose. Language thus plays a part in that stubbornly persistent racism that Martin Luther King called "unconscious." We have largely moved beyond the overt racial hatred that plagued Sylvia's youth. Yet unacknowledged negativity pulls us backwards—away from racial justice—despite changes hard won in the Civil Rights era. The more we underestimate language, the more it powers that retrograde drag.

At the same time, language can work—and has potential—as a progressive force. Despite the unconscious effects language has on us, we can and do change it. We're constantly inventing, adopting or dropping expressions, bending and altering rules. Equally important, factors such as social inequalities and differing histories put people in varying relationships with language. The dominant culture's words and rules occupy our minds differently. And these differences can throw open alternative possibilities.

One morning as Sylvia and I sat in a library meeting room working on the book, I learned that my mother had just passed away. Struggling with this news, I saw in Sylvia's eyes something greater than I could grasp. Something that seemed to reach beyond time and space. I had a word for it. Love. One of those words that academic discipline would ask you to define. Define the word with words defined by other words—in that endless go-round of words and meanings that have no necessary link with anything outside language. Such as the look in Sylvia's eyes. Feeling that Sylvia would better comprehend such a look, I realized more poignantly than ever why I have always considered her a teacher as well as a friend.

∽

In August 1998, Sylvia and I flew to New Orleans, then drove to her Springfield home. We crossed what she called "the longest bridge"—over a flat, yellow-green expanse with a scattering of dead-looking trees. Briefly, Lake Pontchartrain stretched into the distance. Then came forests of tall pines and hardwoods with Spanish moss hanging ghostly grey. We stepped out of the car at cousin

Ben Tillman's. As we walked past his blooming roses, an overcast sky gave the August heat a surprisingly gentle presence.

On Ben's carefully painted porch, he and Sylvia caught up on family news. She fanned herself with a pale blue Chinese paper fan, looking momentarily— and to me quite surprisingly—ladylike. I realized I had never seen her in a skirt before. Ben Tillman, a deacon at Galilee Baptist, gave us a tour of the church. Everything was new, except the pastors' portraits, the cornerstones, and the giant oak still standing out front.

Later, we turned onto the road named for Dock Bell. At first, Sylvia drove past "Papa's house," now half-burned and boarded up. She had not yet seen it like this, had not come here for years. "Gave up," she said, "after the fire." Further up Bell Road, we stopped and borrowed a hoe from brother Henry Bell's widow, Pulu. Back at Papa's house, Sylvia hitched up her skirt and strode into the tall grass, hoe ready for snakes. Examining the house, I could see hints of the remodeling she had done. Here, a glass oval showing above a door's protective plywood; there, a shattered glass sliding door. Sylvia declared that she would never repair the place again.

We drove past the swampy woods where Sylvia and her brothers used to play. Cypress stumps stood in water the color of a new cast-iron skillet. Sylvia pointed out the juke joint where she danced as a teenager, a tiny building now almost completely hidden by bushes and trees. In Springfield, we saw the old store where her family used to buy supplies, one of the few places they were allowed to enter. Further down the road was a school—for both black and white children now, Sylvia noted.

That night, we ate sweet potatoes, hush puppies, and Gulf shrimp at a restaurant in Hammond, where whites and blacks seemed to enjoy each other's company and the white owner stopped at our table for a cordial chat. The next day, at a sandwich place in Albany, we saw hostility in other customers' faces: an older man in the back of the room; young men at the next table. We turned away from them, but met the same look everywhere in the room. Hatred. After lunch, Sylvia said she was glad I had seen that, too. Her sister-in-law, Betty, did not find the Albany experience surprising. "Things change very slowly down here," she observed.

We encountered four generations of Sylvia's kin: from her mother's last living sister to grandnieces and grandnephews. A distant cousin working in the Livingston Parish Clerk of Court's office helped us locate documents. A childhood friend jumped in his car and hurried to see Sylvia. Her nieces and nephews made no secret of their admiration. "Aunt Sylvia is powerful," Sadie declared, "so powerful!"

1

I Thought I Was a Nigger

Growing up in a world profoundly marked by a past of slavery, Sylvia felt effects of that history with little chance to learn about it. Public schools would not generally teach African American history until after the Black Power movement of the 1960s. In the 1930s and '40s where Sylvia lived as a child, the public school system provided a school for whites only, none for blacks. Even if she had not been excluded from schools and libraries, however, young Sylvia would not have had access to accurate information about slavery. Until the mid-1950s, most historians relied on slaveholders' records, dismissed slave testimony as biased, and portrayed slavery as a benevolent institution.[1]

By the end of the twentieth century, studies had exposed the horrific Transatlantic passage; the whippings, mutilations, and rapes; the overwork and inhumane conditions; the millions killed. In a sense, historians cannot overemphasize the brutality of slavery. Yet some of those studies seemed to cast the enslaved as objects acted upon by others, rather than willful, intelligent human beings. Other historians have avoided this problem by focusing on revolts, escape networks, or communities of runaways—or by examining indirect resistance. Slaves countered a system that callously sold away members of their families, for example, by cherishing family ideals and developing strategies to maintain relationships. Some learned to read despite the threat of harsh punishment. Many flouted slave code by raising or making products that they marketed for cash, with or without planters' permission. In Louisiana, slaves gathered moss from trees, baled it, and hauled it to river ports for sale as furniture stuffing.[2] Slaves made what they could of their situation. Focusing there, however, risks downplaying the harm done the enslaved and their descendants.[3] Most important for Sylvia, slavery shaped the racism that

17

has systematically denied African Americans opportunities to prosper and live in peace.

Historians generally agree that trading in African slaves worsened whites' attitudes toward blacks. Some cite striking expressions of earlier positive views. In Ancient Greece, for example, Homer and other writers praised black African cultures and attributed Egyptian civilization to the black pyramid builders of Kush.[4] Early European culture did carry threads of racial prejudice, but certainly did not need racism to make cruelty thinkable. When the African slave trade began, Europeans had stopped forcing each other into slavery, but still maintained class hierarchies that left enormous majorities scarcely able to survive and subjected them to abuse by tiny minorities. Kings and emperors devastated each other's lands in almost constant wars. Religious authorities burned people alive for holding the "wrong" beliefs. At first, then, enslaving Africans fit unexceptionally into a larger pattern of brutality. The elaborated racism Sylvia would later face emerged only with increased pressure to defend slavery.

During the eighteenth century, new thinking about reason, human rights, and humane conduct swept Europe and made slavery more problematic.[5] Across the Atlantic, the United States based its new Constitution on Enlightenment ideals and debated slavery, but ultimately protected it. The slave trade boomed, even as Enlightenment thought strengthened antislavery sentiment. In 1788, London abolitionists produced the well-known drawing of 451 captives packed onto the ship *Brookes*, as Parliament considered limiting ships that size to no more than 454.[6] Yet most abolitionists shared the racial prejudice deepening in the world around them. Race was playing a part in the broad shift away from maintaining social hierarchy by sheer force, as Europe recognized that self-policing by the lower classes worked more efficiently. This modernizing social control operated through cultural means that ranged from childrearing to new institutions such as prisons and schools—to cajoling whites with discourses of racial inequality and practices of racial exclusion.[7] Equally important, the Enlightenment spurred efforts to justify slavery. Apologists answered talk of human rights by using scientific-sounding language to reframe denials of Africans' humanity, intelligence, and moral character. This pseudo-scientific racism pervaded Euro-American culture and, reinforced later by defenders of segregation, directly affected Sylvia's life.[8]

African Americans in the South faced racial hatred intensified by anger about events surrounding emancipation. Before the Civil War, Southerners felt unjustly singled out by abolitionists, since Northerners had amassed wealth by trading in slaves and textiles made of slave-produced cotton. Then, war took the lives of at least 260,000 Confederates and reduced Southern cities to rubble, plantations to wasteland. Although the North had a higher death toll, the South's losses came with the bitterness of defeat.

Southern whites knew that blacks there had prayed and worked for a Union victory. Slaves had spied, refused work, and escaped. By war's end, some 500,000 had sought refuge in Union army camps. When runaway men asked to fight, President Lincoln hesitated, convinced that if slaves joined the army, he must free them. He issued the Emancipation Proclamation in part because the Union desperately needed soldiers. Rejoicing in their freedom, former slaves welcomed the Union army and the Freedmen's Bureau. After the war, Southern whites retaliated. Armed men on horseback rode through the countryside beating and murdering blacks, burning their crops and homes. State legislatures passed laws limiting black people's rights.

Infuriated by this postwar defiance, Northerners elected a new Congress to chastise the South. Despite widespread racism nationwide, anti-Confederate sentiment led to radical steps such as inscribing civil rights in the Fourteenth and Fifteenth Amendments to the Constitution. During Radical Reconstruction (1867–1877), the army and Freedmen's Bureau supervised as Southern blacks voted, ran for office, and won elections. As numbers of federal troops in the region dropped from one million in 1865 to less than twenty thousand in 1868, they could not control the violence. In Louisiana, the Freedmen's Bureau recorded 1,081 politically motivated murders, almost all of black people, between the April primary and the November election of 1868. In Tennessee, Confederate veterans founded the Ku Klux Klan in 1867. Absorbing local groups, the KKK spread throughout the South and killed some twenty thousand people in its first ten years.[9] Outside the region, support for defending black Southerners predictably waned. The nation's first segregation laws had appeared in the North. Anti-black riots had erupted there during the war. After President Rutherford B. Hayes withdrew the army in 1877, the white South could establish a thoroughly abusive racial system without federal intervention.

Segregation by law in the South emerged in the 1880s and '90s, as the Populist movement threatened the power of plantation owners. Populists not only attracted lower-class whites, but also recruited black voters and allied with black political groups. Conservatives responded by campaigning for segregation laws and voter requirements that effectively excluded blacks. Stump speeches inflamed racial hatred. Violence punished those who did not fall in line, black or white.[10] Most critics of segregation went silent.[11] In 1896, the U.S. Supreme Court ruled in *Plessy v. Ferguson* that segregation did not violate the Constitution, if facilities were "separate but equal." Yet nothing stopped the segregated South from setting aside degrading facilities or none at all for blacks. Railroad and bus stations often had no restrooms except for "Whites Only." The police enforced exclusion from public and private spaces—if whites on hand did not do so themselves. Southern segregation laws enshrined codes of racial inequality rooted in the world of master and slave.

Sylvia's words take us to the very heart of these matters. A child's heart. She looks back from a standpoint affected by the Civil Rights Movement and Black Power. Yet she experienced the segregated South as a child trying to make sense of her world. Aware that her father's parents had been "slavery people," young Sylvia did not have enough information to understand those words. She processed what little she heard about slavery into a stunningly insightful conflation of past history and immediate experience. Sylvia recalls seeing herself as exactly what racism said she was—until, thanks to a teacher and a dictionary, she "got to be . . . a human being." Such deeply personal roots sustained one of grown-up Sylvia's most strongly held and reiterated beliefs: that education leads to liberation.

I was born in Milwaukee at County Hospital in 1930, February 10th. My mother, Ruth Bell, had come to Wisconsin from Louisiana at that time—to visit with an aunt of hers. Mama had brought my brother Joseph and my brother Lawrence along with her. Before I was born, Lawrence said, "Oh Mama, you gonna have a little girl and you name it Sylvia." That's where my name came from. My brother Speedy—that's Lawrence, we all call him Speedy—gave me that name. When Mama went back to Springfield, Louisiana, she brought me back to my dad, Dock Bell.

Mama was born in Killian, Louisiana. Her father was a preacher, Reverend Patrick Tillman. He had a church in Clio and his church over in Killian. Or Tickfaw. They really called it Tickfaw, but it's Killian on the map. My mother's Killian would be south of Springfield. There was a river in between there. Or it mighta been a big stream from the Gulf. Not the Gulf but the swamps. In the swamps, you got so many areas that look like rivers. It's just low land, where the water would settle. Lotta water back over there where Mama used to live, around Killian and just south of there, Maurepas, Head of Island, and The Baptist. Nothin' but water. I don't know why them people stayed in there but they did. Where I'm talkin' about is those little islands, where they raise sugar cane. Down there in that bayou, not that far from where Mama lived.

Once in a while we would go to her father's house. Grandpa had a fireplace in his old house. He had cows and he had a runnin' well. We had to go through them woods to get to Grandpa's house. It's different now. Oh God, sometime I don't even know the way my own self. The world has changed so. Sometime Grandpa would send out the horse to get us at the main road. Later, my brothers had this old car that made maybe ten miles an hour. We used to get stuck in the mud goin' back there. I remember my grandfather well. I was ten or twelve when he died. He had a son became a preacher, preached at his daddy's church for years.

My mother's mother died when she was very young and left her with the woman that she came up here to see when I was born, Aunt Oja—her real name was Ojalene—and Aunt Oja's mother, Mama Rose. Grandpa married another woman. I never knew too much about that marriage. I knew the sisters though, my aunties. They had a lotta them sisters in that family, one boy and a buncha girls. Two of 'em are still livin, one of 'em ninety somethin'.

My father was born in New Orleans on December 24th. I don't know if it was 1887 or 1889, but somewhere around that time. He never told me about his parents. Because they had passed away. I don't know who raised him. I can't pinpoint it. I know he say about the Jackson peoples.* The Jackson did so much for him and helped him. But that came . . . oh, I guess when my daddy was eight, nine, or ten years old. His parents had died. I don't know if it was from hard labor or war. They were slavery people, his parents was.

I don't know too much about slavery. Didn't learn about it in school. School was scarce for blacks when I was a child. And there was no black history taught, nothing. I knew Christopher Columbus. Somehow I read that book. But to really know about slavery . . . We didn't have a library to tell you about it. I didn't know how blacks came to the United States.

We never knew anything as children. What we knew was today's livin', the way whites would treat blacks at the time. They would hang the black man or chase the black man and kill him unnecessary. Things like that. I got the

---

* In chapter 14, Sylvia notes that, although she and her brothers called the Jacksons "cousins," they actually were not related except by friendship ties to this family that helped their father so much as a young man. Herbert Gutman suggests that a familial culture derived from African extended family traditions encouraged enslaved Africans to embrace "fictive kin." Such family members were not related by blood, but by caring and otherwise filling in as family. This as people struggled to cope with a system that regularly sold away their biological family members. Herbert G. Gutman, *The Black Family in Slavery and Freedom, 1750–1925* (1976), 220–29.

impression that this was slavery. I remember a couple cousins got killed. Or we couldn't mix, black and white couldn't mix. I thought maybe that was slavery.

I remember some hard, hard things bein' a child—with the white and the black. It really wasn't easy. Down there in New Orleans, they were so screwed up. They were French and all kinds of . . . Well, long as you were dark, you were black. You could have anybody's blood in you, but you're black. From day one, you became aware of that—not taught by my parents now, 'cause they didn't have to teach it. The white peoples would automatically teach you. The word, the "n" word would come up. "That little black n—. You see that little black nigger?" Of course, my parents they used to hate to hear the word. Or dislike it. But that's what they call you.

There was a white man like a mile away from where we live. My father used to go there to help him out. I knew his family. He used to come to my daddy's house to borrow money. And his wife used to tell my dad, "Dock, don't lend him no money. He's an alcoholic." Now this is as a child. I'm a young child. There was whites livin' down the road from us and in the back of us.

To me at that time, Mr. John or Mr. Thomas is white. I'm the nigger. We lived that way. I mean, I was born that way. You see, I thought I was a nigger. Now you know that's bad. I didn't know any better.

I thought I was a nigger until I got to be—oh my God, oh—a human being. That happen when Mrs. Clark, my teacher in school, says to me, "Come here, I wanta show you what a nigger are." And she showed me this word in the dictionary. It said a nigger is a piece of iron. I think you would find it—not think, I know—this word, "nigger," n-i-g-g-e-r, was in the dictionary. I got the meanin' that it was a piece of iron. Then I knew there was this part in the sawmill they would talk about. They called it the "nigger" because it was the hardest workin' part in the mill. My father called it the "nigger," too. So when my teacher showed me the word, I says, "I'm not a nigger. A nigger is a piece of iron."

I say that all the time, right today. It's no such thing as . . . Well, the book did say it was a slang word for Negro. But it's just a slang. It's not a proper word. So that's what made me think, "Hmm, I been thinkin' I was a nigger. I'm not a nigger. I'm a human being. That's exactly what I am."

To tell you the true, I don't know what I am. But I'm human. We are—some say we black, we African American, we . . . I say, well, I'm just a *plain American*. I am plain . . . an American.

So, as I was saying, it was the white taught me what I know about segregation. 'Cause if you go in certain places—Oh, you just didn't know. I mean, you knew. You knew. Okay? They got signs up there: "Colored." [*Long pause.*] And you don't go in this place because . . . Or in the toilet, or sit at the counter, or go inside. The only places you go inside is the store, where you gonna buy food. 'Cause you can point to it, or it's already wrapped. Then you can go in there, you allowed. Not to restaurants, you not allowed to go in there. You stand outdoors and get it at a window. I say, "I don't have to eat there. My daddy is a good cook. I can go to the store and buy me a hot dog and take it home. Papa'll fix it for me." You had to be an independent person.

I was not taught by my parents to live that way, not at all. My parents didn't tell me, "You better stay away from that white person's house." No, that never was taught. It was the white let us know not to come around or not to be involved with them. They let us know and we didn't. You stay away. Like a beehive. I'm not going up to a beehive, because I know what that bee will do to me. So I just stay away. I stay over here. And you stay over there. Unless it was somebody I knew very well.

Up on the road, not far from us was a very nice white livin' there. They used to let us come and do the strawberry patches for 'em. To put the berries up on top of the straw. And they would pay us. We'd make a little money, me and the younger kids. That's Jimmy, Ernest, and Dan. This is as I'm growin' up, eight, nine, ten years old. I would be the leader. We would look forward to that. We work for some nice white folks down there. My dad did too. That's why we survived as good as we survived. Every year we had those little jobs. And them whites would give us, oh, sometime my daddy and my mama would be just so happy, because they would give us bushels of sweet potatoes or meat that they had cured in their smokehouse. Those guys, they were nice. There was a few, some nice one.

We still was black children though. We couldn't go—now, I ain't gonna lie and say all of 'em—but we couldn't go into some of them peoples' house to sit down and eat. After we would be there all day long. We were children, just little innocent kids. But we were doin' grownup peoples' work. And they knew we were good worker. They would fix the food, nice food. They never gave us something that would hurt us. I give 'em credit for that. And some of 'em would say, "You come on in and eat." But some of 'em, they would give you your food on the back porch. Some of 'em wadn't that good, they'd give it to you outside. It was hurtin'. And I just consider this slavery.

Now my dad, did he talk about slavery? I didn't know. I remember he would talk about how they whipped black mens. And womens. That coulda been slavery. But I just thought it was the way white peoples treated black people. They beat you 'cause you wouldn't work for 'em or because . . . My father said they would sit the children up on the block. Or a good black man on the block and sell him.

But never readin' or knowin' or seein', I didn't know how to take this. The word, "slavery," really did not come into my vocabulary until I was a grown woman.

Later on in life, I learned somethin' about it. This one woman were showin' me about not knowin' if the name, that's on my mama's side, was white or black. 'Cause the whites gave my parents they name. That was in Virginia. I guess that has to do with slavery. Another friend told me a lotta stuff about slavery. About how bad it was, the things they did to them peoples. And I saw movies where they had the black peoples down in the bottom of the boat. When they'd get sick or die, they'd throw 'em overboard. I also saw movies about the war, not the World War, but one before that—in the eighteen hundreds. They were still killin' and brutally murderin' then. That's when some of the white womens would take more interest in the black person than the governor or whatever. Slavery. I have saw it in movies. Like *Roots* and there was another movie I saw.*

I had a white friend said, "Sylvia, I want you to see this movie." On television. So I was prepared that evenin' to watch this movie with him. But when I looked at it, I said, "Man, I don't wanta see it." I just didn't wanta watch. I say, "This, this is slavery. This is what they been havin' us in all my life. I been used to 'em beatin' up black peoples, mis-usin' 'em, not lettin' 'em go to school and things like that. All my life."

My dad did talk about what happened back when the blacks was freed. He say, "Sylvia, you won't believe what them peoples did." Well, one time in New Orleans, black people voted and they had black peoples as presidents and governors and this, that 'n the other. This is the true. My father told me this. He said the white got sick of them black peoples bein' in office. So they would go out into the countryside and tell these black peoples, "Oh, I'm gonna give you a barrel of flour, a barrel of lard, and a barrel of sugar." They would put all this sand in a barrel, put a little flour 'n stuff on top and give to them black peoples to vote for them. And I guess that kinda voided the votes. They had these black peoples sell themselves out, voting for this person to get in there. And after they got 'em in, the blacks got down to this part of the food and found out that it wadn't nothin' down there but sand. I think they sold out their rights just for food. They lost it. By voting. That was papa's way of explainin' why they didn't learn to vote too much any more. Because they had been hurt. He says black peoples wasn't—the way he talked—they wasn't really down back then. But they sold they rights to

---

* *Roots* was an eight-episode 1977 TV miniseries based on Alex Haley's book *Roots: The Saga of an American Family*. An estimated 130 to 140 million viewers total, in nearly 85 percent of U.S. homes with TVs, watched all or part of the series, an unprecedented success.

the white man. I'm talkin' eighteen hundred something—was the last time that blacks was allowed to vote.*

That's a natural born fact, because I found that somewhere in the book, too, later on in life. I don't know if this was told to my father from his family or his raisin'. He was born in the eighteen hundreds. But my father told me all that stuff. And when I read it, I said, "Oh my God, the man told me that."

He had one sister. They never knew whicha way she went. I don't know if she got huddled off the street by somebody or what. Or it was some of the relatives dead. These men was snatchin' black peoples up. They would just take 'em 'n kill 'em 'n throw 'em out somewhere in the swamps. Then the alligators would probably eat 'em up 'cause they was treacherous at that time. That's what some of the older peoples would say.

We was goin' to have family reunion one time, eighty-four or eighty something. So my cousin and I were diggin' up some of the black history—of the family. From the library, that's where we went, in New Orleans there. We really didn't get too much out of that. The woman, at the library, she would only allow us to see the books for a while. And we really didn't get a good scene. Listen to this. They was shootin' like they shootin' now, killin' each other like they doin' now. I remember, she said, "Oh Sylvia do you think our family was like that? With guns and stuff?" That was in New Orleans, all that shootin' 'n killin' we found out about.

Papa never liked the big city, which I don't either. He moved to this little place called Springfield, Louisiana. My dad used to tell me this story all the time, about how he got to Springfield. This man, Mr. Joe Jackson, would come to visit Papa's folks in New Orleans. He would come on a horse and a buggy. Oh, I'm talkin', I guess, 1910. The distant from Springfield to New Orleans would be about forty-five or fifty miles. And he would take Papa back with him. It was a good distance and took a long time 'cause they was comin' with horse 'n buggy. This man would go through them swamps. Before they had that bridge. If you are familiar with Louisiana, you know how they have a bridge now at Ponchatoula. This bridge, they built it across that swamp—with all kinds of snakes and alligators and you name it what's up under there. When my father went to Springfield, he enjoyed this place with the Jackson. He wanted to go back out there.

---

* Black Southerners did not quit voting voluntarily, although some of them may have voted for the politicians who then passed laws that disfranchised blacks. I did not find reliable documentation of the particular vote-buying practice Sylvia describes here. But Louisiana was notorious for electoral corruption.

When he met my mother, my father was livin' in Springfield with these peoples, the Jackson. There was a sawmill there. They cut lumber, sawed these pine trees and stuff. My father start workin' there as a kid. Them days they didn't care. As long as you would work, you could work.

Then my dad he met my mother. And he really liked that little woman. He always used to refer to her as "that little woman." They met each other through some of the related families. Church, them days, was where a lot of peoples met. Peoples would walk for miles and miles and miles—we had trails through the woods—to go to each other's church. Mama live like six miles from where Papa was livin'. He fell in love with her. But he didn't have property, didn't have a home at that time.

So my father he bought this land—which we still have the land today. There was an old lady, Mrs. Brakenridgen. She was a very kind woman. And she had all this land for, oh God, miles. They had a sawmill, too. That was not too far down the road where we live. Walkin' distant. There was a little black settlement up in there. "Settlement" they called it. It was all black families livin' there with mucha nothin'. The Hayne Settlement. That's where all the Haynes was. The Hutchison, that was a family that live there. The Towns live in the Hayne Settlement and I guess the Whitaker came a little later. And the Simmons and the Bells was in that section. If you go home today and say, "Where did the Bells live?" They'll say, "Up by the Hayne Settlement." Well, those black peoples would work in the sawmills—as long as they was there.

So Mrs. Brakenridgen, what she did, she told some of the guys who worked at the mill, "If you wanta buy a piece of this land, it's five dollars a acre." It was cheap for land at the time. 'Cause she wanted to keep 'em there. My father bought five acres. Then, I guess this Jackson person bought a five-acre split. Simmons, he bought him one. And the Garners they got them five acres. 'Cause these peoples are all together. I used to wonder how they did it. But since we talkin', it comes to me. It was all Brakenridgen land. They used to tell us that all the time. "This is the old Brakenridgen land." It never occurred to me then. But that's how them peoples got land. 'Cause that woman wanted her lumber. She would come in, cut all the trees down and . . . She was makin' money twice. She made the money on the land after she cleaned off the trees. It was cheap labor for her, too, for that sawmill.

That was the first mill Daddy worked at. Papa had to walk like four miles to get to that mill. And a couple more miles from there to where Mama lived.

So my mother and my father was—what do they call it?—courting. Mama, she was anxious to get married. My dad told her, say, "Well, Ruth, I'm not gonna marry you until I build a home for you. I don't wanta marry a woman and can't give her a home." He was buildin' this house. He got the lumber from the mill where he was workin'. He was steady bringin' this lumber home and built this place. Then they got married. That was 19 . . . , I bet 14 or 15. I don't know if it was a church wedding or a backyard wedding or what peoples did at them times. But they did get married.

2

This Five Acres of Land

Sylvia's father, Dock Bell, bought five acres of land in the early 1920s South, where fewer than one in five African American farmers owned the fields they worked. Half a century earlier, freed slaves had hoped for better.[1] Many believed that the United States government had promised each of their households forty acres and a mule as compensation for centuries of unpaid labor. In part, this idea came from overhearing Southern whites' fears of what a Union victory might bring. The first charter of the Freedmen's Bureau, too, although not widely known to slaves, suggested that emancipated families receive forty-acre parcels of land taken from Confederates. Instead, postwar amnesty agreements returned confiscated property to former owners. Although a small percentage of freed families obtained land under the Southern Homestead Act of 1866, most could only buy land when their ability to pay came together with local whites' willingness to sell. Much worked against such sales in the Jim Crow South. Well into the twentieth century, most rural blacks worked as tenant farmers or sharecroppers, a poor situation, but one that freedpeople had preferred to working in gangs under overseers as in slavery.[2]

Sharecroppers received land, seed, equipment, and mules on credit from the landowner. They paid interest rates as high as 55 percent for this so-called furnish and similar rates for food bought on credit. Landlords often ran the only available store, in addition to controlling land use, farming methods, and the settling of accounts at harvest time. Many did not permit tenants to use land to grow food. At settlement time, an estimated two-thirds of black sharecroppers only managed to pay what they were told they owed—or went deeper into debt.[3] Fewer than 20 percent made any money at all, typically miniscule amounts. Tenant farmers, who paid cash rent for their land, did little better. In 1930, nearly 80 percent of blacks who farmed did so as sharecroppers, tenant farmers, or, worst off of all, agricultural wage workers.

Landless rural blacks had few options. In the 1930s as earlier, attempts by sharecroppers and tenant farmers to unionize achieved little, at a high cost in injuries, lost lives, and jail terms.[4] Insubordination brought violent reprisals or eviction. Those who quit without first obtaining work elsewhere could find themselves held by force and worked without pay—in violation of federal law. Government investigators found patterns of forced labor involving phony debts and racial targeting. Sheriffs would arrest unemployed black men for vagrancy and then contact planters who offered to pay the fine in exchange for labor. A 1908 study estimated that one-third of cotton plantations in Georgia, Mississippi, and Alabama used such labor. Florida's turpentine industry had its own version of the pattern. Although less frequent later, forced labor cases continued to surface in the twentieth century.[5]

The Great Depression worsened the position of landless farmers and agricultural workers, while making it more difficult for farm owners to keep their property. In the 1920s, falling agricultural prices had already cost many farmers their land. As the Depression began, conditions turned catastrophic. In 1930, the year of Sylvia's birth, severe drought hit sixteen states, followed in some areas by grasshopper infestations. Yet farm production did not decrease as precipitously as demand and prices for crops. Cotton growers received nearly seventeen cents per pound for their harvest in 1929, but less than six cents in 1931. As their income plummeted, planters pushed share-croppers off the land.[6] Nationwide, the number of farm foreclosures more than doubled between 1929 and 1933.

In those same years, one third of the banks in the United States failed, wiping out customers' savings and halting the flow of credit. The nation's industrial production fell by half. Unemployment jumped from 3 percent to 25 percent.[7] Those who kept jobs took cuts in pay. Hunger afflicted one third or more of the population. A Congressional committee heard testimony in 1932 that thousands were starving, especially in the South.[8] Throughout the nation, people waited in long lines for food provided by relief agencies. With more than half of U.S. home mortgages in default by 1933, foreclosures were evicting a thousand families per day.[9] Unprecedented numbers took to the road. In 1932, the Southern Pacific railroad reported 683,000 transients caught riding its boxcars. The new vagabonds included some 250,000 teenagers, many because their departure meant more food for younger siblings. Whole families, too, packed up vehicles and went seeking work. Masses of so-called Dust Bowl migrants headed for California. Estimates put the nation's homeless population at 1.5 to 2 million by the end of 1932.[10]

Although historians disagree about the causes of this disaster, most consider other factors more important than the October 1929 stock market crash.[11] Economic top-heaviness, for example, curbed sales of manufactured goods. The top one tenth of one percent of U.S. families enjoyed a combined income equal to that of the bottom 42 percent in 1929. That year, half of the population did not make enough to cover "basic necessities," according to a 1930s study.[12] New forms of consumer credit that helped sell cars and appliances in the early 1920s had put many people over their heads in debt.

In the first years of Sylvia's life, the Depression worsened the already difficult situation of most African Americans. As the economy collapsed, white job seekers displaced almost half of the nation's skilled black workers and took many unskilled jobs formerly left to blacks. The unemployment rate for black men neared 50 percent. The majority of employed black women worked in the troubled agricultural sector or domestic service. In the 1930s, more white women sought jobs cleaning private homes, while many former employers of domestic workers either could no longer afford such services or offered things such as a meal instead of monetary payment.[13] North and South, black people with nowhere else to turn found that some relief agencies gave aid only to whites.

Sylvia's account of how her father made a living calls attention to industries that remained exceptionally open to African Americans through these years. Black workers' share of cargo handling jobs at Gulf ports in Alabama, Mississippi, Louisiana, and Texas grew from 65 percent in the 1920s to 75 percent in the 1930s, even as the International Longshoreman's Union—one of the few labor unions with black members at the time—put a stop to the "casual" hiring system that formerly allowed men just to show up and get a day's work on ships.[14] Although Dock Bell no longer traveled to the Gulf for work in the 1930s, earlier earnings there had helped him develop his farm.

Throughout Sylvia's childhood, her father worked in lumbering, the industry that employed more African Americans than any other during these years.[15] A younger generation of black men had begun to view wage work in lumbering as a possible alternative, not just to sharecropping but also to decreasingly viable family farms. Dock Bell belonged to the older generation that saw the lumber industry primarily as a way to fulfill the dream of property ownership. Purchasing cutover land from lumber companies could disappoint, however. More often than not, buyers found it impossible to overcome difficulties such as removing stumps, and replacing soil nutrients and topsoil stripped off by logging.[16] Although Dock Bell succeeded in making his land productive, he had to keep the sawmill job because five acres would not in itself support a family. Yet, with alternatives such as sharecropping, owning that small parcel of land mattered to the Bells for more reasons than its immediate practical effects on their way of life.

Sylvia's description of the food her family enjoyed contrasts strikingly with the larger picture of these lean years, especially in the South. Dock Bell managed to feed his children, even if he did not earn much selling produce and at his sawmill job. Documents that Sylvia and I found in the register of deeds office in Livingston Parish show that, in 1934, the title of the Bell farm transferred to the state of Louisiana because of $20.13 in unpaid taxes for 1932. The title transferred back when the state received that payment in 1935. Sylvia had never known how close her family came to a very different way of life.

This chapter indirectly sheds light on the strength of the Bells' feelings decades later during their first attempted lawsuit for Daniel's wrongful death. When the court and their own attorney pressured them to accept a settlement that the family did not consider a full admission of wrongdoing, they refused. To Sylvia, her brothers, and her father, settling the case amounted to taking a bribe—and betraying Dan. They held their ground, even after the court threatened to seize the Louisiana property—ostensibly to pay the hospital bill resulting from Dock Bell's collapse in a Milwaukee courtroom.[17] When I mentioned to Sylvia that I had found these documents in the court records, she waved it off, proud to say that they had never taken any of "that stuff" into consideration.

To be sure, neither property ownership, nor that five acres where their father still lived, had grown less important to them in 1960. By then, Sylvia and her brothers had invested hard-earned money buying homes in Milwaukee. Sylvia cites a disagreement over her wish to buy more property there as the main reason for her divorce. She and Joe Bell would purchase plots of land and build dwellings on Wisconsin's Crawfish River. Later, Sylvia would remodel the old family home with her share of the civil rights lawsuit settlement the Bells finally won in 1984. Here, she details the importance of those five acres to her childhood family's well-being, vividly evoking this part of Louisiana's geography and life in the house Daddy built.

In this part of the country was all swampy land—from Ponchatoula to New Orleans. That's what I'm talkin' about, the swampland of Louisiana, where you can see the alligators, the poison snakes. It's wild, but beautiful. I didn't like it then, when I were livin' there. But now, as a grownup, I really enjoy it. The moss on the trees. Have you ever? Oh, that moss would just hang. And the snakes would just roll.

My dad worked in there, in the swamps, as the sawmill man. It was right on the water. Them guys used to go out there and cut them logs, different logs, cyprus and everything. And they would float 'em back in there. They could get these big trees and use the sawmill. Then they could float them logs all the way to the Gulf. They had some kinda barge that they made. It would float through the woods.

Daddy used to run on those steamboats over there in the Gulf, too. He was what they call a fireman. He would throw the wood in there to keep the fire goin'. I don't know how he got there. It was difficult. But they knew how to go through those woods—on tugboats or something they called 'em. Through those swamps over to the Gulf.

As a child, I didn't realize I was right at the Gulf. Even when I left Louisiana, I didn't know. Way later, when I was forty some years old and livin' up North, I said to my girlfriend Stella, "My son is gettin' married in Florida." She say, "We'll drive down there. You got a brand new car." I love to drive. Stella and I, we drove all the way to Orlando. My son, Douglas, was in the Air Force down there. But first we went to Mobile, Alabama, where Stella was from. Honey, when I saw the bay . . . Oh my God, I couldn't believe it. All that water. The sand, it's just as white as snow. I thought I was in Hawaii. That was my Hawaii. All those years I had missed that. I never saw it, never knew how close we were.

That's how—I don't know how to say this—how narrow-minded we were. We lived like—what would you?—like peoples in Africa, I guess. Maybe they live a little better than we did. I don't know. We had no kinda transportation, no road, nothin'. Didn't even know about the Gulf and we were right there.

Papa used to talk about these places. Pass Christianne, Biloxi and Kiln, Mississippi. Today, I know it's about sixty miles from where we were livin'. To get there, he could cross the swamps in these tugboats, him and a group. There was a group of mens that would go to these places. They could work on them big ships to make a little money. It was a certain time of the year they could do that. At that time, Papa's children is growin', his two boys he done had. He would leave home in the mornin' at 4 o'clock and get home that night at 7 or 8 o'clock. He never stayed away—maybe some of those mens did, but not Papa—because he always felt like we might need him. And when he come home at night, he sometime had to go right into the field. He would take a lantern and go out there and plow his ground. So we could—or the boys, the older boys—could plant. That was before I were born. I did not know directly about the tugboats and Bay Christianne and all that. That was told to me.

The second mill he worked at, I knew about that. What he did then was work at night. He was the boiler man. At night he had to keep the boilers goin'. In the daytime, he could leave, 'cause he had up enough steam for the peoples to saw them logs durin' the day. He was the one who knew how to make that.

My father, he was a farmer. Well, he really wasn't a farmer. Down South, if you had—like my father had bought this five acres of land—they called it a farm. And when he bought this land, he learned to plant food on it. First, he had to clear this ground, burnin' out the stumps. It was pine trees. And pine trees really grows down into the earth. That take a long time to clear. But he would clear so much land every year, so he could plant his food for his children. Before the children, he had start plantin' trees.

Fig trees was a big thing. Everybody had fig trees. They would continually spread. So we had a lotta fig trees there right in the backyard where we kids could go and pull off a fig and eat it. Sometime we was afraid to get too close to the fig tree. 'Cause they would get hollowed and snakes would crawl up in 'em 'n make they home in there. Poison snakes or the plain old snake. You never know. There was so many snakes down there. Most times figs would be ready by June. We could barely wait. We would pull one and taste it. But it was really bitter tastin'. And we goin' to just make mom 'n dad mad, pickin' stuff before it get ripe. You had to wait 'til that fig turn brown. When that fig get that way, oh, we just eat, eat, eat figs. Y'ever eaten one? A Louisiana fig? Or the plums would be ready. Pears, plums.

Then we had all this good wild stuff. We knew about it and we would go out and get it. The grapes, some of 'em were small and sour. They call 'em possum grapes. But it's another one, everybody love that grape. Good God. It was a large, blue grape and real sweet. They make the best jelly you ever ate. We would pick, oh they had all kinda different berries. Or mayhalls, please put that word in there, m-a-y-h-a-l-l. We had blackberries, dewberries. In the swamps, these berries are big as a cherry and sweet. But we didn't go to these swampy areas. Not as a child, 'cause if my parents hadda known I was out in the swamps, they woulda kill me.

Years later though—I'm talkin' up in the eighties now, when I would go back home—I would pick berries in the swamps. Oh, the peoples would, say, "Sylvia, you go out in them swamps?" Some of my peoples been down there all their days. They couldn't understand why I would do that. "Don't you know there's rattlesnakes 'n things up under them berries?" Didn't even bother me. I'd get me some boots 'n put 'em on. Don't get me wrong now. I would tell kids right today, "You don't go out there, because you never know when a snake is comin' up. One of those dangerous snakes could bite you or tie around your neck." But I went in the swamps when I was grown. These were things I always wanted to do. And I love those berries. I would get just pails of 'em and make jam, wine, blackberry pie and blackberry dumplings.

When we were children, we couldn't buy gum. What we would do, sometime my dad would put a gap on a tree for his surveyor line. Pine trees. When you chop 'em like that, the milk would come out the tree and turn to rosin. We would take that and chew it. The taste wasn't bad at all. And if we fell or injured ourself, my father would use soap and spider webs 'n things. He mix all of this together with turpentine. Turpentine consist of pine, you know. Believe it or not, peoples would use a little turpentine on sugar to cure stomachaches.

We had the pine trees. We had the magnolia tree. We had oaks, lots of oaks. And these hickory nut trees. They produced a nice nut, too, delicious. We had to crack that with a hammer and take the meat out like the squirrel. Pecans, you could crack them with your teeth. That's why I don't have any teeth now. Down there, they had the most beautiful, the best tastin' pecans you ever wanta eat. When we walk to Springfield, some of the whites, their pecan trees would be leanin' over the fence. We always wanta go that path so we could pick us up a bucketful, or a bagful or a pocketful, because we didn't have pecan trees on our farm. We had the wild persimmon trees. You had to know when to eat them. Our parents would tell us if you eat persimmons while they not ripe, they would tie your mouth up. Well, they wouldn't tie it up but they would have you sticky. So sticky. And it's a long time to get that outa your mouth. Persimmons were so good when they were ripe.

Papa always thought about plantin' or raisin' something. He raised cows. They could graze for acres into the woods. There were rivers that ran maybe two or three miles from our house. And those cows would walk all the way to that water. They ran loose in the woods. Other peoples used to steal 'em, 'cause they were too lazy to raise a cow or somethin'. But my dad always had cows. That's how we got ahold to that much milk. We had cows and pigs and chickens.

My father tried to make things easy for us, where we wouldn't have to go hungry. That man knew how to do anything. He would go buy salt by the hundred pound. Then, he'd kill a pig, cut its throat. He'd take a block 'n' tackle and he would hang that pig up in a tree, let it drain real good. He didn't need no butcher. He would cut that meat up in pieces, put salt on it: layer of salt, a layer of meat, layer of salt, a layer of meat. That is how he kept his meat.

For breakfast in the mornin' before we went to school, we had a biscuit and a piece of my dad's salt pork. He taught us how to soak the salt pork overnight. Then, in the mornin', when you get up, you could fry it. We always had syrup. We could have milk. We could have a egg 'cause the chickens would lay. For Easter Sunday, we would take grass or beets to make dye. And there was a paper—today they call it crepe paper. We used to wrap the eggs in that to color 'em. But my father didn't like for us to use that. He said it might be poison. So we had to stop.

Anyway, we did eat good, 'cause my dad could raise enough food to last us. Papa raised everything, him and them boys. He would plow the ground with the mule. Not the horse, we had mules. The South didn't have too many horses, I think because of the climate. Down there in the summertime it would be a hundred in the shade. Mules could take it. We only had one or two, 'cause a mule, that cost a lotta money, like, oh God, fifty dollars. We grew okra, corn, potatoes, sweet potatoes. Now sweet potatoes was another blessin' for black peoples. We still love 'em. Beans, cucumbers, peppers. Anything. Anything that you eat, we had it.

My father even begin to grow sugar cane. He and other mens would get together and they would grind this sugar cane they grow. They would use mules, one mule, he could walk around. They made up this thing themself, to put the sugar cane in and bring out the syrup. Then you put it in cans and keep it. The syrup will sit and turn to sugar. Big hunks of, it was something like crystal, but brown. And we would take those little crystal balls and put it in our coffee or anything, for our sweetness.

Daddy would raise that food and all what we couldn't eat, he would take it to the 'sociation. He had to do that in order to pay his bills. In the summertime, when his crop came in, he would pay for his syrup cans or for our hundred pounds of flour or our hundred pounds of rice and stuff like that. Papa raised peppers and strawberries to sell. He could get twenty-five crates of peppers offa that place. And strawberries.

Oh, did we raise the strawberries! And that was not easy. Strawberries you have to put straw around 'em. Papa would do that with pine trees' needles. We had to go in the woods, rake that stuff up and get it back home on a sled behind the mule. The strawberries could lay on these pine needles and they wouldn't get bruised or dirty. 'Cause you couldn't sell 'em like that. In the spring of the year, when up North they didn't have strawberries, well, I imagine my father sent a lot of 'em up here. He would take 'em to this "association," they called it.

Strawberries was a big thing in Louisiana, 'specially in the area where I live. So a lotta peoples would come to pick strawberries. From Mississippi. All around. Across the bayou, across those woods. They would come out of New Orleans, forty some miles away. Baton Rouge, they really came from there. To pick straw-berries. They would have little shacks to house these peoples. They have shacks like that around out where I live today, where peoples come in and work . . . to do the nursery out there. So that's the way they used to do down there with pickin' the strawberries. All those peoples was black peoples.

The white would come through once in a while. Just lookin' for a handout or somethin' to get 'n' get goin'. Hobo, they calls 'em. Do you know anything about them? Hobos are peoples, tramps, peoples that just go from place to place to make a livin'. I never saw too many black hobos. White was the hobo.

There was certain seasons. In Louisiana, it's seasons on anything. It was season on killin' rabbits or squirrels. It's—they would say—"season on killin' niggers." Or season for vegetables, pecan season or strawberry season. Cucumber season or blackberry season. Time to harvest the stuff. But "harvest" wasn't the word. It was always "season."

About my home, how my home was built, that's what I wanta finish tellin'. My dad brought that material in on his back. Not by horse and buggy because he didn't have it. With his back and his shoulder. Some days he would bring two boards. Right today I have pieces of those boards. I will not give 'em up for nothin'. Those boards meant a lot to me. I can say my father built that house with his own hands, with his own knowledge.

It was so warm in Louisiana that he didn't have to insulate. The rain would rain in. But my father was always kinda cool. He would take rags and stick 'em in those holes to keep the air out. Or the rain. When my daddy built his house, he had to make a board window. You open the board window in order to look out and get daylight. But that was all right. At that time, it was all right. It was better than what some peoples had. So many peoples, black in particular, they didn't have a little shack like we had.

My father did have us up offa the ground. But we could look through the cracks 'n see the ground. Or bugs could crawl through. My father knew how to keep those bugs from crawlin'. Inside, he would whitewash. I don't know if peoples would know what I'm talkin' about when I say whitewash. Now they use it in barns to keep the disease out from the cows. It was lime. My father would make a paste and whitewash the walls. It made the place look nice 'n made us comfortable. At the time, I didn't know that it would keep bugs away 'n stuff. But he knew what he were doin'.

Oh, just to think of the insects! In the South, you have things they call chinches. There's another bug that crawls into the bed and will bite you. We had the redbug down there. We had a lot of ants' piles. Oh, them ants would just get on you and kill you. We had mosquitoes, too, but not as bad as out there where I live right now. [*Laughs.*] God knows they weren't. Down South, you could make smokes to get the mosquitoes away. You could sit outside with that at night. My dad knew how to do all that.

We had this old wood stove, with the four eyes and the bakin' part. In the wintertime, we made heat with that. We had kerosene lights, not kerosene heaters. My father, he would take the mule and his sled. He would go out into the woods, find these pine knots and bring 'em back home for heat, for cookin'. He would find the good wood, say, for Christmas. Our Christmas is comin'. And my dad would say, "Ooooo, boys we gotta get that winter wood in." They would go out and get oak. 'Cause oak would burn real good for bakin'. "You keep that for Ruth," he would say. "Ruth wanna make these nice cakes." Later, I cooked on that stove. I thought it was really nice 'cause we had a oven on top. You could put your food up in there and it would stay warm.

Our beds were—I guess my father could buy a bed once in a while or get a hand-me-down bed. Then we would get the moss out of the tree. In Louisiana, you got a lotta moss. We had to take that moss and hang it out, let it cure, as they called it. Mama would make the mattress cover. And you stick all that moss up in there. That made us a nice something to lay on. Sometime the old moss would get knotty. Then the boys had to go back out there—snakes bein' up in the tree and everything, they had to be careful—pull some more moss and hang it out. Just about everybody was usin' moss beds, moss pillows. That was our bed. A very comfortable bed.

Runnin' water, we didn't have nothin' like that 'til later on. How our first water came about was from springs. Thank God for the spring! We had to go to the spring to get water in buckets. And my dad would use barrels or tubs to catch water when it rained. We had to drink that water. I can't remember sterilizin' it or anything like that. We had to take a bath in a tub. Mama heat the water on that stove. Or sometime it was warm enough you just take the water, leave it sit outside somewhere and it get warm. We didn't have plumbin'. We had the outhouse.

It was very uncomfortable. But I thought it was comfortable at the time—my father's house. It was a L-shape house. It consist of a kitchen, oh I would say, nine by eight or ten. We had a livin' room and bedroom combined. And we had one big bedroom on the end, where, as we grew up, we had three beds in the same room. We all crammed in there together. My mother and I, we slept together in the same bed. And her babies would sleep in that bed, too. It was a shack, as far as I'm concern today. But in them days, it was nice. It really was.

On Daddy's porch—the garry as we called it—it was shady in the evenin'. That's the way his house was sittin'. Bless my daddy's heart. In the mornin', when we'd wake up, the sun would be on the garry. All right. I'm on the garry. The sun goes down in the west. And when the sun went down, it was on the kitchen. From my kitchen window, I could see the church. You could tell when the peoples was fixin' to start. You could hear 'em singin' 'n everything. That's west back there. I'm sittin' on the garry now, facin' east. The side would be, yeah, that was south. That's right 'cause New Orleans would be that way. So that's where I was.

Straight ahead, you were lookin' into these trees and bushes. That was Mr. Johnny Mills's property, my daddy's lot line. To the south, dead to the south, is the dirt road and them big old pine trees. Some of those trees, they were huge. If that son of a gun hadda fell, it woulda fell right into our house. On the porch, I'm still on that porch with that dirt road to the south. Sometime the ice cream man would come through. He'd be ringin' his bell for you to run out. He's white now. Ain't no blacks around there with nothing.

It was kinda swampy to the south of us. 'Cause it was a branch or a small river back in there. When the river rise up, we would have a overflow of water in there. Livin' in Louisiana, in the swamps part, oh, I have saw alligators not too far from our home. From our house to alligators was like three to four miles. They probably would come in there and have their babies. Then they would leave. They wouldn't hang around by us. Because it wadn't enough swamp. Alligators, they like where it's a lotta food. But whenever the water went up, then we would have anything to come in there. When the water went out, though, we didn't have nothing but the ground, the earth, left.

There was grass, too. Well, to tell you the true, it was weeds and grass. My dad would always cut it. You gotta cut the grass, you know. Some peoples think you crazy, 'cause they just let it grow. But you gotta cut it. I ain't gonna let that grass grow up—because I'm afraid of snakes gettin' behind me. One time, this is in the eighties now, the 1980s, when I were livin' down there in the wintertime. I had bought a lawnmower, 'cause in January, February the grass is still growin'. I had made a driveway, with gravel. So one night, I was pullin' in the driveway. And girl, the biggest snake was right there. Oh that snake was so big! The grass is cut. The driveway is gravel 'n everything. But those snakes was still comin' outa there. So my daddy would always cut the grass. He love cleanin'. Keepin' his property clean. He love that.

We had these chiney ball trees in the front yard. Great big old trees and they grew little chiney balls. I can remember tryin' to eat 'em and they taste so nasty, you had to spit it out. We didn't have lawns like peoples have today. No grass up around the house, 'cause we had too many kids runnin' around in the yard. It was natural born dirt.

On the porch, my dad made a swing. We would swing high 'n low. Sometime if a brother get in the way, he get knocked over. And we have to pick him up 'n put a cold cloth on him or something. Okay, so I'm on my porch sittin' on that swing. The sky look so good sometime. Until I say, "Oh my God, that's up North." I used to think up North was above my head. Because they called it "up." I had relatives livin' there. And they called it "up North." I always thought I had to go up to go North. I thought the train was gonna be elevated, like a mountain or a hill or something like that. I pictured that.

So I'd sit on the garry and I would look at the sky and I say, "Ohhh, that's up North." Then I would dream. Of where I was goin'. Or even of becomin' a nurse. That part came after my little brother Roosevelt got injured and I got chance to go to a hospital. I saw the nurse there, with her pretty white cap. I don't remember seein' a black person as a nurse. But as small as I was at that time, it never occurred to me that it was black 'n white. Seein' that nurse gave me the idea. I would go up North and become a nurse. Oh, I could dream! Sittin' on Daddy's porch.

3

I Was a Girl

Sylvia's family raised her "as a girl," at a time when public discussion had not entertained much questioning of that idea. Most parents viewed masculinity and femininity as natural expressions of biology. Yet masculine and feminine ideals varied with differences in geographic location, social class, and ethnic group. African Americans derived their gender thinking from unique cultural traditions and historical experiences, as well as their thorny relationship with a racist mainstream culture.

By 1930, gender traditions of the mainstream were adapting to significant changes in technology, society, and politics. A decade earlier, women in the United States had won the right to vote. During the 1920s, the range of jobs open to women in cities had expanded into formerly all-male terrain such as secretarial work and new roles such as telephone operators. Urban employment and entertainment possibilities continued to draw the young away from farms and small towns. Mass-market advertising emerged—with its gendered courting and shaping of consumer desires. New appliances were transforming housework for those who could afford them. Modernizing dress codes allowed women to cut their hair, wear shorter, less-cumbersome skirts—and, later, even trousers for certain activities. To be sure, traditional notions about women's "nature" retained much force. People still saw marriage and motherhood as the aim of a girl's upbringing. A "gendered imagination" shaped government policy on issues from work rules to social programs.[1] Yet young women in the 1930s dared to think, say, and do things their grandmothers would not have imagined.

Geography placed people in differing relationships with all of this. In 1930 rural America had few cars, telephones, or radios, and, in many places, no electricity. Although urbanization continued, 44 percent of the U.S. population still lived in the countryside. The South, where Sylvia grew up, had the nation's largest rural sector—as well as a particular set of conservative political, social, and religious traditions.

Being African American added distinctive dimensions to the picture. Although most black people lived in the South, their culture differed from that of Southern whites, especially about gender. African cultural traditions contributed to the difference, even if few African Americans consciously embraced that heritage in the 1930s. Although not egalitarian and quite patriarchal in some cases, societies in Africa generally cultivated competence and economic independence in women. That foundation would have proven useful to black families during slavery and its rough aftermath.[2] In contrast, Europe's upper classes had defined femininity as delicate, dependent, frivolous, irrational, and unfit for decision-making. As the twentieth century began, European American gender traditions cast most women as unfeminine, because their economic situation required strengths, skills, and/or work outside the home. A weak, incompetent femininity had little value for people facing not only poverty but also segregation, racial violence, and discrimination. Yet mainstream culture did affect African American gender ideals.

White society complicated the issue by pointedly excluding black women from its feminine sphere. World War I defense industries gave women men's jobs, but reserved for black women the work that required wearing men's clothes—a sign of disrespect at the time. During Sylvia's childhood years, the tobacco industry treated white and black female employees differently, giving only whites the work deemed "suitable for 'respectable ladies.'"[3] Such examples fit a pattern established centuries earlier, when male-identified work, sexual abuse, and brutal treatment of enslaved women made an ugly contrast with ideals of correct conduct toward white ladies. After emancipation, when former slaves refused to continue working in field gangs with white overseers, planters complained of freedwomen "playing the lady."[4]

Where planters saw emulation of white ideals, however, some historians now recognize a kind of resistance. Freedwomen sought to avoid work sites associated with sexual assault and to devote more time to their families than slavery had permitted. If they claimed the respect society accorded "ladies," black women were countering dehumanizing racial codes. Similar threads of complicated resistance run throughout the story of African Americans' engagement with mainstream gender ideas.

Freedpeople received a strong dose of European American gender codes after emancipation, when Northern administrators, teachers, and missionaries came South to establish schools and run the Freedmen's Bureau. The Bureau designated men as heads of households and recommended that employers pay women less than men. Teachers and preachers promoted white middle-class ideas about marriage, masculinity, and femininity. The message carried more weight when it came from African Americans who had obtained their freedom before emancipation. Experiencing what "freedom" meant in a racist society, many such individuals and their families made a survival strategy of conforming to codes of dress, speech, and behavior that whites admired. Those most successful at living free during slavery served as role models afterwards, especially for the small but influential group on the upper rungs of the African American social ladder.

Privileged African American women of the late nineteenth and early twentieth centuries saw feminine respectability as key to improving the overall situation of their people. Although respectability supposedly depended on following codes of proper conduct, white society did not recognize black women as respectable, regardless of their behavior. For centuries, slaveholders had tried to excuse sexual abuse of slaves by labeling African women lascivious. After emancipation, upper- and middle-class black women strove to disprove the stereotype by strictly limiting their own sexual behavior and preaching the same to the lower classes. Since racism encouraged sexual aggression against any black woman, less-well-off families such as Sylvia's could see the value, if not always the workability, of keeping females in controlled spaces and under escort. Such respectability concerns and the need for social services shaped the mission of groups such as the National Association of Colored Women founded in 1896.[5]

While such women saw themselves as natural leaders of "racial uplift" work, they faced African American men who considered proper femininity incompatible with leadership. Many black men agreed with mainstream culture that decision-making in families and communities should be a male prerogative and that women should stay out of politics. In deference to that opinion, relatively activist middle-class women's groups such as Detroit's Housewives League of the 1930s claimed not to have political ambitions.[6] Even with such gestures, however, African American women did not in any simple way fit the mainstream model of gender hierarchy.

In a book about black families published when Sylvia was nine years old, sociologist E. Franklin Frazier cited an old report of women's daring political behavior in rural Mississippi. During the 1868 presidential election campaign, black women—but not men—reportedly wore the campaign emblem of the candidate that Southern whites opposed. Frazier interpreted this as indicating wives' dominance in family life and said of that era's African American woman that, "Neither economic necessity nor tradition had instilled in her the spirit of subordination to masculine authority."[7] One might, of course, interpret the behavior of those Mississippi women and their husbands differently. Yet with its glimpse into a racialized political struggle that killed more than a thousand black people in Mississippi and Louisiana in just eight months, this story highlights the kinds of historical pressures that have shaped gender dynamics in black families. Frazier's 1939 study described a wide range of family types, including exaggerated patriarchal dominance among the black upper classes and a greater "spirit of democracy" in some urban working-class families.[8]

Across time and social distances, black families remained more likely than white families to cultivate independence in female children. The contrast showed most starkly among the economically comfortable. While well-off white parents typically envisioned marriage and motherhood as the only goals for daughters, such black parents urged girls to get an education and a job. Even highly patriarchal black families encouraged daughters to become independent economically and personally.[9] In part, this was a practical matter. Regardless of rank in their own communities, black males faced discrimination that hindered providing for a family. Privileged black women, too, might face the necessity of supplementing family income through paid work. And most African Americans were born not to privilege but to a lifelong struggle to survive.

In 1910, 40 percent of black women were gainfully employed, compared to just over 15 percent of white women. Around the time teenaged Sylvia left home, the racial disparity had decreased because white women's rate had doubled as black women's reached 45 percent. Throughout these decades, black women had an extremely limited range of job possibilities. Only a tiny fraction had the opportunity to go to college and become professionals. In 1930, nearly four out of five employed black women worked either in agriculture or in private household service. More than half performed housework in other women's homes, a sector still at 42 percent in 1950.[10]

With domestic and agricultural work exempt from labor laws passed to protect women workers in the first decades of the twentieth century, employed African American women worked long hours.[11] The agricultural workday ran from dawn to dusk. Non-live-in domestic work commonly required twelve to fourteen hours per day. This meant that black children more often had to do without their mother's care—and cover grown-up household tasks. When possible, gender norms assigned housework and care of younger siblings to older girls. In poor families, mothering duties fell to younger children, since the older ones worked for pay if possible. As Sylvia grew up, most children, black or white, experienced gender socialization through work as well as play. Being poor and black increased the likelihood of shouldering adult responsibilities.

Sylvia's remarks about being raised a girl emerged in response to questions about how the children played. Her account thus centers on a particularity that she says left her "boyish." All twelve of her siblings were males—in a rural setting where she had no other playmates in the early years. She tells of climbing trees, swinging on grapevines over the swamps, and playing baseball—always in a dress. The fun enjoyed with "them boys" contrasts sharply with the drudgery and restrictions of being socialized as a girl. Sylvia associates her gender role with the end of childhood—at the age of eight—and the responsibility she increasingly assumed for mothering her brothers. She does not, however, suggest that being female placed her at a disadvantage relative to her brothers.

In the 1980s, one of the Bell family's attorneys, Walter Kelly, observed the relationship between Sylvia and her brothers over the course of their civil rights lawsuit. It seemed to him that part of Sylvia's leadership role in the Bell family arose exactly from being the only girl.[12] Here, as she recalls girlhood chores and boyish amusements, she sketches each brother's personality. Dan, the "quiet child." Pat, the "girls' man," who would learn tailoring through the GI Bill and thereafter see to it that his sister's clothes fit properly. Lawrence, whose "brilliant mind" would handle tricky questioning during the family's 1980 depositions and produce some of the most powerful statements recorded in those transcripts. This chapter only begins unfolding their importance in Sylvia's life.

❧ I was a girl. Mama and Daddy brought me up as a girl. But, as a child, I didn't have that little girl, that sister, to play with. I had them boys.

I had six brothers older than me: Henry, Eddie, Pat, Dolfuss, Lawrence, and Joe. After me, my mother and my father still had more boys: Jimmy, Ernest, Daniel, Roosevelt, Walter, and Alfonso. We all are two years apart, pretty well two years. Mrs. Mose Ella, she is the one that brought all of my brothers into this world. I never knew nothing about how children was born, until this one mornin' when my last brother was born. My mother was screamin' and yellin'. Oh my God! Ooooo! My father had went for Grandma Mose, by horse or something or somebody. She was kinda late. I could hear this baby screamin'. And my mother was alone. Those boys was born by midwife, this black woman, Grandma Mose we called her. I can't hardly remember a doctor. There was a doctor, but not when the children was born.* The only child that was born without a midwife is me.

As a girl, I was right with the boys. It took a long time for me to know about a doll. Me and them boys. We playin' in dust and dirt and sand up under the chiney ball tree. We'd sweep all of the dirt away, so we could draw us a hopscotch thing. My brothers, as little boys, they liked to play hopscotch. Papa would make us a wagon and we could pull each other around in it. He would make us a kite when it was time to fly a kite. And jump rope. We used to have the double rope out in the yard. We'd do that and get all dust and dirty. Oh!

We played ball a lot, too. You know baseball is something for blacks from way back. You heard about the Negro Leagues? Well, that come from way back. We had the baseball diamond in our section, where a lotta black mens would go and play some good baseball. I can remember that, as a kid, those guys was really great. And we, them boys, knew something about that—the older brothers. They knew how to make a ball. Or Papa made a ball for them and the bat. Oh, I could bat ball real good. I could hit, throw. Boy, I was a good throwin' person—until I threw this arm out not too long ago.

I became kinda boyish woman, you know, bein' with them boys. I remember this one guy told me—that's later, when I was like forty, livin' in California—this guy took me up in the mountains. And he was fast driver. All California is fast drivers. They taught me how to be fast driver. But oh my God, those peoples drive like that in the mountains. You lookin' down in those canyons. And this guy, he look at me and he say, "Sylvia, I didn't think I could ever scare you. I am really shock. I thought you was the type woman who wasn't afraid of anything." And I was that type of woman really, still am. Because I live with all those brothers and I learn to be kinda tough.

I'm with them boys—with a little dress on that my mama had made out of a fertilize sack. Most of my dresses was made outa flour sacks or fertilize sacks. 'Cause you didn't go to town and buy dresses. And them days, they didn't allow womens or girls to wear—like I do now—jeans 'n stuff. We had to have a dress. And I'd be with them boys. Get my dress caught into the barbwire fence or hung up in the tree, climbin' trees.

* For an African American midwife's description of her work, see Margaret Charles Smith and Linda Janet Holmes, *Listen to Me Good: The Life Story of an Alabama Midwife* (1996).

We would go off to the branch. You know what I'm talkin' about when I say "branch"? Not a branch of a tree. It's where the water run through. My brothers, they used to always wanta take me down to this branch. It was deep, very deep. Snakes and everything else was there. Poor Mom, she didn't know where we was. I would go down there with the boys. My brother Jimmy was always the type kid who wanted to scare you. He would go off into the water and holler, "Help me, Sis. Help!" Girl, I would run out after him and slide right into the water. That's what he wanted to see. He wasn't in troubles at all. It took me a long time to catch on to that.

Or we'd be fishin'—not in a boat now. We probably floated on a log or something like that to be in the rivers or the branches. Sometime my brother would say, "Set still. Don't move." And those big snakes would be crawlin' up in those trees, stickin' they tongue out at us.

Me 'n them boys, we used to play Tarzan. I didn't know anything about Tarzan when I were doin' that. But my brothers knew about Tarzan from comics.* And so we used to pull those grapevines down. They grow here in Wisconsin, too. But down there in them woods, some of them vines grow that thick. [*Gesture indicates two inches in diameter.*] We would swing on that vine all the way across that branch. We were strong enough to do it and we did it. Just swingin' across that. If we fall in there, you know, some of us mighta got drownded or somethin'. But we, by the help of the good Lord . . . Well, the vine wadn't gonna let us down. It was a nice strong vine. And if you know what you're dealin' with, you can deal with it. That was one of our games for the summer.

The funniest thing, when it comes to playin' . . . This is later, when my father had dug a well. Oh, it cost him a arm and a leg. He's gettin' to be better off in life. He dug his own holes. Where you would need a bulldozer to dig 'em, Daddy did it. He dug this well and he could irrigate his garden. He has the water runnin' through pipes. So me and the boys, we would—one be on one end of the water thing. I'd be on the other end yellin', "Hey, man!" We telegrammin' to each other. "Hey Sis, what's goin' on down there?" And just as I moved up to look through

---

* It is ironic that African American children played Tarzan, given the outright racism that pervades Edgar Rice Burroughs's original Tarzan novel (1914), as well as the 1930s and '40s Tarzan movies, radio shows, comic books, etc. Muhammad Ali mentioned Tarzan in a 1967 speech at Howard University. Describing how blacks saw only white role models, Ali exclaimed, "Even Tarzan, king of the jungle in black Africa, is white!" By then, Ali's audience knew that it was not whites but blacks who had reigned as African kings. Sylvia's generation grew up with no such knowledge.

the pipe at him, the snake came out. A water moccasin! Those was the things we had to play with.

Then, from about eight years to bein' a teenager, I had no child's life. This was a absent time in there for me—as a child. I couldn't run out there 'n play. I was busy. I was more of a mother than I was a child.

I had to do all the cookin'. Honey, I started cookin' when I was eight years old. I start because my mama wasn't a good biscuit maker. The boys used to say if we got stuck in a hole with the car, you could put one of Mama's biscuits up under there to get the car out. But my father showed me how to make a good biscuit. Them boys, they would say, "Let Sylvia make the biscuits, 'cause she make 'em better." So then I got to be that type woman—or child really—who had to cook for them boys. I would cook to the best of my knowledge. To make it taste good. Everybody would holler let me do it.

I was doin' all that wash by hand. That's why my hands are so big. I had to do a lotta work. Even when I were very small, I had to help my mother wash the diapers—on the scrub-board or the glass board. We eventually got to the glass board. I had to do it. There was no other way 'round. And I wasn't usin' Ivory Flakes. It was Otakinshee, Otakinsh soap. That was made with lye. I did that myself. That's no lie. I had the strength to wring. I was strong.

I had to clean the boys up at night when they got ready to go to bed, find somethin' to put on 'em. Some of the time they didn't need nothin' to put on. It was just that hot. But Mama always made something for her boys to sleep in, some kinda flour sack thing. I gave 'em their night bath or night bottle. I was makin' Alfonso a bottle with condensed milk and hot water. And Roosevelt, he could tell you, "Yeah, I used to tell Sis to put me in Papa's bed or put me in Mama's bed or put me in . . ." I'd be pickin' him up off the couch to put him in bed. And he would tell me what bed to put him in. Here I thought he was sound asleep.

Roosevelt, he was a explorer. He's the one got burned playin' with the fire. Alfonso was the baby. He was sort of a meany, roughy—but a sweet child. He wanted to be. But he didn't have that right discipline. Them boys needed a mother—as well as a father—and just didn't have it. Now Dan, he was a quiet child. He wasn't a playful boy. Not like Jimmy. Jimmy would go out there and try to drown me in the branch. But he playin'. Jimmy, he's gonna do this or he's gonna do that. But Dan—or Ernest—wasn't that type of a person. They were more thinkin' or mellowed-down person. Dan was more smoother. He always stutter. Never could speak right out. He kept that, stuttered until he died. My dad stuttered a little, too. But you could know what my dad was talkin' about. Dan, sometime you really didn't know. But he was a good child. All my poor brothers was good—to their ability.

Now the older ones, I didn't know as children. Well, Joe and Lawrence I did because they was closer to me in age. Joe, he always thinkin'. As a kid, Joe was a type person who would start to move. Or show how smart he was. We used to call him smart alec. But he knew what he doin'. Joe held his own. We couldn't get along. But he was a good man. Lawrence, now he was another Dan. You never knew. Right today, you can think he's a happy person and he can come up—not the person you thought he was. To me, he—his son the same way—has this brilliant mind. But you never know what he thinkin'. Lawrence was always a more quiet type person. Where Pat, he would wanta see what's goin' on. Or Henry, he was gonna see.

Pat, he was the girls' man, nice lookin'. And he loved to dance. He loved music. He were truly a Bell, not a Tillman. Tillman was more religious or something. Pat was a first class man, first class. He was always kinda smart. With no education, he did well for himself. He went in the CC camp—on his own. Mama didn't want them boys to move. "You stay here." And she was wrong about that. When they went off on their own, that's when they learn.

My brother Dock, he was a very good person. Could be led by other blacks. Poor Dock, he was a slow type. He wasn't a music person like me. When Dock would go to taverns 'n clubs, he would like to just get him a drink and settle in the corner and forget all about it. Me, I love music. And I love to dance. When I go to the bar, I like to go with friends so I can run my mouth, party, listen to good music and dance a lot. But that's later—me goin' to a bar. I'm tellin' you about when I was still down in Springfield, takin' care of them boys.

There were six of 'em younger than I and still at home. The older ones, most of 'em was gone. They worked at Cell-O-Tex or someplace in New Orleans. They would, some of 'em, give my dad money to help us out. Sometime they'd come home on weekends. And they do wanta come home for Christmas. Wherever the family is, they always want to come home for Christmas. The older ones who was livin' at home, they were cuttin' pulpwood. I think Joe was still there. Now Speedy, I don't think he was there, 'cause he went to New Orleans. Or in the service, he coulda been in the service, too. That's when I'm like fourteen. But it was six good ones at home, mighta been seven or eight.

So startin' about eight years old, I was another mama. At first, I rather been outside with the older boys and let the younger ones take care a themself. But I had to help. And I was a girl. As I got older, Mama and Daddy always wanted me to work inside. If I went toward the garden or the field, my dad would say, "Dem boys can do this. You go on in that house and do that work." It was always: "You pack the strawberries neatly in the pint." "You sit here." I would transplant or put everything into containers or something like that. "You do your work inside."

'Cause they wanta raise me as a. . . . "You a lady." Papa say that sometime. And I just wanted to get out there with them boys and cut 'n plow 'n pull. 'Cause I enjoy runnin' my mouth with 'em, listenin' to 'em talk and doin' their things. That was fun for me. I think that's why I really like to be outdoors now.

I did get to be with the boys when we went to town. To do what little shoppin' we did, we had to walk to Springfield. That was like, oh four miles, and it was always with my brothers. To go to Springfield was not to stand around on the corner now. You don't go down there 'n stand on the corner, 'cause it ain't no corner. You got a big old warehouse-lookin' place. Not that big, but big to me at the time. You go in this big store. And they got everything in there. Candy, flour, sugar, cleanin' stuff, farmin' stuff, fertilizer 'n everything in one place. That's John Setoon's place. He was a nice man, too. When you come in, "How's old Dock doin'?" He just as old as my daddy but he call him "Old Dock." "Oh, Mr. John, he doin' all right. He sent us down here to get this list of stuff." Mrs. Ethel Setoon, that's Mr. John Setoon's sister, had the clothes store in Springfield. Her store was about as big as this little room here—with one dress hangin' in the window or a pair of shoes sittin' there in the window. So we get our food 'n whatever we supposed to do 'n go home. In Springfield, it wasn't a lotta black peoples standin' around. You would have a few comin' in 'n leavin', walkin' to the store.

We could also walk to Ponchatoula, eight or nine miles from where we live. Now that was a bigger place, with the sidewalk. In Springfield we ain't got no sidewalk, just gravel 'n dust. Ponchatoula had a lotta stores. When I say a lot, it's 'bout four or five stores. And there was a train we would take sometime from Ponchatoula to New Orleans. I used to look at that other train—the one that goes from New Orleans to Chicago. They called that train the *City of New Orleans.* I would look at it and I say, "Oooo, I wish I could ride on that." 'Cause it was so pretty.

Springfield, Ponchatoula, I can't go nowhere without my brothers. Well, they just don't let you. It sounds strange that I don't go with a girlfriend. But you didn't do things like that in them days. You go with one of them boys. You don't go out there in the streets without, I guess, a man. Everywhere I went I had a brother. [*Laughing.*] You're the girl what said you was gonna make the title of this book, "Brother somethin'."* Well, it sure was a brothers affair. You better believe it. A brother affair.

---

* Sylvia refers here to the initial title I had given the book, *Her Brothers' Keeper: A Sister's Quest for Justice,* with "brothers" in the plural referring to all of Sylvia's siblings, to the Black Power idea of all African Americans as one family, and to Sylvia's inclination to include all people, as she says in chapter 20, "when they are people."

4

That Daddy of Mines

Much of what Sylvia says about her father needs no introduction. We readily appreciate the kind of good father she describes. The reliable protector. The man whose abilities dazzle his children, whose loving care wins their hearts. The role model who has won the respect of his community. Yet one side of Sylvia's portrait here has significance only partially accessible without some knowledge of the lynching phenomenon. This particular form of racial violence never struck the Bell family directly, but posed a constant threat to all African American men in the region where they lived.

According to a classic 1937 sociological analysis, every black male Southerner knew that he lived "under a kind of sentence of death" that might be carried out at any time.[1] Certainly, lynchings occurred in all regions. Lynch mobs killed one black man in Milwaukee in 1861, for example, and murdered three black circus workers in Duluth in 1920.[2] After 1905, however, areas outside the South accounted for only about 5 percent of the nation's lynching incidents. Fewer lynchings occurred anywhere in the nation by 1930 when Sylvia was born. Yet Dock Bell had grown up through the worst years and in a state with a lynching death toll second only to that of Mississippi. As an African American man and the father of twelve sons, he had to keep this threat much in mind.

Historians have two main sources for lynching statistics. One set of numbers emerged from research conducted by the National Association for the Advancement of Colored People. In the 1910s, that newly founded organization began gathering information from newspapers and conducting interviews—some with lynch-mob participants unaware they were talking to NAACP investigators.[3] This process produced a count of 3,625 incidents between 1889 and 1928, all fitting a four-point definition of lynching as: (1) a killing; (2) outside the law; (3) by three or more perpetrators; (4) claiming to serve either justice or tradition. The NAACP numbers thus exclude the many "legal lynchings," where the authorities staged a phony trial and carried out the death penalty—often in just a few hours.[4] The less strictly defined 1931 Tuskegee University report counted 4,761 lynchings between 1882 and 1930. Scholarly reviews of these materials have yielded somewhat different totals.[5] All agree that lynching peaked in the 1890s and decreased in the late 1920s. Other undisputed patterns emerge as well. Before 1900, at least a quarter of the victims were white. From 1905 on, however, the word "lynching" referred to the killing of African Americans in 95 percent of reported cases.

As lynching became more racial, the tradition changed. Violence moved beyond beating and hanging. Perpetrators tortured victims with knives, corkscrews, even blowtorches. In 1916, when Dock Bell was twenty-two, a crowd of fifteen thousand cheered while burning a teenager alive in Waco, Texas. Copycat mobs burned people at the stake in 42 of the 454 lynchings recorded between 1918 and 1928. Participants would collect items such as charred buttons, even body parts, to display as souvenirs. Such openness characterized racial lynchings. The press reported—and occasionally announced—the event.[6] Employers and schools allowed time off. Photographs captured the moment.[7] In 1915, an observer at a Tennessee lynching noted hundreds of cameras taking snapshots. Enterprising individuals made postcards, despite a 1908 ban on mailing them. A man who photographed a 1930 lynching in Marion, Indiana, produced thousands of prints and sold them at fifty cents apiece. Dr. James Cameron, who lived to found America's Black Holocaust Museum in Milwaukee in 1988, narrowly escaped hanging in the incident captured by this well-known lynching photograph.[8]

Local authorities often did not even try to prevent or stop a threatened lynching. Police officers who witnessed these murders rarely made arrests. In many recorded lynchings, they joined the mob instead. Some at first tried to uphold the law, then backed down rather than risk their own lives or offend leading citizens.[9] In its heyday, racialized lynching had the community's approval.

With rhetoric about rape, defenders of lynching tapped a collective anxiety about black male sexuality that intensified in white Southern culture after slavery. Whites convinced themselves that black men posed a constant threat to the "purity" of white women. Some historians suggest that white men's sexual abuse of black women during slavery prompted them to dread revenge. Others point out that talk about black rapists served to keep white women subordinated to men.[10] Whatever the underlying emotions, the white supremacist mentality saw control over sexual behavior as crucial to maintaining racial hierarchy. By custom or by law, the white South defined any sexual relationship between a white woman and a black man as rape.[11] A woman could take refuge in that definition, if caught violating the taboo. She faced society's wrath if she admitted having a consensual interracial relationship. Even when the alleged victim insisted she had not been raped, however, she could not necessarily stop a lynching. Mobs sometimes lynched without allegations of actual sexual contact, if whites felt they saw anything sexual in a black man's behavior towards a white woman.

Lynch mobs saw themselves as taking action to punish crime. Rape or attempted rape was alleged in 24 percent of reported lynchings, murder or assault in about 46 percent. In another 26 percent, however, the mob targeted individuals for non-criminal behavior such as arguing with a white man or behaving "disrespectfully" towards whites.[12] In some instances, mobs lynched black men for doing well economically—and thereby violating the codes of white supremacy.[13] Whatever the accusation, a crowd unable to find the target individual might grab any black person on hand. In Georgia in 1918, for example, a black man killed the planter who had held him in forced labor. Whites responded by going on a five-day rampage and lynching eight people who had nothing to do with the murder.

The force of white supremacist traditions permitted whole communities of ordinary people to commit or condone hideous acts. Although defenders claimed that ineffective law enforcement prompted lynching, analysis shows that incidents occurred as often where a judicial system worked quickly and readily used capital punishment.[14] Lynching frequency correlates to some extent with factors such as inflation, falling cotton prices, and larger populations of white tenant farmers dependent on cotton agriculture. This suggests that economic competition played a part, but with the caveat that whites rarely lynched white competitors.[15] Racial codes made blacks the culturally approved target. Lynching served planters' interests by discouraging interracial labor alliances and by pressing black workers to accept almost any work arrangements. Equally important, a show of power could momentarily ease white fears that blacks did not accept subordination. Lynching participants often talked of restoring racial hierarchy.[16]

The number of lynchings decreased in large part because of a concerted campaign against the crime. Ida B. Wells (later Wells-Barnett) stands out in the early history of this effort. Editor of a Memphis newspaper when three of her friends were lynched there in 1892, Wells began writing fiery articles against lynching and urged blacks to arm themselves for self-defense. When a mob destroyed her newspaper office, Wells escaped to continue the fight by writing, lecturing, and helping found the NAACP.[17]

The NAACP emerged in 1910, as two groups joined forces.[18] The Niagara Movement had formed in 1905, when W. E. B. Du Bois and other African Americans took the then radical position of demanding equal rights—and rejecting Booker T. Washington's politics of acquiescence. A circle of well-off white friends and colleagues, including journalists, social workers, and children of abolitionists, resolved to act against racial violence and reached out to the Niagara Movement. The newly founded NAACP, with Du Bois as director and editor of its journal, *The Crisis*, made eradicating lynching a top priority. While NAACP investigators worked to document and publicize the horrors of lynching, the group's lawyers wrote anti-lynching legislation and carried on the struggle in court. Members deluged the White House with letters asking President Woodrow Wilson to denounce lynching. When Wilson finally made a statement, the NAACP printed and distributed it. Meanwhile, the group lobbied for the anti-lynching laws that proved effective where passed. Lynching nearly ceased in Virginia, for example, after state law made anyone present at a lynching an accessory to murder.[19] With most states refusing to act, Congress failed to pass 257 anti-lynching bills between 1892 and 1951.[20] Yet the anti-lynching campaign made federal legislation seem likely—and thus pressured local authorities to try harder to prevent the crime.

Meanwhile, increasing numbers of Southern whites spoke out against lynching. The Association of Southern Women for the Prevention of Lynching emerged in the early 1930s and managed by 1936 to persuade 35,468 women and 1,799 men, all white Southerners, to sign a pledge against lynching.[21] Businessmen worried that lynching discouraged investors and economic development in the region. In 1937, a poll found 70 percent of respondents nationwide and 65 percent in the South favoring a federal anti-lynching law. While public debate affected attitudes, factors such as urbanization and African Americans' mass migration altered the society that had made lynching integral.

The threat retained considerable force, however. Black families and communities had little choice but to warn young males. Racial killings continued, although less frequently and less openly. Later, a wave of violence met the Civil Rights Movement. The 1964 Freedom Summer voter registration project, for example, endured six deaths, eighty beatings, thirty-five shootings, and thirty bombings. Nor can we consider lynching entirely a thing of the past. The 1998 killing of James Byrd Jr. in Jasper, Texas, fit the NAACP definition.

Despite the decrease in numbers of such incidents by the time Sylvia was born in 1930, lynching lurked in the background of every black man's life in the rural South in those years. How much more so for a man with twelve sons? Although this father never talked directly to his daughter about lynching, she learned from talk in the community about the generalized threat, even knew which tree the mob had used to lynch a black man in nearby Springfield. Later in life, Dock Bell recounted that incident to Sylvia's sister-in-law. The South's lynching tradition helps to explain why Sylvia makes so much of moments when her father stood up, even in the smallest way, to bullying whites. In one episode, he ejects a young white man from the blacks' juke joint with the words, "if I come down there in your town doin' that, you would kill me. You would put me up to a rope." The words of fear she recalls hearing from other adults reinforced Sylvia's admiration of her father's audacity in the face of white supremacy.

Her portrait of him shows us much more, however. We see parenting that allowed children to feel protected from dangers such as storms, snakes, and alligators—as well as poverty, racial hatred, and violence. Sylvia attributes this sheltering effect to her father's "powerful prayer," and to the knowledge acquired by this intelligent man who never had the privilege of a formal education. Describing skills ranging from mechanics to cooking, she emphasizes the importance of those capabilities to a larger community of employers, co-workers, and neighbors, as well as family. Centered in this chapter, Sylvia's tribute to the good father reaches through her entire narrative.

I know this whole thing consist of my father. But that was my life. My daddy was quite a man. He was totally uneducated. Didn't know A, as he say, from Bullfrog. My father had to use a X at his name. Even when he died, he still were putting an X at his name. But that man knew a lot. My father knew everything. Thank God for that!

He knew how to protect us. Sometimes in Louisiana you got the worst storms. Oh! the storm would be white like snowstorms look up here. We'd be sittin' on the floor and Papa would be our protector. The storm would be so strong and so powerful. He got us sittin' in the middle of the floor. We lookin' at the rain comin' in. The house, them boards, they were well put together. But the wind would just rock the whole house. It blew the church away one time. And our house wasn't too far from the church. But for some reason, the good Lord never blew us away. My father prayed when those storms hit.

My dad really wasn't a church man. He believed in havin' a church. He wanted this community. He knew that we hafta have this to live. But to be sittin' up in that pulpit or in the deacon's board—and he coulda been there, right there on the front line—but he was not that type. See, to my dad, the preacher was more like our president, Tricky Dick. I didn't understand life enough to know. But Papa knew. And it was a lot of gossip. So Papa stayed his distant from it all. He never set in church like a lot of peoples did, but he could pray.

As we doin' this, I realize that my father had to be a very, very religious man. Not through the public, but within himself. My father could not read, but he told me so much about the Bible. I don't know who read to him. But whoever was readin' the Bible to my father, that man heard it all. And every night, when my dad would go to bed, he could put up a powerful prayer.

Livin' the way we had to live down there at that time, we were takin' a chance on life just to play or sleep or eat. But we lived—all us children. I can't remember a single . . . Well, one of my brothers, Roosevelt, he got burned. We was out in the field puttin' the straw around the berries. And Roosevelt was throwin' straw on the fire, when it flew back and set him on fire. Before Papa could get there, that poor boy got burned from the waist down the legs. He still limps from that. But that was really the only, the worst incident. How we kids live without a snakebite, I don't know.

Honey, I remember when we had to throw the snake out of the house. The king snake mostly, he would come in the house, or the black snake. The poison snake never came into the house for some reason. I saw what they call the king snake. They were like this, [*Stretches arms out wide.*] them big rascals. They'd crawl up on the porch. But they were homeless. My dad would say, "Don't kill 'em." They weren't dangerous. Now the black runner, I don't know if that was a poisonous snake or not. They would come right to the house.

Rattlesnakes, it was no end to rattlesnakes. As a little girl, I can remember one day my mother said to my dad, said, "Oh Dock, you should go out and see that pile of rocks that them children done piled up in the outhouse." So, my dad say, "Well, let me go out there Ruth." He, that man hear, when you talk to him, he always heard you. He were there for you. So Papa went out there and he said, "My God! Where's my shotgun?" That was a big rattlesnake. He had to kill him with the gun. That's how dangerous it was with snakes livin' where we live.

As the people say, "God is with you." God had to be with us. Them old peoples used to say how we ever made it. How did we ever made it? God had to really steer us. Or we had our guardian angel there. 'Cause for all that went on in our life as kids in Louisiana, I don't know how we got over. But we got over.

It was my dad, a strong man, who brought us through that. Without my dad, I don't know. I really don't know. My daddy was my backbone. He was there.

Papa knew how to discipline us. He did a good job of that. The younger children—when they did somethin' wrong—would have to stand and face the wall with their hands up. Just for a little while, you know. As a child though, that's a lot. He spanked us sometime, too. And when we got older, he had a switch he would use, if we did something really bad. If we would steal something or . . . stuff like that. Sometime, we would run away from him. At least once I remember doin' that. I don't remember why he were gonna whup me. But I ran off into the woods. And when I came back hours later, he was over it. My brothers, they would run off and not come back for a day or two. But still, he did teach us right and wrong. Do right. That was important to him. That was one of the things we learn from him.

My father was a person could tell you how to protect yourself. He could do that for us. He love to fish. But he wadn't gonna go out there on that river and just sit there with all the snakes. He made him a good hickory stick, a sharp object. Then if that snake came down that tree, he would puncture those snakes. He knew to do that and showed us. I already told you how he cut up his own meat. And he knew enough to save the food, as warm as it gets down there. I have often thought, how did that man get brains enough to do that?

I wish I could talk to him. For some of the things that he knew. I don't know where he get his smarts from. I wouldn't call him a dumb man, would you? He didn't wanta stop havin' babies though. Of course, who knew how to stop havin' 'em at that time? And that man sure did know how to do for the children he had.

My dad could cook anything. I don't care what it was, it was good. He could make the best biscuits you ever ate. He worked the dough up good. And it would rise up so nice. He just put so much into it.

The weekends would come up and my father would say, "Oooooo, I gotta make my kids something nice for Sunday." Papa always said, "You don't work on Sunday." Sunday was a holy day. You supposed to sit up and rest. So we did. On Saturday evenin', Daddy would go in that kitchen and take some sugar and eggs and butter and whatever he used. He could make the best—it's something like a cookie—teacakes, they were teacakes. Oh, that was a pleasure for Saturday night, sittin' around the fire or sittin' on the porch.

My father could make so many things. He could take a piece of tin or wood and make something. He loved schooner boats and made them outa wood. Just beautiful. Or you could have a busted tub. "It's no more use," peoples thought. Well, my father would look at that hole and he'd say, "Oh, I know what to do with that." He'd put tin over that hole. And it would stop the water from runnin' out.

Daddy didn't know how to read or write or nothin'. But the things he did know, I often wonder where did he get it?

Wasn't for my father, this man Thomas would've never been able to operate his sawmill. There was something there that would break down, go out. My father called it a arm or, as I mention before, he called it—I gotta use this word—the "nigger." It was a elbow, like when you pumpin' oil outa the ground. Sometime it would slip outa place. And that would shut the mill completely down. 'Cause, for some reason, those mens could not put that arm back together. But my daddy knew exactly what position to hold it in. He would slip the arm right back in there. Couldn't none, the white, the black or nobody else, could operate that mill but my father. Nobody taught him this. He just picked it up. Everbody had to go home, if Papa wasn't there or they couldn't get him there. Yeah, my dad. They all knew Dock Bell was the man who had 'em workin', 'cause he knew how to fix the machines.

Papa never ran into some of the problems that some black peoples had down there. He could buy from this one place, 'cause the white man who own the store, he knew my father really well. He knew my father was the type man who were tryin' to make a livin'. He would say to my father, "Dock, I know you tryin' to raise them children. Now if you want these cans, you can pay me when your crop come in." And sometime Papa had to borrow money. They would let him have the money. See that's one thing about the South in them days. If you was a good black person and they trust you, you could get anything you wanted—almost. Well, not anything you wanted. But like a piece of property. Or money, they would loan it to you 'cause they know you will work.

My father wasn't no pushover either. Like at the 'sociation, where they would take Papa's food and tell him, "Well Dock, these cucumbers are no good, you gotta throw 'em away." But they would take 'em in the back room and keep 'em. "These beans, they a little bit specked. They're no good." And they'd put that in the back room, too. Then they were sellin' it anyhow, just lyin' to him. Keepin' his food 'n not wantin' to pay for it. All they wanted to do was give him enough money to pay—to say he paid—his bill. So my father got kinda tired of that. He told 'em, said, "Well, give me my beans and cucumbers back. I'll just take 'em home and dump 'em over to my pigs and my cows, 'cause they can eat that." So he start bringin' his food back home, givin' it to his animals. And that's not all Daddy did.

My brother had a little shack down there sellin' pops 'n stuff, kind of a juke joint—all black. One time the white boys come in and start dancin' with the black gals. Roughin' 'em up 'n I guess doin' anything they possibly could do. So my father had to step in. He told 'em, he say, "If you don't get outa here . . . 'Cause if

I come down there in your town doin' that, you would kill me. You would put me up to a rope. You get outa here!" That boy says, "You wait 'til I go tell my daddy. You wait. I'll be back." And my father said, "Now come on back. Come back. And I'll blow your so-and so behind . . ." He meant it. He went and got his gun. Daddy got his gun and laid up in them bushes waitin' for 'em. That's the first time I saw him do somethin' like that. A lotta black people said, "You do that Mr. Bell?" They were afraid. But I wasn't.

Later on in life, when I ran into a problem, I was like my dad. Go face your problems. I didn't go with my shotgun. 'Cause I didn't even have one. Well, I guess I had a shotgun or something for a while when I first moved to Waterloo, out there where I live now. 'Cause I remember gettin' out my gun when some kids were drivin' around back there throwin' cherry bombs at my house. I got my shot-gun and I throws a whole load of bullets into the air. I really wanted to blow they tires out, so I could get 'em and beat the piss out of 'em. But I just shot into the air. And they never came back there no more. But that's not what I mean when I say I was like my dad. Not the gun part. Papa would get his gun. He always believe in his old shotgun. Me, I was always afraid of havin' a gun. It just bug me. But the other part, the part about goin' to face your problems, that's how I got to be like my dad.

Like this one night when my boyfriend, Paul, came to my place just so upset. Somebody in this tavern—that's in Waterloo now, in the 1970s—somebody had hit him. So I goes to the tavern myself and I say, "Now, what in the hell happen here?" The bartender say, "Sylvia, I'm the one hit him. I'm sorry. But Paul really brought it on himself." I said, "Man, you don't beat on anybody like that. You just don't do that." Paul is white now. He's not black. And I'm defendin' him. I say, "You do that to your own peoples! What in the hell would ya do to me? Maybe I got no business even bein' in here." He said, "Sylvia, no. It's not like that. Let me tell you." Turned out Paul hit him first. I knew Paul could get nasty when he got drunk. And the man was so nice about it. So that was the end of that. That was up North here, many years later. But I wanta get back to my dad.

My daddy, when he ran into a problem, he would get his gun and go face the problem. Like in that book, *Gatherin' of Old Men*. Remember? Those guys in that book, they all did that. I thought that was kinda sharp. I didn't know other black mens did it that way in the South. But my daddy did.

Another time when he was workin' at the sawmill, the white man wanted him to get up. See, they all up in one of these old vans, a hearse car. It was the sawmill van. They call it the Black Mariah. They all crowded up in that thing together goin' home after work. And the man wanted Daddy to get out of his seat. "You get up, nigger!" Right away the word flies. That day my father musta got up on the wrong side of the bed. He hit that man so hard, the man went out the back door. And the door's shut. The rest of the blacks in there, they got so nervous. "Ooooo, Dock. They gonna kill us." But that was right. Man for man. Papa was tired, too. He wasn't supposed to get up from there. And everybody knew, the other white dudes knew that the white dude my dad hit wasn't no good anyway. Just hangin' around there for a few nickels and then he's gone. Where my poor dad was serious. He wanted his job. And when peoples know you are serious . . .

In the 1950s or so, they named the road for my father. He was the one built this road and the first one lived on it. They named it the Bell Road. That's from Washington, DC. It's really for real. Because my father was a good man. Very good man. He was serious. A lot of peoples liked my father. They honored the old man. They knew what he had done for them. I can remember Reverend Mixon preachin' his funeral. He says, "You see that man?" And he pointed down at my father. He says, "A lotta you peoples in here should learn to live like that man live."

As far as us children are concern, if we didn't have a father it woulda been no kind of a world for us. But we did have a dad. That poor man brought us all up. He was a mother and a father, to tell you the truth.

5

Mama

🔸 In this chapter, Sylvia talks about her ill-tempered and often absent mother. A sense of context can deepen our understanding of what she says from two perspectives. On the one hand, additional information can help to frame her poignant musings about why her mother behaved as she did. On the other hand, when Sylvia describes the troubled relationship between her parents, her words necessarily converge with a public discussion of African American families that affected her whole life. She connects most directly with this debate as she recalls an intermittently single-parent family: a mother's readiness to stay away from her children; a woman's quarrelsome behavior toward her spouse. Of course, white families had marital troubles, too. Theirs, however, did not translate into negative stereotypes about white family life. As one of racism's many narrative threads, erroneous notions about black families have caused incalculable harm. Exposing that wrong by carefully examining and analyzing the evidence, scholarly discussion of African American family dynamics has more than academic importance here. It matters deeply to Sylvia, because disparagement of black families played a part in the most painful moments of her life.

"They seem to lack a sense of family intimacy and interdependence," declared a Milwaukee mayoral commission report about black migrants from the South in 1963.[1] Expressed in this case by a relatively liberal group and at a time of increasing awareness of racial injustice, the widespread undervaluation of family feeling among blacks could have grave effects. Five years earlier, Thomas Grady had unhesitatingly pulled the trigger and then, according to fellow officer Louis Krause, responded to the realization that he had killed Daniel Bell by declaring him "just a damn nigger kid anyway."[2] The mentality dismissive of black family life likewise surrounded the Milwaukee police chief's decision to violate the established policy of never releasing information to the press before contacting the family of a person killed by police officers. Underlying racist beliefs about black families said that no one would care that much.

Negative notions about black families had touched Sylvia's life since childhood. Ugly falsehoods about black family life pervaded the political rhetoric that had led to laws disfranchising black voters and segregating public spaces in the South. Defenders of segregation and lynching portrayed African Americans as dangerous savages with no sense of family commitments, no control over emotions or sexual impulses, no morals. Slavery, said white politicians and social scientists, had kept Africans under control and taught them all they knew about family feeling. Proponents of these views cited as evidence any statistic or anecdotal report of "irregularity" in black family life: divorce; family desertion; out-of-wedlock births.[3] Sylvia's mother-absent family could have served the purpose, too, although not the usual grist. Indeed, the Bells would have gone into the problematic column even for black scholars such as sociologist E. Franklin Frazier, whose 1939 study of black families measured them against familial ideals of mainstream "civilization."[4]

Today, although stereotyping has not ended, such characterizations of black families have been refuted by historians, sociologists, and anthropologists. An abundant literature emerged over several decades, mostly in response to a 1965 government report that called "the Negro family" a "tangle of pathology."[5] We will revisit the debate over that report in the chapter where Sylvia recalls her own choices regarding childbearing, marriage, and family. Here, we will consider the case historians have made against the idea that slavery caused some kind of enduring familial "pathology." This can help us to contextualize Sylvia's experience in a family just one generation away from Emancipation.

Certainly, most historians agree that slavery did enormous harm to families. Slave code denied captives the right to marry and made slaves of all children born to enslaved mothers. Although many planters permitted slaves to marry informally, slavery worked against stable marriages and families. The slavery business facilitated sexual abuse by traders, planters, and overseers.[6] Slaves who formed families could expect to witness violent abuse of loved ones—and to suffer punishment if they tried to intervene. Moreover, any given slave had an estimated 49 percent chance of being sold if she or he lived for thirty-five years—and would see family members sold as many as ten times during such a lifetime.[7]

Yet studies have made clear that family played an important part in helping enslaved people maintain a sense of their humanity. Although their marriages could have no legal status, slaves chose to marry and tried to stay together. They named children after relatives, passed on namesake lore and tried to keep the earliest last name given their family in the Americas. African-rooted notions of extended family facilitated a widening of family circles to include "fictive kin," that is, individuals bound to each other by love and care rather than blood.[8] Slave communities valued forbidden literacy in part for the possibility of letter writing among members of separated families, as well as for recording names, marriages, births, and deaths.[9] When freedom came, former slaves demonstrated the strength of their family ties. They paid to have letters written, bought ads in newspapers, took to the road and wandered for years seeking their loved ones. A form of resistance under slavery, cherishing family thereafter passed from generation to generation as one means of maintaining dignity in a racist world.

Contrary to racist lore, African Americans tapped deep-running African cultural resources to counter slavery's destructive effects on families. They developed strong and flexible commitments that could hold across distances, family ties such as those between later migrants and kin back home. Sylvia's narrative thoroughly supports such scholarly findings. From start to finish, she shows us the very opposite of the family stereotype reiterated in that 1963 Milwaukee commission report about the city's black migrants.

What brings Sylvia's thoughts about her mother most directly into this discussion is that she describes a kind of single-parent family. Her account of an absent mother intersects at an odd angle with the debate about slavery's alleged legacy of fatherless African American families. On the one hand, she confirms the father-present norm found by historians studying statistical records from slavery times through the first decades of the twentieth century.[10] Sylvia takes for granted that hers and other families in the community had fathers heading the household. Unlike these other fathers, however, Dock Bell had to play the role of both parents much of the time. Ruth Bell did not completely abandon the family. Other chapters of Sylvia's narrative place her there to bake cakes, to make Sylvia's flour-sack dresses, pajamas for the boys and covers for their moss mattresses. Yet she stayed away more than most mothers would and, when home, "fussed" at her husband far too much for the children's comfort.

Most of this chapter consists of Sylvia's effort to explain her mother's behavior, to herself as well as to her listener, it seems. As she speaks, possibilities not discussed loom in the background. Her words touch only the surface of issues such as skin color prejudice, social class, and control of family size.

Observing that her mother "sure had some babies," Sylvia stops short of imagining how many more children Ruth Bell might have had if she had not stayed away as much as she did. When Sylvia turned six, her mother had just given birth to a tenth child, Daniel. Could Ruth and Dock Bell have known about birth control? Would they have used it if they did? In 1916, the year their first child was born, the nation's first birth control clinic opened in New York. The authorities quickly shut it down, because laws then forbade even spreading knowledge of contraception. Dispensed by European clinics, the most effective means known at the time, the diaphragm, remained under a U.S. import ban. Condoms existed, but could not legally be advertised or sold for birth control in most states, including Louisiana. By the late 1930s, court rulings had begun lifting barriers. Advocates in Southern states frankly promoted targeting blacks for population control and sterilization. Many black leaders feared an attempt to exterminate their people by such means.[11] Black couples in the rural South may not have heard any of this. Although often in better-informed New Orleans, Ruth Bell may have known no other way of not having more babies than avoidance of her husband.

Sylvia speaks of family relationships seemingly affected by class hierarchy, but does not acknowledge much class difference among black people she knew. Although scholars of the time found it easier to discern social classes in urban black communities, a rare study of rural Southern blacks in 1930 did find such differences and defined a social hierarchy. In this model, factors such as education, cultural aspirations, and skin color entered into class status, alongside occupation, home ownership, and levels of income and/or well-being. Professionals such as doctors "almost always" ranked in the rural upper class, preachers in the middle class only if they made "a comfortable living." Sylvia's family does not exactly fit any of the categories, but would probably have fallen in the "upper-lower class," a group earning "barely enough to live," but not "comfortably"; desiring, but rarely achieving home ownership; differing from lower ranks in aspirations to respectability and education for their children.[12] Land ownership did not count much to social scientists, if just a five-acre "patch."[13]

Sylvia grants that one neighbor seemed of a higher social class, since he owned a bigger house and "because he was a preacher." Although she does not mention it here, we know from an earlier chapter that her mother was the daughter of a preacher with his own church, a man whose home had a "running well." Moreover, Ruth Bell could read and write. She had married an illiterate sawmill worker / truck farmer who owned five acres of land and, an important distinction, earned enough so his wife did not have to work. Yet Dock Bell could only offer an extremely rustic way of life. The family—nine in number with Sylvia's birth—lived in a tiny three-room house with no glass windows.[14] They carried water from a spring and had snakes in the house, a rattlesnake in the outhouse. Sylvia observes that her mother often stayed in New Orleans with her city-dwelling sisters. They might not have lived all that comfortably there, but did have room for Ruth and could board her oldest sons, too, as they moved to the city to work. Urban life offered more possibilities for entertainment, social life, and more prestige than anything "country." Sylvia remembers her aunts behaving as if they considered themselves higher in social standing than her father. She so utterly rejects those status claims, however, that she looks elsewhere for explanations.

Telling this story after four decades of dealing with the psychological damage that Dan's murder did to Jimmy and Ernest, Sylvia wonders if mental illness might explain her mother's absence and behavior. Here, her words touch issues of race, class, and family structure, then move beyond—to the pain of all children who suffer from the behavior of an ill-humored parent and from a troubled relationship between the parents who make their world.

Now you probably would say, "Where was your mom?" She mighta been home. Or she coulda been with her sisters. Or she was kinda ill, failin'. At one point Mama was goin' through the change of life and that was difficult for her. Maybe that's why she went away at that time. She'd go away. Not to work. My mother never was the type who would go to work. She were lucky. My father would overwork hisself so she could stay home with us. He had enough for her to stay home. But she'd go away and stay long as she wanted. Ohhh. Six months, two months, three months, four months. Then she'd come home. And Papa would say, "Welcome."

I never did talk too much about my mom. I still don't, because my mother was . . . My mama, she was a nice person and a sweet woman. But not like that daddy. All I can say 'bout my mama, she *sure* had some babies.

Well, I can say some other things, too. Mama could write. She had real nice writin'. I remember that. She would teach us certain things, like how to wear clothes. She would correct us how we was saying things and how we was doin' things. Mama taught us about manners. Mind your manners. Yes, sir. Yes, ma'am.

No, sir. No, ma'am. Oooo, if we forget to say that . . . Oh! And she would make things.

My mama could make some good yeast bread and bread pudding. My favorite food that she make was rice pudding. I can remember a smell, that odor of the vanilla that she used in there. I really try to make it like she do. But I cannot get that vanilla flavor, good odor. Down there I think vanilla is stronger or better than what you get here. I think that's why that rice pudding was so good. Or her vanilla cake. Mama could make some nice jelly cakes. She had these little tin pans. You use so many of 'em and make these cakes. The way peoples did cakes them days, they did 'em by a handful of this and a handful of that. I try to do that today and it just doesn't work. But she would make that cake and then she would put this jelly on it. Make a stack. You would have four, five little slices of cake with jelly on 'em. It was good to me at that time, real good. The sweet side of life.

But Mama was sort of uh . . . mean. Or she used to be so angry with my dad all the time. I always thought of it as—whew—evil? Honest to God. But talkin' to you, bringin' this back, I realize my mother was the jealous type.

She used to accuse him. Oh, I can remember, as a little girl. This old woman, she used to bring the strawberries to town for my father, 'cause he had no way of gettin' that stuff down there. If we bring 'em to town, we had to take 'em on this sled or something. And they would bounce and smash by the time they get there. So Mrs. G., she would take 'em. She was the only black woman knew how to drive and had a old truck. She would stick it in the road. You had to go push her out. So one day this lady, Mrs. G., came 'n was givin' my dad the receipt from his strawberries. And my mother saw it out of the window. Mama ran out there, say, "Gimme that note that heifer give you." So Papa went in his pocket, gave it to her. It was the strawberry receipt.

One lady used to come to the house talkin' about my daddy. This woman mighta been talkin' to my mother to get my father for herself. To break 'em up. I don't know. Well, I knew better than my daddy were doin' anything. So I told my dad. My mom and my dad, they fightin' because of what this woman said. Mama wouldn't tell Daddy where she got it from. That wasn't fair. So I told him. He say, "I wonder where she gettin' all that from." I say, "Miss Ida." My mama got pissed off at me 'cause I told him. But I thought I was supposed to do it, even if I woulda got a whippin'. I mean that old woman was breakin' up my . . . She was really makin' it uncomfortable. Us children had to listen to all this gossip.

Or my mother would be in New Orleans with her sisters. Sisters didn't have sense enough to say, "Ruth, you need to be with them children." Later on, some of my brothers was down there workin'. The older ones. They were grown up mens and them aunties didn't mind takin' them on, 'cause they were chargin' 'em rent. They had 'em all piled up in one or two little rooms, them boys. That meant a lotta money in rent. Mama was there.

So I had to take care of them kids. That's the only thing I dislike about it. That wasn't my job. Mama wasn't home. Or when she was there, she wouldn't do it sometime. Then she used to get pissed off at me 'cause I were doin' it—takin' her place or something. I would get that, too. She would tell me that. But I had to do it. That was my determination, to help her with the children.

My mom, I'm really thinkin' hard about what could've made her the way she was. What could have? Once I even thought—as a child—this one day a man came to the door, a white man, and he told Mama somebody had put a hoodoo on her. He took her outside and showed her this hoodoo stuff down by the gate. I was there when he say that. And I figured maybe that was it. Maybe that explain why she always fussin'. Maybe somebody hoodooed her. But then Papa come in and he say, "Where my money I had up in here?" Mama say, "I gave it to the man." And she tell him what happen.

Daddy had saw the man. Daddy was out in the field and he saw that white man sprinklin' somethin' by the gate. See, the man put that hoodoo stuff down there. Then he talked to Mama, showed that stuff to her, told her somebody else put it there. Got her to pay him to lift the curse. But Papa saw—which really prove that hoodoo stuff wasn't true. Papa never believe in it anyway. Lotta black peoples believe, but not Papa. He say, if black peoples can hoodoo other black peoples— it's generally black peoples, not white, doin' hoodoo or saying they can do it— Papa say, "If they can't hoodoo the white man, how can they hoodoo the black man?" I say the same thing today. I don't believe in it, just like Papa. Later on in life, a man try to hoodoo me. Believe it or not, it was a reverend had a church there in Milwaukee. Tellin' peoples he's a hoodoo man. He put hoodoo stuff on my porch. But I just walk right by it. Sylvia say, "Hoodoo don't work—no kinda way." [*Picks up a pen and writes, "Sylvia said, 'Voodo don't work any how.'"*]* Be sure you get that in there. But . . .

I was tellin' you about Mama. How I used to wonder, still wonder what made her the way she was. Nobody really told me anything. If there was something, it was a secret.

---

* The literature on Voodoo deals with other aspects as well as "supernatural harming traditions" and, unlike Sylvia, treats it with the respect due a religion. See, for example, Yvonne Patricia Chireau, *Black Magic: Religion and the African American Conjuring Tradition* (2006).

My mom did not have a mother to raise her. She was raise by other relatives. I don't know how well those relatives—okay, okay, okay, okay, okay—treated her. I won't say that anybody was mean to my mother. I won't say that. My Aunt Oja, she appeared to be nice. But Aunt Oja had property down South. And I can remember my father sayin' that instead of givin' this property to my mom, she gave it to some other relatives. My father never could understand that. Ruth got all those children and she is so close and it went to . . . *I ain't talkin' too loud am I?* It went to somebody else. So I don't know how those folks treated Mama.

Mama had a bunch of sisters, half sisters they was. I don't know too much about them. No more than, when they came around, they would ssssssssssssss. This was when I were goin' into my teens. They would be a little sarcastic or uppity up, as my father would say. Uppity up, you know. I think it was because my mother had so many children and we were really poor class of people.

Still, the way Mama was, I don't think it came through this part, class. There *was* families that lived a little better. As I grew up, I could see that. Like the reverend, Reverend Garner. He had a car. This is gettin' up when I'm older. The Garners had a nice board house, bigger than ours, because he was a preacher. But I don't think of Mama's sisters as bein' above my mother—not any of her people.

My mother's sisters, some of them got married and went to New Orleans. Which was a little better place to live. Or they went North. Aunt Edna, one of my mother's sister, she was housekeepin' up North. Now if she hadda went on to school and became Miss President or Miss R.N., I'da gave her a lotta credit. But to come up here to scrub floors! They were makin' a little extra money. They went to the big city and got a pretty good housecleanin' job. But they wasn't doin' nothin'. They never was big wheels like I know now. None of them peoples was a teacher. If they was a teacher, I coulda look at, "Oh my auntie." Or if they was a nurse, "My auntie was a nurse." 'Cause these are the things I wanted to be: a teacher, a nurse. I had nobody to look up to. I wanted to be a nurse on my own. Not that my auntie was.

Was Mama dominated by her sisters 'cause they was uppity uppity up? Well, some of her sisters was that way. But my mother had *more* than some of those womens had to offer. They could come to my mother's house. And there were food on the table at all times. I could go and visit them 'n couldn't even get a piece of—Well, we never had bread, but cornbread, biscuits. My mom, she did not have to want for those things. It was there. If it wasn't there, she couldna raised twelve boys and one girl. If my father wasn't a good provider.

See these are the things I think about now. What a good provider this man was, when he was havin' so many difficulties, so many arguments with my mother.

Alfonso, one of my little brothers, he say, "Oooo I'm not gonna eat any of that. Mama made it. It's fussin' gravy. It make you fuss." That came out the mouth of a little boy. When she cook sometime they would look at it and say, "Euuh, that's fussin' gravy." I said to myself—this is now, it wasn't then—I say, Lord, if I had to live with a man like my poor father live with my mother, I would never get married. Never. It was kinda sad.

I do have brothers identical to her. And I have to live with those boys. You don't know how much hell I had to go through with some of my brothers. To try to help 'em. Or to try to make 'em a man. Or to try to tell 'em about school. I really had it hard with some of 'em. Alfonso, he just treat peoples like a dog. I was so hurt the way my poor baby brother were treatin' people. I prayed for him one time. I really did. Then he came back to me and he just was so different. I said, "Fonzo, you know I prayed for you." I was so happy. He come to me as if something had really told him somethin'. Just as happy and huggy and everything. I say, "Man, I sure prayed for you. I prayed that you would change." But it didn't change him forever, just for a while. I've said a lotta times I wish my mother was here to see what she raise.

I really don't understand this. Then maybe I might can understand something about it. The only thing I know is the mental illness. That flashes in my mind like a great big sign—anytime I start talkin' about it. Somebody told me that my mother's mother suffered from mental illness. Mama's half-brother became mentally ill too, after preachin' for years. And with my brothers Jimmy and Ernest bein' in the mental hospital. So when I think about Mama, I can see this word, "mental illness."

Still, I have wondered sometime. Was I really? Then I don't want to say it. Was I born and my mother wanted a little girl and she saw a little child over there and another woman wanted a little boy and says, "Ohh. . . . I'll trade you . . ."? I do look like my mother. I'm not light-skinned like Mama. I look boyish, more boyish than that little typical gal, my mother. But I do have my mother's features. Of course, they say that grow on you. I wonder about that sometime. One of my sister-in-laws say to me, "Sylvia, *why* are you so different?" I say, "Girl, I don't know. Maybe I'm not a Bell." But my father and I, we could pass for twins. And some of them boys, me and my brothers, we look so much alike. I have my mother's features, but look like my daddy. Daddy is a dark man.

My daddy told me this. He says, "Sylvia, I'm gonna tell you why your hair is so nappy and so kinky." Say, "When Ruth was carryin' you, she would always see these womens. These black womens." Well, he didn't say black women. They were black, though. She would always see these womens sittin' out there on the river fishin'. And she would say to him, "You quit lookin' at them little nappy-headed black womens." He say, "Your mama used to make fun of them womens so much." Until one day he told her, said, "Ruth, stop makin' fun of them womens, 'cause you going to have a baby. And that baby gonna come here lookin' just like that woman." My father always used to tell me that. He say, "That's why your hair don't look like your mama hair." Or, "That's why you are the little *black* one in the family."

My mother, she was that little cute, long, light-skinned woman, nice pretty hair 'n everything. My mother was a beautiful woman. Oh, she were pretty! She was entirely . . . You had to know my mother. Thank God that my dad was there. We had that daddy, even if my mom was the way she was.

6

Jim Crow Schoolin'

Sylvia grew up where outright oppo-
sition to the education of African Americans had strong historical roots. Less
than a century earlier, laws throughout the South had forbidden teaching slaves
to read or write, and prescribed harsh punishment for any caught learning.
After Emancipation, violence targeted missionary and Freedmen's Bureau
schools. Planters would resist educating blacks well into the twentieth century,
because they feared losing workers or finding them harder to control—and
because children worked the fields. Nearly half of Southern black boys aged
ten to fifteen and 30 percent of girls that age were gainfully employed (compared to 23 percent of white boys and 7 percent of white girls) in 1900, a
rate still at 46.6 percent for black children of both sexes combined in 1910.[1]
In the 1880s and '90s, as state legislatures disfranchised black voters, they
cut funding for the black public schools established during Reconstruction.
States including Louisiana permitted local officials to give white schools
the funds allocated for blacks. Spending disparities jumped further with an
early twentieth-century push to improve schools for whites.[2] In the 1910s,
the South overall spent an annual average of $4 per black pupil to $11 per
white. Louisiana averaged $1.81 black to $16.44 white.[3] Southern politicians
campaigned against using any tax dollars for educating African Americans.[4]

In this context, Booker T. Washington came to prominence urging black
people to limit their educational aspirations and learn the work that white
society wished them to perform. Washington's Tuskegee Normal and Industrial Institute minimized academic subjects and required teacher trainees to
practice manual labor, including fieldwork. White enthusiasm for these ideas
significantly increased black school funding from Northern philanthropists.
The South's all-out hostility toward black education moderated a bit in these

Washington-influenced years, but not the white-supremacist mentality.[5] As Southern states opened "industrial" black secondary schools in the 1910s, a Louisiana official could tout the curriculum as resembling slave training on antebellum plantations.[6] Some black contemporaries, notably W. E. B. Du Bois, did not accept Washington's approach. Nor did this period of extreme hostility extinguish African Americans' desire for education.

Resifting and rethinking documents from slavery times, historians have traced how slave families and communities developed cultural traditions that prized the education forbidden them, associated learning with freedom, and overcame considerable obstacles to obtain it.[7] Literacy skills nurtured hopes of freedom and directly helped those preparing an escape to write fake passes, make maps, and so forth. Frederick Douglass learned to read and write as a child, later conducted clandestine classes for fellow slaves, then ran away North to become a powerful voice against slavery. During the war, white observers reported black soldiers and fugitives in Union army camps studying, reciting the alphabet, and reading aloud from spellers around their campfire. "The men are actually clamoring for books," wrote one army chaplain.[8] Bibles and spellers figure prominently among the items slaves possessed. Some people freed legally during slavery later marked anniversaries with ritualized readings of the treasured bill of sale or letter of manumission. An act of defiance, learning to read and write empowered an individual to help the group resist dehumanizing effects of slavery. With preservation of the family at the heart of that struggle, literate slaves recorded marriages, births, and deaths, as well as writing and reading letters.[9] An estimated 5 to 10 percent of the enslaved learned to read, in communities that valued—and concealed—their literacy.[10]

Enthusiasm for education surfaced with Emancipation. Where Freedmen's Bureau schools opened, former slaves impressed teachers by walking long distances to school and avidly pursuing knowledge. During Reconstruction, black voters and elected officials played a significant role in instituting the region's public school systems.[11] Yet many rural African Americans would have to provide their own schools. A 1909 study found that black Southerners contributed most of the funding for black schools called "public" and privately owned more than 40 percent of the schools their children attended. Between 1914 and 1932, the Chicago-based Julius Rosenwald Fund helped build nearly five thousand public schoolhouses for African Americans in the South (about 20 percent of their schools), but only where communities could match contributions. With or without such help, rural black taxpayers commonly double-taxed themselves to supply or establish schools.[12]

Poverty limited what such efforts could achieve. Schoolhouses often had only a single ill-lighted room, inadequately protected from weather and lacking basic furniture. Parents and teachers provided almost all supplies, except textbooks salvaged from the white school's cast-offs. With large classes in the agricultural off-season, teachers faced such unreliable attendance numbers that many did not keep records.[13] Conditions in all-black schools came into focus in the 1930s and '40s, as scholars and lawyers developed a case against segregation. A brief phase of school improvement followed court rulings that states must admit blacks to all-white schools or create substantially equal institutions. Spending for black Southern schools was 288 percent higher in 1954 than 1940.[14]

More changed—including some conventional notions of North and South—after the United States Supreme Court declared segregated schools inherently unequal and therefore unconstitutional in the 1954 *Brown v. Board of Education* case. "White Citizens Councils" formed throughout the South. Mobs tried to prevent black students from entering Little Rock's Central High in 1957 and the University of Mississippi in 1962. Behind the televised scenes, whites opened private "segregation academies," privatized public schools, and eliminated the jobs of an estimated thirty-one thousand black teachers.[15] Outside the South, local civil rights movements of the 1960s made a key issue of school segregation.[16] In 1970s, the media spotlight turned to whites in cities such as Boston protesting court-ordered busing plans with violent displays of racial hatred. In the ensuing backlash, the desegregation effort effectively ground to a halt.[17] By the 1990s, studies found school segregation—accompanied by disparities in spending and conditions—on the rise nationwide, but most markedly outside the South.[18] Fifty years after the *Brown* decision, the nation's most segregated schools were in New York, New Jersey, Illinois, Michigan, and California.[19]

Such developments challenged conventional thinking only because the battle over race in Southern schools had overshadowed a history of racism in education elsewhere. In the nineteenth century, courts upheld school segregation laws in Massachusetts, New York, Ohio, and California. By the twentieth century, school boards outside the South no longer relied on law to keep black and white children apart, but rather on residential segregation and manipulation of school district boundaries.[20] Racial separation of elementary and high school students in the North increased as large numbers of black migrants arrived.[21] Where smaller black populations necessitated mixed schools, racism worked other effects. Educational policies in vogue by the 1930s put students on different tracks—with assessment procedures that limited horizons for black children.[22] Textbooks communicated negative racial attitudes.[23]

Mixed-race schools rarely had black teachers, since officials did not want blacks teaching whites.[24] In New Jersey and New York, parents fought to improve schools for black children as early as the 1920s—without the national attention later given extreme conditions and struggles in the South.[25]

Sylvia offers an inside view of Southern public schooling in the 1930s and '40s. When she was ten years old, public schools in the region spent an annual average of $21 per black child, compared to $50 per white child.[26] Although all states had compulsory elementary education laws on the books by 1918, Sylvia reminds us that, as late as the 1930s, parts of the South still permitted black children to grow up without any school at all or with only the schools their parents cobbled together. Not all poor rural communities could muster what it took to create and supply their own schools. Sylvia's narrative shows us the limitations of such community-generated schooling: the short school year; the sole teacher for large numbers of pupils; the mix of ages and levels; and, most important, the outcomes for students. Sylvia felt the inadequacy of her early schooling throughout her life, as she tried to pursue her dream of a nursing career. Several of her brothers emerged without basic literacy skills.

Testifying for their 1980 civil rights lawsuit, Daniel Bell's siblings suffered painful effects of that educational deprivation. Although they managed to make a few powerful statements, their depositions contain multiple examples of attempted testimony confounded by unfamiliar words and tricky questioning. When one of them needed a question reworded, all were subjected to an objectifying and humiliating exchange about their "intelligence" engaged by two attorneys. Above all, Sylvia and her brothers could never forget that Dan did not have a driver's license when he was pulled over that night—because he could not read. Convinced that education would have prevented her brother's untimely death, Sylvia makes this one of her most passionately articulated themes.

There was no school provided for the black children, as I was growin' up in Springfield, Louisiana. My parents was taxpayers. But we didn't have any school. They had a nice brick school down in town. We could've walked to that school. But it was just for white children. From my father's time, there was no school for blacks. I wonder, how could they take that tax money from my dad and not give us *some* kind of an education? That is sad. 'Cause if we had've had a little support . . . You know even some of the whites wasn't as smart as we were.

They just didn't want you to have a education. Sometime I say they figured you was gonna get ahead of them—of the whites. I can't just say "them," I gotta say who it was. Maybe they figured like this: if the blacks get a good education, they can't clean our floors, or they can't clean our bathrooms. They never thought: "Let that black person get an education and won't run into these obstacles that we got today." They never thought about that. Your big wheel, your little wheel, the president or the governor, they were just thinkin' about themselves. In certain parts of the South—New Orleans, I'd say—blacks did get some education. But out where we lived, in the country part, there were no schools for black children.

There was black peoples that knew about education—including some who had no education themselves, like my father. They start thinkin': "Well, we better get these kids to know a little education." My father, he often talked about education. They *wanted* education for us. The little school that we had, our parents had to dig that up. It was started by Mrs. Clayton, Mrs. Townser. The government did nothing. It was helpin' ourselves with that school, our parents. They knew that education was important for black people. That was the only way you could really get ahead in life. They knew we need education and they tried to give it to us the best way they could. They set up a little system through the church. I think they had to pay quarter a week or something like that. You had to pay. It wasn't free. Nothing was free.

My schoolhouse was the old church. On Sundays, we would use it for church and . . . Come to think, we did get a schoolhouse later. But my very first school-house was the church. Later it was an old hall. They called it "the hall." The parents got together and they repaired this old buildin'. It wasn't nothin', just an old country shack. Some of the kids used to say it was haunted. The church not too far from this old hall. I think in the old days some of them blacks would meet there. They would have they meetin', pertainin' to—not church but other things. I just can't recall what it was all about. But this old hall, that's where they sent us to school.

Somehow, through the church, some of our peoples knew how to get ahold to a teacher. They finally found some lady from Denham Springs, I think, to come in 'n start teachin' those children. They had to pay her, a quarter, fifty cent. She would always stay with somebody in the neighborhood who was capable of keepin' her. My parents, they couldn't keep her because we just had a little three-room shack.

The way we got books was the older black people, they went to the board down in Springfield there, and told 'em that these kids need books. Can we have some books for these children to read? The only books that they gave us was the ones that the little white children had tore the pages out of. I can remember so well one book that we got. We had to begin off with, "Yippity-yip, Bob and Nancy can ride." We didn't know what was before. I do know now, because later on in life I did see the book. At the time, we just learned a part of the books. I guess my parents had to give a little money for this.

We had at least a hundred children going to that school. It grew and grew. Certain time of the year, the teacher would have a large group of kids. We went to school durin' the wintertime. They had old stoves, wood burners. They would heat the place with that. October or November, we started school, maybe November. Then we had a lot of the children. Because then, your vegetables wasn't comin' in. You had crops but not as good as they was in the spring. Your spring crop was really nice for us kids to work and make money.

Our school would end in April or May. Berry season, strawberries. We had to help pick strawberries. The old peoples, they knew the strawberries was comin'. So school would end. Berry season, that was a time when you could make money to get your little Easter frock or your little Easter shoes. My daddy had only five acres. But we could go off to the neighbors, after we get through with my dad strawberries. We could make our own money. We had to—and we wanted to— work in the field. So therefore school was a limit.

Kids would go to school 'til they were—twenty? It didn't matter. You could be eighteen and you in first grade. I can remember they wasn't kids. Children was goin' to school. But we were goin' to school as adults, as children, all in together. We didn't have no separation, no separate rooms. Never had two teachers. Oh, I can't remember the day that we had two teachers. The poor teacher would say, "Well, I'm gonna start here, with the smaller kids." And she work up to the bigger kids. Or some of the older kids would even help the teacher with some of the smaller kids.

Now my older brothers, after they got a certain age, they drifted off to wherever they could find a little work. They didn't stay in school. But me and most of those boys, we went to school.

Us, we was right at the school. We could see the church from our kitchen window. But some kids was walkin' from, oh my God, how far back over there? Girl, maybe five, six, eight, ten miles just to come to that little school. That's how far those poor children had to walk.* Where the white kids, they had a bus to pick

* When Sylvia and I met one of her childhood friends in Louisiana, he recalled living with his grandmother in Springfield every school year because his home community, Killian, had no school. His wife reported that, in nearby Maurepas where she grew up, black children received no schooling at all.

'em up 'n take 'em to school. They did make sure those white kids rode that yellow bus. They would pass us on the road and throw rocks, stones. Even the bus driver sometime would try to run us over. As children! We tryin' to walk to our school and them kids ridin' to their school.

The white man did let us have his bus to go to the state fair. Not us 'n the white kids, noooo. We weren't on there together. Nope, no, no, no. Just us. Our teacher would tell us, "I'm gonna take y'all. A dollar 'n a half." A dollar and a half to go to the state fair to see all the animals. Not to bring our animals to show off. I had a old rooster. He was so sweet, just like a good dog. He would play with you, protect you. He would listen to me. But I couldn't take my rooster to the fair, 'cause I were black. We still went to that fair. The white would provide a bus, 'cause he was gonna get the money. A dollar and a half was a lotta money then. They want the whole community to turn out. Black or white, they don't care who it is, long as they get that money.

Gettin' back to school, I'm gonna tell you about it now. I'm in the school. I really don't remember doin' my ABCs. However, I remember this one woman. Whatever she did, she taught us very well. Mathematics. Or arithmetic. What did she call it? She used to have us to go to the blackboard. We did have a blackboard. We had to really be careful with the crayon—to keep from breakin' it—so that we could always do our one plus two plus. I don't remember usin' a book for math. We had maybe one book. And she had to keep this book so that she could teach us. One plus one equal two. After I learned to do my one plus one equal two, then I learned the time tables. I can remember the signs. I got to the dividing sign.

My teacher would say, "Sylvia, you are doin' *good*. We gonna move on." I still was maybe third or first or second grade. But I was movin' on. See that's why I know my brains shoulda went further. I know that.

She used to always try to correct me with my language, which is very poor right now. Oh, she used to always get on me about "thee," the word "thee." I don't know if I was sayin' "thee" or "thou." She had the language books and she would try to, she did teach me. "He," "she," simple words like that, or the noun. What was a noun? And what was the other one that she taught us? That was our language. Very, very poor. I didn't get too far. But I learned to divide. I learned to multiply. I did learn time tables.

When I would go home, I would write it all down. By lamp lights. We did not have electricity. I would write down on a piece of paper all my time tables and keep 'em for myself. I would show it to my brothers, try to help them. Sometime it worked and sometime it didn't.

Them boys, it was very hard for them. Some of the kids at school was not good at learnin'. Boys mostly, the problem was boys. Girls, too, some of 'em. My brothers, they did not like school as much as I did. Or they liked it for play or to associate. But they didn't learn very much. My dad, he tried to tell us, how important it was to go to school. I guess my mom, too. Mama had I think a fourth grade education. She could read a little bit and she could write. And I can remember a few words that she say, "Now you not sayin' that right." But for some reason, I don't hear her mouth too much on school. My father, oh he would raise . . . Not to me, 'cause I was the type that like school. Everybody would tell you who know me.

I learned to help Miss Clarke teach the other children. Some of 'em are old mens today. I was in my thirties or forties, when one of 'em say, "Sylvia you showed me how to do my name. You taught me how to do this. You taught me." I say, "I sure did." One girl, she always wanted to copy. She would say, "How do you spell that word? I'll give you my sandwich." I would spell it backwards. And she would spell it backwards. Then the teacher would look at me. She could see her askin' me, you know. I would do it backwards because I felt like, "You should learn to spell just like me. You are comin' to school thinkin' I'm gonna do the lessons for you? No. That doesn't work." That girl, she was so uppity up, a child and just uppity up. I think she was that way because her parents would let her run around a little more. My parents wouldn't. And I was boyish too, from bein' with them boys. Those girls would call me nappy-headed, raggedy and all that kinda stuff. "You thinkin' you're so cute. I'm not gonna show you anything." Of course, there was kids I did show and help—all they math, they fraction 'n stuff. I wanted to help the next black child like Miss Clark was doin'. That was important.

Some other people around there, they would try to help us. Miss Anderson would come to our house. She probably taught me as much as my teacher did— just a neighborhood woman. Or Mrs. Clayton, she would teach you. Mrs. Clayton was a very religious person, her 'n her husband both. He was a preacher there. They were all kinda educ- . . . Well, nobody was *educated*. To tell you the true, when I look at it now, a lotta peoples in them days, black or white, was uneducated. The white had the opportunity to go to school. But they was a buncha dummies, too. They, we all talk the same. They really had a drawl accent. And us, we had ours also.

I know the blacks never use the proper words. What do they say, right now? "Cool." We been usin' that for years. "Cool, that's cool, man." In school, I learn that those words we were usin' was more of a slang. I don't think we should even use the word "cool." It's not the proper language. It's a slang, right? But today, for today it's cool. That's cool. That's cool. So where were we?

That school. School was so important for me, the most important thing in the *world*. I just loved school. When your parents are sendin' you, you can go to school and sit down with joy. It is nice, children, to go to school when your parents are sendin' you. They makin' your meal. They buyin' your clothes. They takin' full control of you. It's so good to go to school at that time. You don't have to worry is your light bill paid, your gas bill paid, your house note paid. But when you tryin' to go to school on your own, which I tried to do when I came up North . . .

I did try. I really tried. I went to MATC* at Eighth and State. They called it Vocational at that time. Voc' has my records. They will show you where this little black gal went to school for dinner, breakfast, and supper. I'm studyin' the books. But I'm workin' at Walgreens. It really wasn't easy for a person to do that.

I did learn quite a bit at Vocational, but not enough. I would've learned faster by sittin' with the children in school. That's where I shoulda been goin'. Because Vocational wasn't givin' me what I really needed. I needed basics. Like my verbs, my nouns, my pronouns, my proper nouns and all that kinda stuff. When I needed it, I couldn't get it. And when I got so far gone, I didn't know one noun from another or one this from the other. Oh, it's just sad.

My poor brothers could not pass a driver's test, because they didn't know one word from the other. That make me cry sometime, how them poor mens . . . I was the only one . . . Well, Pat could read and write pretty good. Joe, too. Me and Joe, we did okay at Vocational. But my brother Dock, he could barely write his name. And when Dan came to Milwaukee, he didn't know how to write good. Readin' was completely out. He went to school down there. But it wasn't a school where children could really learn, because the teacher's teachin' a hundred children. Nothing to help bring the brain out. It was sad. I tried to help them boys pass that test. This is later, in Milwaukee. I used to try to get the test for them and read it to 'em. It was hard. They just couldn't pass.

My brother Dan, if he hadda been educated enough to take the test for his driver's license, I don't think he'da been dead today. It's a shame when peoples do not educate peoples. Them peoples who don't wanna be education, okay, you can kinda blame over that. But them peoples who want it, who had to suffer the consequent . . .

* Milwaukee Area Technical College.

7

Galilee

When Sylvia recalls the importance of the church to her rural Southern childhood and the changes in her faith over time, she places herself in a story begun centuries before her birth. Forbidden to practice their own religions almost everywhere in North America, enslaved Africans did not immediately convert to Christianity in large numbers. Slaveholders saw danger in any kind of slave gatherings and in parts of the Bible such as the book of Exodus. When the wave of religious enthusiasm called the Great Awakening swept the colonies in the 1740s, however, missionaries broke through this resistance by arguing that conversion would make control easier. They preached obedience and portrayed slavery as ordained by God, but in the framework of a religion with more to offer. Slave converts numbered perhaps thirty thousand in the early 1790s and neared half a million by Emancipation in 1865. Forty years later, the count of black Christians approached three million nationwide.

It is difficult to imagine the racial violence, educational deprivation, and poverty surrounding black churches such as Sylvia's Galilee Baptist when founded in 1884, or the churches pastored by her grandfather, Reverend Patrick Tillman, in nearby Clio and Killian. A study of black Christianity in the Mississippi Delta in these years examines the many ways churches helped people survive a hostile world: by organizing community-wide aid networks, for example, or through activities that cultivated notions of freedom and respectability.[1] At the center of social life in the rural South, black churches would play a part in events such as the Great Migration and, later, the Civil Rights Movement.

Black scholars of the early twentieth century discussed the political potential of the "Negro Church," but doubted whether the institution could help improve black people's overall situation without eliminating its particularities in faith, worship, and preaching styles. White-supremacist discourse had long cast black religiosity as a threat to "civilization" because of an "emotionalism" rooted in primitive African cultures. Striving to disprove demeaning stereotypes and "uplift the race," most well-educated blacks believed that they could not obtain full participation in society without cultural assimilation to a white mainstream that saw anything African as inferior, savage, uncivilized. Although W. E. B. Du Bois traced African American religion to the mother continent, few of his social class wished to make that connection.[2] By the 1930s, a somewhat more assertive and self-affirming African American identity had emerged. Yet esteemed black intellectuals such as E. Franklin Frazier still maintained that no African cultural "retentions" had survived slavery and that blacks must jettison folk cultural "peculiarities" if they wanted equal treatment.[3]

Today's scholarly discussion of African American Christianity emerged after the dramatic transformation that brought forth Black Studies. The Black Power movement raised its own questions about religion. How could a religion that slaves adopted from their oppressors have met their spiritual needs, much less those of modern-day African Americans? Black Power theologian James Cone replied that enslaved Africans and their descendants could authentically embrace Christianity because Jesus Christ "sided with," indeed fully identified with, the most oppressed. Thus, Jesus was black. Cone further clarified his Christology by stating that those who called themselves Christians embodied the anti-Christ, whenever they did not do everything in their power to eradicate racist oppression.[4] Shaking the theological establishment, Cone's 1969 book, *Black Theology and Black Power*, caught the attention of Black Power leader Amiri Baraka, formerly LeRoi Jones, whose African name expressed the moment. Invited by Baraka to head a workshop at the 1970 Congress of African People, Cone found himself assailed by young black nationalists who denounced Christianity as oppressive, dismissed him for defending it, and then fell to arguing among themselves about what religion, if any, would satisfy.[5] A new phase of discussion about African American religion had begun—in a context unthinkable to earlier generations.

With a changed mindset and a trove of long-neglected slave narratives, historians bolstered the argument that African Americans made Christianity their own. Evidence showed enslaved converts connecting their adopted religion with hopes of earthly emancipation. In a letter from 1723, an anonymous slave asked the Bishop of London to help free a group of Virginia slave converts for reasons of faith, including the point that bondage prevented them from keeping the Sabbath.[6] Planners of the 1739 Stono Rebellion knew that Spanish Florida offered freedom to runaways from English colonies if they converted. Bible reading helped fuel insurrections led by Gabriel Prosser in 1800, Denmark Vesey in 1822, and Nat Turner in 1831. Plantation communities held clandestine preaching sessions in woods and swamps, where literate slaves used their forbidden skills to share Biblical passages. One such reader, Frederick Douglass, recalled double meanings in slave spirituals. He and others preparing an escape bolstered each other by singing, "I'm bound for the land of Canaan," and such while doing their plantation work.[7] "Wade in the Water" told runaways what to do if pursued by bloodhounds.[8] "Go Down Moses" retold a story so loved that one Union Army chaplain complained of runaways in army camps emphasizing Exodus more than the gospels.[9]

Black Power enthusiasm fired historian Albert Raboteau's sweeping study of slave religion's African influences. Christianity helped to keep those roots alive, he argued, in a "process . . . broader and more complex than simple retention."[10] Most African religions had the idea of one God—alongside beliefs in immanent deities, spirits, revered ancestors, a sense of the divine in Nature and the sacred in everyday life. Christian baptism resembled African rituals of immersion in bodies of water. Great Awakening missionaries welcomed seeing "the spirit" take possession of an individual. Africa's "danced religions" entered Christian worship, in the full-blown form of the "ring shout," or in foot tapping, hand clapping, and call-and-response patterns in preaching. After Emancipation, horrified Northern missionaries tried to banish all such Africanisms. Reviving the African connection later deeply affirmed black identity, not only for scholars and students but for individuals such as Sylvia as well.

Another question raised by Black Power dissolved in later work that reconnects the discussion directly with Sylvia's religious life. Had black churches historically acted as a force for change or for maintaining the status quo? This debate went beyond the obvious issue of pastors' attitudes about civil rights activism. Radical voices considered it insufficient to provide dispossessed church members with concrete help getting by, as well as a sense of "somebodyness."[11] Others saw resistance running through the entire history of African American religion.[12] Historians later observed that this discussion centered on church leaders, most of them male, better educated and better off than the poor and female majorities of African American believers.[13] More important here, a scholarly shift of attention from doctrine and institutions towards "lived religion," that is, "religion as practiced" by ordinary people in their everyday lives, has expanded notions of what constitutes the church, resistance, religion itself.[14] Such work can help to illuminate Sylvia's evolving religiosity.

With an eye to "lived religion," a study of black Christians in the Mississippi Delta between 1865 and 1915 found "a popular sense of the divine and the supernatural . . . not easily contained by creed," and a religiosity expressed as importantly in the activities of everyday life as in church. Such religion helped people to resist violent oppression in ways that ranged from practical networking and cultivating humane values to singing gospel lyrics about freedom trains.[15] Under quite different forms of oppression in the post-civil-right era that surrounded Sylvia's narration, a study in cultural anthropology asked black women in 1990s rural North Carolina about their faith and its effect on their lives. The women recount a few instances of outright protest, against racial unfairness by employers, for example, and many "everyday forms of resistance," in personal as well as community life. Attending to spirituality itself, the analysis glimpses how faith can shape notions of a self capable of effecting change and can drive compassionate engagement with the community.[16]

Connecting further with Sylvia's words here, the womanist theology of the 1990s opened visions of Christianity to Nature-based religious perspectives deeply embedded in African, Caribbean, and Native American cultures.[17] Moving past arguments about the historical church, these theologians ask what God and salvation can mean presently to those suffering brutal poverty, racism, and sexism—and find answers in the old African American saying, "Making a way out of no way." Monica Coleman defines this process as beginning with "unforeseen possibilities" and what one does with them; moving toward Divine goals of "justice, survival, and quality of life," and challenging any "existing order" that works against those goals.[18] A vanguard in African American religious thought at the time when Sylvia looked back and told her life story, womanist theology resonates with themes in that life and in this chapter's narrative of unconventional religiosity.

Recalling childhood years at Galilee Baptist Church, Sylvia focuses on the social role of the church, bringing people together in the community and across geographical distances. Her words make clear that the sense of "somebodyness" church activities provided represented a very real countering of racism and poverty, especially for children. Although she recalls growing increasingly discontent with the limited theology expressed in sermons, Sylvia came away from Galilee with a deep faith that would sustain her through a lifetime of struggle. A faith adaptable to urban environments, to her intellectual maturation, to her streetwise Black Power incarnation, and to her heartfelt return to Nature. A lived religion strong enough to help her maintain her own moral compass and keep love alive through the anguish of her brother's death and her family's bruising challenge to the existing order in pursuit of justice.

The church was important in our life because that was our schoolhouse, that was our education, that was our sociable thing, to get with each other. I was baptized a Baptist. Our church was named Galilee Baptist Church. Back in nineteen hundred, I think, they built that little church. It was like twenty-four by twenty-four, with a steeple and a bell that you pull to ring. When somebody died, the bell would ring. When they gonna start the service, the bell would ring.

As long as I can remember, Reverend Mixon was our pastor. He came from Hammond, eight miles away. Mrs. Mixon, she was our choir director. It was seven o'clock to go to church or Sunday school in the mornin'. Mrs. Walker, she would play the piano for introduction to the preacher. Then they play the pastor's song. The song I used to like so much was "I Need Thee." [*Sings.*] "I need Thee. Oh, I need Thee. Every hour, I need Thee." The rest of it I done forgot. She would play the song and you'd sing.

We had some good choirs. I used to be pretty good at singing, 'cause that was our pleasure. And I hoped. I wish I coulda got with a group that could've sung abroad. I did sing with a group: my cousins. Most of us was kinda cousins. We didn't have friend friends like today. A few friends but not a lot. We were glad to see each other, real glad. When we get to church, we had our little area. We would pray and we would sing and we would whoop and we would holler. I don't know how serious we was, but we were there.

We were very serious with our voices. We thought we could be the—can't remember the name. These boys who had this name, they were good singers. And they had 'em on this washin' powder box. They were black. All black. We thought we could be like them. Well, we could have. But we had nobody to help us. Those guys was livin' in New Orleans, right with the publicity. We were fifty miles away, back out there in them woods. The people wadn't comin' out there to hear us until, oh baby, around forty somethin'. Then they found out there is a Galilee Baptist church.

Then our church grew differently. It's a big brick church now, with big ten-maid-of-honor marriages. We had to walk all the way out there in them woods to get to the river to baptize each other. Now they got a swimmin' pool that they roll back.

Back then, it was small but it was a big part of our life. We had the choir and we had plays that we act in. I had some beautiful plays in my life. We had one play of gettin' married. I played the preacher's part 'cause my voice was always kinda heavy. I said to the young man, "Who give you the rights to marry this woman." And the boy came up and say, "I did, I did, I did." Oh, we just had so much fun. We were kids. Plays the public schools and other places threw away, we would take 'em and make something out of it.

See, that's why I'm sayin' if somebody coulda carried us further. At that time, these brains was open. They were ready for anything. They graspin'. Now the brains are close for years. It is very hard to get 'em back, girl. When they close up, you just as well dig your own hole and tumble in. 'Cause you down. But while they open, they are graspin' things. That's why I say to children, "Please, do it. Go to school. Get interested." But that ain't what you asked me about . . .

Okay. We would have these big church rallies in Maurepas, Head of Island, back over there where my mama used to live. Nothin' but water over there. When I grew up and went back to Louisiana, I went over there. Oooo, there was the most beautiful place! Girl! It was a very few black peoples left in there. The whites had moved in and they had all these big boats docked out there. They put up all these big buildins. When the hurricane go through it tumbles 'em over. They bought that property, probably bought it for nothing offa them poor black peoples. I know a lotta peoples sold they property and got outa there. Back then, I can remember the big logs down in this water with the church sittin' up on 'em—like you build a pier into the water.

The white man would let us rent them busses to go to Head of Island. They know that was a big church affair, somethin' like your convention. You know, church peoples have convention. It was black. All the black Baptists would get together. It wouldn't be at the same church every year. It would go from church to church. Head of Island would be one. Then maybe we'll have it; your year gonna be five years from now. We just kept goin' around. And we could communicate with peoples that way, communicate with Louisiana. Every year.

When we'd go to those rallies, we'd leave at six o'clock in the mornin' or five o'clock in the morning, 'cause daylight break around that time. Our pastor would go, our choir too. Some of us kids, we would have a little part to play—kids who were smart and knew how to read or perform. We all went. Oh God, there was hundreds 'n hundreds of peoples, at least hundred fifty, two hundred, three hundred. 'Cause we would get maybe two busses, big busses with fifty or sixty peoples or a hundred peoples. And then other party would get the same from Killian or Albany or Maurepas or the Head. Peoples that I knew so well. Some of your family. Or the other person family. You really know these peoples. They're miles 'n miles away from you. But this way you stay in touch. That was the only way to do it.

That was a good cookout. Everybody would bring cakes and pies. Oh my God. Some of them womens could really cook. That's one of our main thing was to go to eat. You get a chance to really eat. Which was important in our life, 'cause we wasn't gettin' this every day. To get something like that was almost like going to heaven. That was a big thrill. But they watched us children. We couldn't just run up there 'n snatch 'n grab. I had to be about fourteen the last time I went there.

Church was meaningful. But as far as I'm concerned today, the preacher really didn't know too much to preach to us. He would read parts out of the Bible that he had read over and over and over again. Tell me something different, Rev. I wanta hear something different. Just like an old record, he would wear it out. God was crucified. He died up on the cross. He'd do that to me every Sunday. Now this is enough. Because I have read the Bible, too. I've read where Jesus was crucified. My father didn't know how to read, though, and he had got kinda sick of hearin' God was crucified on the cross. We know that. Give us something else. That's all I'm askin' for. My preachers was almost as dumb as I was, but they were preachers. And you supposed to honor. So I honored 'em.

But today, it's entirely different. If you stupid, that's your business. But I don't wanta be bothered with you. I can go on to somethin' a little better. See baby, today the world isn't based on lyin' to peoples, or tellin' peoples what you think. You tell people what you know is the facts. That "think" stuff do not work. Take a tip from me. Okay? I'm takin' a test and I think this is correct. It does not work. Sometime one word can tell you the whole answer. And if you don't know, you be screwin' around there all the time. Pardon my French. But . . . we were supposed to talk about church. Okay.

Church. I did go to church. When I got up North, too. Oh, yes. Every Sunday, Aunt Oja and I, we had to go to church. Every Sunday. It was New Hope Baptist Church. Later on in life, the pastor, Reverend Lovelace, he married me 'n my husband at the church. Wait, I better get that right. Mount Zinah Baptist Church, yeah, that's the one I belong to. There was a New Hope and there still is. New Hope and Mount Zinah is different. I'm just kinda rememberin' them together, 'cause we went to different churches. New Hope and Mount Zinah and Tabernacle, all those different churches that we were affiliated with. A number of churches, but all Baptist. I was more of a Baptist person.

In Milwaukee, I became a member of Mount Zinah Baptist Church. Mount Zinah was not a small church at that time. They had members like, oh my God, five or six hundred. That was a nice organization. I used to sing in the choir there a lot. I were singin' pretty well. And I met a lot of friends there, young kids like myself. I was seventeen when I first got there, you know. We would go off some-time to other churches, singin' and praisin' God and havin' a good time. 'Cause we kids, it was sort of a gettin' out thing for us. Instead of goin' to the tavern, like some young peoples would do. I'm not gonna say I didn't go to the tavern. Because I did go. But I feared on Sunday. Sunday was always a day to worship. And I really did my part of worship.

Every Sunday, go to church. Go to church, goin' to heaven. Go to church, goin' to heaven. You go to church to go to heaven. How do that sound? Do you go to church to go to heaven? Or do you go to church to hear something different?

Don't get me wrong now. I'm not sayin' I didn't believe in God. I knew there was a God, because my father taught me. Papa knew.

Oh, I sincerely believe in God. I know that God is lookin' after me. I do not use God until I need God. When I need God, I ask God—seriously—to help me. And He respond. Like the time I lifted the tractor offa my brother, Eddie.

I was in my kitchen—that's out where I live now, it's like a quarter of a mile from Eddie's place—and I heard Eddie's tractor runnin'. Then all at once it was goin' pook, pook, pook. And I heard somebody sayin', "Help! Help me!" I just dropped everything and ran out the house. My truck was sittin' right there in the yard, key in it and everything. But that old truck couldn't go up the hill fast enough for me. I saw the tractor was turned over on his leg. I could see him. So I jumped outa the truck and ran up that hill.

I says, "Eddie! I gotta call somebody." I was startin' for his house, to call on the phone. Had to get help. I say, "I gotta call the rescue squad. I gotta." Eddie says, "I can't wait." I looked at him. Then I looked at this tractor. It's all steel. It had a rubber tire, but it's this big hunk of steel. I looked at that tractor. Then I looked up.

I say, "God, give me strength!" And I picked that thing up. I don't remember liftin' it. I don't remember the weight. All I remember is Eddie sayin', "Put it down, Sis. Put the tractor down." He had crawled over a little distant. "You can put the tractor down now, Sis." I got on my knees and crawled right behind him. I don't know why I couldn't walk. But I crawled. Later on, at the doctor's office, Eddie said that was the second time the tractor fell on him. The first time, there was three or four mens out there. And it took all them mens, every one of 'em, to lift that thing up offa Eddie. But I lifted that tractor offa my brother all by myself.

I just can't believe what I did. But I did ask God. And He gave me strength to raise that tractor up. I looked to the sky. It was pretty and blue. It was beautiful. He was there. And I needed Him. There's that old song, "Oh Lord, I need Thee. Every hour . . ." I don't need Him every hour. But I sure needed Him that hour. It's not that I'm asking God to give me something to eat or to give me money or to give me . . . I don't do that to God. But the day I picked that tractor up offa Eddie, I did it to God. And God did it to me. That was God above who did that. And I thank Him.

Oooo, I get that good feelin'. Some people say they go to church and they pray and they holler and they whoop. And then they get the good feelin'. But right now, Jody, I have that feelin' runnin' through my body. Right now as I'm talkin' to you. Who else can do that but God Almighty? Me and my God, we get along fine. I think of Him in the mornin' when I get up. Oh, this mornin' was a pretty mornin'. I don't know if you noticed it. It was a beautiful mornin'. And that was my God. He were there. Lookin' after me.

Us poor black peoples, if we didn't believe in God—and sincerely believe—we woulda never made it through all we been through. The slavery peoples, they couldna made it out of slavery—out of hell and destruction—without God. They had to have God. Oh, we are deeply concerned about God. We are communicatin' with God. Yes, there is a God. Our Survivior.

8

Teenagers

Sylvia entered her teens in the early 1940s, when the word "teenager" was just entering public discussion. Teenagers emerged in a world their grandparents could not have imagined. Although the 1920s had brought greater urbanization, technology such as home radios, burgeoning entertainment industries, and a new enthusiasm for modernity, most Americans still spent their teen years not in school but contributing to their parents' income by working a paid job or for the family farm. When the Depression eliminated such jobs, hundreds of thousands of teens hit the road looking for work. To curb youth unemployment, 1930s New Deal programs helped build high schools and provide the young part-time work so they could stay in school. By 1936, an unprecedented 65 percent of U.S. teens attended high school, where they developed an age-specific culture. To be sure, how individuals experienced the advent of the teenager depended on factors such as geographical location, social class, and race. To African American youth such as Sylvia, the advent of the teenager mattered less than the emergence over several decades of a more positive and assertive "New Negro" identity. That new sense of self has received much scholarly attention, the teenager's early history very little. A brief look at both will help frame Sylvia's memories of her teens.

In the United States, high school played a central part in germinating mainstream teenage youth culture.[1] Besides instruction, many high schools offered team sports, clubs, activities, and entertainments such as dances. Educational policy experts aimed to keep teens contentedly under adult control. Mass high school attendance had something of the opposite effect, however. Brought together at school, 1930s teens "learned to look to one another and not to adults for advice, information, and approval." With an impatient desire to run their own lives and a growing sense of "teenage rights," many dared to disagree with parents about clothes, friends, movies, and music.[2] As the economy improved, teen consumers, particularly girls as consumers, gained importance. At the dawn of the 1940s, swing jazz inspired the "bobby soxer" craze that swept the nation with its irrepressible dancing, its signature look and lingo incomprehensible to adults. Manufacturers adapted product lines to teen tastes. Advertisers of soft drinks, records, movies, beauty products, and clothing encouraged the development of this new demographic group.[3]

Teenagers had widely divergent experiences of this phenomenon. Rural high school enrollment rates remained lower in the U.S. Both technology and ideas reached such areas more slowly. Not quite 50 percent of the nation's farms had electricity by 1942, although nearly all would by 1952. Traditional notions of parental authority remained strong in cities, too. Large numbers had little money for non-necessities and could scarcely dream of fulfilling consumer desires. Then, World War II weighed down dancing bobby soxers with rationing, serious responsibilities, and worries. High school enrollments fell for the first time in decades, as teens too young for military service went to work in defense industries. Yet even in Germany and Occupied France, where Nazi governments banned swing jazz because of its African American origins, rebellious teenagers danced to forbidden music in clandestine nightclubs.[4] Whatever the obstacles, many connected with the trend well before the 1950s brought the teenager into full bloom.

Two studies conducted around 1940 provide a sense of what "teenager" might have meant to African American youth.[5] Researchers in the South's rural Black Belt found most teens not in high school. Blacks there had few secondary schools and inadequate elementary schools where children's fieldwork limited attendance. Many of high school age remained in lower grades or left school to help families earn a living. About 17 percent of the surveyed households had radios and electricity; 26 percent had phonographs; 21 percent automobiles. Some had never heard a radio or seen a movie. In contrast, young blacks in a study of Washington, DC, and Louisville all had access to media such as radio, records, magazines, and movies. These city-dwellers all attended high school. The urban study defined three distinct classes that differed in views as well as consumer spending. Almost all interviewees in both studies said they loved dancing. Black Belt teens complained that their churches banned dancing, even expelled young members for it. Yet dance they did, at homes or the local honkytonk. In the cities, black youth could more openly enjoy this quintessential teenage activity. They had school-sponsored dances, as well as dancehalls and radio or records at home.

The music enjoyed by both black and white 1940s teens had roots reaching back to Africa. Musical traditions had come through slavery in channels such as the "ring shout," a danced form of prayer permitted by some Christian missionaries.[6] With drums generally forbidden because they could communicate from one plantation to another, enslaved people kept the African beat alive with a thigh/foot slapping gesture called "patting Juba." In exceptional New Orleans, Africans performed the music of their homelands for large outdoor audiences. In 1817, a city ordinance restricted this activity to one day a week, daylight hours and Congo Square only. Two years later, a visitor wrote that, on Sundays, slaves would "rock the city with their Congo dances."[7] Soon, however, Congo Square featured a musical mix brought by newcomers sold South.

Reworking music borrowed from whites, black musicians flattened notes to make them "blue"; added beats, offbeats, and shifts in meter. Ornamenting melody with pitch-wavering, bends, slides, and extra notes, they wove in call-and-response patterns.[8] By the beginning of the twentieth century, jazz had spilled out of its New Orleans cradle, spread through the black South and gone North with vaudeville performers. Access to guitars brought forth wandering country blues singers who worked gambling houses, saloons, or speakeasies and brothels. Migration carried the country blues to cities such as Chicago. In the 1920s, women blues singers toured with tent shows, played big-city cabarets, flaunted their "wild" ways and made records.[9] Respectability concerns kept the first major black-owned record company, The Black Swan, from signing artists such as Bessie Smith and Ma Rainey.[10] White companies, however, rushed to record such music after 1920, when Mamie Smith's "Crazy Blues" sold a million copies in less than a year. The blues remained "race music," marketed primarily to blacks. Jazz had white fans—even whites-only jazz venues such as Harlem's Cotton Club.

African Americans faced far worse than the insulting exclusion, however, as racial hostility flared between the World Wars. The late 1910s and 1920s brought a wave of particularly hideous racial lynchings where mobs burned people alive or inflicted other tortures. Anti-black riots occurred in cities throughout the nation—more than twenty in 1919 alone. Chicago rioting that year ended with 38 dead and 537 wounded. A 1921 rampage left Tulsa's black neighborhood burned to the ground and took an estimated 50 to 300 lives, the numbers covered up by local authorities then openly connected to the Ku Klux Klan.[11] In the 1920s, a revived KKK with some three million members nationwide gained control of several state legislatures, staged enormous rallies, and encouraged mob attacks on blacks in cities such as Detroit.[12] Such abuse prepared the ground for Nation of Islam founder W. Fard Muhammad's 1930 emergence in Detroit, teaching that whites were innately evil mutants "grafted" by a wicked scientist.[13] Racial violence had a long history. African Americans' response, however, was taking a new turn.

Historians agree that World War I contributed to the emergence of a more assertive "New Negro" identity. In several postwar riots, armed black veterans used their wartime training to defend black neighborhoods. "Over there" during the war, soldiers from the South experienced a relatively nonsegregated world. Falling in love with the jazz bands accompanying all-black regiments, the French did not object to black soldiers eating in cafes or dancing with white women. Many men brought home raised expectations. More important, the war opened industrial jobs in American cities, encouraging mass migration from the South. Half a million made this move during the war, tripling to 1.5 million by 1930. These migrants joined communities with all social classes—including a small topmost group of highly educated world travelers—segregated into all-black neighborhoods. This sudden gathering in modern urban settings fostered new attitudes. The expression "New Negro" and self-affirming discourses such as Pan-Africanism had emerged earlier, mostly among the privileged few. Now those ideas received a wider hearing.

Between 1916 and the mid-1920s, Jamaican-born Marcus Garvey built a popular movement on Pan-Africanist ideas. Garvey urged people to love their blackness, empower themselves through education, and return to Africa—or at least create self-sufficient, all-black enclaves. His organization attracted millions of members and sympathizers nationwide. In the Black Belt youth study discussed above, one interviewee seemed to echo Garvey, when she declared it best to be darker because "if you're black you look more like an African and people know you got pure blood."[14] By the time U.S. authorities deported Garvey, he had drawn strong criticism from other black leaders, most notably W. E. B. Du Bois of the NAACP, head of the U.S. Pan-Africanist Association since 1900. Opponents of segregation were appalled that Garvey not only preached racial separation, but also tried to ally with the KKK in order to achieve it. Garvey's popular but much-disputed movement calls attention to the complexity and struggle that characterized the emergence of the New Negro.

Class differences complicated that process, as did divergent generational perspectives. Notions of "high" and "low" culture made it difficult for upper-class devotees of the Harlem Symphony Orchestra to recognize the importance of cabarets, dancehalls, blues and jazz clubs in birthing a self-consciously African American culture.[15] Established black intellectuals mentored and promoted "the younger generation" that philosopher Alain Locke described as "vibrant with a new psychology."[16] Yet some brilliant black artists of the 1920s displeased elders who had fought to counter degrading stereotypes. Writers such as Claude McKay evoked stark ghetto realities in their poetry. Zora Neale Hurston breathed life into her fiction with folklore material she gathered as a cultural anthropologist in the South. "We younger Negro artists" declared Langston Hughes in 1926, "intend to express our dark-skinned selves without fear or shame." Pleasing people, white or black, did not matter.[17]

The Negro Renaissance/New Negro phenomenon unfolded across several decades, in Harlem certainly, but also in cities from coast to coast. Black communities encountered the new literature in NAACP and Urban League journals; received visits by national leaders and artists. People engaged locally in artistic, intellectual, and political activity—and danced to a more self-consciously black music.[18]

Connecting this directly with Sylvia's experience, a Chicago study argues that less-educated migrants from the South, particularly as consumers, played a central role in the creative intellectual work that brought forth a new, more affirmatively black identity.[19] This complicated process took place in multiple arenas. Black filmmakers struck chords with the new urban con-sumers, for example, as they shifted from trying to "uplift" popular culture and began producing dramas about interracial love, racial violence, and abusive class relationships. Proliferating beauty colleges and shops worked a problematic interweaving of hair-straightening and the recognition of black beauty. Blues musician Thomas A. Dorsey systematized a melding of that "devil music" with down-home hymn singing. Careful discipline of moves and music made the modern gospel choir eventually marketable even to established black churches that had preferred European music such as Mozart. As diverse communities of African Americans contested their way toward a new apprecia-tion of themselves and their own culture, migrants embodied that news when they went back South to visit relatives.

Sylvia recalls such visits in one of her vignettes about teenage friendships, all with cousins. A relationship with the cousin next door has a simple sincerity, almost as if the "teenager" had not yet touched their rural world—except that these two teens have a system for deceiving their parents and flouting dicta against their "girl talk": a mix of boys, music, things they'd like to buy. With her New Orleans cousin, Sylvia remembers dancing—on double dates with boys—at a teen club. That conduct would have horrified her parents, who forbade even listening to such music, much less sneaking out to dance at the juke joint down the road. A third cousin whose family had migrated earlier came South from Chicago for visits. She dazzled local people black and white, impressed young Sylvia with her beauty-school looks, her spending, and bold actions such as taking her very black cousin into a New Orleans department store. Sylvia ends the tale with a prophetic twist on a pair of patent leather shoes.

I still ain't brought out no friend. So I'm going to Gladys. My cousin Gladys and I, we could talk about everything—our mamas, our daddies, our brothers, our sisters, everything. See, when I was five, six, seven, eight, I didn't have this person to talk to. She was back across the branch at the time. They lived where, when the water come up, oh my God, you had to have a boat to get outa there. Her daddy was a preacher. He used to go off and preach. But when that water go up he couldn't move offa that little knoll. Later, he done moved up in life, even bought a car. He got him a house built just west of me, right over the fence. As I say, my kitchen was to the west. And Gladys, her kitchen was facin' my kitchen. We could see each other house through these patch of trees 'n bushes, me and my cuz.

So, a lotta time—this was my telephone now. I still don't know what a telephone look like but this was my telephone—I'd go to the kitchen window, to my back door. And I'd go, [*Whistles two notes, twice.*] "My gal." I'm sayin', "My gal." She would hear it and come back: [*Whistles.*] We called each other "my gal." We both had the same whistle. And we know to come to the window. If she can, she run to the fence. And I run to talk over the fence. See? From a distance, she would see me and she would come. Oh! She would whistle back to let me know she's free.

Me, I always was a busy child. Gladys, too. Our parents taught us we had to do work. We wasn't the type who could just sit around, pick up a book 'n read it or go out there 'n play. In a day, I had a full day's work. My brothers was supposed to have a full day's work, too. But some of 'em didn't have as full a day's work as I did. It was washin'. Cookin'. Cleanin'. Goin' to get water. It was something to do all the time. This was when I was like twelve, thirteen. So she probably was fifteen or sixteen. 'Cause she's older than I. That's when we started that talkin'.

If we were talkin', my parents wouldn't like it. He, they would say, "Oh, you out there talkin' about them old boys." He never realize that we had to have . . . Girls wanted to do girls' talk. I guess he figured girls' talk was 'bout meetin' some boy or bein' with some boy. I don't know. I never really ask 'em, about it. But the way they approach me was, "I bet you was talkin' about that old boy, L.C." Or some old boy.

I wouldn't tell 'em, "No, I wasn't talkin' about that. I were talkin' about . . ." I wouldn't say that. They say I was talkin' about it, so I thought they knew what I were talkin' about. And I just go along with their program. 'Cause if you argue with 'em they might: "Well, I'll put the switch to you." So you don't do that to your parents. You just shut up. That's exactly what I did. Shut up.

'Cause we really would be talkin' about the boys. Or we'd be talkin' about a dress or a piece a material that, if we could get it, we'll take it to Miss Helen. And she'd make us a dress to wear to church. Or where we was gonna meet 'n stuff like that. And then one of Gladys's sisters got married. Well, that sister was younger than the one I were talkin' to, closer to my age. Her parents let her marry this guy. She was, I don't know, fourteen, fifteen or sixteen. Young, very young.

My parents, they were fussy. They didn't want other peoples tellin' me about life. I imagine they wanted to tell me. And they didn't tell me nothin' either. [*Laughs.*]

So if my parents wadn't around, I would whistle to her to let her know. If she was free, we can come to the fence 'n talk. We would whistle: "My gal. My gal." I would hurry up 'n run to the fence. She'd hurry up 'n run. That's the way we did to talk to each other about girls' talk. We could talk our business up under a tree. And sometime we would sing. Gladys 'n them—she had sisters—we used to sing a lot together. Later, we wanted to talk about our little boyfriends or our little personal things. Oh, that was our gossipin' hour.

Girl, I saw that guy so and so. You did? Now what are you gonna wear Sunday to church? When is you gonna get your hair done? Or can we? When are you gonna walk to Springfield? 'Cause we maybe could meet. And we'd go look through the window of Miss Setoon's store and wish we could have this dress. Of course, I gotta take my brothers with me. Her sisters would go with her. But we really enjoyed that.

My gal. Did I leave her or she left me? Lord have mercy! To tell you the true, I don't know. I think she left before I left. Because she became pregnant by one of the church members. So I think she left first. I'm almost sure. It took years and years for me to find that girl.

When I went to live in California, peoples was tellin' me, "Your cousin Gladys live in Oakland." I say, "Oooo, I gotta go up there 'n see her." And the minute—I don't know if she came to me or I came to her. But we used that whistle. We sure did. Yup. [*Whistles.*]

So we were visitin' each other in California. It was like, "Oh girl, I wanta see this and I wanta see that and I wanta." Next thing I heard, she was in them mountains up there out of Oakland or San Francisco, takin' care of peoples or doin' housework or something up there, when her car broke down and she tumble off the mountain. Fell and killed herself.

Never will forget that whistle. It was, "my gal." We were sayin', "my gal."

Then, I had another cousin named Gladys. Not my gal. Another Gladys. This Gladys lived in New Orleans—Gretna really. We called it New Orleans though. My mama would let me go down there and stay maybe three or four days. I could always go to New Orleans to this big Mardi Gras. Oh, that was just beautiful! Whenever I went to my cousin place in New Orleans, I could go to the juke joint. That's what they call 'em, down South. You could dance 'n you could really . . .

This Gladys was younger than I. And she loved to dance. Me too. But Gladys, oooh, she knew it all. She could do everything. She were just too excited. She would have her boyfriend and find me a boyfriend for when I'd come down. There was a young kid that liked me, too. We would go out to this party place for teenagers. And we would dance.

One night, I never will forget. I was in bed sleepin'. She was still outside with her boyfriend. I did have a fella that walked me home too. But I gave up and came on in the house. Then my auntie came in and she said, "Sylvia, where's Gladys?" I said, "She's outside." Pretty soon Gladys come tearin' in that house—with my auntie just hittin' at her. Gladys says to me, "You shoulda stayed out there with me." I say, "I couldn't. Those mosquitoes was just eatin' my legs up and I wadn't gonna stay out there with nobody."

Gladys, she could be up all night. Party all night long. She only had to do her little chores around home, which wasn't that much. I couldn't stay up as late. I wasn't the type person who could lay in bed. I had to get up and work, take care of my brothers. I guess I was tired most of the time.

She used to make fun of me because I was that way. "You are just country." Those was her words. She would really make fun, call me all kinda names. Even when we were grown she still referred to me as "country." Then I say, "Well, if I'm country, I kinda like it."

This Gladys, she drink. I can remember one time when she gave me a drink. This is, I'm in my teens now. I say, "Ooooo, I don't want this." She says, "Oh, you just plain country." I said, "No, I'm not, because my daddy . . ." My father would let me have a glass of beer sometimes. I knew how to drink beer. But all this hard liquor! Whew! I never fool with a lot of alcohol. But I did love to go out and dance. I did know how to dance.

When I was growin' up, we had a little juke joint out near where I lived. This white lady had this place. She would let you play a lotta black music and dance. I had to slip in there, 'cause Mama and Daddy woulda never let me do stuff like that. I'm still at home with my parents. And my parents, they don't like for you to dance or sing the blues, because they are religious peoples. Yeah. First time you hear that?

I guess that's why I couldn't jump right off to tell you about the music part of my life. I loved music. I especially liked the blue part of it. Oh, I can remember the song, [*Sings.*] "Open the door, Richard." There was a lot of blues. [*Sings.*] "Open the door, Richard. Richard, why don't you open that door?" Was that by Little Richard? I done forgot who it was by. But I really remember that song.* I always got that blues singin' on the radio station.

You couldn't go 'round that house and sing blues songs. You couldn't even pop your fingers. They said if you do that, you against God's rules. You just don't do that. Not a normal young person. Old sloppy womens and whorish womens will go around poppin' they fingers 'n singin' the blues. You don't go around listenin' to these old blues songs. Any of these blues songs. That's how they thought. You do that and you ain't goin' to heaven. Really. My peoples was very, "I better not catch you poppin' your fingers or shakin' your booty or dancin'."

We had one of them old radios. If the wire came loose on it, the ground wire, you couldn't get nothin' but one station. That was pretty sad. But it was a radio. Later, one of my brothers went to the service or someplace and sent us a pretty good radio.

One day—Honey, this is funny—the radio is on. The radio set way up there high, so we all couldn't get to it. But I could. I'm listenin' to that song what I was talkin' 'bout, [*Sings and pops her fingers.*] "Open the door Richard. Richard, why don't you open that door?" And my daddy was outdoors hearin' me. The radio is goin' and I'm goin' behind it. You know, you like some song and you singin' behind it. Daddy came rushin' in there. He say, "Who were you talkin' to?" I say, "Aww, I, I, I." I didn't know how to lie out of that. I didn't know what to say. I says, "I wadn't talkin' to nobody, I was singin' that song." He say, "You ain't goin' to heaven! I done told you about singin' them blues songs. You don't go singin' blues

---

* "Open the Door, Richard," first recorded by Jack McVea, reached number 1 on Billboard's list of hits in early 1947. Several other versions went to the top of the charts that same year—one by Count Basie and one by Louis Jordan, the "father" of rhythm and blues.

'n stuff like that! *You*. You don't do that! You're a lady. You don't do that. I don't teach you that kind of teachin'." And all that kinda stuff. Oh!

It was a secret thing to sing the blues. Or to learn to dance. Or to listen to the radio, to the blue part. You could listen to "Inner Sanctum"—you know, the squeakin' door—or the news on the radio. But not the blues. Or that juke joint in the neighborhood. We used to go in there and dance and party. We would just dance, dance, dance. But I had to slip in there. Or when I went to New Orleans. My parents better not hadda known I was down there dancin' 'n swingin'. But I was. That was one of my ways of havin' pleasure when I was a kid.

Another cousin of mine, Odile, lived in Chicago. My mama's sister, Edna, went to Chicago when Odile was a little bitty girl. I can remember as a child that my mother would get these packages—for Christmas and Easter. Aunt Edna would send us a nice package. From up North. Seemed like to me it would even smell different. You could smell something. The clothes, everything was really refresh-like. There was something about this package. As simple a thing as a apple or a orange or the candy that they had . . . Oh! Aunt Edna would send girl clothes, my cousin Odile's clothes, because she was older than I. I wore what she wore. I can't remember the boys gettin' this stuff. But the treats 'n all would come for everybody.

Certain time of the year, my Aunt Edna and them would come down South. I think it would be fall or spring, when it isn't too hot. So they would come down and they would *appear* to have a little money. Never looked into their bankbook. If I hadda looked, I'da saw they didn't have nothing. I had saw different cousins come home with all the fancy clothes or the fancy this. And, oh my God, look at 'em how they spend a little.

My cousin, Odile, she could spend money. She were workin' at some packin' house in Chicago. Well, she was makin' a little money and she gave me the impression that, "Oooo, I just *live*." Later, she became a beautician. She finish high school and went to beauty school. Her mother probably was providin' money for this girl to go to school. Aunt Edna was housekeepin'. They say her job was housekeepin'. At the time, I didn't know what they were talkin' about. I didn't know that word meant workin' in the kitchen for the white woman, scrubbin' floors, cleanin' house for her. I felt like these peoples were up North. Up North. They would look so nice 'n so dignified.

My cousin Odile, she was very light-skinned. And my mother's sister, Rosy, was very light, too. She didn't have straight hair. But black people straighten they hair 'n it looks like it's straight. There was twelve or thirteen girls in the family. And Rosy was the baby sister. She was about the same age as my cousin Odile. So Odile and Rosy, they just kinda flocked together. Everybody thought they were two sisters. That was Odile's auntie. So Odile 'n Rosy would come down. And these white guys would bring them out to where we live. It wasn't a cab them days, but somebody standin' around 'n, "I'll take you out there to Dock Bell house." When they got off the train in Ponchatoula from up North, white mens would bring 'em. They didn't know if these girls was half-white or white, or what. Because they were different, comin' from up North. They were stacked, too. So those guys would be flirtin' with 'em. Then my cousin would say, "Oh, Uncle Dock." And the white guy was shock that my daddy was black.

This other girl, Rosy, was already beautician. So they could make a pretty good livin'. When they come down there, they always had money to go to—where was that? D. H. Holmes. Ooooo. Me, I never got to go into a D. H. Holmes store. It was in New Orleans. Odile would take me. That's one thing about her. I was a little black gal. But she would definitely take me into D. H. Holmes.

We would take the train down to New Orleans. Somebody would always take us to Ponchatoula. It's just forty, fifty miles to New Orleans. Odile would take me to Canal Street. That's how I learn Canal Street and Maison Blanche and all those big—oh I tell you—them stores. They small now to compare. At that time, I thought these was just huge. We would go on Rampart and Canal. Honey, they had this very exclusive black restaurant, where they really let black peoples *in*. I think it was black on one side and the whites on the other. They serve all these shrimps 'n crabs 'n gumbo 'n oh my God. We'd go in there and sit down and eat. *Sit down and eat.* That food was some good. To me, New Orleans was just unbelievable—the New Orleans Odile showed me.

One time, Odile sent me a pair of her shoes. Or my auntie sent 'em. They wasn't high heels, because I don't think my parents woulda allowed me to wear high heels. But they were black patent leather. Black patent leather is so pretty. It looks so good on your feet.

I tried to wear them to church. I can remember walkin' in those shoes. They were actually hurtin' my feet. Too small. But I wanted to wear those shoes, even if they did hurt me. And I mean they hurt. I can remember the hurt right now. Every time I buy a pair of shoes and they begin to hurt, I think about that day when I put my foot in Odile's shoes. Which gave me a good feeling because they were, oh beautiful shoes. But they hurt. I'm wearin' these pretty shoes and I'm very uncomfortable. But I wore them. I walked through the woods. It was gonna be baptism. So we had to walk back into the woods to the river. And I wore those shoes.

I was . . . how would they say that? I was walkin' in her shoes. I'm walkin' in Odile's shoes. I guess life was tryin' to tell me somethin'. You got your foot in her shoes and they hurt. Just because she up North, that don't mean that it was easy for her. Up there. It wasn't as easy as I thought. There might be a hurt.

9

My Roosevelt

At the Southern Conference for Human Welfare in November 1938, First Lady Eleanor Roosevelt did something unheard of. The conference had been organized in response to a presidential report on Southern economic conditions. Although the U.S. economy had recovered significantly during Franklin D. Roosevelt's first term, the South still suffered the nation's lowest industrial wages and an agricultural economy characterized by tenant farming, sharecropping—and extreme poverty. Calling this "the nation's worst economic problem," the president sought solutions. The twelve hundred attendees of the Southern Conference for Human Welfare, about 20 percent of them black, included college students, professors, businessmen, journalists, lawyers, political and union organizers, even sharecroppers. They met in Birmingham, Alabama, at a time when Southern law and custom kept blacks and whites separated. On the second day of the conference, police officers came to enforce local segregation laws. Participants reluctantly moved to one side or the other of the tape that the police put down the middle of the auditorium floor. Arriving later, Eleanor Roosevelt seated herself on the black side next to her friend, Mary McLeod Bethune. When an officer told her she must move, the First Lady placed her chair in the aisle, on both sides of the tape—and insisted she would stay there.[1] African Americans would remember this gesture as one of many signs that they had friends in the White House under FDR.

That relationship had its complications. Loyal since Emancipation to the party of Lincoln, African Americans who could vote in 1932 had backed Roosevelt's Republican opponent two to one. By 1936, however, three out of four black voters joined in giving Roosevelt a landslide, despite the president's failure to take a stand for civil rights or even anti-lynching bills. Roosevelt carefully avoided challenging Southern Democrats about white supremacy and segregation. He needed their votes to get his New Deal programs passed—and had their cooperation, at least briefly. The programs that resulted brought enough practical help to African Americans that they could feel included in FDR's plans to do something for "the forgotten man."

Under Roosevelt's leadership, the federal government made unprecedented efforts to lift the nation out of Depression. An array of new programs put unemployed people to work building parks, hospitals, roads, bridges, dams, and levees; extending electricity to rural areas; teaching, providing medical care; creating artwork. Besides jobs, this brought healthcare and education to many who had never known such services. The Works Progress Administration employed almost eight million people by the time it ended. The Civilian Conservation Corps set up camps where 2.5 million young men ultimately received food, clothing, shelter, and $30 a month for work in forestry, erosion control, and such. Some 250,000 blacks participated in the all-male CCC and 300,000 more, including females, in National Youth Administration programs. By 1935, about 250,000 black adults worked in WPA projects. The New Deal expanded money relief, as well as the distribution of surplus commodities. By the end of 1935, about twenty million people in the United States, almost one in six, had received public assistance.

When historians turned attention to how these efforts affected African Americans, they emphasized that, in many ways, New Deal legislation hurt rather than helped.[2] Efforts to drive up cotton prices by paying farmers not to plant reinforced an exploitative plantation system and spurred evictions of black sharecroppers. Moreover, as Roosevelt pushed through the federal minimum wage law, unemployment insurance, and Social Security, he permitted the exemption of agricultural labor and domestic service, a loophole that effectively excluded two thirds of the black workforce.[3] Southern businessmen negotiated a regional exception to the minimum wage law that permitted racially tiered pay scales. Even so, many refused to comply or fired all black workers rather than raise their pay. Under local administration, race commonly determined the distribution of relief, commodities, and jobs. The national director of the CCC kept the camps segregated and refused requests from states such as Wisconsin to integrate them. Studies of such failings grounded newer work that explores how individuals working to implement the New Deal did what they could within its limits.

The 1932 election brought an enthusiastic crowd to work in Washington, DC, many of them young, a few with a long record of seeking racial justice.[4] Most important, the Roosevelt administration hired some forty-five African

Americans, more than ever before, and in positions of real influence. Eleanor Roosevelt's friend and director of Negro Affairs at the National Youth Administration, Mary McLeod Bethune, invited a group of then young, later renowned, individuals to social gatherings that metamorphosed into the administration's so-called Black Cabinet.[5] On macro levels, these black advisors brought indispensable perspectives to the administration, while using their expertise to formulate improvement strategies for New Deal programs. On micro levels, their presence permitted friendships that convinced at least some white liberals that the New Deal could not succeed without addressing racial injustice.[6]

Progressives found indirect ways to further the cause of civil rights through New Deal cultural programs. These WPA projects permitted artists to move from the relief rolls to painting murals for public buildings, staging theatrical productions, playing concerts in the park, writing state tourist guide books, and so forth. In addition to employment, this brought African Americans opportunities for countering stereotypes. Black historian Sterling Brown wielded influence over state guidebooks as national editor for all Federal Writers' Project writings about blacks. The FWP also conducted interviews with former slaves, producing more than two thousand narratives and unearthing hundreds of photos. Federal Theater Project "Negro Units" in twenty-two cities staged plays including the outspoken original, *Turpentine*, where black workers rebel against conditions in Florida forced labor camps, as well as "blackened" versions of Shakespeare's *Macbeth* and the Gilbert & Sullivan *Mikado*. A popular success that had audiences dancing in the aisles, the *Swing Mikado* exemplifies FTP work that, although not daringly pointed, felt political to participants.[7] After 1939, such energy shifted to the Office of War Information and the War Department.

Charged with rallying the entire nation to the war effort, these agencies had to include blacks in ways acceptable even to the segregated South. Heavyweight boxing champ Joe Louis embodied a solution. In 1938, Louis defeated German boxer Max Schmeling, dubbed "the Nazi" by the U.S. press, in a highly publicized event that included meeting with FDR at the White House, anti-Nazi pickets around Schmeling's hotel, a full Yankee Stadium and perhaps seventy million people worldwide listening on the radio. In 1942, officials disseminated newsreels of Louis's induction into the army and a poster of his uniformed image with the words, "We're going to do our part and we will win, because we are on God's side." Without mentioning rights issues, Louis represented their cause to African Americans. Stars such as Lena Horne and Louis Armstrong subtly did the same in wartime agency productions including the radio variety show *Jubilee* and films such as *Stormy Weather*.[8] The Office of

War Information used photos of black defense-plant workers to contrast American ideals with enemy ideologies.[9]

"We Loyal Colored Americans Demand the Right to Work and Fight for Our Country," declared a banner for the huge Washington, DC, protest march that would have taken place in 1941, if FDR had not quickly issued a ban on hiring discrimination in defense industries.[10] As this new war began, African Americans made clear that they would rally, but did not accept second-class citizenship. Many embraced the *Pittsburgh Courier*'s "Double V" campaign that urged people to fight for a double victory: one against the nation's enemies abroad, another against racism at home. Alert early to Nazi discourse and signals such as Hitler not shaking hands with black medalists at the 1936 Olympics, the black press highlighted the hypocrisy of fighting a war against Europe's regime of racism and segregation, while permitting homegrown versions to continue. Although top officials pressed the president to halt such talk from a press sector with more than 1.25 million readers, the attorney general persuaded Roosevelt not to censor black journalists' speech.[11]

Roosevelt ignored demands for equal rights to serve in the military, however. In 1940, the Army and Navy permitted only a small number of blacks to enlist, kept them segregated, and limited their roles. The Marines did not accept blacks at all. Only part of this changed as the need for men required mass conscription. On the fringes, Nation of Islam leader Elijah Muhammad and thirty-seven followers went to jail for refusing to enter the military.[12] Overall, more than 700,000 blacks served in the Army, approximately 165,000 in the Navy, 17,000 in the Marines, 5,000 in the Coast Guard, and 4,000 women in the Women's Army Corps. While serving, they faced segregation and racial abuse. Standard military policy put white Southerners in command of black units, a practice that could lead to mistreatment. In one of the worst examples, white Southern officers forced black ammunition loaders to work unsafely at Port Chicago, California, in 1944, causing an explosion that killed 250 men.[13] In Europe, segregation of the U.S. Army permitted Nazi propagandists to work the racial divide with targeted leaflets playing to whites' racial stereotypes and to blacks' unease about what awaited them back home. When Sylvia recalls one brother's account of eating with whites in the army, it suggests that he participated in the military desegregation experiment ordered by the Allied high command in order to maximize efficiency for the push into Germany.[14] Yet most blacks knew only a segregated war.

Sylvia helps deepen understanding of African Americans' favorable view of Roosevelt, despite his equivocation on racial issues. This chapter poured forth in a flood, when I asked if she remembered FDR's radio addresses. Her words make clear how much difference the New Deal could make to a disadvantaged family. Sylvia and her brothers embody the strengthened sense of citizenship rights that historians see emerging in the 1940s, not only among African Americans who served in the military, but also those who experienced the rhetoric and made the sacrifices wartime brought on the home front.

World War II returned to Sylvia vividly on September 11, 2001. Working in her kitchen that morning, she watched the attack on live TV. "It brought it all back," she told me on the phone, "the war. The war. All over again." Then she added, "I'm not a big United States person, you know, never have been. But when I saw that plane hit that building, my mind changed direction." Beyond its evocation of wartime memories, that moment resonates with a complex configuration of African American patriotism that Sylvia illuminates. In this chapter, she speaks frankly about racial injustices unresolved both as the United States entered the war—and when her brothers returned. Indeed the entire narrative of this woman who identifies as a "plain American" bespeaks a deep, historically rooted attachment to notions of freedom and democratic ideals that African Americans have cherished despite their country's broken promises.

You ask me did we listen to President Roosevelt on the radio. Well, we did have that radio and my dad he would listen when Roosevelt came on. At the time, I was kinda young. So I can't remember what Roosevelt said. I don't know how much interest I really had. Now if you asked me did I listen to some song or another, I'd say, "Oh yeah I heard that. I know when that came out." My dad mighta said, "Listen to this, 'cause someday it gonna come up." And he would tell us about what he heard.

Now my father, he didn't vote. It wasn't no voting down there until—no, no, no voting. We know better than that. We didn't think about tryin' to vote. Black peoples only got they voting rights, not too long ago, I think about the time of the Martin Luther King thing. But Papa used to tell me . . . There go that daddy again. 'Cause my mother never told me anything like this. She would tell me to keep my dress-tail down 'n stuff like that. But that daddy of mines would tell me about President Taft, how bad he was. Or Hoover. Oooo, he was unexplainable how he kept black peoples down. Then comes Roosevelt.

And Roosevelt says, "All you black mens, we gonna do these roads up." Before that, the roads through there never was paved. I didn't know what a road was. I thought the ditches 'n the mud was what it was supposed to be. The roads was just old rocky roads. You gotta go way back, to know what I'm talkin' about. You walked down these roads and you would see big holes. And mud. Your wagon or car or truck would get stuck in the mud. Oh, it was just hell. But it was normal. I thought this is the way you supposed to live. Until Roosevelt come. That's when I begin to walk on a road.

It was right around then—I guess I was about eight or nine—when we got the first mail route. Not by our house. We still had to walk a mile to the one mailbox out on the road. Everbody who lived in that settlement had one box there. Miss Anderson, she would go over there to the box and pick up the mail. You come to her house and get it. She was nice enough to do that. That was right after Depression, when mail start comin' in there.

We had to walk to Springfield to get mail before they put in a route. And we had to build the roads ourself. We didn't have the government to do something for us. Where was our government? I do not know. He musta been out in Hawaii or someplace. To do something for us—nobody.

But then Roosevelt came and he started this commodity thing. Oh, he gave us flour. Sometime the flour was . . . ick. But it was flour. And then I'm sayin' ick because that was whole wheat flour, which we didn't know anything about. We only knew about white flour. Or they gave us yellow corn meal. We didn't know too much about that. It was always white corn meal. There was grits they gave us—which is known in the South. He gave us raisins, prunes, powdered milk. We used that. It was a blessin'.

I think that's when Social Security came in, too. Before then, I don't know how that was, Social Security. But I know my father did pay some kind of a tax. That I do know. We had to pay property tax, 'cause we had property. And you don't keep property down there—they will take it from you—if you don't pay those taxes. But my father was always clear with his. He would tell you today: "Pay your taxes." I pay mines. Simply because he taught us that. Otherwise they'll take it away from you.

That was Depression time. But Roosevelt reached down and he gave these black peoples that stuff. And gave them jobs out there on that road. It was like a chain gang, not jail-like but, that's the kinda . . . I can't remember exactly. Some of my brothers was old enough to work in this program. Roosevelt stepped in there and he gave them peoples . . .

That was the only time in life that I can remember that *anybody* gave my father *anything* for nothin'. I guess my poor daddy's prayer . . . At that time, things just lit up for him. He improved his property. He built a little addition to our kitchen at that time. Honey, my father put windows in like this with all the little . . . [*Points to window panes.*] You could see outside—glass—when that happen. I could see everybody goin' down that road. He bought him a decent horse or mule, or a plow, or rakes, or a little fertilizer to fertilize his farm. He built him a little shed to put his sweet potatoes in and a shed for his strawberries, so we can sit and pack the strawberries, while the boys pick 'em. It was a *great* improvement at that time. I remember that well.

My daddy started doin' a heck of a lot better. That's after he had preached to me about Roosevelt. His kids was leavin'. I guess he could grow enough food to make a little money with at that time. As far as his job concern, they needed my father, believe you me. But, when it come to money, givin' him a raise, I don't know. For the white man to give a black man something worth something was very difficult. The only time I saw improvement is when I told you—after my Roosevelt.

President Roosevelt, I think he was in there when my brothers went to the war. Now we movin' up in time a little bit. My brother Pat, he was in the CC camp, down in Florida there someplace. That meant get a little money. And they were helpin' to build up different places. He had been in the CC camp for years and years. He had to go right from the CC camp to the war.

My brother Speedy were seventeen years old. He had no business in the war. But he had put up his age so he could work, so he could make some money for the family and for himself. He was workin' at Cell-O-Tex or somethin' in New Orleans. He wadn't even eighteen and he had to go to the war. You know how they send out registration? Well, they were doin' that at that time. I don't care if you were black or white, when they say, "Get up and lets get to this war," you better get to the war. That was in the forties. Speedy is sixteen, seventeen. So I am like thirteen years old.

Then they called Eddie to go to the war. I guess they sent him a letter. But Eddie, instead of going to the war, he went someplace down there where they were cuttin' cane and got him a job. He was workin' at the cane mill, sugar cane. They found him there, handcuffed him. Say, "You either go to war or we gonna throw your behind in jail." He said the way they were kickin' him around, he rather went on over there to that war than to stay here in the United States. They sent him to Fort Bennin' Georgy for trainin'—of how to crawl around on that ground and how to pull the trigger and how to kill peoples. They were trainin' them boys for, oh, six weeks. And then sent 'em to that war.

Eddie, Pat, Henry, and Lawrence were in the war. My brother Dock had bad eyes. We used to call 'em cock-eyed. But they were cross, cross-eyed. Otherwise, we'da had five fellas in there.

They was in the service at Pearl Harbor, the bombin'. Yeah, I think one or two of those boys was in boot camp at that time. Down in Georgia and Alabama. I'm not sure. But I think that's when they start gettin' 'em all in there. I think those boys was away because my mama became so upset. Ohh, the bombin' of Pearl Harbor! And she didn't know.

Or did we get a letter that one of the boys was killed? Or it was gossip that one of my brothers was killed. Because so many of the other boys was over there also. Boys that was from the neighborhood was right there and they had saw each other. I think somebody wrote home and said they thought Eddie Bell was in this regiment that got bombed away. But it wasn't true.

Pat never went across the sea, because he was in the aviation. Henry, Eddie, and Speedy were in the army. They sent 'em all across that water—to Germany. Little Speedy went to Japan. *Uneducated boys.* Uneducated, just can sign their name, just. You oughta see how they sign their name today. It's unbelievable. But they did write home. Oh, yeah. They could barely write. But you could understand whatever they were tryin' to say on that paper.

They sent my mother a little money. And she bought the property down the road for the boys. So when they come back home they would have a place—if they got married—for they wives. She did that. I can remember there was a big who-shot-john about that. "I'm gonna buy them boys this land." The white man who sold it to her took the money and didn't pay the other part of the family. So then that part of the family took the land back. I remember my dad kept tellin' 'em: "You gotta watch them richy neighbor boys, 'cause they will take it from you." They took it from her. I think them boys had to repay, to get it cleared up. My dad had told my mama: "You have to have things done right." But that wasn't what we was talkin' about.

The war, the war. We did have that radio at the time. You could hear a lot. We were well aware. My father would hear different things about the war. Like about Hitler. My dad knew all about this Hitler mess. Evidently he was listenin' to the radio. He really knew. At that point, I myself did not know.

I didn't learn about that until years later, in the seventies, when I had this boyfriend, Paul, from Czechoslovakia. He was a citizen here when I knew him. But he fought in that war against the United States. He was the one that told me about Hitler and how they burned the Jews. He was the one laid it on the line to me. Because I didn't know. My brothers, they might have mention it, 'cause they were there. Wasn't this Holocaust durin' the time when them boys had to go to Germany to fight? But they never brought that out. Kinda wiped it away.

They did tell me things though. They told me how they crawled in the foxhole. I ask, "How did y'all get over there?" They said by boat. They didn't have airplanes to fly over there at the time. Just to bring over cargo. Eddie told me how they bombed this bridge in Germany to keep them Germans from goin' across from one side to the other. He told me how they slaughtered them people. That's the way he talk. He still have nightmares 'n stuff like that. That was pretty hurtin'. He say they took the bulldozer and they covered them mens over. He relives that today. It's sad.

He said, "But you know one thing? You wasn't black over there. You ate in the same place. You were—it was a different world—you wasn't a nigger over there." Even he said the lieutenant—and he's deep outa the South, the lieutenant—if one of them boys would say the word "nigger," the lieutenant say he'd shoot the boy and kill him hisself. Eddie say it was a different world, the war.

The German people were so nice to me, he says. The Germans they told the black mens that when they get back to America, "They gonna kick you niggers in the ass 'cause that's what they call ya." Some of them German peoples say, "When you go back to the United States, they gonna misuse your behind. Just like you over here misusin' us." Eddie, he kinda admired those German peoples. I think he coulda stayed there, if he hadna been afraid. But I think Eddie figured he couldn't stay over there. I don't know if he coulda. Over there in Germany during the war, they told the German womens—'cause the German womens like the colored mens—the white mens would tell the white womens over there, "Don't fool with them niggers. They got tails like monkeys."

When you get on the battlefield it was a different story. But the boys say, some of 'em said they was afraid because they didn't know what the white would do to 'em after the war. They might throw 'em overboard when they got through with them. Throw 'em right out there in the sea somewhere. So they were nervous. Because they didn't know what was happenin'.

If the white person told 'em over there what to do, oh, they did it—with pleasure. "Because we are fightin' for our country." And what country? Eddie says, "When I come back to the United States, I couldn't even go to the bathroom." I said, "Well, didn't that tell you enough you had no business comin' back here?" They did come back, my brothers. They all made it through that war and came back home.

After the war, my brother Henry got married. Big church weddin', right there near our house. My mother had built a house for her boys on that property she bought for 'em down the road. Henry is gettin' married to this girl. And that's where they was gonna stay.

That night—the night of the weddin'—I went down the road to that house Mama had built for them—to get something she had sent me down there for. I had been all the way to the house and was on my way back. It was gettin' dark. And here come my brother Jimmy, with his lyin' ass. He says, "Sylvia." I say, "What?" He says, "Mama say for you to come 'n go back down there with me to pick up the pail." He didn't wanta walk that dark road in the woods by himself.

"Mama said . . ." So I turned around and went back with him. Now we, me and Jimmy, we comin' back.

As I got almost to the spot where I had met Jimmy before, Mama come down the road. And she tore into me! 'Cause I didn't do what she say and come right back. She was gonna hit me with somethin'. I don't know what she had. But whatever it was, she threw up her hand to hit me. And she fell into a stroke.

I had to bring her home. I picked her up and said, "Jimmy! Jimmy go get . . . Go get Papa!" And the wedding is goin' on this night, too. I forgot all about that weddin'. We got her to the doctor. And the doctor say that was a stroke. She went to come down on me, to hit me, and she had that stroke.

So then, all of my people said I was the cause of my mama's ill. I said, "Jimmy, why don't you tell 'em what happened?" He never told. Never told 'em that he lied. I had to live with that. That I was the cause of my mother havin' a stroke. I made her mad. Then some folks they'd say, "Well, she had the stroke because she didn't want Henry to marry Pulu." I say, "Well, say somethin'. Get it offa me, 'cause I'm tired of listenin' to that." I say, "'Cause God knows that boy told me to go back with him."

After she had that stroke, Mama got along pretty good. And I helped. Now that's gettin' close to my seventeen years old. And I'm gonna leave soon.

Sylvia remembered that her brother Pat, who had learned tailoring through the GI Bill, worked on this "sack dress" outfit that was the height of fashion at the time, late 1950s.

Detail from a photo snapped at a Milwaukee night club, late 1950s or early 1960s.

Sylvia emphasized that what she holds in her hand here is not the registered nurse's diploma she always wanted. It is a nurse's aide certificate, awarded, she thought, during her California years.

Bottom left: Sylvia standing in front of her Palmer Street house, late 1950s or early 1960s.

Haynes Settlement sign. Springfield, Louisiana, August 1998. (photo by Jody LePage)

Bell Road sign. Springfield, Louisiana, August 1998. (photo by Jody LePage)

Bottom left: Sylvia at the old Bell family homestead. Springfield, Louisiana, August 1998. (photo by Jody LePage)

Sylvia holding a portrait of her father. Springfield, Louisiana, August 1998. (photo by Jody LePage)

Dock Bell. Close-up of the portrait in Sylvia's hand. (photo by Jody LePage)

Daniel Bell, January 1958. Photo taken just before Dan was killed.

Sylvia at the grave of Daniel Bell. Springfield, Louisiana, August 1998. (photo by Jody LePage)

Sylvia Bell White and Patrick Bell leaving the courthouse after the favorable verdict in their civil rights lawsuit. (*Milwaukee Sentinel*, December 16, 1981, photo by Dale Guldan, © 2012 Journal Sentinel, Inc., reproduced with permission)

Sylvia Bell White and Patrick Bell at the final review of the documents settling the civil rights lawsuit, nearly four years after the jury verdict and three months after the higher court ruling. Prior to this meeting, the mayor announced to the media that he would let the settlement in the Daniel Bell case go into effect without his signature. (*Milwaukee Sentinel*, December 1, 1984, photo by Dale Guldan, © 2012 Journal Sentinel, Inc., reproduced with permission)

From the front cover of the *Milwaukee Sentinel* entertainment section, "Let's Go," for the opening of the Milwaukee Repertory Theater production of *An American Journey*. (*Milwaukee Sentinel*, January 11, 1987, photo by Michael Sears, © 2012 Journal Sentinel, Inc., reproduced with permission)

Sylvia with her son, Douglas Lamont Bell, at the opening of the Milwaukee Repertory Theater play *An American Journey*. (*Milwaukee Journal*, January 18, 1987, photo by Brian Poulter, © 2012 Journal Sentinel, Inc., reproduced with permission)

Touching the Liberty Bell. Philadelphia, Pennsylvania, November or December 1988. Sylvia was in the City of Brotherly Love for the Philadelphia Drama Guild production of *An American Journey*.

From left to right: Curry First, Sylvia, and Walter Kelly, at the Wisconsin State Bar Association Convention. Madison, Wisconsin, June 2000. (photo by Jody LePage)

10

Goin' North

When Sylvia went North, she participated in an event of tremendous scale and significance in African American history: mass migration from the South. In 1900, more than 90 percent of the African American population lived in Southern states; by 1970, only 53 percent did. Between 1910 and 1970, 6.5 million African Americans left the region.

The first great wave—the phase that historians call the Great Migration—began in the mid-1910s and lasted until 1930. Greater numbers would move later, but with less suddenness and less dramatic effect. In two years beginning in 1916, some 400,000 African Americans departed the South, at an average rate of 16,000 a month. A thousand people reportedly quit the tiny town of Newborn, Alabama in a single day. Some areas lost nearly all their inhabitants. By 1930, almost 1.5 million people had left.[1]

White Southerners did not passively accept this movement. State legislatures banned labor recruitment. A Louisiana lawmaker even proposed forbidding African Americans to leave the state, although no such law ever passed. Here and there, the police did prevent black people from boarding trains or forcibly disembarked black passengers. Some towns closed their railroad stations. Some stations refused to accept prepaid tickets from blacks, since migrants often had fares paid by relatives who had migrated. A chorus of voices warned black Southerners that they would freeze in the North. A few suggested making the South more attractive by curbing lynching. Others encouraged blacks to stay by taking measures such as the land sales in Sylvia's home community. Once underway, however, the Great Migration seemed unstoppable.

Why did so many people suddenly leave? Migrants themselves gave reasons such as lynching, Jim Crow laws, the denial of voting rights, and poor schools. Since all of this had long tormented black Southerners, historians have asked what prompted a mass departure specifically in the 1910s. Early studies debated the relative importance of "push" and "pull" factors such as the boll weevil that pushed sharecroppers out of the South, or the pull of job openings in the North. Critics of this push/pull discussion objected to reducing human beings to objects moved by phenomena beyond their control.[2] Noting that economic forces such as job availability affected males and females differently, women's historians have focused on gender-specific reasons for migration.[3] Others emphasize human initiative by studying how individuals made informed decisions, carried them through and helped others to do the same.[4] Some observe that the Great Migration created its own momentum, inspiring people to leave as the growing numbers generated excitement. More recent work examines community formation in destination cities.[5] Efforts to pinpoint a single answer have given way to exploring complex and dynamic processes that turned a small stream of migration into a tidal wave.

A significant change in job opportunities certainly played an important role. Before World War I, European immigrants had entered the United States at a rate of a million a year and provided cheap labor for Northern industry. Employers could pit ethnic groups against each other, since a newly arrived nationality would work for less than groups already settled. After 1914, World War I halted immigration from Europe, while increasing demand for goods. Northern workers saw this as a chance to obtain better pay, safer conditions, and the eight-hour day. Employers could ignore those demands, however, if they had another labor source. Accustomed to low wages and excluded from many jobs, blacks in the South strongly desired work. Before the war, Northern industry had occasionally used black workers to break strikes. Now companies looked to hire African Americans as regular employees. Some even sent recruiting agents South.[6]

Labor recruitment jump-started the Great Migration, although recruiters actually played a less important role than either black or white Southerners thought. Whites overemphasized recruitment in part to avoid admitting that Southern racial traditions drove blacks away. Reports of recruiting spread like wildfire through African American communities and developed into a folklore of hope. The vast majority of migrants never saw a recruiting agent. As the wave of migration grew, those thinking about it could rely increasingly on information and help from people they knew who had left earlier. Family members and friends provided train tickets, temporary lodging, or at least information about housing, churches, and jobs. Those who migrated wrote letters to loved ones left behind. Many returned to visit—and impress—the folks back home.[7]

Although lived experiences in the North rarely matched the migrants' expectations, they tended to report successes—whether real or embellished—rather than disappointments. Some were deeply moved when their train crossed the Ohio River out of the Jim Crow region. They celebrated by praying, stopping their watches, or singing.[8] Richard Wright wrote of moments such as the first time a white person sat next to him on a Chicago bus. He recalled a scene in the restaurant where he worked, when a white waitress arrived late and, finding him nearby as she emerged from changing into her uniform, asked him to tie her apron strings—quick! The still-recent migrant froze, mindful of how dangerous such an act would be for a black man in the South. Realizing that no one around him gave it a second thought, he mastered his feelings and tied the strings.[9] Most migrants felt they could hold their heads high in ways not permitted blacks in the South. Northern wages impressed Southerners, even if the money bought less. Their children went to better schools. Many urged others to migrate.

Institutions, too, played key roles in the Great Migration. Churches came down on both sides, with some preachers standing opposed, others helping organize the move. Three pastors from Hattiesburg, Mississippi, reunited their entire congregations in Chicago. Some churches provided the *Chicago Defender*, perhaps the most energetically pro-migration example of an increasingly favorable black press. Information and help also came from some 100,000 African American railroad workers and their labor union, the Brotherhood of Sleeping Car Porters. People listened to these men whose jobs showed them more of the world. Where whites tried banning the *Defender*, black railroad workers hid the paper in bundles of merchandise that they pushed off the train at secret backcountry pickup spots.

No source reached more people with word of the Great Migration than the *Chicago Defender*. A migrant from Georgia, Robert Abbott, founded the paper in 1905. In one decade, it grew into the most widely read African American weekly. By 1920, the *Defender* was selling some 200,000 copies, read by an estimated 1.5 million people. Two thirds of those readers lived outside Chicago, many in the 1,542 Southern localities on the *Defender*'s shipping list. Copies would pass from hand to hand and could reach illiterate people when others read aloud. As more and more people migrated, officials in some

Southern localities prohibited the sale and mailing of the *Defender*, even arrested people for possessing it—thereby deepening faith and interest in the paper.

The *Chicago Defender* promoted migration in articles, photos, cartoons, letters—even a staged event called the "Great Northern Drive." In February 1917, the paper began telling readers that a mass departure so-named would take place on May 15 of that year. Rumors spread about special trains or cheaper train fares. Although nothing of the sort materialized, greater than ever numbers of migrants did go North that week. The *Defender* tapped powerful emotional energies by gleefully reporting the magnitude of the Great Migration and taunting white Southerners who were trying to stop it. Even the paper's "do's and don'ts" for new migrants had strong appeal for Southern blacks. One such article instructed workers not to call whites "Boss," telling them to "leave that word dropped in the Ohio River." An entertainment section paraded attractions such as nightclubs, music, dancing, movies, and baseball. Most important, the *Defender* filled its pages with success stories, descriptions of schools, and want ads calling for workers.[10]

In the 1910s and '20s, migrants could find work through the Urban League. Formed in New York in 1913, the Urban League united groups of middle-class blacks and whites that had been helping black migrants to Northern cities. Within five years, the League had offices in thirty cities. With a significant sector of its highly educated membership drawn from sociology/social work, the League excelled at gathering and analyzing information. The organization also taught rural people how to deal with city life; found them housing and jobs; helped them deal with police and courts. As opportunity grew, job placement became the League's specialty. In 1918, the Chicago office placed nearly seven thousand people in jobs; in 1919, more than twelve thousand. At the height of the Great Migration, Urban League representatives greeted new arrivals at train stations.[11]

By the time Sylvia went North in 1947, no such welcome awaited. During World War II, defense industry jobs had drawn another wave of black migrants from the South, many of them headed for California. They arrived in Los Angeles at a rate of six thousand a month at the height of the wartime influx in 1943 and totaled more than 200,000 by 1950. Oakland's black population increased from about eight thousand in 1940 to more than twenty-one thousand in 1944. After the war, however, defense production dropped off sharply. Oakland's shipbuilding industry went from 250,000 workers at the peak of wartime production to just twelve thousand in 1946.[12] Although reconversion to a peacetime economy ultimately meant good jobs for many

Americans in the 1950s, that prosperity did not translate into the kind of demand for black workers that had drawn migrants during the two World Wars. Yet black people continued leaving the South in large numbers—about five million between 1940 and 1970.

Sylvia's narrative suggests possible explanations for the persistence of this movement. She makes clear that she went North because she felt certain that she would have a better life there, get an education, a good job, make a career. In Sylvia's world, the successes of an earlier generation gone North continued to fuel high hopes, despite the downturn in real opportunities. Those predecessors directly encouraged and facilitated the move as well. As Sylvia grew up, she knew she had a place to stay in Milwaukee—with a relative who had left Louisiana during the Great Migration, married a railroad worker, and later lived in her own home. Older brothers went there first and found work. Then, a gender-specific issue—her parents' equivocal response to a marriage proposal—precipitated her departure. Here, we see migration through the eyes of a teenaged narrator not impressed by moments that moved her elders—such as crossing the Ohio River. A teenager more focused on indications that her brother and friends didn't like her clothes. Most important, the sensibilities of a seventeen-year-old bring particular clarity to this account of hopes and disappointments shared by so many migrants North.

❧ I decided to come up North at seventeen years old because I figured I could get a better job. I could go to school. I could become a RN. That's what I wanted to become. A nurse. Or I didn't really know what I could be. But I knew I could improve myself, if I could get away from the Jim Crow state. I still thought of North as upward.

Well, 'bout that time, my brother Joe had came up North to Milwaukee. I had gave Joe the money to come up here. So he was gonna give me my money back by buying me a ticket. He said, "Oh Sis, I'm gonna send for you." I say, "Okay."

Well, my mom 'n dad was very happy because then me 'n Dirk Taylor wouldn't have to get married. Me, I figured, "Well, I'm not too particular about marrying him. I'm just marryin' him to get away from home." Yeah, just to get away from home. Not because we were in love. Isn't that sad?

This man, Dirk, he was maybe a year older than I. I met him, 'cause you know everybody. You gonna know if somebody comes around. He came back from the service. And we just little girls likin' peoples. We all would go to church and we would pick our boyfriends out, whoever we thought we would like. "Mmm, I like him." Or, "He likes me." Or somethin' like that. Our parents don't know nothin' about it. There was a fellow before this one. We used to hold hands and that's about it. Because I was like fifteen. Now when Dirk came along, the one that asked to marry me, I was sixteen or seventeen.

So this guy he got serious about me. He say, "Sylvia, I'm gonna ask your mother and daddy for you." That's the way peoples did in them days. He came to the house and asked about could he date me. My father really didn't like the guy because the family . . . My daddy called 'em drifters, if you didn't have a piece of land. See 'cause that's the way some blacks are. The black who was tryin' to be progressive, if he ain't got nothin', don't fool with him. It rubs off on other peoples. You gotta watch that. Daddy had often say, "You know nothin' from nothin' ain't nothin'." This man didn't have nothin'. But Daddy let us date.

So then Dirk, say, "Sylvia, come on. We'll get married. I'm gonna ask your mom 'n dad can we get married." I say, "Well, you ask. But I'm goin' North." I was. Then he really asked my mother 'n dad could he marry me.

I remember that so well. My mother looked at Papa and she say, "It's up to Dock." My daddy looked at my mother and say, "It's up to Ruth." Say what in the hell are they talkin' about? You either tell the man yes or no. Then I really got disgusted. I says, "Now, I'm goin' up North anyway, 'cause my brother is sendin' me a ticket." He was definitely sendin' me that ticket. "I don't care if you let me marry or not." That's where I formed the impression I just wanta marry to get away, to get the hell away from here. I was tired of takin' care of children, cookin', cleanin' up. I had did ten years of it. That was enough. And I figured if I married him I might wind up with a buncha babies, too.

I had explained it to him though. He was station in Kentucky. So I told him, "Now, I'll go with you to Kentucky, but I'm not gettin' offa that train. Maybe I'll come back down there or you come up North." 'Cause I think he was gonna get discharge. He just had to stay so long. The war was over. He coulda rode on the same train that I was gonna ride on. Then he coulda gotten off and reported to service. And I could've came on up North. Because that was the route. Anyway, we didn't get married.

When my brother sends me the ticket, my mom and my dad say, "Well, you goin'." I say, "Oh yeah, I'm goin'. If I have to walk out there to take the train, I'm leavin'." I jumped the train. Dirk got drunk somewhere down in New Orleans. I came North.

When I got ready to come up here, they say, "Oh! You gonna take the *City of New Orleans*." That was really beautiful. But the train ride, I cannot describe that— not like if you asked me, "Oh, how was Paris?" I mean that's a different thing. I don't remember that I had any fear on the train. It was, I imagine, fun. But you know I still don't like a train. I can still hear the grindin' in my ears. It was something about that. I don't think I could sit here and lie about it. I were just doin' it because I thought I could get the education. I thought I could get the job. I thought.

I can remember the Jim Crow section, where you're Jim Crowed until you get across the Ohio River. You sit in a certain section. Then when you cross the Ohio River into Illinois, you are no longer Jim Crow. You could move around. But you just stay where you are. I did go to the bathroom. It was colored 'n white down South. Then all at once, when you cross the Ohio River . . . There's this big curve. That's when you can look back and see the back of the train makin' that horse-shoe sign. Then, they say, you're no longer Jim Crow. They don't tell you that on the train. But that is what I experienced. And so my family said—that you're no longer Jim Crowed when you get across the line. At the time, it didn't even bother me—was I Jim Crowed or not Jim Crowed—'cause I'd been Jim Crowed for almost eighteen years.

I came to Chicago first because the *City of New Orleans* stops there at the Illinois Central station. It don't go any further. My brother Joe and my cousin Odile, they met me at the station. How well do I remember!

I got off the train. And it's cold. June and it was cold. You would consider this cold, comin' from the South. I had on them—they called 'em ballerina skirts and the little ballerina shoes. I thought I was lookin' all sharp. They said, "Ooooo, we gonna buy you some clothes! We gonna buy . . ." That's the first thing they holler. I wadn't dressed proper as far as they concern.

My brother Joe was workin' at Cudahy packin' house in Milwaukee. Them days you could come up here and get a job. Or the mens could anyway. My cousin, she's oohh all dressed to kill and my brother he done bought his clothes. "We gonna buy . . ." They took me, I guess to Chinatown. Pickin' clothes, seemed like whatever I liked, they didn't like. So I had to buy what they liked, my brother Joe and Odile. I'm seventeen and I think they . . .

They takin' me someplace that night. I think it was to hear some of the old blues singers around Forty-seven and Wabash. Yeah, Forty-seven and Wabash. Muddy Waters or—a couple more guys. I just can't call they name right now. Oh! I had heard these guys on radio but I had never saw 'em. So that was nice for me. I like music anyway and I really enjoyed that part. I think I even danced a little bit, quite a bit, with my brother. Later, I got tired. And my brother said to me, "Girl, we stay up all night." I say, "Man, you know I'm not used to stayin' up all night." I just couldn't do it.

Honey, I don't know what they did all night. Whatever they did, it was stuff that I didn't like. Lotta drinkin'. Clubs or taverns or what have you. It wasn't my cup of tea. Of course, I liked to go to places where they had dancin'. That's why I had my ballerina skirt on. We gonna dance away. But all this drinking! They took me back, so I could go to sleep. And they partied.

We left Chicago after a couple days, 'cause Joe had to be back to work on Monday. We had to get the train or the bus. I'm not sure which. So I come to Milwaukee with my brother.

I like ta froze. Girl, it was cold.

I came to Milwaukee because Aunt Oja live there and she say, "You send them kids on up here." Mama knew Aunt Oja had a nice big house to put us in. Anyway, when we said we goin' up North, Mama never did say, "Well, stop in Chicago by my sister Edna." We stopped. But Mama never insist on us stayin' there. When we said goin' to Milwaukee, that was all right. But Chicago, it wasn't too kosher with her. I wonder why though. I think I coulda done a little better in Chicago than I did in Milwaukee. My father, after we was goin', he didn't care whicha way we went as long as we tried to make somethin' outa ourself. But for my mom, it always was, "You stay where I say stay or you don't go."

When we get to my auntie house, Aunt Oja welcome me in. She say, "Hey! Ruf little gal." 'Cause she and my mother was pretty tight. She put me in the same room with her. She had other rooms, but she had my brothers. I think my brother Lawrence was there and my brother Joe. Them is the two guys who were there with my mom when I was born.

Ojalene McRae wasn't really my auntie, but my mother's cousin. She helped to raise my mother. She was older. She'd be sweatin' in her chair rockin'. She smoked a pipe, too. She was a good old woman and had money. Nice bank account. Her home was paid for. Her husband used to work for the railroad. He wasn't there when I were there. He had died way before. So her home was probably automatically paid for when he passed away.

She did have a nice place there, one of them old-fashioned houses, up 'n down, in Milwaukee. She had a one, two, three, or four bedroom house downstairs and then the same thing upstairs. There on Somers, 839 West Somers, right across the street from Yaeger Bakery.* I could look out the window and see the beautiful trees. It was nice big old trees in front of her house.

---

* Reuben Harpole, later a well-known community leader, grew up on the same block of Somers Street. Some years younger than Sylvia, he didn't meet her when she lived there, but described Mrs. McRae as "dear to the neighborhood" and remembered the pies she made with rhubarb from her garden. Interview with Reuben Harpole, August 1999.

I could see all the people, all these—I don't wanta really emphasize on white—but all these white people walkin' down the streets on Monday mornin'. I say, "Where they goin', Auntie?" She said, "They are goin' to Yaeger's Bakery." Right up under us. I mean, it was a nice little black community there. That was about as far as blacks went. Okay, you got Vliet street, that was all kinda black. Juneau, it was mostly black, but with white businesses, a little bit of everything in there. Somers Street though, Somers was black. And oh, it would be just droves of white peoples comin' in there, passin' right by us, goin' to Yaeger's Bakery or Wonder's Bakery. Wonder Bakery were down the street, too. I say, "Oh my God! Look at all those peoples, Auntie. Maybe I can get me a job over there." She said, "Not hardly. Them white peoples been walkin' down that street for many and many years, right up under us. They do not hire black."

Here I'm up North now. I was almost ready to 'bout face and go back. I'm up North and couldn't even work at Yaeger's Bakery? I went to Yaeger's. I tried. No. No. It was whites comin' down them streets.

So then I says, "Oooo, I sure wish I could get me a job out at Patrick Cudahy." That was the packin' plant where my brother worked. But it was so far. You had to get up at four o'clock in the mornin', get your bus at five and get to work for seven. Joe, he say, "You should try to get a little job around here." That's why I say, "These bakery jobs is right up under me, why can't I go right there?" This is up North.

Up the street there was Vliet Street. *Am I talkin' too loud?* And there was a shoppin' area. The big store, Schuster, were there. Walgreen drugstore was on this side. Down a little bit was meat stores and . . . It was really where peoples would shop. White peoples. Wadn't too many blacks around, but a lotta white.

So I went on in Walgreen's and I say, "Are you doin' any hirin'?" 'Cause I saw these girls, the white gals wearin' they pretty white uniform with their little cap on they head. They were waitin' on tables. I thought I was gonna get in to do something like that. They put me back in that kitchen, washin' dishes. Cuttin' my hands up. When you cut it, Mr. Bailey would come. "Oh well, come on. I'll take you in the pharmacy and bandage you up." Mr. Bailey would—a very nice person. But it was no money. I think I was makin' between seventy-five cents and a dollar an hour. To wash all them nasty dishes—by hand, not by a machine at that time. They would bring 'em in and throw 'em in the window to ya. You'd clean 'em off and wash 'em. They furnished us nice white uniforms. But by the time you get through, you be sloppy, so nasty. You don't wanta come out in the front for anybody to see you in that predicament. You needed a different uniform. But they say, "You can't use all these uniforms."

I kept askin' for better positions in there. Those little white girls—girls my age—could wait on tables. But I could not do that. I could only wash dishes. This is Milwaukee, Twelfth and Vliet.

I say, "My God, I just left the South with all this stuff. I come up here and . . ." I'm up North now in this Promise Land. Oh, sure. I had heard it called that. Some of the older peoples, maybe even my father mighta said, "Oh, that's the Promised Land." Or, "That's Canaan land." Because he didn't know what it was like. He had never been up North.

Mama, she never said too much to me about up here where I was born. One thing she would say, she says, "When you go up North, you keep your mouth shut." I wondered why she said, "Keep your mouth shut." That kinda bug me. When I saw the environment I was in, I say, "Well, I guess this what she meant." I kinda hate to mention it. I guess it's one of my—or her—little secrets.

Aunt Oja, she ran one of these little transom houses. That's the secret part. She had peoples that drop by and she would rent 'em rooms for a short period of time. Just for the night or a few hours. And then there was policy—that's what they call it. It was gamblin'. You buy a ticket and you pay thirty-five cents for a number. If the number came out, you would get the full amount of money that they collect that day on that number. There was quite a bit of that goin' around in Milwaukee back in forty-seven, forty-eight, even in the fifties. I used to play numbers, too. Aunt Oja would ask, "When was your daddy birthday? Your mother birthday?" And sometime we'd catch a little something. I didn't get rich over it. But Aunt Oja, she made nice money on that stuff. And then goin' to church every Sunday.

In the meantime, I'm workin' at Walgreens, doin' the dishes. It was two of us. The other girl, she would be there from eight in the mornin' until four. I would come to work at twelve and work 'til two. The lunch hour. Then I'd come back at four and work 'til they close, ten at night. I worked there . . . oh, I don't know how long. Durin' that time, I said, "Oh I'm gonna buy Mama a washin' machine." With my little dollar an hour. Well, my brothers kicked in somethin' on that, too. We sent Mama some money to get her a washin' machine.

Then I start goin' to school. I don't know who told me about it, but someone did. They say, "You always want to go to school." I say, "I sure do! Where can I go?" They say, "Vocational." So then I say, "Auntie, where is that school somebody were tellin' me about, that Vocational school?" It was not too far from where we live. I could walk. Or if I had money, I could take the bus. I say, "Maybe I can get me a better job, if I go to school." This was my whole thing. I started goin' there. They said I was equivalent as a fifth or sixth grader. That was my equivalent when I went in there. I took English, math and what else? Some other subject. You could only cram three in the time that I had. I had to get to Walgreens by noon.

So, all right, Christmas was comin'. It was very cold and everything. It was my first Christmas away from home. I say, "Aunt Oja, I'm goin' home for Christmas." She says, "Why you wanta go home for?" All this snow and cold weather, I guess. Back there it was muddy and wet, but it wasn't as cold. And I really wanted to tell my mama what she had sent me into—the environment. But I didn't tell Aunt Oja. She never knew. I said, "I just wanta talk to my mama." Aunt Oja say, "Girl, you stay here."

11

Let Me Go Home

🎗 Many African Americans shared feelings such as those that motivated the attempt to return home that Sylvia recounts in this chapter. Those who migrated to the North generally did not find that the region met their expectations. In the 1940s, however, their disappointments rarely prompted efforts to go back South.

After World War II, frustrations ran high among African Americans everywhere, especially those of Sylvia's and her brothers' generation. Men and women who had served in the war felt more strongly than ever that such risks and sacrifices warranted full citizenship rights. That meant, of course, that segregation and mass disfranchisement of African Americans in the South had to end. By the mid-fifties, a civil rights movement would call on America to fulfill its democratic promise. Less well-known efforts had gone on for decades inside and outside the South, too, where black citizens fought race-based exclusion from schools, housing, jobs, and spaces such as libraries and restaurants. Impatient for change and more attuned to the media, young people keenly experienced these times that would both raise and dash new hope of movement toward racial justice.

The war had brought unprecedented changes in rhetoric and some real political progress in racial matters. Established to enforce FDR's 1941 executive order, the Fair Employment Practice Committee had sent posters to all defense industry factories declaring it "the policy of the United States that there shall be no discrimination in the employment of workers . . . because of race, creed, color, or national origin."[1] The very idea of the FEPC mattered much to African Americans. Rhetoric vilifying Nazism had cultivated, albeit unevenly, notions of an American way opposed to overt racism. One member of Congress turned such language against conservatives' push to terminate the FEPC, for example, calling that effort an anti-democratic attempt "to perpetuate a Hitlerite concept of race supremacy in this country."[2] As the decade ended, President Truman desegregated the military and set up his own commission to deal with racial issues. Nationwide polls showed changing attitudes regarding racial discrimination during these years, at least outside the South. Yet, as we will examine more fully in the next few chapters, these apparent changes only heightened disappointment with what unfolded in employment, housing, and response to the civil rights movement.

Everywhere except the South, the disconnect between talk about race and actual practices gaped wide. To be sure, all regions had a history of outspoken racial prejudice and violence. However, Northern whites often did not frankly admit their racism, expressing it in ways that African Americans dubbed "James Crow." Richard Wright wrote of "the daily horror of anxiety, of tension, of eternal disquiet" that came from never knowing what to expect from whites in Chicago.[3] In a Milwaukee oral history of 1940s migrants, one interviewee compared the Northern way to someone throwing a brick at you from behind and then pretending not to have done anything. At least "you knew where you stood" in the South, said another.[4] Although many shared such feelings, few chose to go back until the "Whites Only" signs had come down.

In 1998, when Sylvia narrated this chapter about her thwarted attempt to return South, three of her brothers had already migrated back to the region. By then, the migration tide that had originally brought them North had fully reversed, a turn that began in the late 1970s.[5] Between 1985 and 1995, nearly 500,000 more African Americans moved from North to South than went the other way. Even the magnet state of California lost more African Americans than it gained by the end of the 1990s. Dubbed the "New Great Migration," this mass movement has included all social groups, with the college-educated participating at the highest rates.[6]

Several factors contributed to the reversal. By the 1990s, as Sylvia notes, Southern blacks had developed a significant political presence, with higher percentages of elected officials, especially at local and state levels. Increasing economic opportunity in parts of the South corresponded with decline elsewhere. In the 1990s, the Midwest had the highest percentages of blacks living in poverty. In Wisconsin, 40 percent of the African American population lived at or below the poverty line in 1990, up from 28 percent in 1970.[7] Black employment rates were higher in the South than the North throughout the 1990s.[8] Some of the new migrants have chosen rural areas, however, foregoing urban job prospects in favor of a sense of community and what they hope will prove a more wholesome environment for children. Living away from the

South, many African Americans maintained strong family ties to the region and viewed rural communities there as home.[9]

Family feeling clearly had much to do with young Sylvia's 1940s attempt to go back South. Her mother had just passed away. She worried about her father and brothers. Yet her 1990s retelling focuses more on opportunities that the intervening years persuaded her she had lost. She expresses strong convictions about a changed South. Not surprisingly, Sylvia saw much significance in the improvement of Southern black schools. Telling of her brothers' postwar behavior, she confirms historians' observations of greater assertiveness then among black Southerners, especially returning soldiers. Sylvia insists that the war changed white Southerners' behavior and attitudes as well—and supports that point with a tale one brother told of his arrival home from the war. A dramatic tale that illustrates one of the many reasons for desegregating the military. The chapter ends with the powerful father who could send his strong-willed daughter back North, even if he could not convince her that she and her brothers would live better lives there. Trying to explain that decisive moment, this woman so rarely at a loss for words finds none to name what her father meant to her.

Then my mother passed away. She passed on January 29, on her birthday. I had just came up North. I had been up there not much more than six months. I was about seventeen. Mama died from another stroke. She was a young woman. Just forty-five and she got babies. Alfonso, the youngest, was like five years old. And Walter, he mighta been seven. There was Roosevelt and *Dan, the one who got killed.* Dan, Ernest, Jimmy and me. We was all just kids. That was our first death in the family, was Mama. And to see her go with all these kids. That was my hard part, my hard, hard, hard part. What are we gonna do?

When I went to my mother's funeral, I told my dad, I said, "Papa, I wanta stay *home.* To help you with these boys." God knows I wanted to stay home with him. But he say, "Well, you up there got a little job." Here I wadn't makin' but a dollar an hour—washin' dishes. I say, "Oh Papa, I can stay." He said, "No."

There was that fella that really likeded me. I think my daddy thought that I wanted to stay home to be with that man. I wasn't thinkin' about this man. I was thinkin' about my *father.* And them boys. I coulda kept all them last boys at home, made 'em go to school, been there to wash them dishes and clothes. I coulda made some nice mens outa them guys. I wadn't thinkin' about this man. I was thinkin' just like my dad. This black man didn't have shit. What did I want with him? I tried to explain it to Papa.

You can't explain things to certain black people. They got it up here and you can't pull it outa their head. Like me, I got certain things in me. I don't sweep the dirt outside after dark. What is it gonna do? I don't know. But Mama say don't sweep the dirt outside after dark. I can get right to the door, but I won't do it. In my seventies and I won't sweep the dirt outside after dark. I guess she said it was bad luck.* But that's not what I wanted to say about that.

What I was sayin' is that some peoples are like that. They wants to say that you care for the man even if . . . I didn't. I didn't care that much for him. It wasn't no big deal. I coulda forgotten about the man. But I guess my dad figured I would *never* forget this man, 'cause I was gonna marry him at one time. And the man was there. Well, naturally when you come back home, all the friends is comin' around. I was still a young girl. And this guy, he likeded me so much. But I don't think we were even dating each other. But Papa, he just knew. My father figured to get her away from the man let her go back North.

At that time, I was concerned about the well bein' of my brothers. 'Cause I knew when they came up North it was gonna be different. 'Cause I was washin' dishes and that was the best job I could get. After I got up North, I saw that you couldn't get a job unless you was educated. Or you knew something. You had to pass a test.

Oh, I went through a lotta tests. Everyplace in Milwaukee, I takin' a test to try to get a job. I took the test. I fail the test. I took the test. I fail the test. I took the test. After while, I knew. The meanin' of words is so important when you are tryin' to take a test. Words that sound alike, look alike is not alike or is alike, you know. I couldn't take a written test for a long time, before I knew. You couldn't pass a test, you couldn't get the job. This is why I hound on that education.

---

* Sylvia delighted in the two explanations we found for this belief, both of them reaching deep into the African American past. One points to African religions that envisioned a world inhabited by spirits: spirits of plants, animals, bodies of water, etc., as well as human beings living and dead. Some believed that the spirits of living people wandered at night, so that one could sweep out the spirit of someone sleeping in the house. Another explanation comes from the experience of slavery in South Carolina rice-growing country. While separating the grain from the chaff, slave women would let rice fall into the folds of their skirts in order to increase their family's food supply. When they unhitched their skirts at home, they gathered the precious grains that fell to the floor, but could easily miss a few. If they swept dirt out the door after dark, they risked losing food and getting punished, since the rice grains would be visible in daylight to overseers or slaveholders.

The driver's test was the big problem for my brothers. They came outa the South—uneducated. They knew how to drive, but they didn't have driver's license. Down South, you didn't need no driver's license. Or if you did need it, those white folks didn't bother you about it. That's where I have to give the police down there a little credit. If the police hadda saw them boys doin' somethin' down there, they would come to my father and say, "Now Dock, you know them boys is doin' this. You better talk to 'em." It was discuss. Everybody kinda knew everybody. They knew those boys couldn't pass the test. But I never remember that you had to have a driver's license. My brothers could run around there without it. Or I think they would give 'em a test on the road. Long as you could drive good, they give you a driver's license. 'Cause when they came up North, some of them guys had driver's license from down there. But when they got here, they had to . . . What is that light there, flashin'? [*Police car lights visible through the window.*]

That is where the police come in. The police up North, they throwin' them boys in jail, 'cause they out there drivin' without a driver's license. Them guys knew how to drive well. I said, "Now why couldn't they give peoples an oral test?" They rather for the cop to catch 'em and throw 'em in jail, send 'em to Waupun.* Oooo, it was awful. That's a lot for a person to think about. I can see why some black peoples went on 'n died. It was easy way out. Because—for what you have to go through . . .

Of course, I didn't know yet all what we was gonna go through up North, when I was talkin' to my father about comin' back home. But I did know my brothers needed education. Already I knew they would need it even more up North.

So I told him, I say, "Papa, I should stay here with you to help you with these kids." Which I'm sorry I didn't. You know, I still wish I coulda stayed home. Because I had been there with them kids. I had wash clothes. I had cook. I had cleaned up. I was a mama. I made them boys' bottle. I had taught, I was teachin' those boys how to read, how to write. Or I would read stories to 'em. I would read to my brothers. I did that for those boys. So I knew I could help my father with those children. I knew that. I would have.

If I stayed at home, I coulda built the house up. Hey, it was cheaper down there. Peoples woulda gave me a big loan. Or I coulda become a postmaster. Before I came up North, this lady, Miss Grace, she had me workin' in the post office for her. I hadn't signed up but she was givin' me four, five dollars a day. And she were just as happy with me! I coulda just went on into the postal business,

---

* Waupun Correctional Institution is Wisconsin's best known prison.

without all this test, and without all this . . . Because down there it's, "I know you." Good recommendation and you get places.

That woulda been nice. I would've became somethin'. I could've turned it all around. My niece, my cousin, my friends they went to school. They were grown but they went to school. A number of my cousin's children, they are professors of the school. They got all them good degrees like you have. Some of those black peoples got swimmin' pools in the back. Not that a swimmin' pool was what I had in mind. Of course, I would love to have mines in the backyard, too. But what I mean is, they start doin' so good. If I took you to some of my relatives homes . . . I don't wanta even bring 'em to mine, 'cause I don't have shit to compare. My brother has a brand new brick home and another nice home that he rents out. That's Henry, the one who just passed away. They had such a funeral there for him! They had to have a special semi-truck to bring the flowers from the church to the grave. [*Laughs.*]

See, the South start to change in the forties. Yes, in the forties. The war was over then. My brother Eddie says, "When I came back, they still had that sign up." Ohhh. Colored. They were in the train station, just comin' back. Eddie say, "I had to go to the bathroom so bad, until my captain . . ." They all, a buncha them boys, black 'n white, was from Louisiana. Eddie said, "That white boy got so mad with that station man. He say, 'This was my buddy. We laid in that foxhole together.'" That's when things change. Really. That white boy took that sign and tore it down. He say, "*I'm* takin' him in the toilet. If you kill him, I'm gonna kill you." Eddie says it was the biggest mess. He say, "I still was scared to go in that bathroom." Just back from Germany.

They still had the sign up: "Colored Peoples." They did have that sign up. But after the war, my brother Eddie, my brother Pat, my brother Henry, they improved their lives. Right there in Louisiana. The governor or someone high up decided to tell them boys they could go to school. My brother Eddie went to school right with the whites. Eddie say he walked in the classroom. And them white guys say, "Nigger, what you doin' up in here?" He say, "Sir, Uncle Sam said for me to come here go to school. Here's the papers." So he went back and he made a issue of it that they called him "nigger." The black and the white was goin' to the same school. Henry and Eddie took up agriculture. My brother Pat became a tailor. He learned upholstery, down South, not up North. Those boys, they gave 'em they rights to go to school, to take up trades. The GI Bill of Rights. That's all they got outa the GI Bill of Rights. They didn't get a home. But they did tell 'em they could go into this school. They gave 'em money, too—after the boys had fought for their country.

That's when the thing turn. Oh yeah, it was a big turnover. That is when the black and the white people start gettin' along a heck of a lot better. In the forties, right after the Worlds War. Yes, yes. They were better down South than they was up here.

I know I was segregated. But that was all right. Well, okay now, I knew my position in the South. I knew where I stood. I knew I was black. And you stay back. You don't go there even askin' for . . . no kinda freedom. You don't ask. You just keep your mouth shut. Whatever we—like school—whatever we dish out to you, you accept. I knew that. Or whatever position we give you. If it's diggin' a hole, you dig it. You knew to dig that hole. You wadn't sayin', "Well, the white person ain't diggin' no hole. Why do I have to dig it?" The white person told you to dig it, you *dig* it.

Then everybody, a few peoples run up North and tell you it's this and it's that up here. I learned different. I was well adjusted to the situation down South, because I'm in it. I thought I was gettin' out of it, when I came up here. And I found I got right back in it, but worse. I mean, it was worse to me. Because I thought I'm really gonna begin to live. You come North. You think "Justice. Oh, I'm free." No. It was no freedom. It wasn't free. I think it was worse. I could've just stayed where I was. It was Jim Crowed. It was difficult. But still I woulda been a better person.

I knew I should stay home. It had change. The white man wadn't tellin' you to dig the hole. He were tellin' you to go to school now. 'Cause then, they wanted they kids to come up with a good education. The black ones and the white ones. They had got that stuff together. We can't keep Tom down over here and Harry down over there. That's when I shoulda stayed home, 'cause I coulda went to school. And you didn't have to have that high school diploma. Have whatever you got 'cause we need you now. The tables turned—that *we* need *you*. We need you to teach the black children. It turned just like that.

The South was changin'. Not much, but a little bit. School was changin' a little bit, too. Although it was rough, they said, to go to school down there. But it change. I can remember in the fifties I went home and they had a better school for black peoples. Because they wanted to keep the blacks out of the white school. Now that they wanted to do. So what they did, they build a school in the Hayne Settlement. Through Congress or through somebody someplace somewhere, they decided that they was gonna build a school there for black children. I think that school is still there.

There was a lot of problems down there. Okay. But today is entirely different. Entirely. Of course, today it's still, you black and I'm white. But it's not as bad. The South was bad, at one point. And it still could be bad at another point. 'Cause you still got the Ku Kux Klans. You got this; you got that; you have the other. But oh, you have the same thing here. You do.

You had a bigger problem up here than you had down there. A lotta people wasn't seein' it. They say, "You shut up. I'm makin' more than I was down South." But that wasn't my problem, makin' more. I still couldn't get a education up here. Here's where you had the problem. You still do.

If you go down there now, you will find out that the jobs the white peoples do here, nobody do it there but blacks. Black peoples down there are not on somebody's comp money, they on their own jobs. Fifty percent of your blacks or more. If you notice, all your big black representative come from the South. Washington will tell you that. Tell me how many black representatives we have here in the state of Wisconsin. You can count 'em on your fingers. But if you go to Texas or Louisiana, Georgia, Alabama . . . Now you got some black peoples down there that I wouldn't trust as far as I could throw a rock. Or not that far. But you do have intelligent, great black peoples in the South. All your banks are run mostly by black people. Yes. All your big business. It's a different world. And that all started in the forties. That's in the forties, that they let them peoples out of the dungeon.

We ran up North, thinkin' we was gettin' away from it. We ran right into a brick wall. I got some papers I was gonna show you. These was papers back in thirty-two, thirty somethin'. They were knockin' black peoples then, up here. "You dumb," they said, "all them dumb Negroes." That's what they called us up North. This is the true. I'm glad for somebody to put this on paper. The whites up here would call you dumb, stupid. What else could you be when you ain't had a chance to get educated?

I hadn't been up here too long. So I told my dad, I beg my dad. I said, "Papa, I should stay down here. I should stay with you, with these boys." But my father, he thought I was doin' a little better. I was on my own, takin' care of myself. He say, "Oh no, you take that boy. He wanta go up North with you." That's where I made my mistake, by not stayin' home with him. But I couldn't argue with my dad. You don't argue with your . . .

12

What About My Career?

🐾 Here, Sylvia recalls experiences as a young woman making decisions about childbearing, childrearing, and marriage. This part of her story took place in the 1950s, a time commonly remembered for conformity to conservative norms, particularly regarding gender, sex, and family life. Although broadly accurate, that view also over-simplifies this decade when a hardship-weary generation, keen on enjoying prosperity, nurtured children who in turn identified the era with rock and roll. Regardless of generation, African Americans lived a different 1950s. Main-stream culture affected black families, but less so than their own traditions and the intrusive forces of discrimination in employment, housing, and policing.[1] We will address those major problem areas in the next few chapters. Here we focus on culture and families in this complicatedly conservative decade, when activism against Southern segregation brought racial injustice to national attention as never before.

The era's familial ideals and family life unfolded in a world redefined by nuclear weaponry, the Cold War, and television. Novelties such a televised atomic bomb test and backyard fallout shelters brought this home. As foreign policy strove to "contain" communism, Senator Joseph McCarthy and the House Un-American Activities Committee conducted a publicized hunt for communist spies and sympathizers—not only among left-leaning labor and political groups, but also government employees, academics, writers, artists, and entertainers. The Cold War climate discouraged dissent, while distracting people with consumerism. World War II had ended with broad agreement among politicians, economists, labor, and business that economic well-being depended on maximizing consumer spending. Televised images empowered that push, whether in commercials for automobiles or sitcoms modeling family life in well-furnished suburban homes. The nation had fewer than fifty thousand TVs total in 1946. By 1953, more than half of U.S. households had television; nearly 90 percent by 1960. Auto sales quadrupled between 1946 and 1955, as consumers who had the means enthusiastically fueled the economy.

Historians have explored how this context shaped notions of the family and contributed to increased marriage rates, earlier marriage, and higher birthrates. One line of thinking emphasizes the "containment" politics of a time when officials worried aloud that loose women, misguided maternal behaviors, and homosexuality could lead to communist subversion. Cold War family models cast woman as the housewife and man as the breadwinner who "wore the pants," but not as in the past. Young housewives saw themselves as far more modern than their mothers, even driving the family car. And the ideal modern family would supposedly better "contain" feeling and sexuality by allowing them healthy expression within the home.[2] Another approach observes how various aspects of reconversion to a consumer economy—from legislation to advertising, the emergence of credit cards and shopping malls—tended to reinforce gender hierarchy. Several scholars pinpoint the televised "Kitchen Debate" between Vice President Richard Nixon and Soviet Premier Nikita Krushchev at a 1959 Moscow exhibition of U.S. products. Alongside a model kitchen, Nixon extolled consumer choices as "what freedom means to us." Asserting that this put U.S. closer to "the ideal of prosperity for all in a classless society," Nixon expressed the era's wishful thinking about the happy housewife and an American dream that in fact left out many families.[3]

Other work adds nuance to this picture. Studies point out how actual U.S. families deviated from the 1950s ideal: the 80 percent jump in numbers of babies put up for adoption by unwed mothers between 1944 and 1955, for example; or the frustrations women felt with their role.[4] Scholars observe at least some outright contestation, including the rare publication that dared defend homosexuals. Less peripherally, Business and Professional Women's Clubs, even the Tupperware phenomenon, encouraged women in the non-domestic sphere of business.[5] Broad areas of "subversive consensus" underlay the conservatism of the times.[6] Philosophy, theology, and psychology contributed to new notions of self and heightened reverence for the modern artist. Many Americans believed sexual repression unhealthy. The striking popularity of Benjamin Spock's child-care book points to a liberalization of childrearing.

Those children who reached their teens during the 1950s transformed mainstream American culture through their consumer power and love of rock and roll. These teens made box-office hits of James Dean's *Rebel Without a*

Cause and Marlon Brando's *Wild One*, but mostly did not carry their own wildness so far. In a culture that increasingly saw adolescent rebellion as a normal "phase," teens and adults could find common ground. Many girls reassured their parents, for example, by preferring the exaggeratedly wholesome Pat Boone to Elvis Presley.[7] Elvis exemplified what the 1950s adult world liked least about the new rock and roll: its black origins and its sexuality. White teens had discovered R&B, as a few radio stations turned to what they called "race" programming. Hanging around Memphis blues clubs, young Elvis learned the sound well enough to please black audiences of Beale Street Amateur Night.[8] By 1956, his appeal to the teenage market would bring unheard-of record sales. As rock and roll took off, segregationists banned records and issued dire warnings against this "Negro" music, whether performed by whites or by Little Richard, Chuck Berry, and Fats Domino. Adults not so worried about race also disliked rock and roll. Many objected to innuendo-laden lyrics, sexual rhythms, and dancing that teens found irresistible. As record companies, performers, and the well-mannered daily fare of "American Bandstand" fostered acceptability, the first generation of teenage rock and rollers left mainstream American culture a little blacker and a little more sexually forthright.

African Americans stood in different relationships to all of these mainstream developments. Rock and roll illustrates the complexity of response. Particularly in the South and in rural settings, the polarity between church people and blues people remained alive—and strong enough to draw Little Richard off the rock stage at the height of his success in 1957. In black neighborhoods of Northern cities, churchgoers felt less torn about dancing at house parties and nightclubs. Among people already enjoying blues and R&B, rock and roll did not belong so exclusively to teenagers. Nor did it divide generations so much.[9] Black teens loved the music, dancing, and fun of youth culture, but also took a serious interest in civil rights actions, such as the 1957 battle over black students' admission to Little Rock's Central High School. Cognizant of rock's black roots, black audiences might appreciate performers such as Elvis, but also knew that black originators did not get a fair share of radio and television time or money. Pop hits such as the Silhouettes' "Get a Job" hit home quite differently where job discrimination put painful pressure on family relationships.

A large literature that sheds light on 1950s black families and familial culture emerged in answer to a 1965 government report on the topic. Examining statistical trends since the 1940s, report author Daniel Patrick Moynihan described white families as stable, but black families as "crumbling," indeed "approaching complete breakdown," as a result of "illegitimacy," overly powerful females and "broken homes."[10] Moynihan saw a problematic deviation from mainstream norms in numbers showing one in four black families with no fathers present and, in those that did have two parents, mothers earning as much or more than fathers.

As we have seen, historians countered by tracing historically specific strengths of African American familial culture. Sociologists emphasized the complexity of black communities and variations in family ideals, gender dynamics, and survival strategies.[11] Placing African American families in their own cultural frame of reference, anthropologists recognized African roots nourishing a vibrant extended family; a treasuring of each birth as a gift; a refusal to ostracize unwed mothers or to label children born outside of marriage "illegitimate"; customs of keeping adoptions of babies, as well as care of the elderly, within the family.[12]

African Americans' own familial culture manifested certain differences from mainstream behavior. Although both black and white birthrates among unmarried women increased from 1950 through 1965, black rates started higher, beginning at 18 percent and ending at 25 percent, as whites' went from 2 percent to 4 percent. Black marriage rates ran somewhat lower and divorce rates higher. Gender definitions differed, most visibly in expectations of female competence and contribution to family income. As the 1950s began, one-third of married black women worked outside the home, compared to one-quarter of whites. While mainstream magazines, especially those targeting women, looked askance at the woman pursuing a career, black magazines such as *Ebony* celebrated career women and dual-career families.[13] Yet some upper- and middle-class African Americans had gender traditions closer to mainstream norms and tried to create their families accordingly.

No family-related issues mattered more to black America than racial injustice. Discrimination made it less possible to make ends meet with a single breadwinner, to realize the dream of a new house in suburbia, or to even choose freely as consumers where segregation blocked access to stores, restaurants, and lodgings. It was a family matter, then, that civil rights activism stepped into public view in the mid-fifties.

As in other large U.S. cities, the Cold War context literally ringed 1950s Milwaukee, with conspicuously placed Nike anti-aircraft missile sites. When the city's first TV station appeared in 1947, less than 1 percent of households there had TV sets, a rate that leapt to nearly 55 percent in 1951, and surpassed 97 percent by 1957. Sylvia at first settled into Milwaukee's increasingly overcrowded black neighborhood. Called Bronzeville by its inhabitants, the area had its own commercial center with stores, beauty/barber shops, dry cleaners, auto repair shops, restaurants, taverns, and nightclubs. Nightclubs such as The Flame and Moonglow had nightly floor shows with local performers during the week and travelling acts, occasionally national celebrities, on weekends. The number of female owner/operators in the Negro Business Directory confirms women's importance outside the home. In 1956, black Milwaukee elected a woman, Vel Phillips, the city's first black alderperson.[14]

Sylvia remembers her dreams of a career in nursing, her pursuit of that goal through adult education at Milwaukee's Vocational School—and the derailment she feared when faced with pregnancy. The choices she made and her family's response confirm what scholars have said about specificities of African American family culture. This chapter brings us more deeply into Sylvia's familial world. She also connects here with 1950s rock and roll culture, commenting on her marriage to O.C. White, Milwaukee's first black deejay. Later a local celebrity and station manager of the city's first black-owned radio station, WAWA, White would found the O.C. White Soul Club that used War on Poverty funding to distribute food, establish a community center, and provide youth jobs and training in home repair.[15] He began his deejay career with a 5 a.m. to 7 a.m. slot, because black radio programming received only unwanted airtime in Milwaukee at that time. Audiences liked White's way with words, as well as the mix of music he played; a mix, Sylvia notes, that included the black sound of Elvis. As she tells it, their marriage broke down in large part over issues of property ownership, an imperative ingrained in her as a child. Yet Sylvia also makes quite clear how far she stood from any ideal of subordinate feminine domesticity.

Okay, so I'm back up North. Papa really thought I would do better up here. And I'm still thinkin' maybe I am gonna begin to live. I'm gonna be the nurse I wanted to be. I still thought I was gonna become well educated. And I woulda been, if I'da had somebody to back me up.

I'da done better at Vocational, if I'da been involved with your educated people. When I came to the North, I came to rock 'n roll, good time, boozin'. You work five days a week. The rest you party. You go to the tavern. It wasn't you go to school, make something outa yourself. I was hangin' on a bar. The weekends come. "Oh girl," say my brothers 'n my friends, "Come on. Let's go to the Flame." Let's go to something like that. Nothing educational. If I'da just had that person to say, "Hey, we goin' to a class somewhere." Or, "I'll show you."

And I gotta work. I wasn't goin' to school full time. I might go in the mornin' from nine 'til eleven—every mornin', year after year. I didn't get this eight grade diploma overnight. I got it over years.

I can remember we had a big graduation class. I think I was the only black person—or maybe . . . There was a few, not a lot, but a few of us. The rest was whites and them people from wherever, from across the water. Polish, Czechoslovakian—a lotta different nationalities, the foreigners from the South Side of Milwaukee. They were learnin' to speak English.

I notice, too, all them peoples that couldn't speak English, they had jobs downtown, scrubbin' floors in the banks at night. And in Gimbels, Boston Store, all those different places. It was a lotta stores down there on Wisconsin Avenue at that time. Now scrubbin' floors was okay with me. But if you black, you could not get in there 'cause those peoples, they got the job first. You wasn't trusted enough to scrub a floor in a bank or clean it up. And I'm up North now, up where—what'd they say?—you get the honey, the milk 'n honey.

So I got the little eight grade diploma. I were like nineteen at the time. After I got it, I advanced at Vocational. I had a very good teacher. He was white. But he were nice. That man knew. He tried to help me. Mr. Jacobsen. He taught me the math part. He say, "Oh, Sylvia, I don't know why they can't push you along a little more." I wasn't pushed at all. I had to sit on the fraction. They never gave me algebra. They see I could do divisions. I knew how to do all that stuff. No problem. Well, some of 'em didn't know. And I had to sit along with them. I had to some-time sit in the back of his class, because I was a smart person. They saw I was progressive and everything. But they never said, "Move her up to another level." It was disappointin'. It took so long to get one subject done. I shoulda went on.

Well, I guess maybe I couldna went on because I gotta work and go to school. I musta spend six, seven, eight years down there. A lot happen in my life durin' that time.

I had a child, Douglas. The way I met Douglas's father—I was goin' to Voca-tional at the time. This fella would see me standin' on the corner all the time gettin' the bus and he finally talked me into bein' a friend of his. He was a very nice guy. He would invite me to meet his auntie and other folks at their home. We just got involve. One relationship and I got Douglas.

I start feelin' sick. And he said to me, "Oh, you pregnant." I'm in school. I'm really wantin' to be successful woman. I say, "What? Man, don't tell me that." I said, "I don't need any children. I raised my children." Later on, my son wanted me to have another child. I say, "You better be glad *you* got here." Then I went to Doctor Carter, a black doctor in the neighborhood. He says, "Yes, you are pregnant." I was so upset. I were just sick about it. My folks couldna felt any worse than I did. 'Cause I thought this was it for my career. I'm really on the road to be successful, to get an education, and I come up pregnant.

I went back to the father and told him. He says, "Well Sylvia, we can get married." I wasn't thinkin' about gettin' married. I wanted to go to school. So I say, "I don't know what to do." I had to quit school before I start to show. I did work though—a little housework. Douglas's father, he said, "We could get an apartment and give it a try." To get married. He really wanted to. I said, "No, I don't think I wanta get married." I wouldn't. I just wouldn't marry him. My son was born out of wedlock.

Why I could have my life like I wanted was I had this auntie I was livin' with, Aunt Oja. She says, "You're not the only girl had a baby." And my father, he told me the same thing. He says, "There's a lotta young womens who have babies." So that gave me the feelin' it's okay to have this baby. Simply because my father agree. And Aunt Oja was takin' care of me pretty good. Then I had my brothers. They were married and havin' babies. Lawrence Junior was born in August, Joe's Ida in November, and my Douglas in December. I was twenty. Douglas always tell me, "Mama, you were twenty when I were born."

Now my brother Henry 'n his wife, Pulu, they had been married for years and never had a baby. They said to me, "Bring the baby down here. We'll take care of him for you." They were livin' just down the road from the old house where my father was. So I says, "Okay. That'll give me a chance to go to school and work." I took my boy down to them. Douglas was like two months old at the time. I would go down 'n see him and send him presents 'n stuff. Douglas, he knew his mama. They told him, "This is your mother."

When Douglas was a year 'n a half or so—he was walkin'—I went and I say, "Can I have my baby?" Henry said, "No. I will never give you this baby, because I raise him. You gonna hafta pay me money to get this baby back." I say, "But you told me to let you have the baby just while I . . ." I didn't give Pulu my child. No kinda legal papers whatsoever. I just let her keep the little boy until I got chance to take care of him. Henry say, "No. I'm not gonna give you this baby." I would go down there and try again. Go down and try again. They would not turn that baby loose. And I didn't know how to fight him to get the child. I coulda took my kid, just picked him up 'n walked on outa there 'n said, "To hell with you." But I didn't wanta hurt nobody's feelin's. Henry kept that baby until he was almost five years old.

Pulu did take good care of him. My dad, too. Years later, I was askin' Douglas, "Did you know my father?" He say, "Oh, Mama, I knew Grandpa very well." I say, "Really? You were so small." He say, "I used to be over at Grandpa house a lot."

He say, "Grandpa used to boil the Irish potatoes, the little bitty one, and he would put butter on 'em." He were tellin' me how my father could fix a good meal for him 'n stuff. He say, "I spent most of my time with Grandpa." 'Cause you see Henry and Pulu was in the field. From what Douglas said, I come to a conclusion that Grandpa were takin' care of him more than Henry was.

Then, all at once, Pulu had a baby, the boy. And she got pregnant again, had a little girl. Some time after that, my brother Speedy went South with his son, the one who was born the same time as Douglas. That child and Douglas, they got together and you couldn't part those children. The little boy, he wanted Douglas to come back up North with him. That's how I got my child back, through my nephew, Man. We called him Man.

My brother Speedy came to me and he say, "Oooo, I got somebody out there for you." I say, "Who? Papa?" My dad was livin' at the time. Speedy brought Douglas in. I could not believe. I says, "How did you get him?" He say, "He wanted to follow Man-boy. And I brought him up." I say, "*Thank you!*" I was so happy, I didn't know what to do. Or what to say. That was a beautiful day, when I saw that little black boy walk in that house. I couldn't believe my eyes.

I say, "What happen?" Then I thought—they had two kids and this one probably was gettin' up under they skin. Maybe that's why Douglas was stayin' so much at Grandpa's house. They let him go. I didn't have to pay. I didn't have to do nothin'.

By then, I was married. That happen when Douglas was still down South. I married this guy—not Doug's father. I married O.C. White. He was a nice man and he loveded me. Oh, he would bring me roses and everything. He really loved me—more than I loved him. I kinda married him to spite another man. Tell it like it tis. It didn't matter to me if our little marriage ended or what. We stayed together for two, three years.

The way we met was at the Riverside, a big place where the whites would gather for wrestlin' matches and roller skatin'. When big bands like Lionel Hampton would come, they would go there and play. Every year we'd go there to see the Harlem Globe Trotters. And one night a week the blacks would go there for roller skatin'.

Now this guy and my brother Jimmy had got into a fight. So one night when I was skatin' at the Riverside, Jimmy says, "That's the man who hit me in my eye." I say, "What?" I roller skate up to him and I says, "You son of a bitch. Why did you hit my brother?" Oooo, I raised so much hell about that. I just went off on the man. He say, "Now wait a minute. Wait a minute. Girl, let me tell you. Jimmy kicked me—in my privacy." Jimmy's right there and he kinda admit. . . . The man was so nice about it. He was the bouncer at the roller skatin' rink. After that, every time I'd go skatin', he would meddle me. He would always ask me to go out 'n stuff. That was O.C.

I don't know if you ever heard of O.C. White. He was the disc jockey, the one with all the mouth, there in Milwaukee. He worked hard in his music—not his own music. It was playin' all these records on the air. He was a construction worker, a cement finisher. He would play this music in the evenin'. He play oh, blues songs, jazz or jazzy music, any of that kinda stuff. I really know a lotta music but I can't think of that old music right now. It was, oh, Muddy Waters, Jerry Butler, Bobby Blue Bland. He even played the Hound Dog and that was Elvis Presley. 'Cause the Hound Dog really sound like black people's music. He played all that music. Later on O.C. finally got his station. I think that was WAWA.

He wasn't into music as much when we were married. But he did have his radio show. And we used to go see the black musicians. Riverside always had 'em. I have saw a lotta musician. Anybody big, I were there. And we had records. Honey, I had stacks of records 'n still got some. Any of the black musicians.

I liked music just as much before I married O.C. White. I love music. I told you how I loved the blues when I was a kid down South. But it's after I grew up that I got to know music. When I came to Milwaukee, I used to love to hear Billy Eckstine or Fats Waller or Louis Armstrong. I wish I could remember 'em. Jimmy Witherspoon. Nat King Cole. I have saw Nat King Cole. Oh my God girl, any them musicians. B. B. King. Most of those blues singers. And some of the good jazz musicians. I used to know 'em—they music I mean—very well. Me 'n O.C., yes. But me 'n my brothers, too. We all really liked a lotta music. My brother Pat love to dance. We used to go to Chicago where they would have all those big bands. That was when I'm eighteen, nineteen. Pat 'n them was twenty, twenty-one. I could go out with those guys. That was real nice to go out with men, even if it was your brothers. You got somebody to dance with. Somebody to sit 'n talk with.

And my brother Walter. Ohhhh! Walter went to Roosevelt school in Milwaukee, where the teachers found out that he was a very good person for music. Walter wanted to blow sax. So we all chipped in, me 'n the brothers, and got him a saxophone. Bought that big saxophone off Wisconsin Avenue, Sixth and Wisconsin. They had a beautiful music school there. He start takin' music, the only black boy blowin' sax by music sheets. He really was gettin' his music basic. And he became, oh that boy could get up there and he blow that sax. I didn't want my father to know that because they always say that kinda music was the devil's work. But Walter never heard that, 'cause I took Walter as a child up North. I never taught him that was the devil's work. It was a different life for him. We were very proud of him, me 'n the brothers. 'Cause we got him that saxophone. And he coulda become a big jazz star. Oh, he could really blow sax.

I have a lot of family that is very good at artwork. One nephew of mines should have a museum. But there is obstacles that keeps him from doin' it. It's sad. Even my brother Walter, after he got older, the boys would drink 'n party and have a good time. He laid his saxophone aside. Never tried to make it a career. I don't know what happen to black children that they can't see things as a good career. Even me myself, I tried to see, but just couldn't do it. Maybe they are tryin' to see, too. I couldn't get to be the nurse that I wanted to be. If you say, "Well, Sylvia, you doin' all right," I say, "I'm not satisfied. I could've done better."

Okay, back then, back in the fifties, Douglas came to me and I put him in school. He was ready for kindergarten. So I enrolled him into Victor Berger School. He was a very good student. I went to parent/teacher meetings up there, participated in everything. After he finish Victor Berger, which was sixth grade, Douglas went to Robert Fulton. By then, me and O.C. was divorced. I gotta backtrack to tell you about that.

Before I got Douglas back, me and O.C. bought this little one-family home. It was like six thousand—forty or fifty dollars a month for payment. Now when Mr. Steinheifer, one of our neighbors, got ready to move, he said to me, "Sylvia, wouldn't you like to buy my house for eleven thousand dollars?" A brick up 'n down. I says, "Yeah." 'Cause we had half paid for what we had. The brick home had apartment you could rent upstairs. Huge. Four, five bedrooms, beautiful livin' room.

So I told my husband, I say, "Come on, O.C. Let's buy Mr. Steinheifer's home." I'm workin' at County Hospital. He's workin' construction. I figured, "What the hell, we should buy." I was that type of woman, never the type who would say, "Oh, we can't have this and we can't have that." I say, "O.C., let's buy the house. We both workin' and we just got this one child."

He say, "I'm a young man and I don't need all that. I'm too young for that." I said, "Man, this is the time you start buyin', when you young." I say, "We buy. We buy." I just wanted property. My father brought me up that way.

That's one reason why I got so upset with the husband. He told me he a young man. He had enough. So I saw there were no future with him. Because that was the place for us at that time. Beautiful brick buildin'. He had to have his Cadillac. And I couldn't have that house because he said "No."

Honey, me 'n him, we couldn't get along no more. We started fussin' and fightin'. He was a turd, too. Well, he wasn't really a turd. O.C. wasn't a bad person. When I said "turd," it was a way of expressin' how . . . You couldn't tell O.C. nothin'. That is why I call him a turd, I guess. Like O.C. and football. He loved to play football. Every Sunday I had to go to these football games, 'cause if I didn't he would get awful angry. He was really good at football. And there was some man was tryin' to get him to go to the university so he could become a professional football player. He coulda went to the university! This man, Shapiro, was gonna help him. But that man couldn't tell O.C. anything. I couldn't tell him anything. He never heard me on stuff like that. So that's where I say, "turd."

He could have been somebody. Everybody thinks he was. O.C. got to be the big wheel—to ride up 'n down the black parade. One time he was in the parade for Juneteenth day—mister of ceremonies, big wheel—and he saw me out there. I was there sellin' barbecue. He saw me and we both, "Oh, hi!" So when the parade was over, he politely walked all the way back down there to see me. He say, "Oh Sylvia, I want you to meet Joyce." That's gonna be his third wife. He introduced me to all his wives before he married 'em. He had three: me, Bernice, and Joyce. So I says, "Oh man, I look like this." He say, "I don't care. Just come on." So I met her. And he had me get up on the stage and say "Hi" to everybody, too. Okay. O.C. was kind of a leader, leadin'. He had them young boys paintin' 'n stuff like that. I don't know too much about that, because I were my distant. I know he did a lot of things for the community down there. But I say he wasn't the person he coulda been.

Anyway, I divorced him. When the divorce was almost over with, he say, "Sylvia, are we goin' back together? 'Cause that divorce is final on the twenty-seventh." I never will forget them words. He says, "Cause I have found me another woman. And if you don't want me back, I will marry that woman." I say, "You do that. You go right on and marry her. You have my best wishes."

My attorney called me and he say, "Sylvia, don't you bite off your"—how is that?—"bite off your nose to spite your face. You should take the man back." I guess he had been goin' to my attorney and everything. The man did love me. He really likeded me. But I said, "No, no, no, no, we just can't get along. We can't. I'm not gonna take him back. I'll just live my life without him." That was the end of that husband.

I coulda married again. My son's father wanted to marry me. He was a nice guy. But I was afraid to try marriage again. 'Cause I was doin' what I wanted to do. And to get involved with other peoples, you know, you have to go along with they program. What? Why go along with somebody's program when you—when it just doesn't work? You almost know it's not gonna work. So you just go by yourself. That's what I did. I was on my own.

I was still tryin' to become that nurse. I had to quit school for a while when I got Douglas back. 'Cause I had to take care of the kid. I was runnin' out the house, workin' at night and leavin' that child. Just get home early enough to get him to school. I had to give that up, because if they catch you leavin' your child like that . . . Later, I got a different job and went back to school again. Oh, I spent years in Vocational. It was only two to three hours a day. I wish it coulda been a full-day course. But I had to work. I couldn't study as hard or as much as . . . I'm workin'. And I got the kid. It was such a squeeze. But I just wanted to go to school and become a RN. That was my goal.

13

Get a Job

Sylvia began looking for one of Milwaukee's "good jobs" at a time of raised expectations among African American jobseekers. Before World War II, racial traditions had generally excluded blacks from jobs that whites wanted. Black workers made inroads during World War I. But their employment remained more precarious, their work more dangerous and disagreeable. Black men labored nearest the blast furnaces and the molten metal in steelmaking, for example, while black women received assignments such as cleaning intestines in meatpacking plants. Many labor unions kept their membership exclusively white and fought to keep blacks out of skilled positions. Employers could blame discriminatory practices on their workers, citing incidents such as the walkout that occurred when a Milwaukee steel company hired blacks in 1934. During the Depression years, whites took black-identified jobs as janitors, railroad porters, and such. Then, in just two years between 1940 and 1942, mobilization for war brought jobs to nearly 5.5 million of the nation's 8 million unemployed. That spectacular improvement had little effect on black unemployment rates.[1] Black activism and labor shortages would soon change the outlook, however.

As 1941 began, well-known labor leader A. Phillip Randolph urged African Americans to travel to the nation's capital for a protest demonstration that summer—an idea proposed by an unknown woman delegate to a 1940 civil rights convention in Chicago.[2] By May, the March on Washington Movement announced that fifty thousand people would march—unless the president used his executive power to overstep Congressional obstruction and address the unfairness in war preparations. As presidential advisors tried to persuade Randolph to cancel the event, the estimated crowd size grew to a hundred thousand. Convinced that such a spectacle would hurt the nation's reputation and morale, FDR issued an executive order on June 25 that prohibited racial discrimination in hiring for government agencies or in defense industries. A new agency, the Fair Employment Practices Committee, would implement the ban.

With enemies in Congress and limited powers, the FEPC nonetheless made its presence felt. Tested by a November "hate strike" in Ohio, the committee helped there, as it would in scores of cases, to persuade whites to accept hiring or promotion of blacks. The FEPC publicized the president's order, investigated complaints, held hearings, and issued cease-and-desist orders—the threat of contract withdrawal always looming, but never actualized. Exemplary hearings in Chicago in January 1942 interrogated five Milwaukee manufacturers. Three admitted that they did not hire blacks, one bluntly refusing to comply. Within two years, all improved their statistics. Even the defiant company hired 802 black workers by the end of 1943.[3] Historians disagree about the importance of the FEPC in bringing about such progress. Most give more weight to labor shortages.[4] Failing predictably in the South, the committee proved ineffective in some cases elsewhere as well.[5] FEPC findings against California shipyards and the shipbuilders' union had no effect until the state's Supreme Court ruled against hiring discrimination. Oakland's transit system exemplified the common tactic of agreeing to comply, then stalling.[6] Terminated by Congress in 1946, the FEPC ultimately reported success at resolving 42 percent of about twelve thousand complaints received: 66 percent in the Northeast, 62 percent in Midwest, and 55 percent in the West.[7] With its unprecedented mission, the agency arguably had a part in the changing patterns of race and jobs.

During the war, large numbers of African Americans found work where they formerly could not get hired. A scattering of statistics suggests the magnitude of these wartime employment gains. Between 1941 and 1945, the executive order helped raise the count of black government workers from 60,000 to 200,000. Their numbers in industry more than doubled to about 1.25 million. Black union membership tripled to 750,000.[8] In the Milwaukee area, about three thousand black workers held industrial jobs by war's end, roughly one third of them in companies that had previously hired only whites. As Detroit area auto plants shifted to producing war materials in 1940, black workers held only 3 percent of jobs in the auto industry; a share that reached 15 percent as the war ended. Nationwide, African Americans went from 2.5 percent of defense workers in 1942 to 8 percent in the last months of 1944. Those who secured a foothold in defense industries during the war earned substantially more in 1950—if they managed to stay in those industrial jobs.[9]

Not everyone reaped such rewards. Black women found it far more difficult to get industrial work, or even to register complaints with the FEPC.[10] Male or female, those who did land defense-industry jobs might not keep them. In one example, a St. Louis arms manufacturer with 3,600 black workers in the summer of 1943 cut about a third of them by the end of that year.[11] Mass layoffs due to production cutbacks and demobilization included more African Americans, because discrimination put them among the last hired. Postwar oversupply cost thousands the California shipbuilding jobs they had only recently obtained.[12] At war's end, some companies fired all their black workers. Others folded or closed, retooled and then rehired, but downgraded blacks to less-skilled positions.[13] Union membership could provide job protection, but not at the expense of organized labor's commitment to seniority. Nevertheless, the wartime employment boom permitted young people such as Sylvia to envision a lifetime working secure, well-paid jobs in industry or government, or even as professionals.

Public opinion about race and employment also seemed to be improving. Over the postwar decades, one research group repeatedly asked people nation-wide if blacks "should have as good a chance" of getting "any kind of job," as opposed to whites having "the first chance." In 1944, only 42 percent of respondents said they agreed with equal opportunity so articulated, a sector at 47 percent in 1947. By 1963, the same wording elicited 83 percent approval of "as good a chance," an upsurge that reached 87 percent in 1966.[14] At the very least, these polls point to new discomfort with saying openly that race should affect a jobseeker's chances.

For many African Americans, such changes did not translate into better employment chances. Indeed, between 1953 and 1962, black unemployment rates more than doubled from 4.4 percent to 11 percent. The jobless rate for black youth reached 20 percent by 1964, as employers proved more ready to take a chance on inexperienced young whites than blacks. While some black workers did maintain industrial employment and prosper in the robust con-sumer economy of the postwar era, significant numbers found such opportu-nities blocked by racist attitudes, policies, and practices.

Trends that had less to do with race worsened the situation. Technological innovations wiped out jobs in industries that had been major employers of African Americans. In the late 1950s, maritime shipping changed from using crates handled by gangs of men to truck-trailer containers lifted by cranes. Railroads lost ground to trucking and automobiles. With improved refrigerated transportation, meatpackers moved their operations to livestock-raising areas, shutting down huge stockyards and meat processing plants in cities. By 1963,

Chicago had lost more than 90,000 of the jobs located near black neighborhoods six years earlier.[15] Between 1947 and 1963, Detroit saw 140,000 manufacturing jobs disappear.[16] The city of Oakland enjoyed 50 percent of Alameda County's industrial jobs in the 1950s, less than 30 percent by the 1970s.[17] Entwined with the racial attitudes that drove white flight to suburbia, the shift of manufacturing away from city centers disproportionately affected blacks.[18] Within a few decades, little would remain of the booming U.S. industries that had raised Sylvia's hopes in the 1940s.

Sylvia migrated to Milwaukee envisioning a nursing career at a time when few African Americans in the city worked in such professions. In an unpublished oral history of 1940s Milwaukee migrants, one interviewee recalled her high school "Career Day" turning away black girls who tried to attend the nursing session.[19] The first African American nurse graduated from a Milwaukee nursing school in 1950. That year, with a black population of 21,000, the city had only 177 black professional or technical workers. Milwaukee's famous breweries had just opened to black workers.[20] The local Urban League found that numbers of black employees in industry had decreased after 1945, most sharply among women. Of the 308 Milwaukee companies returning the Urban League's 1949 questionnaire, just 171 said they hired blacks.[21] Employers that did hire African Americans commonly denied them promotion and training opportunities.[22] In 1960, two-thirds of Milwaukee's employed black males (compared to just over one third of white males) were at the bottom of the pay scale in less-skilled jobs. Almost half of the city's employed black women performed service work such as cleaning.[23] Eight years later, the Allen Bradley Company faced a federal lawsuit for hiring only "friends and family" of current employees, a policy that yielded only twenty-five black employees out of a workforce of 7,500.[24]

Sylvia helps to put a human face on such numbers. She recounts the extraordinary lengths that she and her brothers went to as they tried to get jobs and stay working in Milwaukee. Applying at factories and food-processing plants with masses of employees coming and going, she felt certain that their numbers alone disproved the "no jobs available" refrain. Sylvia recalls personnel practices that worked against black migrants: written tests that eliminated the educationally deprived; policies requiring birth certificates that many Southern-born blacks did not have. When she found work, she faced what historians have called the "front-of-the-house / back-of-the-house racial line" that separated black employees from the public: washing dishes rather than waiting tables; moving stock rather than sales in a department store.[25] Her narrative of years cleaning private homes sheds light on reasons for continuing a type of work considered demeaning, but shared by so many black women. She speaks forcefully about the welfare programs that she saw as truly degrading, a trick to dampen ire about discrimination. Perhaps most important, Sylvia provides a profound sense of how all of this felt: To have her application crumpled up and thrown in the trash in her presence. To rejoice that a new program would give nursing training to aides at the hospital where she worked and then see only whites admitted. To find herself at retirement age without a pension—and almost no Social Security—after a lifetime of work.

After my divorce, what I had to do was get a better job. And that was hard, really hard for blacks in Milwaukee at the time. Oh, I can tell you a lot about that!

I know I already mention about Yaeger's bakery, about tryin' there when I was livin' with Aunt Oja. They was always: "No jobs available." That big old bakery, two or three stories. Other ones, too. Them was some *big* bakeries. And Jay's Potato Chips was right there. I could walk out the door to work in them places at that time. But it wadn't a single black in there. Well, at Yaeger's they had one black boy workin'. He was unloadin' that flour. But that was the only black person I saw. I went there all the time tryin' to get a job. "No jobs available." I'da liked to have job there. 'Cause I know they were payin' good money. But I never could get in. Never. *Never* could get a job—out of all those bakeries or the potato chip place.

When I married O.C., I was workin' at County Hospital, at the mental hospital. I got that job because the whites didn't want to work there with their own peoples. Most of our patients was white. But they were crazy and the whites didn't wanta be in there with 'em. So then they start hiring blacks. That took years. I was tryin' to get in there for years. Couldn't pass the test. They finally cut the test out, 'cause they needed help. And we black womens were glad. Honey, we were glad to take care of them peoples. Although they were callin' us niggers and doin' us dirty—would throw shit on us and everything else. But we . . . that was a job.

Mrs. Field was the only black nurse in that geriatric buildin' where I worked. She had got her RN down South somewhere. At County, they were givin' her hell. Some of the whites wouldn't even listen to what she had to say. They just misused her like you push a board around. You black, you stay back. This is up North now. It was very painful.

And listen to this. I'm workin' in the County Hospital and the county says, "I want you girls to become a practical nurse." Oh, thank God! I'm in. But no. The white gals got them positions. We were trained well enough to do anything. There were black womens who knew everything. But they did not give it to us.

By the time of my divorce, I had resigned from the hospital—mostly because this doctor committed suicide out there. This doctor were tellin' me about "long-term workin' here . . ." He gave us a lecture on long-term workin'. He was stayin' on the premises and that's where he killed himself. We had to pass his place. Then, too, I was so disappointed with how they were trainin' you for a little ol' practical nurse right there and they didn't let any blacks have that. Whew, I just can't believe that! It was hurtin'.

So I got a job downtown at Gimbels—as a stock girl. That's the best you could do there. Or you could go down in the kitchen and wash dishes. Or you could vacuum the floors. You couldn't be a sale person, when you lookin' at all these black peoples buyin', shoppin' there.

What the hell? You gonna pay all this money for clothes? Girl, I was goin' to the Goodwill and rummage sales. As I said, my brother Pat became a seamster after the war. When he came up North, he showed me what he knew. I used to go to the Goodwill and get them nice gowns. He would put me up on a table like this, cut them things off and hem 'em for me. Just beautiful. I were pickin' up Saks Fifth Avenue clothes at them places. I knew what Saks Fifth Avenue was by workin' downtown. Workin' there did give me time to go to school. But I wasn't makin' enough money to be payin' all those house notes.

That was after my divorce. I had left O.C. in the house, 'cause I didn't wanta be bothered with it. I had a job, but I had the child, too. I moved to another place. Then my attorney call and say, "He haven't paid those notes over there at the property." I say, "Well, what is I got to do with that?" He says, "Put him out." So we went back to court. The judge said, "Mr. White, don't you know you can't stay in the house without payin' the rent?" He said, "Judge y'honor, give the property to Sylvia. I will not argue. She can have it."

After you got three or four hundred dollars worth of bills! It was about seven months of not payin' the house note. That's fifty dollars a month at that time— not much compared to now. But that's a lotta money, when you ain't got no money. Payin' this. Payin' that. Your light bill, your gas bill and all that kinda stuff. Now I'm stuck.

I says, "I'm gonna get outa this rut some kind of a way."

At the time, I'm seein' all these jobs up on the board at Vocational. I says, "Oh my God, let me try to put in for this job." That was at the police department. Girl, the man took the application, crumbled it up. "Oh no! You got a child." He crumbled it up, *boom*, right in front of me. They don't care if they hurt you or not.

After that I goes to City Hall because they got all these jobs posted. Lotta work. Honey, I took the test and I *passed* it. The man call me in. He says, "Miss

White, you passed that test. And a buncha them children from over there at Marquette University, they didn't even pass." I say, "Oh, thank God for that! I got my position." He say, "No. You ain't got no job. You ain't got no high school diploma." I said, "Mister, that's what I'm goin' to school for." I'm still at Vocational. I says, "Call Vocational. They will let you know that I'm all workin' on a high school diploma. Ain't that good enough?" I begged him. I say, "Mister, I need the job. I got my child. And I need the job so I can pay for my house. I'm goin' to school. I'll get my high school diploma."

Honey, I missed that job. Damn good job, too, workin' for the school board. I coulda retired from that job with some pretty dollars in my pocket. I did not get it. Because I didn't have a high school education. I just cried. That was a shame—when you pass and you can't get a job! He coulda say, "Well, you can't have that job. But here let's see can we work you in with cleanin' the floors." I woulda accept that. Because it was city. That was a retirement.

So I goes to the employment office. The employment office says, "Would you clean?" I say, "Yeah, I would do anything." See 'cause now I got this kid and I want this property saved. I wanta pay my house note. I wanta live, all right? I'm not going to welfare, that's for sure. Didn't even know what welfare was.

Well, I did know. That's how my child was born. When I got pregnant, I had to go on welfare because they said, my family says, "Well, you can go downtown—you pregnant—and get on welfare now." So I did. That's how I got all my medical care. When I took Douglas down South, I could get off welfare and I did.

So I did know what welfare was. But after my divorce, that welfare never occurred to me, 'cause it wasn't nothing. Two, three dollars, five or ten dollars a month. That's the way this crap was. I was gonna settle for that, when I could make a dollar an hour cleanin' floors?

So I would go out in these neighborhoods like Whitefish Bay and Fox Point. They was mostly Jewish, the ones who were hirin' us. You got with some of them Jewish womens and they were nice to you. Now I can tell you that. They say Jews ain't no good but that's a damn lie.*

---

* On the relationship between African Americans and Jewish Americans, see James Baldwin et al., *Black Anti-Semitism and Jewish Racism* (1969). Cornel West and Michael Lerner elevated the tone of discussion in *Jews and Blacks: A Dialogue on Race, Religion, and Culture in America* (1996). See also Paul Berman, *Blacks and Jews: Alliances and Arguments* (1994); William M. Phillips Jr., *An Unillustrious Alliance: The African American and Jewish American Communities* (1991); Jonathan Kaufman, *Broken Alliances: The Turbulent Times between Blacks and Jews in America* (1988).

I saw that man on TV. I can't say his name, starts with a F. F something. You know the man I'm talkin about. He sayin' all this stuff about Jewish peoples. Got his hair slicked down and. . . . I say, is this man black? Is he really black? Don't seem like it to me. His mind is so . . . so warp.*

Them peoples was the nicest peoples I ever met in Milwaukee—was my Jewish nationality. They had these stores—right there with us in the neighborhood, the black part. And they would let you . . . I couldn't go down to the Boston Store and say I want that dress but I don't have the money to pay for it and get it. But them Jewish stores, they would let you do that. I have saw little children go in there and get that piece of penny candy. And that child would bring that penny to the man the next day. Penny candy! It's a small thing. But small things mean a lot.

And them Jewish peoples I went to work for—cleanin'—they was so nice. They wasn't lookin' at me as a nigger either. They looked at me as a *human being*.

When you meet one Jewish person and they like you, you meet the full family. I worked for Joyce. She had just got married to this man, this attorney, Jack. Then Jack's mother, she was so crazy about me. She saw how I helped around that house and kept that house clean. "You come work for me." Then I met this other Jewish attorney, he lived somewhere out there. "You come help me." Oh, I was in with some nice peoples.

That man's mother, one day she say, "Oh Sylvia, I got all them plums out there and I'm gonna show you how to make a pie. You bring 'em in here." I say, "Okay, Mrs. C." We peeled 'em and took out the seeds. She say, "You take these plums and you put 'em in the bottom of the dish. And you just sprinkle a little vanilla or cinnamon—whatever you would like—sprinkle it over 'em and a little sugar, too." Then she says, "You take one cup of sugar, one cup of flour and one stick of butter." Easy to remember. You mix all that together and crumble it on top of the plums. That makes the crust. Girl, I make the best apple pie outa that. My brothers' children would come by me all the time and I taught them kids. My nephew, anytime they have a big get-together, he got to make that apple pie. The other one,

---

* Sylvia refers here to Louis Farrakhan, head of the Nation of Islam, a man much in the media in the 1990s, most notably for convening the "Million Man March" in October 1995, where speakers included Maya Angelou, Rosa Parks, and Cornel West. That same year, the daughter of Malcom X, Qubilah Shabazz, made headlines when arrested for allegedly conspiring to have Farrakhan killed for the role she believed he had played in her father's assassination. Not long before this conversation in October 2000, Sylvia had seen Farrakhan on TV making anti-Semitic comments at odds with her own experiences.

he make the yum-yum cake. That's a Bell thing, the yum-yum cake. Anybody asks for the recipe, we do not give it out. Okay, so gettin back to . . .

Them peoples would keep me on they property for twelve, thirteen, or fourteen hours. That meant fourteen or fifteen dollars. One day would pay my light bill, or maybe light bill and gas bill. I'd go out in their yard and work. I love doin' things in the yard. I'd do anything them peoples asked me to do because they were nice to me. They would have these big parties. Oh, I could fit right in there, makin' those different thing, settin' it up 'n gettin' the party goin'. Joyce would say, "Sylvia, you can't go home tonight. Can you stay 'n help me out?" Well, that meant extra hours. Those was little blessings that I really needed. Other ones who knew me would do the same thing.

So I scrubbed floors. That was heck of a lot better than washin' dishes at Walgreen's. Because I was scrubbin' those floors in beautiful surroundins'. Or people would say, "Come on, Sylvia. Let's sit down 'n have lunch." Sit down 'n do this. Sit down 'n do that. Or the babies need a-changin'. Or, "Syl, I'm goin' out to shop, you take care of the babies. You don't have to do anything." And my money is still goin' on. Cleanin' floors for some of them womens was better than workin' for anybody. 'Cause I could pick my shift. Or if I had to bring my son along, he could sleep in the boys' bed and play with the boys. It wasn't, "No, you don't bring him out here." It was, "If you need to, you get on the bus with that boy and bring him on out here, too." I say, "Yes, I do. I ain't got nobody to keep my child." See, it was advantage, not disadvantage. Then I was out in these nice neighborhoods, where they was havin' all these rummage sales. My sister-in-laws and me, we would go pick up clothes for the children.

I never knew peoples could be so nice. They were so nice. Yet they could be . . . No, I can't put down on those peoples. Because they would give me all they clothes, they excess clothes. They would give me they shoes. They would give me food. They would give it to me. I could get they old used car. That was the good old days.

Now, too. It's a Jewish woman gave me my computer. Brought it out to my place and set it all up and everything. She's a doctor, retired, one of my market peoples. They come out, her and her friend—every week, if the weather isn't too bad. They drive out to my place and teach me how to use that computer. Girl, I am havin' so much fun with that. Oooo, that computer gets mad with me sometime. At first, I was afraid to touch it. But they kept tellin' me just go head on and try stuff. That won't break it. So I'm readin' the book and . . . She says to me, "Sylvia, don't you ever tell people you are uneducated." 'Cause I were readin' the book that come with the computer. I don't know a lotta the words. But with the pictures and the words I do know, I . . . That's another Jewish person. Now I wanta get back to talkin' about back then . . .

It was a good long time that I worked with them folks. Then Joyce, she move out somewhere further away. Her husband built her this mansion, all white carpet. Oh, she wanted that white carpet. Joyce was my girl. I still can go to her house 'n sit down 'n chat with her just like I'm chattin' with you. Joyce, and I had other peoples, too. They were really nice folks. But I didn't get Social Security, cleanin' floors for them peoples. I didn't get benefits, retirement and all that stuff. So when Joyce move, I'm branchin' out in life. I'm gonna try for these good jobs.

I'm talkin' in the 1950s, while I'm livin' on Palmer Street. I says, "Well, I'm right here on the bus line." Holton Street bus would take me right to Allen Bradley. Allen Bradley, with the big tower. Every time I look at that, I get sick to my stomach. I went in there. They would not hire you. Them womens and mens was pourin' outa that place, shift by shift, just like you would turn loose a buncha cattles. And they said they had no jobs.

So then, okay, right up on Center Street, Masterlock was there. They was in full speed. They gave me a test—dexterity—movin' blocks 'n stuff. "You ain't fast enough," they said. Oh! Who was any faster? Girl, when I worked at the packin' plant in Waterloo, I ran the hell outa that wiener machine. Some of the white womens, they didn't like me runnin' that machine so fast. That was later, years after I took that test at Masterlock. And they said I wadn't fast enough. Who in the world would they have any faster than I? But you can't . . . I had to take another kick in the behind. So I went to Allis Chalmer. I went to American Motors, before it moved to Kenosha. I went to all nice places, where I thought they will need work for years 'n years. The last one I went to was Briggs & Stratton. They were makin' pieces for—was it the Viet Nam war? I don't know which war it was. This was in the fifties. I went there and I almost cried for a job. But they didn't need me.

While I'm thinkin', let me tell you what happened to my brothers, Eddie and Dock. This took the cake. I'm talkin' durin' the fifties, when American Motors took that plant to Kenosha. Them boys, they say, "Oh, they hirin' in Kenosha. We gonna drive all the way from Milwaukee to Kenosha to get a job." But they wouldn't hire 'em, if they didn't have a birth certificate. That way they could discourage blacks from the South. 'Cause back when the boys were born, them peoples down there really didn't give you a birth certificate. Eddie had his discharge paper. He thought that would take him all the way to heaven. 'Cause he went to the war. They say, "No, you got to get your birth certificate."

So Eddie went to his attorney, attorney Murray. Murray says, "You gotta go to the judge." Murray took 'em to the courthouse. The judge says, "Well, you gotta have somebody older to say that you were born." Eddie could say that Dock was born, 'cause Eddie was couple years older. But Eddie didn't have nobody to say that he was born. The judge looked through this stuff. He felt sorry for the man. And he says, "I'll just let it go." Just let it go! See, they didn't really even *need* all that stuff!

My brother Eddie retired from Kenosha. He moved out to Waterloo after I moved there. And he drove all the way to Kenosha for twenty some years. That's like eighty or ninety miles. Dock, he worked there too for quite a while. So they did get the job, but only after gettin' a lawyer and goin' through all that.

Are you followin' me? That was the difficulty that we had—tryin' to get decent employment, to become good citizens. Now some peoples didn't try like we did. They just went on welfare. Welfare would give 'em that money—not money, some change—instead of education and a job.

They say black peoples was lazy, triflin', no good. They taught them black peoples to be that. They taught 'em with the way they do welfare. The more babies you had, the more money they would pay you. So these womens was sittin' home, gettin' fat and havin' babies. Me, I had one, too, out of wedlock. But I sewed up the thing after that. Some of them womens just kept havin' 'em and tellin' the welfare that they didn't know who the father was. "Father unknown." Now Douglas, that boy's father is on his birth certificate. If anything happened, Douglas got his father. "Father unknown." Some of them poor children today is out there in the street mad about that. Welfare taught these womens that.

Welfare never reached out to say, "I'm gonna send you to school." They wouldn't do nothing but give you that little money. Just to keep your mouth shut. And they built them old project houses to stick 'em up in. To paralyze those brains worse. Then they start buildin' the jailhouses. That jailhouse doesn't do nothin' but just ruin. Welfare ruin.

Oh, girl, I looked at a program the other night about this welfare mess that they started today. Now they turnin' all them black womens offa welfare. Uneducated. Uneducated peoples can't do anything. And they kicks 'em offa welfare. Them womens are out there standin' on the corner, goin' to bed with mens for a nickel and a dime. I have saw women and children sleepin' in barrels over there where I sell stuff. These people are really suffering. It upsets me.

Okay, I was talkin' about how I went around lookin' for a good job. Which related me to the welfare thing, 'cause if it wadn't so hard for a black person to get a good job . . .

I have went everywhere to try to get a job. I ended up workin' in nursin' homes. Oh, I was continually workin'. I never went back on welfare. I've always worked. And that wasn't easy, tryin' to work for some of these people. They will kick you in the behind or say something, just to make you get off the job. Then, if you jump up 'n leave, it ain't nothin' they loss. It's your loss. Oh God! What a life! I tried. I tried and tried and tried. But I never got one of those good jobs where you get retirement. And when you get my age . . . See, what hurts me now is I don't have retirement money from a job. I coulda had it. There was no reason why I shouldn't have had a good job.

14

House on Palmer Street

Two years after Sylvia arrived in Milwaukee, a racial drama flared across the pages of the city's newspapers.[1] That summer, housing administrators assigned a lot at the county-run Greenfield trailer park to Albert Sanders, a black World War II veteran enrolled at the Milwaukee School of Engineering. On July 7, 1949, Sanders, his wife, Rogelia, and their children, aged 3 and 5, moved their trailer to the all-white park. In the evening, an estimated 125 of the park's 1,800 residents marched on Sanders's mobile home and threatened violence to his family and property. Three sheriff's deputies who dispersed the crowd offered Sanders protection—and escorted the family out of the park when they chose to leave.

Word of the incident mobilized the local NAACP and Urban League, as well as state and city human rights commissions. The next morning, they organized a meeting where religious, labor union, and other community leaders joined the district attorney, the sheriff, and housing administrators in persuading Sanders to return. As sixty-five sheriff's deputies escorted the family back to their trailer, the afternoon's *Milwaukee Journal* ran a front-page story and photos: a large shot of the angry white crowd and a smaller one of Albert and Rogelia at their door. An editorial emphasized Sanders's wartime service and blasted the incident as a violation of "good Americanism."

At an open-air meeting held by the human rights commissions at the trailer park that night, seven speakers castigated racial prejudice. The commander of the local American Legion, a man with the unbelievable name of Christ T. Seraphim, called the treatment of Sanders "un-American."[2] A Catholic priest from Marquette University decried the outburst as betraying Christianity. Some of the four hundred listeners booed and shouted objections. Booing also erupted when the segregationists took a turn at the microphone and demanded a parkwide vote. Small groups argued into the night. Photos of the event filled nearly an entire page in the next day's *Milwaukee Journal*.

With the Sanders family staying at the park and the "Trailerites" split into factions, human rights commissioners tried to negotiate. The group bent on excluding blacks demonstrated daily. Their spokesmen claimed to represent the majority, but refused when the other side agreed to a vote. After two days of stymied talks, commissioners requested prosecution of the intractable segregationists under Wisconsin's 1895 civil rights law. Without mentioning the toothlessness of that old law, the district attorney said he preferred charges that would more certainly lead to conviction.[3] That night, the ring-leaders went to a priest and said they were sorry.

On July 13, both newspapers described a scene where, after a verbal reprimand from the district attorney, seven men and one woman apologized to Sanders. One man explained that he had never seen anything but segrega-tion, in the New Jersey town where he grew up and then in the army. "I am not a Ku Kluxer," he declared, but "just a plain American citizen who let a few things go to my head that weren't so." The woman spoke of fears among women residents who had no experience living with black people. Several said that they would not have behaved as they did, if they had known the laws. Now a *Milwaukee Journal* editorial congratulated the city and the human rights commissions for using "democratic reasoning" to uphold "basic American fairness." The story dropped out of the news.

Coverage of this incident did not reassure Milwaukee's African Americans. Sylvia remembered only the initial aggression, not the outcome. In fact, the city had serious—and worsening—racial housing problems. Three years earlier, a study found nearly 68 percent of Milwaukee's black housing substandard. Segregation continued to increase. In 1930, blacks were the majority (56.5 percent) in only one of the four wards where most lived.[4] Some sections reached black concentrations of 75 percent by 1940 and would exceed 90 percent twenty years later. With the black population at 62,485 in 1960, a *Milwaukee Journal* article suggested that the ninety black families living in white neighborhoods signaled progress.[5] Yet Milwaukee later placed among the nation's most segregated metropolitan areas and made national news in 1967 for the ugly racism that met open-housing marches.

The Greenfield trailer park story touches on important aspects of the race and housing picture in the postwar United States. Dramatic photos in the Milwaukee newspapers foreground a longstanding and widespread white hostility toward residential integration, as well as the threat of violence that often materialized in worse disturbances. Milwaukee's "Trailerite" episode resembles those elsewhere, not in its positive ending, but rather the backdrop of increasing segregation and the aggressors' obstinacy—even when officials, community leaders, and journalists supported the black family. Yet in that official support, this narrative also exemplifies the era's peculiar mix of progress with retrogression in racial matters. Notions of an American way opposed to Nazi-like racism emerged in rhetoric about the trailer park incident. That saga also featured human rights commissions established by the mayor and the governor in the mid-forties, a time when officials nationwide set up such groups. The GI Bill made it possible for more black men to attend institutions such as the Milwaukee School of Engineering. Those who managed to join the growing percentage of black families able to buy property, however, still faced a daunting array of obstacles.

When Sylvia bought a house on an all-white block in 1950s Milwaukee, she joined the relatively small numbers testing the promise of the times—with mixed results. Despite signals of change in polls and rhetoric, racial separation continued deepening in these years, as a tremendous wave of city residents—almost all white—moved to the suburbs. Diversely motivated, the new suburbanites certainly did not all share the "white flight" mentality exemplified by the 1948 Michigan campaign slogan: "Keep Negroes out of Dearborn."[6] Yet the new communities growing around cities typically excluded African Americans. Wherever they wished to buy, black people with reliable incomes and a down payment could less readily realize the dream of home ownership than whites.

Most historians emphasize the role played by government agencies and programs in that inequity.[7] The Federal Housing Administration boosted the nation's rate of homeownership from fewer than one in three families in 1930 to nearly two out of three in 1960, but hurt far more African Americans than it helped. The agency's system for guaranteeing home loans discouraged mortgages and property improvement loans in black neighborhoods. Color-coded FHA maps provided to private lenders assessed city blocks for building quality, social class, and race. Black residents on a block made buyers there less eligible, as did racial mixing in itself.[8] Likewise, black veterans received fewer VA insured loans. Favoring new housing, FHA and VA criteria spurred white flight, as did construction of the interstate highway system that began in 1956.[9] Highway building further overcrowded black neighborhoods by razing buildings without adequate relocation provisions.

Realtors played a blocking role as well. In 1957, the National Association of Real Estate Boards still openly advised barring black buyers—whatever their income and education levels—from white areas.[10] In a mid-1950s survey of Chicago realtors, 83 percent said they never sold to blacks in white neighborhoods. Twenty-two percent would not deal with African Americans at all. Another study that decade found racial "restrictions" among 80 percent of realtors interviewed in San Francisco.[11] When baseball superstar Willie Mays bought a home in that city over neighbors' objections in 1957, the realtor famously backed out of the deal. A credit system unfavorable to blacks added economic incentives to the mix of individual realtors' feelings and a segregationist professional culture.[12]

Through the 1940s, both realtors and the FHA encouraged the common practice of drafting property deeds with agreements not to sell to blacks. Most early suburban developers had such racial covenants covering all property they built, sold, or rented. In 1948, the U.S. Supreme Court declared it unconstitutional for courts to enforce the agreements. After the FHA began refusing to guarantee loans for covenanted property in 1950, the agreements lost importance among weapons against integration.

Nothing in that arsenal communicated more spectacularly than the housing-related violence of these decades. From New York and Philadelphia to Santa Monica and Huntington Beach, hostile neighbors burned crosses on lawns, hurled rocks and bombs through windows, burned down homes, formed threatening crowds, assaulted and killed people. A 1940s wave of fire-bombings turned deadly for two Chicago children and a family of four in Fontana, California. Most often small in scale, the aggression occasionally involved crowds of thousands. In Detroit, four such mass attacks occurred in 1925 alone. Thousands of Chicagoans rioted in 1949 over mere rumors of blacks moving into a white neighborhood. In nearby Cicero in 1951 and Levittown in 1957, the National Guard had to break up violent segregationist crowds.[13] A deterrent to black families, such events increasingly repulsed mainstream America.

Well before the postwar era, Americans both black and white recognized the conflict between democratic ideals and the practices of segregation. Even in notorious 1920s Detroit, Clarence Darrow could bring an all-white jury to see racial injustice in the case of a physician charged with murder for returning perceived gunfire and killing one of the mob besieging his home. By the 1960s, domestic activism and international politics put enough pressure on the nation's racial fault line to elicit action. An executive order issued by President Kennedy in 1962 and the Civil Rights Act of 1964 banned discrimination by federal agencies and all federally funded programs. The Fair Housing Act of 1968 addressed home financing, as well as racial screening of buyers and renters.

Without strong enforcement provisions, this legislation could not succeed. Already in 1964, opponents passed "homeowners' rights" ballot initiatives in Detroit and California. In 1977, the Supreme Court required proof of intent to discriminate in housing discrimination lawsuits. Politicians courted the white suburban vote with veiled language and policies aimed at avoiding integration. Problems of segregation and substandard housing in U.S. metropolitan areas continued or worsened.[14]

In this larger frame of reference, Sylvia tells a relatively positive story. She mentions the violence that others encountered when moving into white neighborhoods; but she had trouble only with one neighbor, whose abusive behavior remained nonviolent. Sylvia indirectly unfolds how it felt exposing visitors to offensive speech and gestures, as she devotes much of this chapter to recalling joyfully her family and friends—the Christmas celebrations and such—associated with her Palmer Street home. Describing changes to policing as more blacks moved into the neighborhood, she focuses on the discriminatory ticketing later admitted by a former Milwaukee police officer during state hearings of the U.S. Civil Rights Commission.[15] Sylvia ends the chapter with a tale that displays not only her feisty personality, but also a growing awareness of civil rights activism among African Americans not directly involved in the movement.

During that time, I lived on Locust and Palmer. I was the only black person on that block for years. Before that, me 'n O.C. lived on Walnut Street. But I didn't like livin' over there. It was so congested. Just a hole that you had to live in. I am the type can get out of the ghetto. It don't take me long. I'll get out in a minute. My father used to say, "Nothing from nothing leaves nothing." And when I see there is nothing, I wanta get away. 'Cause I think there should be somethin' somewhere for somebody. I don't care what color you are.

So I figured I would move out. My brothers, my brother Joe and my brother Lawrence, they had moved to Locust 'n Chambers, which wasn't too far from Locust 'n Palmer. I wasn't followin' them or anything. But it was not too far. You could walk to my brother's house. He had three or four kids. My son, Douglas, was goin' to school by then. So they were all goin' to the Chambers Street school. They was the only black kids in the school.

It was mostly an all-white neighborhood when O.C. and I bought that house. Coincident—one of the detectives who was in my brother case lived on my street,

Vorpagel. I didn't know this at the time. The mayor, he was in that section, then, too. I don't know how they sold us the house, but they sure did.

It wasn't run down either. It was perfect, pretty floors and this, that 'n the other. It was nice at the time, nice for me. I had been workin' in some really nice homes out in Whitefish Bay. But my little house was decent.

We fixed that house up a lot, too. The boys, some of my brothers, they really knew how to do things. And I had a friend who knew how to build 'n stuff. You know those big attics they have in a house? I wanted my son to have his own room. So I made him a bedroom up there. Douglas had his privacy and, later on, his little television somebody done give me. He enjoyed his bedroom. I got twin beds because he got all these cousins who wanta come 'n stay. I made my main bedroom up there, too. Then I had a little bedroom downstairs. And we did the basement up nice. So I had a lotta room in that one-family house. I always had a couple roomers.

I think I was keepin' my brother Pat's son. Pat's wife had him down South, 'til Pat say, "Well, I want my child." Something about my family, they kinda stick together with they children. His wife say, "Yeah, you can keep him." She didn't mind. Then Pat's daughter, it didn't take her long to get up here with her daddy. Pat did have a place. But for some reason the son moved in with me for a while.

We found our cousins, the Jackson, in Chicago. We called each other cousin but we was not really related. As I said earlier, they family helped to raise my father. When they came up North, they let my father farm Joe Jackson place in Louisiana. I think one of my brothers from down South came up and said, "Syl, all them Jackson peoples live in Chicago." So we found out where they live—my brother Pat in particular was good at lookin' people up—and we went over there.

Bernice and Marguelee were just a little older than I. Bernice said to me, she say, "I'm a . . ." What is a foot doctor? That's what she was. Marguelee, she was workin' for IRS. Everybody there had good jobs. Oh girl, they just had everything. They had money. They had a home. They had nice cars. They had television. It was just so comfortable. I say, "Why didn't I meet these people before?"

Bernice said, "Oh, since you up there, I'm comin' up to visit you." I said, "Well, come on, Bernice." So they drove up with they children. They didn't have no girls. It was all boys. And I had the boy, too.

Then they say, "Oooo, we goin' to the Dells." I say, "You goin' where?" I didn't know nothin' about the Dells. They say, "Come on. We gonna take the boys up to the Dells." So we goes up there. And those girls, they pitch tent. I stood and I looked. I say, "It's good to be educated. You can do things." Then I joined right in, because I wanted to learn how you put this tent up. That was so much fun! It was simply beautiful.

We got to be so close. They liked my brother Pat and my other brothers, too. And Douglas, Bernice would call and say, "Sylvia, the boys want Douglas to come over the weekend. What do you think?" She says, "Just put him on the bus. We will pick him up at the station." Douglas could go over to them peoples in Chicago—every weekend if he wanted to. He was involve with nice people and he was gettin' a good understandin'. Oh, we always was together. We spent a lotta our Christmas together. For Christmas these folks would buy they children airplanes that you put together and all those battleships from the World War. They needed glue and other stuff to put them ships together. Then, when they had this stuff, them boys would do so much. My little Douglas would put them airplanes together just like you would put. . . . like you gonna put this story together. I say, "Boy, where you learn that?" My Douglas was a pretty smart little rascal.

He love airplanes. He used to go to Billy Mitchell Field in Milwaukee to see all those airplanes come in. I didn't know he was doin' that at the time. He know every airplane they ever was. He really like airplanes. I guess that's why he went into 'em. He became a airplane mechanic and then instructor for airplane mechanics. I think he coulda been more than that. But he would say, "Mama, you still ain't satisfied." No, I ain't satisfied. You still didn't get the A. My brothers always say, "You gotta get the A. Otherwise Sylvia think you haven't done anything." Anyway, those Jackson boys became engineers or somethin' good. Doug, my son keep up with 'em more than what I do. Bernice is still livin' but Marguee died a while back. But that wasn't what I was tellin' you. Okay, gettin' back to about my neighborhood . . .

Most of my neighbors treated me all right. I had one white person across the street from me, a very nice woman. And the Steinhafels on the corner, they was nice people. Very religious. And they wasn't poor people. They had their furniture store on Third 'n something. There was a police livin' right next door to me, a young guy. His mother, I have to say, she hate black people. I really believe the peoples who sold me the home, sold it to me because they wanted to put somebody next to her who was a different race. As a way of gettin' back at her.

Mrs. Parks, her name was. She hate black people. Oh, she despise black peoples. You couldn't even walk on the other side of your house to put your storm window in unless she was callin' the cop. Or you couldn't park in front of her house. 'Cause you takin' up her space. If you got company—you know how that is—a big Christmas deal or something. Well, she could insult your company. She could really hurt your feelin'.

Her son was in the police department—way before my brother got killed. So I wonder sometime, did this have something to do with it? I would speak to him.

Sometime he would speak; sometime he wouldn't. His mom, she was nasty. And we right there, neck for neck. It wasn't easy livin' there with those folks.

We had bought a piece of property where there was a back house and a front house. One person owned the back, Mrs. Teasedeal or something like that. She was white, but really a nice person. Her buildin' was right on the alley. I had the buildin' in the front. She would always walk through my property to get to the street. And her son picked her up all the time. Her son could park on the street anywhere. That was okay with Mrs. Park next door. But for me, I had to really park in my . . . "Stay in your place." That's the way they say it, "Stay in your place."

I live with that, with her. There was arguments—me 'n her. And the cops would come out. The police came out a number of times and they couldn't find anything wrong with what I was doin'. I would just tell 'em, say, "Well, what am I supposed to do? Sell my place and get outa here?" That was very hard, livin' with all that torture.

That was right there in Milwaukee. This was in the fifties, durin' the time when Reverend Martin Luther King 'n Rosy Park was havin' all that trouble in the South. They had started down there with the bus thing. But I experience more segregation, more downgradin' black people, in Wisconsin than I really . . . Honest to God, this is the true facts. There was a lotta downgradin' in the South. But, to me, I really didn't come in contact with it as much as I did in the North.

They don't let black peoples in they neighborhoods, if they can keep 'em out. Anywhere. They don't want you there. And you better understand that. They'll burn you out, set the fire. They didn't do that to me. But they did do it to some blacks them days. Me, I only had trouble with Mrs. Park. She was just determined to get me out of there. And I did leave before she did.

Now Mr. Steinhafel sold his home on the corner. That was later. He sold his home to a black woman. Then we had a few more blacks movin' in. The blacks are movin' in to my neighborhood, the whites movin' out. And when blacks start movin' in, the police department moved in. Before that, they did have a little police department further down there on Hadley, which was just an old house or somethin'. It was like a little village police department. But when the black peoples start movin' in, they throwed in that big Locust Street police department building. Ooooooo, that was just, "What is all this?" This is quite a police department here. But blacks are movin' in.

Then they started to say, "You cannot park." Black peoples couldn't park in front of they house, their own property. We poor black peoples could hardly afford to pay our telephone or light or gas bill. Now we gotta worry about this. We got another bill on us. You gotta pay for a permit—to park in front of your house.

I had live there all those years with them white folks. And, honest to God, you didn't hafta have a permit. I worked out in Whitefish Bay and Fox Point and places like that. Them polices out there did not bother you about a ticket. I'd go out there 'n stay all night long. I'd say, "But my car." "Oh you ain't gonna get no ticket out here." You wadn't gonna get no ticket out there. But down where I lived, you would. When the blacks move in, the whites move out. Then they make you pay. Pay for parkin' in front of your house when you payin' taxes! I could not understand it. So I got into a big argament.

They gave me a ticket for parkin' in front of my house. You had to get up in the middle of the night to move your car. And I did not have a garage to put it in. So I got this ticket. I got this bill, three or four dollars. Coulda been less. Parkin' ticket. I didn't pay it.

Then this one police came to knock on my door and tell me that I owed this ticket. He says, "Miss White." I say, "What?" He says, "You owe a ticket. And I'm here to arrest you or you pay this ticket." I say, "Well, I really don't have any money. So the only thing I can do is accept the arrest." He says, "You makin' a bad name for yourself." 'N stuff like that. I says, "Well, that's all I did. I didn't kill nobody. If I hadda murdered somebody, then I'd be makin' a bad name," I say, "but I'm not makin' no bad name for myself. By goin' to jail for a ticket? You gotta be kidding." He's tellin' me that. How stupid can you get? I says, "Mister, I do not have money to pay this ticket. And I have a child. What can I do now? Set in jail?" For the ticket, 'cause it's a couple days in jail, you know. He says, "Oh no, you got to pay that ticket. You call up your friends or your family or somebody to help you pay." I says, "Well, my family don't have anything either. How can I call 'em to ask 'em to pay the ticket?" Oh! Him 'n I we had such a go-round about that ticket. I say, "I'll just go to jail for the ticket. Can I bring my little boy in there with me? Or you gonna send him to school? He goes to school right there on Chambers, right up the street there." He says, "You gotta pay." I says, "I don't have the money. I'll sit in jail."

So then he says, "Should I call the wagon?" I say, "No, you don't hafta call the wagon. I'll walk down there." That's how close it was to my house. I say, "You can save the city that gas. I'll walk down there." Down to that big new police department. I say, "We will walk. That give me chance to talk to you some more." Me 'n this officer, we walkin' down there 'n fussin' all the way. 'Cause I was teed off.

When he push the door open and me 'n him is walkin' in, he says to the other man there, "You got a doozie here." I say, "I'm no doozie. I'm Sylvia White." They all white. You ain't got no black in the office then. I says, "This man pick me up. He come to my house to arrest me for this ticket." And, oh, I started. Oh! Did I start in that place. I says, "I do not have any money. And I do have a child to support. He's at school and he'll be home pretty soon." And he woulda been home pretty soon. I says, "What are we gonna do? 'Cause I do not have the money." I says, "I won't have a little change until I get paid and that's about two weeks." Then the man say, "Well I'm gonna take you back there and lock you up." I say, "Yeah, do that. Or do somethin' so I can get this ticket over with. And you, you gonna see about my child. I have a child there and he's in school. You gonna see about him. 'Cause if I stay in jail . . ."

Girl, I raised so much sand in there with that officer. I says, "The minute black peoples move in, then you start givin' tickets. I been livin' here for many years and nobody got a ticket for parkin' on that street." So many years, they never gave a ticket in that neighborhood. 'Cause I were there. I was the only black person on that block. I say, "Now I have a black neighbor and then I have another neighbor black across the street over this direction. And the minute black peoples move in the neighborhood, this is what you do." I say, "What I need to do is call the NAACP or somebody. But I'll call my brother and see can he bail me out." He says, "Well, call your brother." Then I remember, "My brother ain't home. He's workin'. I just have to go to jail. I'll sit, 'cause I don't have no money."

This other man sittin' in the office heard me. He was sittin' back there in the next room. He said, "Come here, Miss White." I go in there and I says, "Yeah?" He says, "Gimme the ticket." I say, "Okay." And he changed it. He discarded or he did somethin' to it.

But see, I didn't do what I shoulda really done. What I shoulda done was went to somebody to see could we stop some of this givin' tickets in the neighborhood. What I should've done was really call the NAACP or somebody. 'Cause I knew what was goin' on with Martin Luther King and them. I knew what was comin' up, that black peoples was . . . But that was my first experience.

15

The Killing of Daniel

Before we try to see the killing of Daniel Bell in its own historical context, it would help to take a brief look at race and policing in more recent times. When the issue came to public attention more than three decades after Dan's death, what had not changed seemed striking. The Kerner Commission of the 1960s and the Christopher Commission of the 1990s—both formed in response to ghetto riots—uncovered remarkably similar attitudes and behavior. Despite larger numbers of black judges, prosecutors, and police officers in the 1990s, the law enforcement system still convicted blacks more readily, sentenced them more harshly, and subjected them to more frequent police stops and arrests—encounters that more often resulted in injury or death.[1]

Public opinion, however, showed signs of change. Polls following the widely publicized 1991 beating of Rodney King in Los Angeles, for example, found more white respondents than ever agreeing with blacks on the abusiveness, even the racial character of a policing incident.[2] Meanwhile, racial profiling struck empowered individuals such as Washington, DC, attorney Robert Wilkins. After Maryland state troopers pulled Wilkins over in 1992, his lawsuit prompted a study of area interstates that observed 93 percent of drivers violating the law, with African Americans making up 17 percent of all drivers, but more than 70 percent of those stopped. Troopers found illegal drugs as often in whites' cars, but searched and arrested more blacks—then used those arrest statistics to defend racial profiling.[3] Although cases of profiling and abusive policing still continue to emerge and polls still show a black/white perception gap, 1990s media spotlighting stimulated a more probing public discussion of police behavior toward minorities.

Quite different public attitudes framed the killing of Daniel Bell. In a 1959 example with striking similarities to the Rodney King beating, a group of Detroit police officers furiously punched and kicked a sixteen-year-old black suspect on a police station garage floor, as reporters watched through the open door. "Gentleman cops don't solve crimes," quipped a detective to the journalists. Detroit's police commissioner said he saw nothing wrong with the officers' conduct.[4] Nor did national news outlets make much of the story. Meanwhile, a TV series, even a game show, celebrated Los Angeles Police Chief William H. Parker, despite the racism he expressed in his official capacity.[5] When the LAPD later acknowledged its racial history under Parker, commentators cast the late chief as not unusually racist for his time.[6] In fact, a late-1940s Philadelphia study found white law enforcement officers and officials there, like Parker, viewing blacks as innately inclined toward crime.[7] Although attitudes were changing by the late 1950s, many whites still shared such outright prejudice. More broadly, white people considered policing fair. In a 1960s Milwaukee survey, 89 percent of whites agreed that police treatment of blacks was either "just right" or "too soft."[8]

Not a major scholarly topic in the 1950s, race and policing received attention in a 1957 University of Pennsylvania study that surveyed Philadelphia police officers. That city then employed 150 African American patrolmen out of 4,224 officers total. Nearly 60 percent of the white officers said that they would object to riding in a patrol car with a black officer or taking orders from a black person. In the group expressing those views, 75 percent admitted treating black suspects "more strictly" than whites. Fully 87 percent of the interviewed officers, both white and black, believed black arrest rates higher than they actually were.[9] Comparative statistics on police departments in the nation's largest cities showed tiny percentages of black officers, with only one captain (New York) and fewer than one hundred lieutenants and sergeants in all departments combined. Milwaukee's 1,130 officers included only eight blacks, all in the lowest rank.[10]

Incidents of racialized police misconduct came to light when the U.S. Civil Rights Commission began holding hearings on policing issues in 1960. A black plainclothes officer with the Detroit police department testified that white officers had beaten and severely injured him in 1955 and again in 1960, attacking both times without checking his identification and accompanying the beatings with racial insults. In Chicago, a 1958 police raid at the wrong address subjected a black father, mother, and children to rough physical treatment and racist verbal abuse, and then ended with the man taken to the station for ten hours of interrogation without being permitted the phone call required by law. In 1959 Cleveland, after chasing and pulling over a black driver who had tried to flee, a motorcycle patrolman walked up to the open car window, shot the man point-blank, and then threatened witnesses who had seen that the victim did not reach for a weapon, as the officer would claim. The commission selected these and other stories for its published report, calling them "typical" of the 1,328 incidents reported between January 1958 and June 1960.[11]

It was in this context that Milwaukee police officers Thomas Grady and Louis Krause, two motorcycle patrolmen on duty separately, encountered each other at about 8:30 p.m. on February 2, 1958. As Krause would later recount, Grady said he needed more arrests and was going to the city's black neighborhood in order to "arrest some niggers."[12] Just then, they saw Daniel Bell driving a car with a burnt-out taillight, pulled him over, and pursued when he tried to run away. After a brief chase on foot, Krause commandeered a passing car and picked up Grady. They neared Dan and jumped out of the vehicle with guns drawn. Grady caught Dan, pressed the gun to the back of his neck, and pulled the trigger. According to Krause, when Grady realized the man was dead, he said, "He's just a damn nigger kid anyway."[13]

Knowing they could not justify the shooting as it happened, the two officers made up a story. Since the law permitted a police officer to shoot a "fleeing felon," they stated that Dan jumped out of the car shouting, "You sons of bitches will never catch me. I'm a holdup man." In case that weren't enough, Grady took a knife from his pocket, opened it, folded the fingers of the lifeless right hand around it, and placed the hand back in the snow. To the ambulance crew, it would look as if the man had been holding a knife when he died.

Back at the station, Grady and Krause wrote initial reports saying Daniel Bell had a knife in his right hand as he exited the car. A second set of reports said Dan slashed at them with the knife. Chief of Police Howard Johnson explained to the press that he himself had "noticed there was more to it" and asked for a rewrite of the reports. The newspapers and the 10 o'clock television news showed Grady's plant as "the knife." Chief Johnson violated department policy when he released the story to the media. With any death, families were notified first, in order to minimize shock and suffering. One police official said later that he had never before seen that policy ignored.

More of what went on inside the department emerged in the testimony of Russell Vorpagel, the former detective who later said he quit the MPD because of the Bell case. On the night of the killing, Detectives Vorpagel and Edwin Shaffer were the first to arrive on the scene. Grady did not yet mention the knife, but only told them that he had shot a "fleeing felon." Vorpagel measured twenty-three feet nine inches from the spot where Grady said he fired to where the body had fallen. He drew a diagram and wrote a report.

The next morning, Inspector Rudolph Glaser called Grady, Krause, and Vorpagel into his office, told them their reports did not match and ordered them to meet him at the district attorney's office. On the way to the meeting, Chief Johnson questioned the likelihood of shooting from twenty-three feet away. At the DA's office, Grady began saying he had shot from six feet. Captain Leo Woelfel and Inspector Glaser told Vorpagel to change his report to include a knife threat and to replace his diagram with one that put the gun closer to Daniel. Vorpagel refused. District Attorney William McCauley upped the pressure by angrily throwing the reports down, pulling out Vorpagel's, and handing it back to him, saying, "I want these reports to be consistent." Vorpagel considered this an order to change his report, but still did not do so.

Later that day, Captain Woelfel had armed robbery victims brought to the morgue and shown Dan's body, looking for someone to identify him as their assailant and thus produce a more credible "fleeing felon." Woelfel told Detective Vorpagel to pick up one victim known to police as an alcoholic—and to buy her some drinks before taking her to the morgue. Vorpagel did not prepare the woman with liquor. Nor did the morgue visits succeed in implicating Dan in a holdup. The one person claiming to "identify" the dead man had been robbed January 17, while Dan was in jail for driving without a license.

Vorpagel later explained that he disobeyed Woelfel because he believed racial prejudice impaired the captain's judgment. On an earlier occasion, Vorpagel wanted to release a person who had been arrested and then cleared, but was told by Woelfel to keep the man in jail overnight because he was black. Vorpagel's testimony shed light on the racial climate outside as well as inside the department. After the killing, he recalled, Grady bragged around the department about letters he received from Milwaukeeans who applauded how he dealt with blacks. He proudly showed Vorpagel a letter containing the word "nigger"—and explaining that the two dollars enclosed were for more bullets.

The police department subpoenaed witnesses favorable to their case on February 10, but waited to serve William Hochstaetter until the February 14 inquest day, at a time when he was not home. Hochstaetter lived across the street from where the killing took place. He had heard the noise and come out to see what happened immediately after the shooting. Despite the lateness of his subpoena, he made it to the inquest and testified that he saw the dead man's hands—black against the snow—with no knife. Vorpagel's report and on-scene diagram went unmentioned. Grady testified that he shot from less than six inches. State Crime Lab Director Charles Wilson testified that the gun seemed to have been pressing the fabric of Daniel's coat when fired. The six-man, all-white inquest jury "hand-picked" by the sheriff, declared the killing "justifiable homicide."[14]

More than twenty years would pass before the Bell family heard most of the above account. The story Sylvia tells here entangles with what she learned after the case reopened. Yet no new knowledge could soften the emotional impact of those first hours, days, weeks, and years. Sylvia's words take us deeply into the family's experience. At the time, Dan's left-handedness gave the Bells certainty of one falsehood in the police account. Nor did they believe that Dan would have said and done what the officers claimed. Besides making some of her strongest statements of feeling, Sylvia communicates powerfully here by bringing alive certain moments. The joyful birthday party they'd had for Dan just the night before his death. The haunting coincidence of driving past the killing scene. The guns dominating her memory of the police station that night. The inquest room. The anguish of seeing her father—to her a great man—unable to answer on the witness stand and begging her to speak for him when courtroom rules required her silence. Silent no more, Sylvia helps fulfill her father's prediction that truth would one day surface from under the lies. More broadly, she helps us understand how families might feel in cases that do not take so remarkable a turn.

❧ My brother Daniel was killed on February 2, 1958, right after his birthday party. He was twenty, twenty-one. That weekend we had all got together and had a party for him. We said, "Oh, we gonna give Danny a birthday party." Because the younger boys was growin' up and didn't have the mom there or the dad. So some of us, we kinda played mom 'n dad. I made cakes and this, that 'n the other—brought it over to the apartment on Tenth 'n Wright where my brother Pat and them were livin'. We had such a good time that night. Music goin', dancin', food 'n . . . oh, a party, family get-together—and friends, too. I left like twelve o'clock—came home and went to bed, 'cause I got my child and my job. I was workin' nights out there in South Milwaukee at a nursin' home. I don't think I had to go to the job that night though.

I do remember clearly that I had to work the night that Dan was killed. Earlier in the evenin', my girlfriend, Stella, came to my house. She say, "Where you goin', Stick?" We called each other "Stick." I say, "I'm goin' over by the boys' house to pick up my dishes 'n stuff." She say, "I'll go with you." So we went on over there. The boys was all there but Dan.

After while, I say, "Girl, I gotta go home, 'cause I gotta get to work." I had to take Center Street back. And where Dan had got killed was right offa Center. He was on his way to my house, where he live, when all this mess started. He had a taillight out on the back of his car. As me 'n Stella were comin' back, I say, "Girl, that look like Dan's car down there." She says, "Oooo, where them police lights were?" I say, "Yeah." We saw the lights flashin', me 'n Stella. But I had no idea, no idea. Didn't go over there or think much more about it at the time. I was anxious to get back home.

A little later, I was gettin' ready to go to work. My child, he were lookin' at television. He said, "Mama!" I say, "What?" "They killed Dan!" They just flashed this on television. I say, "*Oh my God. Oh my God*, lemme call Pat 'n them 'n tell 'em. Did they hear?" In the meantime, they heard, too. The TV was blastin' about the killin' of Daniel Bell. That was ten o'clock news. They had been killed Dan a couple hours before. They put his name out right away, "Daniel Bell."*

They said he was flashin' at the police with a knife in his right hand. In his *right hand*. The baby was left-handed. He woulda never tried to cut nobody with his right hand, 'cause he did not use that hand. He would write left-handed, he would . . . And his knife was layin' right there in the bathroom of my house. I say, "They done killed that boy for nothin'. They killed him for nothin'." When I was on the phone to my brothers, they said, "The police are here now." So I told 'em, "I'll be right there."

The cops took us downtown. We all piled into the car: me, Pat, Lawrence, Jimmy, and Ernest. When we walked in their police department, they had they guns out. Guns like this—pointed—big old guns all up 'n down the hall. *Yes*. They had them guns pointin' 'em at us. We said, "We didn't come down here to . . ." I says, "I know I didn't come down here for nothin', 'cause I'da came down here with a damn bomb. I sure wouldn't pull a gun on you." And I meant that. At that moment, if I'da had a bomb, I'da brought it in there, got right in the middle of 'em

---

* Of course, it is impossible to measure how much this violation of MPD policy affected the Bell family's grief. Several of Sylvia's brothers recalled the emotions of those first days in their 1980 depositions, as the city's attorney asked if they had initially discussed the wrongfulness of the killing. They described an intense grief indistinguishable from what anyone would feel upon learning that a beloved family member had been gunned down under questionable circumstances. Both Henry, the oldest, and Alfonso, the youngest, reported fainting at the news.

'n let 'em have it. Me too. It woulda been quite all right with me. I was willin' and ready, 'cause I knew them peoples just *lied*.*

We say we wanta talk to the captain. They told us somebody hadda go downstairs and identify the body. Jimmy and Ernest went. Me and Pat, we goes to the captain, the man who wears the *brass*. I forget his name. White shirt with the big brass on it. He said, "Whadda you want?" We say, "We came down to see what happened to our brother." "Your brother was lungin' at the cop with a knife in his right hand." I say, "Officer, you just *lied*." He say, "Don't you call me no lie." I says, "I don't believe a thing you said. My brother was *left-handed*." And I told him I had Dan's knife. Pat said somethin' to him, too. So then, he says, "Can't tell you niggers nothin'! Get outa here! Get out or I'll throw you all in jail!" I says, *"Oh my God."* I looked down the hall and there was all the guns. Just *guns*.

Then I saw them boys comin' from the basement. My poor brother Jimmy and my poor brother Ernest. They never told me was it Dan or wasn't it Dan or anything. I still don't know today what happen. How did he look? I know the jury, one man passed out. But Ernest or Jimmy never respond to me anymore. Never lived a real life after that. *It killed 'em.* They were hurt. They, both of 'em, spent the rest of their life in the institution, mentally ill. Them boys, whatever they saw . . . Whatever they saw, I'm kinda glad I didn't.[†] Because maybe I coulda got the same reaction that they got.

---

* In a phone conversation shortly after September 11, 2001, Sylvia said, with characteristic honesty, that she really had wished she had a bomb in the police station the night they killed Dan—but that the TV coverage of the 9/11 attack made her feel "terrible" about having had that feeling.

[†] Until the year 2000, Sylvia believed that some unspeakably gory sight had caused Jimmy and Ernest to lose their sanity. In fact, the photos taken of Dan in death show only a single bullet hole in his upper back near the base of his neck. His head remained intact—a look of terror frozen on his face. Ernest and Jimmy had always felt closer to Dan than any of their other siblings, a feeling Ernest expressed during his 1980 deposition by claiming they were triplets. Ernest's testimony included insane ramblings that poignantly communicate the harm done by the killing. He recalled returning to work at the meat packing plant, but having to be taken away from the assembly line, because he felt "they was killing people out there." Asked whether he'd seen the knife on TV the night of Dan's death, Ernest took off with the image. "I seen where they pulled the knife out of him," he said, "stuck it up in his heart like that, pulled it out of him." "In his heart?" the questioner echoed. "Yes," said Ernest, "up in his heart and pulled it out of him. I see that on TV, the knife, it was green, green stuff come out of him, the cop pulled the knife out of him." From a distance, one might appreciate the poetic accuracy of turning the knife into a weapon the police used

We didn't know what to do, 'cause we never had anybody to get killed by a policeman before. We calls attorney Murray. My brothers had used him before as an attorney. I call any attorney I know. They all seem to be hesitive, very much hesitive at that time.

They buried my brother down South. I didn't go down there with the body because they was gonna have the inquest. Me and my brother Joe, we stayed here to see what they's gonna do. They had that inquest a few days later. The jury was all white. Which doesn't mean. In a way, it means and it don't mean. But every one of 'em sittin' there was white.

That day they had a little room—I think maybe it was twelve by twenty-four—to put all them peoples in it. Crammed up in there, in that Safety Buildin'. We had little chairs, the few who could sit. Nobody hardly. We had one or two chairs to set on in there. I mean, we couldn't get in there. But they had room for the jury, for their policemen, that gang. It was very hurtin'. When I first looked at it, I said, "Now this isn't right. I don't know what kinda court this is." It was *nothing* to compare to a courthouse. I had been in the courthouse. I know what the courthouse look like. But that day, we had a little room.

Our attorney, attorney Murray, I would give him notes and he would read 'em 'n kinda hold 'em up to see could he get question. He couldn't. And he was white. There was a black attorney there, too, Hamilton, Attorney Hamilton. A black fellow we knew. We asked him to come and set in for us, please. Those guys had very few words to say because they was not allowed. They didn't want them to say anything.*

Now Grady—that's the one who killed Dan—he told his lies. You'll see all the lies he told. You wanta hear 'em outa my mouth? Grady says, "He lunged at me." He say, "He's ran and he hollered, 'I'm a holdup man.'" And, "I told him to stop." Oh, Grady just lied, lied, lied, lied on my poor brother. I'm sittin' there listenin'. "He lunged at me with the knife in his right hand." That's when I begin to write and say to my lawyer, "He's left-handed. My brother is left-handed. He did not use his right hand." And they had evidence that he were left-handed, 'cause

---

against Dan. Those closest to Ernest could only feel their loss of this brother, too, as his testimony jumped back to the meat packing plant and went on about "knives, nothing but knives, all kinds of knives, trick knives . . ."

* Inquest procedure did not permit the family's attorneys, Milton J. Murray and George W. Hamilton, to cross-examine witnesses, ask questions, or even raise issues such as Dan's left-handedness. For a recent *Milwaukee Journal Sentinel* discussion of such problems with inquests, see Gina Barton, "No Sense of Justice," May 22, 2005.

he had signed his name at the courthouse couple time—when he was arrested before.

Now I've got to stop again.

They complainted that Daniel Bell had been arrested a number of times. Because he was caught drivin' without driver's license. And the reason why that baby was caught drivin' without driver's license, was because he couldn't read or write proper. He couldn't pass that test. They did not let black peoples go to school down South. That is one of the reason why that child is dead.

See here's where I get emotional with education. If the polices hadda been educated and my brother hadda been educated . . . The police who killed my brother didn't have but a six or seven grade education, not even a high school education, I don't think. If the police hadda been smart enough to know that the boy . . . Well, they all was boys, the cops and my brother. Did I tell you they was all young? They were all children. The boys who kill my brother, they was just about the same age as Dan, not much different in age. But the baby was black 'n they were white. Hadn't been on the force that long either. If them peoples, all of 'em, hadda been education, that would've never occurred.

Grady didn't have sense enough to say, "Well, this man is keepin' me workin'." He didn't hafta kill him. That cop was lookin' for a better position. *A better position.* That's why he killed my brother and lied and put that knife in his hand. Tried to put it in his hand. 'Cause after a person is dead, stupid, it's nothin' you can do with that person.

At the inquest, there was this one guy. He was a gun person to tell you exactly what's wrong, what happen. He just put a beautiful light on how my brother was killed. He had the coat there and he put it on something where it could show the complete bullet wound. He says the fabric . . . the gun, it was pressin' the fabric of that baby's coat. He says you had to be standin' . . . The man had to put the gun right in his back. For the man to pull the trigger with the gun pressin' the fabric of the coat here, he had to . . . He blew his head wide open. I guess that's what them boys saw. That guy came from here, from Madison. They sent him from the capital.

This one white person, he lived direct across the street from where the shots was fired. He heard the shots and he came outa his house. He says, "I walked out and looked and I saw he was a black man." "What kinda position was he layin' in?" He says, "He was layin' like this with his hand flat on the snow." 'Cause it was snow. And he say, "I could tell he was a black man because of the white snow. "Did you see a knife?" He say, "No, I didn't." He say, "But I saw his hands." He could see his hands layin' out like that. Flat. The man didn't see a knife. That was important. That one man did not see a knife. And them peoples still say justified homicide.

What they did, they had all these other little witnesses, other police officers and other . . . One says I saw that; and the other say I saw this. The ambulance man said, "When I picked up the body, he dropped the knife." It's impossible. How could my brother have a knife gripped in his hand, when the ambulance got there? He woulda been dropped the knife. When a person die, they automatically let all muscles relax. I worked at County Hospital with the geriatric peoples and I saw a lotta peoples die. Honey, sometime they be pull like this, all crinked up, and they straighten out at they last breaths. I couldn't see how that police department overlooked all that. "When did you discover that Daniel Bell"—not Mr. Bell, they didn't say Mr.—"had this knife?" "When we went to pick up the body, it fell out of his hand." I say, "Oh, God Almighty."

"Which hand?" "The right hand." He's left-handed. Peoples, he's left-handed. He's *not right-handed.* I'm writin' little notes. *"He's left-handed."* They still hollerin', "Which hand." "The right hand." 'Cause they know black peoples are always right-handed. Well, the average person is right-handed. That's why they said right hand. We sittin' there listenin' to this stuff. So then they gave the verdict. They found it justified homicide.

That was another day I wish I'da hadda bomb. I'da blew up that buildin'. I was sick. I was very hurt. I had never . . . My mother 'n dad had twelve boys and me. And we lived in the worst place. They said the worst place in the world was down South. But nobody had kill one of my daddy's children or mama's children. Them boys, it wadn't a single brother had even been to a jailhouse. Until they came to Wisconsin. Then they went to jail. That's a lot for me to tell, Honey love. I mean them boys didn't have no record down there. Did you hear me? Not a single brother of mines had a record. But when they came to this state, they got records like this. They got the impression—like today—if you in a different neighborhood, the cop is ridin' your back. That's up North here.

When we came up North, we thought we were comin' to the right place. That's somethin' like when they killed all them Jews. They say, "Hey! You leave outa here, you can go into the right place." And they got 'em all in there and they smothered 'em to death. So that's the way we were. Too bad they didn't kill all of us off to get rid of us. Then we wouldna had to go through some of this shit we are going through.

I do have quite a bit of hatred for the South. Not hatred, Lord Jesus, 'cause I don't. I don't have no hate. Dislikes. And not just for the South. You want me to tell you the true? It's for the whole United States. Maybe it's a shame for me to make this remark. But what did they do for black peoples but aggravate them, misuse them, and tell 'em to go back to Africa? Africa? You can't go over there. We wasn't born in Africa. We were born here in America. We are Americans. We were brought here as slaves. We had to crawl. We had to walk—as slaves. And I'm sittin' there in that inquest room thinkin' I'm still a slave. Because there is no justice. Justice is still hard to find for a black person, very hard to find.

I saw what happened in court for my brother back in '58. I saw what them peoples did. Of course, some of what they did, what they admitted later, I didn't know at that time. But I did know enough to say that my brother was left-handed. That was at that inquest. They coulda settled that then. They didn't have to wait.

Okay so we goes on home and we all said, "This is really . . . This . . . somethin' is wrong." So we decided to appeal the case or to have it brought into court. I think anytime they have inquest, you can go to court or something. We got this lawyer, Resnick, and he got us back into court. To sue. But they said there's nothin' you kids can do with your father livin'. Your father's the one who hafta sue the city. We did what we could do to get it goin'. Then we had to go down South, get my dad and bring him up here. When we found out court date and everything, I brought my daddy up.

When they got my father in that courtroom, Ooooo, they just riddle him so.* Papa knew as well as we did what had happened to Dan. But in that courtroom, my poor dad didn't understand one thing from another. He couldn't even . . . They be askin' him, "Well, is this your son?" He couldn't answer 'em about nothin'. He was a slow talker. Wasn't a fast talker like me. They talked big words to him. My poor dad just didn't understand what they were sayin'. And he was afraid, I think. Then again, I won't say Papa was afraid, 'cause he wasn't that type of a man. But at that age, he was gettin' older and frail. And he just didn't have the ambition like me. I'm still young and I'm: "You just go head on kill me, 'cause I'm gonna say what I have to say. You're wrong. You are wrong." But Daddy, the poor man just couldn't come up.

I felt so sorry—you don't know how—lookin' at my father. How my father talked and how he had to suffer. Couldn't explain himself. When they would ask him question, he wouldn't know *how* to answer this person. Not that he, "I'm gonna lie." Or "I'm tryin' to think of a lie." He couldn't explain hisself, because he

---

* Since the law did not permit siblings to sue if a parent was living, Daniel's father— who could neither read nor write and had never been out of the South—faced the city's attorneys alone. No transcript remains of exactly how they "riddled" him. They may have questioned whether he was really Dan's father. The file contains the report of an unsuccessful search for Daniel Bell's birth certificate.

didn't have . . . He didn't know what they were talkin' about—some of the words that they use. They vocabulary and his vocabulary. He never been to school. This man didn't know what a education was. The words he did learn was the ordinary words.

And I'm still tryin' to say, "Why?" Why couldn't we be educated so that we could understand? For my part, I could've handled my brother's case better, if I was more educated. I probably wouldna needed a lawyer. Well, I would've needed a lawyer. But I would've known a lot more details about this, when it happen.

At that moment though, I wasn't allowed to speak. Not at all. It was Papa had to speak in that courtroom. He would even yell out to me sometime. My father would say, "Sylvia, you tell 'em. You tell them peoples. You know how to talk to 'em." Things like that. And I would be just in tears. It was nothin' I could do. I couldn't burst out because if I do, you goin' to jail. You don't burst out. It was hard.

They riddled him until the poor man took sick. That still wasn't enough. They made him so sick, he wound up in the hospital. They took him to County Hospital. That got him outa the courtroom. Reskin or, well, I think more the judge or someone said, "This man is disabled to really testify."

Then they saw that they were wrong. When my dad got ill, they said they was gonna offer us eighteen hundred dollars. They would give us eighteen hundred dollars and we would just settle the thing. We had asked for eighteen thousand or something like that, because that was the limitation for people's life. You didn't get much money at the time.

My attorney, he says, "Sylvia, you take this burial money. 'Cause this is all I can get." I say, "Man, I will *never* bury my brother with that kinda money. You *keep it!*" Case was never closed. Never closed by the Bells. That was way back there. "You take that money." No. That money *stayed* down there.

I didn't take it. Some of my brothers say I did or said that when the case came back up. And television said that they won't be able to open the case, because the sister took the money in nineteen so and so. The *Milwaukee Journal* called me too and made me kinda angry when they said that. I say, "Where in the hell did you get that from? Baby, you barkin' up the wrong tree." Oohh! And I had to live through all that with my family thinkin' . . . See us blacks, we have a lot on ourself, too. We do. We talk about each other or pull each other down. Not try to help each other up. It's kinda sad. See, with family, too. This goes into what I was sayin' about different ones in the family. Nobody gettin' along. Nobody hardly gets along in this world today. I don't care if you're black or white, it's kinda hard to get along. Anyway, I never saw check. I never went back to that courthouse. I never sign papers.

I say, "Oh, no. Oh, no." We wouldn't accept that money. So then the case was out of court. It wasn't settled. Until this case came up the last time, the case was *never* closed.* Because we didn't accept the money. We just walked out. We politely walked out. Say, "You keep it!" Reskin our attorney, he just insist, "You take that money." We say, "For what? For the killin' of my brother? Sell my brother down the drain like that? No. You *keep* it!" And we left. That was the end of that.

I used to lay in my bed at night and I would cry. I would cry *so hard about my poor brother* that I would wet my pillow. It seem like sometime he would say, "Sis, don't cry no more. That's okay. *Don't cry anymore, 'cause it won't help.*" I knew it wouldn't help. But I just . . . Dan touched me. My brother touched me for years and years. Up until the night—it was seventy-something—when they retrial Grady 'n them.

Papa didn't live to see that. He didn't live too much longer after that first case. My father stayed with me durin' the case time. We tried to keep him here as long as we could—to show him the love, you know. I took him to see *The Ten Commandments*, the movie. I knew Papa would enjoy that. So I took him. And Papa said, "Them white peoples was bein' bad waaaaay back." He were talkin' about how they was fightin' and stuff in the movie. That part really impressed him. He did enjoy some things up here. And we tried to make him as comfortable as we could. But one day, he says, "Sylvia. I gotta go home." He says, "I'm tired of bein' up here. I wanta go home." And he says, "I'm goin' home to die." He went home. And I don't think it was too long after that that he died.

I saw him a few more times. I would drive down there. My poor dad, he was so hurt. I can still see his head—drooped. He says, "You know I been in Springfield all these years and I never had a policeman to shoot my child down like they did up North." And he says, "That hurts That's dirty." He was failin'. After the death of Dan, he really went down. Henry, he tried to do all he could for him. I did too, but I was a distance from him. I didn't think he would go as fast as he did.

We all went down to Papa's funeral. All of us except Dan. Before he died, Daddy said, "There's layers 'n layers 'n *layers of lies* on that boy's grave." He said, "But one of these days, the truth *will* come to the light." He said, "He gonna push, Dan is gonna push all them lies right offa his grave."

---

* Since the family's attorney convinced the judge to proceed without a signature, the case went on record as settled. *Dock Bell vs. Thomas Grady and the City of Milwaukee*, 1960 (Milw. Co. Case No. 286 538).

16

Marches, Riots, and Martin Luther King

On Monday, August 28, 1967, one hundred open-housing demonstrators crossed the half-mile Sixteenth Street Viaduct that linked Milwaukee's overcrowded black neighborhood to the nearly all-white South Side. In the lead walked members of the NAACP Youth Council and their advisor, white Catholic priest James Groppi, himself a native South Sider. The group had obtained a permit and publicized their plan to cross over, then walk about a mile and a half to Kosciuszko Park. Just onto the bridge, the marchers—almost all young African Americans—encountered "Welcome" signs carried by some South Siders from Father Groppi's former parish. On the far side stood about three thousand people, many of them hostile. The demonstrators moved through to the park under a hail of garbage, bottles, and rocks. Press photos and reports document the Confederate flags, Nazi slogans, shouts of "Nigger," signs such as "Bring Back Slavery" and "A Good Groppi Is a Dead Groppi." At Kosciuszko Park, a larger crowd swept around the marchers. With injuries and arrests mounting, Father Groppi stood on a picnic table and announced that the demonstrators would leave, but would be back the next night—and every night—until the city had an open-housing ordinance.

When two hundred people marched across the viaduct the following night, the crowd on the other side numbered about thirteen thousand, their placards, chants, and thrown objects much the same, their mood more aggressive. Father Groppi advised the marchers: "Keep cool. Walk fast. Girls in the middle. Don't be afraid. If we were afraid to die we wouldn't be good Christians."[1] As the mob surged out of control and attacked, Youth Council "Commandos" stepped forward to defend the demonstrators. Police officers fired shotguns into the air, used tear gas—and urged march leaders to go back. Someone began singing "Ain't Gonna Let Nobody Turn Me Around." The marchers pressed on to the park, where Groppi praised their courage, exhorted them in the name of Christ not to hate their attackers—and then led a hurried retreat. Back home, the demonstrators saw their safe-haven "Freedom House" burn down.

As these events put Milwaukee in the national news, the city's two major newspapers and local TV stations editorialized with words such as "shame" and "disgrace." Many Milwaukeeans agreed, but diverged about where to lay blame. In fact, majorities nationwide opposed civil rights activism in the 1960s. A 1963 Gallup poll found 63 percent against the March on Washington; Harris polls found 63 percent in 1966 and 82 percent in 1967 against black demonstrations generally.[2] Nearly a third of Milwaukee voters had backed segregationist George Wallace in the last presidential primary. Faulting the marchers for the white mob's behavior, the mayor imposed a ban on night demonstrations. Those arrested for violating the ban included Alderwoman Vel Phillips, the only African American on the city council, who had brought open-housing ordinances to a vote four times since 1962. Demonstrators—including many whites—crossed the viaduct every night for two hundred nights, their numbers peaking at five thousand on September 10. Local politicians refused to yield until shaken by the April 4 assassination of Martin Luther King Jr. As violent reaction erupted elsewhere, Milwaukee's NAACP Youth Council "Commando" patrols kept peace there in honor of King. About twenty thousand Milwaukeeans participated in a memorial march on April 8. At the end of the month, the Common Council passed an open-housing ordinance—with four of six South Side aldermen voting in favor.

Ten years earlier, Sylvia, her brothers, and their supporters had met with no such response. The Bell case struck on divisions within black Milwaukee, particularly between established residents and newer arrivals. At the first meeting about the case, some of the 450 attendees agreed with a pastor who called for mobilization to improve behavior of migrants. Another group followed Calvin Sherard, a young auto worker, who founded the Citizen Committee to Protest the Case of Daniel Bell. Their meetings at New Hope Baptist Church led to the announcement of a "prayer protest" at the courthouse. But other black leaders—including Vel Phillips—persuaded New Hope's Reverend Lathan to cancel. Lathan's cousin, Birmingham civil-rights leader Reverend Fred Shuttlesworth, later led no more than seventy-five protesters in a march confined to the black neighborhood. Ready to "go down in flames" over this failure, Sherard and friends began getting themselves arrested picketing businesses that didn't hire blacks.[3] Meanwhile, media images—students taking abuse at lunch counters, the firebombed bus and bloodied but determined faces of Freedom Riders, Birmingham protesters struggling to stand up to fire hoses and dogs—helped move many more Americans to action.

In Milwaukee, a new activism had emerged by 1963. Five busloads of Milwaukeeans joined the estimated 250,000 demonstrators for the March on Washington that August, as sit-ins in Milwaukee protested racist comments made by a member of the new metropolitan commission on urban problems. Meanwhile, state NAACP director Lloyd Barbee launched Milwaukee's campaign against school segregation and "intact busing"—a policy that transported children from overcrowded schools to those with extra space, but kept whites and blacks strictly apart.[4] While Barbee pursued a federal lawsuit, activists in Milwaukee and other Northern cities organized one-day school boycotts to protest the school segregation still widespread in the tenth year after the U.S. Supreme Court had declared it unconstitutional. James Groppi took a leading role in the "human-chain-ins" of 1965, where people linked arms or chained themselves together and stood in front of "intact busing" vehicles—until hauled away to jail.

Pastor of an inner-city church, Father Groppi had participated with other priests and nuns in several Southern civil rights actions. Increasingly radicalized, he returned North with ideas such as creating a "Freedom House." The NAACP Youth Council liked Groppi's hot-headed talk and readiness to back up words with action. As advisor, he cultivated democratic decision-making processes and a strong sense of black pride. With Black Power slogans proliferating on Youth Council T-shirts, buttons, and protest signs, the white priest celebrated mass in his black cassock and changed church decor as a statement that "Black is beautiful." He encouraged youth initiatives such as a 1967 "textbook turn-in" by high school students demanding inclusion of black history.[5] Groppi also declared that activists had a right to defend themselves. After the Ku Klux Klan bombed the city's NAACP office in August 1966, the Youth Council posted armed guards at their Freedom House and formed a corps of unarmed marshals called "Commandos." Identifiable in uniform sweatshirts, the Commandos shouldered responsibility for controlling and defending demonstrators—a tall order in the urban climate of 1967.

Less than a month before that first Youth Council march across the viaduct, ghetto rioting added Milwaukee to the unprecedented count of more than 150 cities where such outbreaks occurred during 1967. Milwaukee's toll of five dead, one hundred injured, and half a million dollars in property damage left its mark, although small compared to the forty-three deaths and at least

$40 million in damages in Detroit. Images of a burning Motor City with troops and tanks in the streets filled the TV news, just days before the Milwaukee riot. Using the National Guard and a citywide curfew, Mayor Maier took credit for preventing a worse outcome and echoed constituents blaming "so-called civil rights leaders who have been encouraging defiance of the law." Commando Prentice McKinney saw quite the opposite. "Milwaukee didn't burn," he said, because Groppi "provided young minority people with an opportunity and a constructive manner to vent those frustrations and to say to the system the kinds of things they wanted to say."[6] The open-housing campaign begun immediately after Milwaukee's riot certainly exposed the underlying cause of such outbursts: the racism that barred African Americans from jobs, subjected them to police abuse, and confined them to the worst housing in the city.[7]

This Milwaukee story might have remained largely buried in the archives and in participants' memories if civil rights historians had not shifted focus beyond the Southern struggle.[8] Of course, attention rightly surrounded prominent individuals, groups, and actions in the South: Martin Luther King Jr., his philosophy of nonviolence, his rhetoric, his radicalization—and FBI efforts to discredit him; the Congress of Racial Equality (CORE), whose Freedom Riders gripped public attention when they barely escaped alive from encounters with extreme mob violence in Alabama; the Student Non-Violent Coordinating Committee (SNCC), its lunch counter sit-ins that swept the South in 1960, its nonhierarchical decision-making and daring actions such as resuming CORE's 1961 Freedom Rides and registering black voters in rural Mississippi.[9] A vast literature testifies to the extraordinary number of heroic individuals and moments in this American epic. Civil rights history had more to unfold, however, more even than the many accounts such as Milwaukee's that emerged as the geographical scope expanded.[10]

Historians extended the scope of the movement to include less-studied groups, actions, and places, as well as a time-frame before the mid-1950s. Studies of women in the movement not only recognize overlooked individuals such as those who handled logistics, but also shed light on preexisting Southern organizations such as women's rape-prevention groups. Other important work has shifted focus to less-known places, local circumstances, and local individuals who arguably did as much to effect change as national figures and organizations. Scholars have also examined the role of television, photographs, print media, and the radio then so important to rural Southern blacks.[11]

Equally important, historians have deconstructed the conventional narrative that portrays a nonviolent and integrationist early Southern movement turning into a violent and separatist Black Power movement later, under urban and non-Southern influences. To be sure, events of the mid-1960s strongly affected the movement. When Watts erupted in August 1965, many civil rights activists immediately understood that their movement had raised expectations, failed to alter unjust conditions that infuriated ghetto residents, and heightened anger with media images of whites abusing non-violent black activists. That same year, the assassination of Malcom X gave new emotional force to his words, "by any means necessary." Yet many activists had listened all along to the brilliant spokesperson for the Nation of Islam, as he mocked their efforts to wrest racial justice from white society. Nor did the NOI stand alone in rejecting civil rights activism and racial integration. Black separatism reached back past Marcus Garvey's movement. Traditions of armed self-defense accompanied the civil rights struggle throughout its long history and its wide geography—including the supposedly nonviolent Southern phase. In 1959, the NAACP suspended one of its North Carolina chapter presidents, Robert Williams, for telling the media that civil rights activists should "meet violence with violence." Even as Martin Luther King Jr. publicly refuted that stance, he privately had armed bodyguards in his home. In Louisiana, the Deacons for Defense formed in 1964 to protect civil rights activists from Klan violence. In Mississippi, some Freedom Summer activists followed the lead of local people and carried guns.[12] When speakers began shouting "Black Power" in 1966, the words generated great energy in part because they connected with pre-existing feelings and ideas; in part because "Black Power" meant different things to different people.

The Milwaukee civil rights story makes its own contribution to this evolution in the literature. Most striking, in-depth study of Milwaukee's NAACP Youth Council finds seemingly untroubled mixing of Black Power ideas/practices with nonviolent action against segregation. Moreover, these young people who identified with Black Power refused to let Groppi's whiteness pose a problem—well after SNCC felt it necessary to expel white members. At a Washington, DC, conference in September 1967, black nationalists vociferously rejected the Milwaukee delegation for having a white advisor. The Youth Council talked back to such critics and continued asserting that Black Power did not mean separatism or hatred of whites. This story shows "a much more fluid connection between concepts" commonly considered polar opposites and works against "easy characterization" of any part of the struggle for racial justice.[13]

For the first year of our work together on this project, whenever I asked Sylvia about the Civil Rights Movement, she talked only about Reverend

Martin Luther King Jr. In the end, what she says here raises issues about knowledge and memory. How much Sylvia wished to know and remember about civil rights seems at issue, as well as what she ever knew and what she could remember later. She expresses negative feelings, even about keeping up with civil rights news. Certainly not negativity about the cause itself. Nor only because she worried about her brothers' participation in actions such as the Freedom Rides. Most of all, Sylvia recalls how much it disturbed her to see televised images of civil rights activists taking abuse. She strongly felt that they should strike back. Yet she admired Martin Luther King Jr. exactly for his nonviolence. Such seeming contradictions—and significant inaccuracies— characterize her recollections of "civil rights stuff." A few years after her family's attempt at protest, Sylvia left Milwaukee and stayed away as activism peaked there. Ultimately, in her nonparticipation, her mixed feelings, and her factual incorrectness, she resembles many other African Americans of the time whose attitudes and behavior are also part of the civil rights story.

In the spring of the year my brother was killed, we got together and we had a march. There was Reverend Lathan and a number of my black leaders. I'm sorry I can't call they name right now. We wanted a march on the square right at the courthouse. That's where we wanted to march. But they told us we wasn't allowed across North Avenue. "Don't come to that courthouse." We did march pretty good. It was about, oh I don't know how many of us.

That was in '58, the march for my brother. I were there. I think they have newspapers clippin's 'n stuff like that that you can get to prove this. There was a black paper around North Avenue or someplace. I don't remember the name but I'll get it for you. A black paper that would write up. And the *Journal*, that *Milwaukee Journal*. For some reason, they was on track. The *Milwaukee Journal*, I give 'em a lot—and the *Sentinel*, both of 'em. Even the little opinion part—peoples givin' their opinions—I thought was real nice for us. Some of the time. Sometime it wasn't. They'd say, "Let the niggers go back South." That was their word. "Nigger, go South, where you belong." And, "You come up here, a buncha dummies." That's what they would say sometime.

So we had our little march. We did get down to . . . Well, I think he said Walnut Street was far as we could go. They didn't want us to come downtown protestin' nothin'. They said, "It was justified homicide and you don't come here." Everybody was very hurt. It was not justified homicide. Some of the reverends and other leaders was with us for that march. Oh, a number of the kids.

We wanted Reverend Martin Luther King there. But he couldn't make it. He sent one of his representatives. I forget the man's name. I should have that somewhere around the house. Christian, that was the name of the organization. Christian something, Southern Christian. This one person did come to represent Reverend Martin Luther King. It was Abernathy, I think. Or no, maybe . . . I really don't remember for sure. But someone came.*

We had meetings at churches. But we never could really hit the streets with it. Some of the black peoples was afraid that it was gonna cause . . . And the whites, the police department made sure that we didn't do anything about it. They told us, "Don't come down there with it." Otherwise they was gonna arrest. This is the facts.

I know you probably wonder about the NAACP. We was contactin' the NAACP. I look to the NAACP like I look to Reverend Martin Luther King. I figured, "If you are out there protectin' us, you should be able to take us right on down to this courthouse." They didn't. I don't know what happen. I guess they did something, but not an awful lot. They wasn't a Martin Luther King.

Reverend Martin Luther King is my idol. I wish I could've had him to follow. I would have followed him. I'da been right there. Because he was such a powerful man. My dad woulda been that type person, if he hadda got educated. You know, the only person that really call me was my poor dad and Reverend Martin Luther King. If I hadda been like Martin Luther King, I coulda went to the capital and protest about my brother. Which I thought about writin' to the president at the time, to tell him about the murder of my brother and this was unjust.

I remember Reverend Martin Luther King, when he was tryin' to get black peoples to ride the bus without standin' all the time. Most of 'em was workin' in white neighborhoods or white homes, cleanin' houses or cleanin' stores or whatever they were doin' for the whites down there. Then, on the bus they refused to let 'em sit. And blacks figured—why did they have to stand or sit way in the back, when there was seats in the front that they could ride on?

Which I know that myself 'cause I were there. If you ride on the streetcar or the bus, you had to go to the back. There was a lotta seats in the front. You just couldn't sit in there. The seats, the bus seats was made the same from front to back. But you could not sit on 'em. You had to ride in the back. Then, if a white

---

* This was Reverend Fred Shuttlesworth.

person got on the bus and no more seats left up front, they'd move the screen back. You were sittin' in your seat and you get up. You get up, not the white person. That was pretty dirty, when you are payin' your fare. That white man probably didn't even work, probably out there someplace drinkin'. 'Cause I remember I used to see things like that happen down South. You had to get up and let him sit down, a drunk. And you done came in from work. Who wants to do that?

So Rosy Park, she got on this bus—I don't know when—and refused to get up. That is when all hell broke loose down South. It's a wonder they didn't kill her. Down in Alabama, Montgomery, Alabama, I think that's where it started. That is when the bus stoppin' and stuff like that really started in the South. With Rosy Park. Then Reverend Martin Luther King, he heard about it and he joined her right away. Because he knew she were right. So King won that. He won the bus segregation stuff.

Then he went on. He decided to go with the school business, started goin' to the school door. That's when they had to call in National Guards and stuff like that. That's when they start touchin' the presidents of the United States, when they started that.

Kennedy helped him out, John F. Kennedy, quite a bit. While Eisenhower 'n them, they said it was wrong—different ones said it was wrong—but they didn't give him that good old moral support like Kennedy. He gave him a little more. Now Kennedy could've done better. He act like he was afraid, too. That's my opinion, not nobody else's. 'Cause I says, "Well, why don't he throw in the troops or why don't . . . ?"

That was when George Wallace . . . I never will forget George Wallace getting in the school door. He was in a wheel chair at the time. Or maybe that was later, the wheelchair. Anyway, he kept those little kids from comin' in that school. He got in the door and said, "You niggers, you don't go to school here." This was shown on TV. I says, "How could you be so powerful and so *dirty*?" That was sad. See, that's why they're wrong when they say black peoples don't want education—when they talk about black peoples today. All black peoples was not alike. Some black peoples wanted an education. They knew how important it was to get an education. Even down there.

Reverend Martin Luther King had got all his schoolin' and education. He had been all over the world. When Kennedy took the seat at the White House, Kennedy told him, he says, "Reverend Martin Luther King, I would like for you to be my vice president." He says, "No, I have too many things to do for my peoples in this world." I know that from articles in the paper. Or maybe somebody told me that. He refuse. Because he wanted to help his people. Years later, as I was readin' his book, I thought about that. I said, "Oooo, this man has been everywhere and he's reachin' down to help us." To really help us black peoples. He was black himself, which everybody knows that. But that's . . . Oh! I just cry.

Reverend Martin Luther King, he had an education and he knew how to handle problems. He got throwed in jail. He got beat. He got kicked. Got tear gas on him. They did everything to that man. But that man could survive. And he never struck back. Never. That just tell me again about this education part. If you know how to handle people, regardless to what they do, if they crucify you like Jesus Christ. And that's just what they did to King. They crucified him. I wish I could remember some of the words that he would use, as they did all that stuff to hurt him. And he never hit back.

My girlfriend Stella took me down to where he was from. Mobile, Alabama. No, Atlanta. Wait, where was he from? Mobile or Atlanta? Alabama. When we got there, I say, "Stella, I wanta get out. I wanta kiss the ground." Because this is the ground that Reverend Martin Luther King talked about. He had talk so much about the hills of Alabama, the clay. I saw the pictures that the man drew as he talk. I had never been to Alabama in my life. But when I drove into them hills of Alabama, that's when I saw what he were talkin' about. I say, "I got to stop my car and kiss the ground." And I did. Because he really praised it. Oh, the way he describe that place! He saw so much in those hills. And the minute I approached those hills, it was unbelievable what I saw. It was just like seein' a movie. The granite was like blocks with silver in it, this granite that he was talkin' about.

He say, "When you look to the hills"—I remember in the 27, I mean Psalms—you would "look to the hills with cometh my help." Oh! I see him and I hear him talk about where the little black kids of Alabama and the little white children of Alabama will be holdin' hands and singin', "I'm *free*! I'm free! Thank God Almighty, I'm free at last!" That's Martin Luther King.

Now you keep askin' me—girl, you sure do keep askin'—about this other civil rights stuff. I wasn't down South at the time, you know. I wasn't there. I only saw that stuff on TV. Whatever they wanted to show—and run it by you so fast you can hardly see it. But I saw it. I did. To tell you the true though, when they start talkin' 'bout civil rights I would just get upset. Yes. Yes. 'Cause I don't like to see 'em beatin' on Martin Luther King and the rest of them peoples. Children, too. Just beatin' 'em up and kickin' 'em and everything they did to 'em, killin' 'em, too. Ridin' them buses . . .

My brother Walter, he rode them buses down South. Freedom Rides, they called 'em. That stuff just got me upset. To see what they did to those people. Walter, he would go without tellin' me. Then he would tell me about it later. He went to Selma, too. Or no, not Selma, Washington. They took a busload of young peoples from Milwaukee to Washington. I couldn't even think about goin' 'cause I was too busy workin' for a nickel and a dime. With a child, tryin' to pay the house note and everything. If I'da went to Washington, they'da shut off my lights, shut off my gas. They woulda. I had to work. So I couldn't get into that stuff the way Walter did. He was younger, him and Alfonso. He could go and he went.

I saw it on TV, though. I saw 'em sittin at the lunch counter, children, college kids. And them white peoples doin' everything to 'em. Dumpin' ketchup on they heads and pepper and stuff. Burnin' 'em with cigarettes, yellin' at 'em, beatin' on 'em. I'm watchin' this on TV and I'm wishin' they would just hit back. But they didn't, you know.

Like Martin Luther King. Martin Luther King, he was studyin' . . . uh, it was somethin' biblical . . . It was . . . "Turn the other cheek," that's what he were sayin'. Turn the other cheek. Jesus said that. But I wasn't raised that way, to turn the other cheek. I was raised to hit back. That's what you hadda do down there where I come from.

Like that time them white boys stopped me and my brothers on the bridge on the way to Springfield. I told you that story, didn't I? As a child, I'm talkin' about. It was me, Jimmy, and Dan that day. Them white boys stopped us and said, "No niggers is gonna cross this bridge." I say, "My daddy sent me to go to town and buy some food. And I am goin'." I got me a stick, hickory, that's a good strong stick, just like daddy taught me. And I went at them boys with it. I hit at 'em and chased 'em with that stick, scared 'em. They got so scared they ran into the swamp with the alligators. And we went to Springfield like Daddy told us to. Never heard nothin' more about it. That's how you hadda . . . Hit back. That's how I were raised. That's why if I hadda been at that lunch counter or on them bus rides, I woulda hit back. But I know Martin Luther King, he didn't want you to do that.

One time a white woman hit me and I didn't hit her back though. That was in Milwaukee at the employment office. We was standin' in line. And she hit me. She really did. 'Cause I was poppin' my gum. That's what she said. I was standin' in line there poppin' my gum. That aggravate that woman so much, she hit me. And I didn't hit her back. You know what I did do? I stop poppin' my gum. I don't do that. To this day, I don't.

But gettin' back to civil rights, it seem to me that people was afraid to talk about it too much. Up North here. Afraid to do anything, get anything goin' here. You couldn't get black people together to do anything. In Milwaukee, I mean.

Later, they had marches and stuff in Milwaukee, too, you know. Stella used to tell me quite a bit about that stuff. I can remember when Father Groppi tried to cross the Sixteenth Street viaduct. That was a commotion between South side and the North side. I think the police and everybody else was involve—to stop him on that Sixteenth Street viaduct. I heard some of the people say how he really tried to . . . I really don't know too much what happen. No more than what I heard on the news and from my friends. 'Cause I wasn't livin' there at that time. I was livin' out here in the country.

Durin' the riots in Milwaukee, my girlfriend Stella came out to see me. And she say, "Girl, you ain't allowed to go outa your house. You're not allowed to do this or to do that." I say, "What d'you mean?" She says, "You gotta be off the street at a certain time at night, the curfew." They were arrestin' and, oh! What else did she tell me about that riot? She say, "Them peoples is just burnin' down things." They were doin' everything. They stealin', grabbin' stuff as they would burn the stores, snatch it out and re-sell it. I don't know if they were shootin'. But it sound like it was *terrible*. Different friends of mines, they would come out and say, "Oh, we gotta buy some bread or we gotta buy . . ." 'Cause I guess they didn't allow the trucks to come in to deliver things. That was pretty rough the way it sound.

I sure didn't go back 'n see. What could I do but get in trouble there? I never tried to go down there and see what them peoples did. Maybe because I just didn't give a hoot. I cared for what happen to the black peoples. I cared for the problem it was for them. But I had just got through with my brother's killin'. And the blacks coulda blew up Milwaukee far as I'm concern.

Some people say, "Well, they were just burnin' down the black neighbor-hoods." That was true. But a lotta whites had business in those neighborhoods. So I think that's what they was aimin' at, to get them outa there. Which didn't do too much good. People say, "Well, they ain't got no business riotin'." But when the riots broke out, that is when it got to Washington. That's when they see. You know, it was very hard for presidents and governments 'n stuff to see a black person. Very hard. This is experience, my own experience. Not the riots. I did not experience any of that. Thank God above.

17

Crawfish River Hill

When Sylvia ventured into rural Wisconsin in the 1960s, she took a step most unusual for African Americans at that time. In the nineteenth century, however, the few who came to the region more often chose the countryside. A black man founded the rural community of Freedom, Wisconsin, in the east central part of the state in 1830. In southwestern Wisconsin, two small but vibrant black farming communities formed before slavery ended. One group gathered after a Virginia couple came to Wisconsin's Grant County in 1848 and bought land in Pleasant Ridge. The other settlement in Vernon County's Cheyenne Valley began with one 1855 migrant from North Carolina and grew to seven families by 1860. Like most Wisconsin farmers then, residents of these two communities made little money, but produced their own food, shared skills, made and exchanged goods. In Cheyenne Valley, black and white settlers scattered evenly across the land. Working and socializing together, they also intermarried. In Pleasant Ridge, blacks and whites lived apart, but joined in projects such as building the church where they worshipped together. Both areas had integrated schools. In the mid-1970s, after these communities had dispersed, former members interviewed by a state historical society researcher described a life of hardship, but untroubled by racial prejudice.[1]

Other work about African Americans in the rural Midwest paints a more mixed picture. A study focused on Michigan examined local newspaper archives and found degrading stereotypes, as well as praise of black rural residents. Former inhabitants of Michigan's black settlements recalled minimal contact with whites. They described prejudice within their own communities, where darker skin meant lower social status and individuals who had lived free during slavery considered themselves superior to those freed at Emancipation.[2] An

Indiana study found similar internal tensions. Large rural black communities there shared kinship links and general characteristics with settlements in Michigan and Wisconsin. Although a few individuals prospered in the nineteenth century, most black farmers owned less land and remained poorer than their white neighbors. The difference mattered more as a broad shift to commercial farming favored those who could buy more land and expensive equipment.[3] In the twentieth century, subsistence farming proved increasingly difficult. Necessities came to include electricity, motor vehicles, and fuel. Radios touted consumer products and urban entertainments. As smallholders struggled to keep their farms, their children moved to cities.

By the time Sylvia moved from city to country, African Americans had been making the opposite move for decades, especially as they came North. A history of black Minnesotans asserts that almost all went to urban areas there and observes dwindling numbers of black-owned farms in Upper Midwestern states by 1920.[4] In Wisconsin, the 1940 census found only 800 of 12,158 black inhabitants living in rural areas, just half of them in farming households.[5] As the state's black population grew to 74,546 in 1960, the governor's Commission on Human Rights reported on the shrinking rural sector. Researchers focused on 150 "representative" families, only twenty-eight of them farming at all, most in dairying. A strawberry grower described clearing forested land and building the irrigation system that placed him in the vanguard of Wisconsin agriculture at the time. A retired farmer in Grant County represented descendants of the earliest black settlers. Another group had left cities during the Great Depression, in order to grow their own food. Wherever they lived, black interviewees reported better relations with local whites than with outsiders such as tourists.[6] The commission's report exemplifies a sparse and largely nonscholarly literature on African Americans in the rural North.

Fortunately for our effort to contextualize Sylvia's story, one unusual study documents a 1960s struggle over civil rights that occurred in Watertown, where Sylvia lives now, and just a few miles from the home she bought in rural Waterloo in the early 1960s.[7] This source speaks about the time in multiple ways. In a program instituted as colleges and universities nationwide answered student demands for a more "relevant" education, an undergraduate student from the University of Michigan–Ann Arbor went to Watertown in 1970 and interviewed key figures in the recent "crisis" there. Besides shedding light on local racial attitudes, Lynn Eden recorded testimony of small-town America confronting the cultural changes and political movements of the era.

Shock waves from the open-housing struggle fifty miles away in Milwaukee rocked this town of fifteen thousand people. The population had included one black family for twenty years, a fact cited by more than one interviewee to defend Watertown against charges of racism. The elderly father of that family, Walter Goodie, told Eden that he and his wife had decided to raise their children in Watertown, because they expected to find "less prejudice" there than in larger cities. "Well, not prejudice," he qualified. "That's here as much, but . . . if someone talks up against you, twenty people or more will defend you."[8] The Goodies stayed out of the race-related furor that split the town into hostile camps in 1967. During that fracas, Watertonians ostracized each other. People feared losing their jobs. One church fired its pastor. Three other ministers resigned.

The turmoil centered on twenty-nine-year-old Reverend Alan Kromholz, brought to Watertown in early 1967 to lead a congregation that included the mayor, the chief of police, aldermen, and prominent businessmen. The new pastor preached forcefully that Christians must do everything in their power to eradicate poverty and racism. Thirteen local ministers and two priests signed a similar statement that year, as the town council considered a model open-housing ordinance sent to municipalities by the state's attorney general. Kromholz carried his commitment further than the other clergymen, however. He participated in Milwaukee's open-housing demonstrations, urged his church members to do the same, and invited Commandos from the Milwaukee NAACP Youth Council to speak in Watertown. These actions—coming on the heels of riots in Milwaukee, Detroit, and Newark—provoked an emotional reaction. Rumors said that Kromholz would bring busloads of blacks to riot in Watertown. He and his supporters heard racist invective and threats issuing from their telephones. In this climate of ill will, the town council refused to pass the open-housing ordinance in December. The dismissal of Kromholz in May 1968 dampened, but did not extinguish, the anger.

The anti-Kromholz side decried what they saw as his effect on Watertown youth. In response to the new pastor's sermons, a number of high school students had asked parental permission to march in Milwaukee. Parents who refused faced angry teens. Some who permitted marching complained that their sons and daughters returned criticizing society and challenging adults. Exasperation peaked when the congregation's youth discussion group used church facilities to publish an underground newspaper entitled *Soul*. The first issue harshly attacked the "unreasonable dictatorship" of adults. Criticizing the school dress code, writers jabbed at "bald" administrators who forced boys to have short hair and girls to wear skirts. Articles blasted parents who forbade marching for civil rights. "You, the ADULT, will never give the Negro a chance," said one. "But you will die. And then WE will give him what he is entitled."[9]

Some horrified adults blamed Kromholz. Of course, much about *Soul*—the personal freedom issues, the moral politics of civil rights, the confrontational tone, the word "underground" and the newspaper's campaign for a coffee house—pointed to the countercultural youth movements then burgeoning on a national and international scale.[10]

A few landmarks recall how young people's revolt against racism, war, and restrictive cultural codes had developed by 1968. Early in the decade, college students had seized the civil rights initiative and rejected adult leadership models in creating SNCC. The Berkeley Free Speech Movement answered university rulings against Freedom Summer volunteers recruiting on campus. Students for a Democratic Society went into inner-city neighborhoods to try organizing the poor—and then turned attention to the war. With the troop count in Vietnam surpassing one hundred thousand in 1965, campus antiwar teach-ins and rallies proliferated. Much more widely, rebellious youth embodied the era's chafing against cultural restrictions on everything from dress to sexuality.[11] Young fans popularized protest singers such as Joan Baez and Bob Dylan—and made superstars of the then shockingly long-haired Beatles. In June of 1967, the first international satellite TV broadcast featured the Fab Four wearing garb unthinkable for males a few years earlier, surrounded by flowers and singing "All You Need Is Love."[12] In the United States, many made the pilgrimage to California and found friends in countercultural enclaves emerging in cities from coast to coast. Antiwar feeling grew, as the president sent eighty thousand young men to Vietnam in 1967, bringing troop levels to 465,600 and the year's death toll to 9,378. In October, a youth mobilization against the war held protests nationwide, the main event drawing at least fifty thousand to Washington, DC. During their March on the Pentagon, protesters placed flowers in the rifle barrels of soldiers arrayed against them, an iconic moment in what some historians have called the "utopian" phase of the rebellion.[13]

The Watertown story highlights the presence in these Sixties political and countercultural movements of groups given less attention in the literature. Eden herself exemplifies the many participants in the era's innovative movements who, as she assured one of the wary Watertown adults she interviewed, did not belong to groups such as SDS. Making an affinity less predictable than that of better known children of big-city New Deal liberals or the so-called red-diaper babies born to the nation's few Socialists and Communists, conservative small-town parents had raised Alan Kromholz, as well as some of the teens involved. Kromholz recalled sharing his parents' views, organizing a chapter of Young Republicans, even joining an extreme right-wing group.

Such individuals entered countercultural movements only by overstepping the bounds of their socialization. Eden's study showcases the kind of world-view they left behind, since most of her adult interviewees expressed the Cold War conservatism that defended the war, as well as the racial status quo, against youthful questioning.

Discussing the research for this chapter with Sylvia in 1999, I asked her if she had encountered or heard anyone else mention young white activists trying to organize people in Milwaukee's inner city in the 1960s. She replied that, when she was still living in the city and weekending at her country place, a college-age "white girl" had surprised her by knocking on the door of her Palmer Street house and asking to rent a room for a while. Sylvia remembered teaching this unusual boarder how to cook "Soul Food." The young woman left the house each day doing something that Sylvia could only vaguely recall as not a job. Although the thought remained purely speculative, Sylvia saw one possible explanation for her mysterious roomer in the SDS activism I'd found in the literature.

Sylvia's narrative here certainly resonates with its Sixties frame of reference. She counts young people among the first and most enthusiastic residents of the Waterloo area to befriend her, help her find a job, even take a stand for her. Inclined to keep up with what's happening, Sylvia touches upon white youth trends when she talks about the Beatles and about her family naming their dog after Ringo. Yet she also recalls building relationships with individuals of all ages around her rural home. She began this process with a beloved Wisconsin tradition, the beer party. A quick-witted conversationalist and great listener, Sylvia has a real talent for joking around. If you say something she finds funny, she has a repertoire of creative ways to express and perform her mirth. With that fun-loving sparkle and an abundant feistiness comes a genuinely giving character. Over time, Sylvia managed to disarm people who harbored racial negativity, as well as some who kept their distance. Her memoir unfolds an individualized process of getting acquainted, where she found opportunities to rebut racist thinking and reveal the personality that ultimately won over her community.

A friend of mine, he was workin' for the city as a garbage collector down through there where I live. I say, "Whoa, I didn't know we had any black peoples collectin' garbage." He said, "Girl, I'm the only one." I'm talkin' back in the early sixties. Then one day he said to me, "I'm buyin' me a little piece of land." This fella told me that you could buy plots of land like three point five acres—from river frontage to the top of the hill. "Crawfish River Hill," he call it. He were already buyin' his. I say, "Really, man? *You* on the river? A *black man*? A black man got a river front?" He say, "Yeah, I'm gonna bring you all the information." Ten dollars down and ten dollars a month. It was a good deal. I just couldn't believe it.

When I contact Campfire Land Company, they respond that I could buy. So then I told my brother Joe. Worst move I ever made—goin' in with him. But I'll tell ya 'bout that later. I said, "Joe, what do you think? You wanta see the land?"

It was a little community buildin' up back there. Not for blacks. It was whites in there. Well, one neighbor was something else. I still don't know what. It was mostly whites. But they sold to us.

We bought the land, Lot One, the one that I'm still on. 'Leven hundred dollars. That was how we start buyin'. They had other plots all around back up in there that nobody had. So we went to the back. Those plots was three hundred dollars with three point some acres in it. We bought one, two, three of them, because we could do it—together. I'm workin' full-time at Mount Sinai Hospital, nurse's aide. My brother Joe, he's workin' too.

At the time, they were tearin' all those houses down in Milwaukee for the interstate to come in. And Joe say, "Girl, we pick up some of this lumber, we can build us a nice lil' cabin." So when them peoples would push them buildin's down, we goin' in there 'n pullin' out the best two by fours or two by sixes or whatever. There was so much material layin' around. They wasn't crushin' it and breakin' it all up. We could get a truckload.

So we built a place where we could stay. It was very nice, with panelin' 'n everything. We could pick up inexpensive panelin' in Milwaukee. So we had us a nice little L-shape house. It was cute. We didn't have no water. We had to bring that from the well further down the road. But we had this portable toilet where you put all your chemicals in. We had our tub for baths. We had a very nice little weekender. It was fun.

At first, I went to Waterloo because there was a river, the Crawfish River. I love to fish. I am a fishin' person. I still had my home on Locust and Palmer at the time. And I was workin' weekdays in Milwaukee. So on weekends we would take off. I imagine the only black person in Wisconsin takin' off with the rest of the peoples comin' up North. It wadn't but sixty miles from Milwaukee, but we called it "goin' up North." We start makin' a big garden and raisin' a lotta food. And we would fish. Oh, it was good fishin' in that river! Good God Almighty! Them days, it was something.

Now Stella, my best friend, Stella, oh, did she love the country! And fishin' too. So Stella had to come out every weekend, her 'n her husband and two or three kids. I had friends comin' all the way from Chicago. They would bring out they little camper and they would camp up under the trees. Oh, it was just something. We would all party and socialize—and with people we were startin' to meet out there, too.

Now, my most important person that I met is my neighbor, Ruth, and her husband, Bob. When I met Bob 'n Ruth, they had a big farm, about a hundred eighty acres. They had cows and they were milkin'. So we could buy milk from them.

I met Ruth right away. Ruth was . . . how would I put Ruth? Ruth was the type that would meet anybody and know everything. She saw us comin' out. It was, "Hey, hi." And "hi" back 'n then we just . . . Maybe I might've said, "Can I get some water from down here?" Or through buyin' the milk. Then we got to where every weekend it was, "Hey, Sylvia!"

Ruth and Bob love to drink beer. They were beer guzzlers. Well, I was too. We would bring out a lotta beer. On weekends that was our thing. Big party at my place. We just camp out, lay right out there under the trees with the coolers. It was unbelievable, the gang that came out. White, black. Whites from the community there and other ones, too. It was a close-knit thing. It wasn't you black 'n I'm white. Well, it was you black 'n I'm white. But it was more of a agreeable type thing than a fightin' type thing. Of course there were moments when you really had to tell a white person off. Or a black person off. Both ways, both ways.

Ruth would tell me, "My brother-in-law, he had such"—that's the way she would say it—"he had such experience with black peoples when he was in the army." I never likeded it. But she would tell me that. Sometime I would say to her, "Ruth, that man has never had the experience with black peoples in the army like I have with white peoples in the United States." I say, "Honey, if I had to feel that much—I can feel the pain that this man is havin' with his little experience with black peoples in the army—to compare to the pain that I have had with white peoples in the South, in North." I say, "Honey, I would be hatin' white peoples the *resta my life*. But I don't." I say, "I *don't*, okay?"

She never really told me the experience that he had. But you know that must not've been very much. My God! When that man was in the service, black boys could go in the toilet. But when my brothers was in the service, you couldn't. When Eddie or Pat or Henry was in the service, the blacks slept in one area 'n the whites slept in another. It was segregated. Look at the pain! I say, "Girl, if I had to tell you about how I had to live with *white people*, you would really have some pain." And she say, "You know, my mama don't like black peoples either." So that kinda hurted me a little bit more.

Now her husband never say *nothing* about what incident he ever had with blacks. I think he said we was the first black peoples that he ever come in contact with. I have never heard him say his mama didn't like 'em or his brothers didn't like 'em. It was Ruth that come in with this black/white stuff.

Still, me 'n Ruth got to be close. She really likeded me. Today, I would call her my child. See, I wouldn't criticize her about how she kept her house or how she kept her children. But her mama would really bug her with this kinda stuff. Ruth told me that later. After I grew a little older and I guess after she lost her mother, she call me "Mama."

I became a grandma, too. Her kids call me, "Grandma Syl." That's the way they teach they children, that I'm Grandma Syl. "Oh, this is Grandma." That's all they knew. Me 'n Ruth had our little black/white difference. We had our little arguments about black versun white, like her brother or her mother 'n all these little doo-dee-watts, doo-dee-watt. But we never discuss this mess in front of those children. We never did that to 'em.

After I moved out there, I started spending New Years 'n Christmas with Ruth 'n her children. Sometime I didn't even go back to Milwaukee with my family. Ruth would say, "You can come down here and see the Rose Bowl." I love the Rose Bowl on television. I went over there to see that every year. Like family, that's Ruth 'n them.

It was also some young mens like seventeen, eighteen would come around us. One was from down the road not too far, Dave. Dave just loved us. He was the sweetest thing I ever met. I don't know if Dave knew black peoples like fish or what. But he say, "Sylvia, do you know a certain time of the year these buffalo fish runs?" Spring of the year, that's when the buffalo run. He showed me where they catch 'em. So we get boots on to our waist, Dave 'n I and the other boys. We would chase those things, catch 'em, bring 'em back to the house and deep-fry 'em. Those kids would say, "My God, I never ate anything this good!" Then Dave fell in love with my niece, Shirley. He would say, "Shirley comin' out?" He really loved that girl. Shirley kinda liked him, too. But she didn't like the country. She eventually got married to somebody else. Anyway, Dave would be around us, oh just like one of our kids. His grandma was raisin' him.

His grandma, she had a old farm house with a beautiful old wood stove in it. She was so sweet! I could go in her house. Honey, she showed me how to make the best pickle outa these big old cucumbers that turn yellow. She say, "Oh, you make the slippery jim with these." She taught me how to pickle the buffalo fish, too. Grandpa, he was another sweet person. He could make the best dandelion wine. They had a well at they home, an artesian well. That's where we would get water. So with Dave and Grandma and Grandpa, we became a family-like. They were very nice. I went to they home. These are my neighbors.

Another family near us had a buncha dogs that they wanted to get rid of. Pretty little dogs with spots. I took every one of 'em. At the time, the Beatles had just made their first big hit. The Beatles, they was white. But I liked them. And these dogs was kinda cute like the Beatles. So I named them dogs after the

Beatles. It was Ringo, Stingo and uh . . . Ringo was the main Beatle. I mean, I knew he was a Beatle. Ringo was the drummer. So we named the dogs that way. And Ringo stayed with us forever. Oh! He was another child. He was smart, very smart. My family took the other dogs back to Milwaukee. When everybody come out on weekends, they would bring they dog. Oh, it was simply beautiful, that group of dogs. That man, he would always say, "I see you still got them old dogs."

After a year or two, I just wanted to stay. I liked the country. In Milwaukee, they were givin' me tickets for parkin' in front of my house. The blacks is movin' in and tickets are movin' in. Expensive. It's goin' up. Tax, tickets. It's gettin' worse, not better for me. And after the killin' of my brother, I just . . . There was no peace. As the old peoples used to say, "There is no peace in the valley." Or, "there *will* be peace in the valley for you and me." But there was no peace in that valley. I says, "Now why I wanna stay here in Milwaukee? Give me one reason why I wanna stay." So I started stayin' out in the country. At first, I still had a job in the city, so I was livin' in both places.

Then, out in Waterloo, this other white child, Arbor, came to me out of the clear blue sky. Arbor would come by and say, "Hey, Sylvia." And then bla, bla, blab. He was so nice and—a talkative child, no more 'n eighteen at the time. He brought his wife back there, too. They were both very young. They my children I say. Later he had a couple pretty little blond-haired girls, Brenda 'n Tammy. Them kids, they grown womens now. But I am still they grandma.

Okay, so Arbor was workin' at the packin' house there in Waterloo. He say, "Hey Syl, you wanna work at the packin' house where I work? I make those weiners 'n stuff." I say, "You think they'd hire me?" He say, "I'll bring ya up there." 'Cause that was Arbor. Arbor was demandin'. "You gonna hire this black woman. She wants to work. And you gonna hire her or I won't work. I won't smoke them weiners." So Arbor took me on up there. And they hired me.

I say, "Oooo, I don't have to go back to Milwaukee now, never. This is it. I got me a job right here." I came out to Waterloo and got a little more than I did in Milwaukee as a job. I worked in the wiener room, makin' them wieners on a machine. It was fun. Oh, I ran that machine. So fast some of the white womens, they didn't like me doin' that at first. But me and my boss-lady, Lila, we were just *peas*. We got to be very close. Lila was the sweetest thing in the world. She still livin'. And there was Pearl. We became very close friends, me 'n Pearl. She has a farm out there. We would go to each other's farm and butcher chickens. And another person there, she the one who clean these old casings down there down in the basement. You know what casings are? So we all work in the plant. At break time, we'd all go sit in the break-room together 'n we would laugh 'n tell jokes. Then too, Tupperware was really a big thing at the time—for us to gather together.

About three or four years ago, we had a reunion of the packin' house, a big reunion in Firemen Park in Waterloo. That was quite an occasion. We had a hundred 'n some old employees. We all in age now, in our seventies, eighties. Some was in wheel chairs. We was all huggin' and kissin'. Oh was that nice! They all ask about my brother Dock, 'cause he worked there, too.

After I got that job, I could really live out there. I already had roomers at my house in Milwaukee. Some of my brothers would say, "I'm gonna stay upstairs, Sylvia, 'n pay you a little money." Now I say, "Well, fine, 'cause I got a job in the country." Later I rented my whole house out to some very nice people. Then I sold it. I was the type of person that knew how to make a dollar with a piece of property.

My son, Douglas, really wanted to attend certain schools in Milwaukee. That's just like my nephew, Joseph. He don't wanta come out here to finish his high school. His mama got to let him stay in Milwaukee with his 'sociates. So Douglas was staying with my brother's family. They had him in Robert Fulton Junior High, the new school they had just built on Center Street.

Later on, Douglas did come out and start goin' to school in Waterloo. My niece and a nephew, too. It came on the news—I guess around the riot time in Milwaukee. The news said there was three black children admitted in Waterloo school with no incident. That was that. But the kids say they didn't get along with the teachers, 'cause the teachers thought this and thought that of them. It really didn't last that long, them goin' to school out there. Because I split. I left. That kinda ended that. But it's the beginnin' of Waterloo what I'm tellin' you about. Movin' out there and gettin' along with the folks.

I start livin' out there in that little place. I didn't realize that I had to insulate until winter hit my behind. When winter hit, my neighbor, Ruth, she says, "Sylvia, has you got any insulation in this house?" I said, "No." She said, "Oooo, me, Bob, we all gonna get together and pull this"—it wasn't plywood, it was that white sheet rock—"down. And we gonna insulate." Oh, did that make a different! It was comfortable. And the fuel bill wadn't so high. We had those space oil heaters. And I had electric stove.

Did I tell you about how I was the person got 'em electric back there? Well, Ruth 'n them had electricity—on the big farm up from me. But the rest of us—it was just three peoples on the road at the time, Mrs. Sykon, Lois, and me—we did not have it.

So Elliott said to me—Elliott was Stella's husband. And he was fairly educated. I don't know if he went to college or not. He was from Mobile, Alabama, both him 'n Stella. They went to high school. I used to tell 'em, say, "Wow! Musta been better where you was than where I was." I'm sayin' this to tell you about the electric. But education is really my problem in this whole deal. Because my brother woulda never been dead, if he hadda known how to read, how to write. So I'm gettin' back to the electric . . .

Elliott said to me, he say, "Sylvia, I took up electrician when I was in the army. I can wire these houses back here for alla y'all." He says, "Where is the Wisconsin Electric company? I'll go talk to 'em and have 'em bring the electric line in." Elliott, by him bein' in the service and takin' this course, he could get okayed through the electric company to get us electricity out there. So everybody got they electric. That was me, Sykon, and Lois.

Mrs. Sykon, she was white, from Chicago. On weekends, everybody from Chicago come to Wisconsin. Mrs. Sykon, she would stay. She had her summer home fixed up nice. Her husband was comin' out on weekends. He was a bakery man in Chicago. We would, all of us, be glad to see Mr. Sykon, 'cause he would bring this good bakery. He share it up 'n down the road. And Mrs. Sykon, she was the sweetest thing in the world.

Now the neighbors next door, Lois and her husband, I could never talk about like that, *never*. When I moved to Waterloo, this woman next door, she came over and told me, her 'n her husband said, "The Klu Kluck Klang says no niggers live on this hill."

What I did, I got in my car and drove right to the police department. I told the police chief about it. That Lois 'n them said, "The Klu Kluck Klang says no niggers." I say, "I'm not a nigger." To him. I didn't tell her nothin'. I just say, "You get outa here." Then I went and told the chief of police. Because I had a shotgun and I was ready to fire. If Klu Kluck Klang or anybody else come back there 'n bother me, he woulda got a assload of bullets. He told me, he say, "Sylvia,"—this is the chief of police, not one of his sidekicks, the *chief*—he says, "now I see y'all done moved a lotta lumber back there, them two by fours." He say, "When they come back, you grab one of them two by fours and beat the hell out of 'em." I said, "Thank you." And I walked outa there.

Sure enough, they did come back. That weekend when the family all comin' out, here she come steppin' across there. 'Cause they always ready to eat 'n grab a beer. Then wanta talk all this stupid talk to you about the Klu Kluck Klangs. When she came up, I grabbed a two by four. My brother Joe grabbed one, too. I say, "Get your ass outa here." I was crackin' her ass. Honey, I hit that woman on her big fat A. Yes. I had to hit her, give her one lick. 'Cause then they know I was *serious*. Yes. Yes, because she were tryin' to make trouble. The Klu Kluck Klang. I hit at her and she fell. They left and never came back. I never heard from a policeman.

I had to hit her, you know. The Klu Kluck Klang. I hadn't heard of a Klu Kluck Klang since . . . I guess I might've looked at television or somethin' like that and heard of a Klu Kluck Klang. But my mind was completely emptied of Klu Kluck Klang. You should see the torture she put us through, bringin' that up.

She was the most filthy thing I ever ran across. She had two children livin' in a little attic crawl spot. It was hot, cold. She would sent the boy to school with one odd boot on and . . . The teacher at Waterloo would call me and say, "Sylvia, Kenny talks more about you . . . about how you are such a *good* person." I say, "Yeah, Little Kenny 'n I, we get along good." She say, "He talks that you told him this or you taught him this." I say, "Yeah. He comes over here. But the mother, I do not 'sociate with her. 'Cause she don't treat them kids right." Ohhh. I don't know why they didn't do something 'bout that. But they didn't. The boy is retarded now from that situation. I stay my distant from her. Still do.

That was the only problem person. Out of all them other peoples, you didn't hear me say one word about the Klu Kluck Klang. Some of 'em, at first, they were a little bit hesitive. Today they are nice. But at the time, they were kinda friendly and kinda not.

And one time in town, a little kid told me I were dirty. So I washed my hands right there to show him that I wasn't. God made me this way. That's my color. I can't help it. That kid told me later in life that I did teach him a few things. The older kids did come out there and throw them little cherry bombs. They did do that— until I shot the gun off that time. Oh, and we would hear the word "nigger" some- time from the kids goin' up 'n down the road. Heck, I just say, "Kids, kids, kids."

About the worst incident that I encountered in Waterloo happened at church. Listen to this. I had went to number of the Christmas program at the Lutheran school where Ruth's kids was goin'. One year it was the bigger boys gonna sing in the choir—in church. This was later, after I left and came back from California. Ruth says, "Come on Sylvia, we'll go to the program and after that we'll come back 'n open up the Christmas present at the house." So I went. The kids sang 'n we applaud 'em. Then the program is over. The "Silent Night" has been played and everybody is in a good mood. We all goin' out. And the pastor's standin' at the church door. We all going out and he is shakin' everybody's hand. I'm walkin' out the door. He reach for my hand, then kinda went back, jerked his hand back. It was disgustin', to come from a *pastor*. I guess I jerked my hand back, too, when he jerked his.

I haven't forgotten that. Like Ruth brother-in-law hadn't forgot what happen in the service. That was in church, in the eighties. That was bad. But still, my Waterloo was better than my Milwaukee. The white people that I knew out there, some of 'em, most of 'em, was very nice.

Even Ruth's mother. After what Ruth told me, I always avoided her mother. I live with all this fear. Ruth would say, "Mama is comin' down. Are you comin',

Sylvia?" I'd say, "Oh no. I don't want. No, no, no, no. I won't do that." I don't know how many years I live not knowin' that this woman liked me. I remember one time Ruth was at my house with the kids. And this lady walked in my little shack. It was nice in there. Really nice. She look surprise. Seem like she wanted to stay. I were just shock. Then she saw me at Ruth house, babysittin'. Ruth had to work. And she had four babies. So I said, "I'll babysit for you." She said, "I can't afford it." I say, "Well, you could pay my light bill once a month, couldn't you?" She say, "Yeah." I say, "Well, okay then I'll babysit while you work."

So one time, Ruth's mother came in when I was over there. I had clean the bathtub out. It was pretty dirty. Country water will turn everything yellow 'n moldy. I would do things like that, babysittin' for Ruth. You got a farmhouse here. I can help you clean up a little bit. Her mama came in when I had cleaned up that bathroom. I had them children in the tub, givin' 'em a bath. I guess that's when she . . . No, it was that next summer, when Ruth 'n Bob needed somebody to take the kids over to her house. I still didn't know how the woman took me. So I was just gonna drop the kids off and get outa there fast. But she invited me into her house. She insist. I went in. That's when she told me. She say, "Sylvia, you do so much for them children. I just love you, Sylvia."

A lot of my black peoples said to me, "Well! You livin' out there with all them white peoples. How can you do that?" I said, "This is *America*. You supposed to live anywhere you *want* to live." So I thought. I don't know. Maybe I'm thinkin' wrong, huh? But those are my thoughts. As long as you pay your tax, your this, your that, you live anywhere that you can afford to live. So don't come tellin' me how can you live out here with these people. I can live with anybody if they let me.

18

Freer in California

In 1968, Sylvia headed for California, the geographical center of Black Power and Sixties countercultural movements at the time. Although historians of Black Power have emphasized the significance of actions and people elsewhere, California did give rise to important groups and leaders. With the state's higher education system then tuition-free, student groups played a key role in cultivating ideas and leadership. Future leaders of major Black Power groups participated earlier in an all-black Bay Area group that discussed writings of African revolutionaries, started a business manufacturing African garb, had a radio show, and gave speeches on ghetto streets.[1] UC-Berkeley students sustained protests against the war in Vietnam. Youthful counterculturalists from across the nation travelled to California. Sylvia settled in Los Angeles, where the black population had been growing faster than in any large Northern or Western city.[2] Motown Records moved there, too, during her five-year sojourn. Through popular culture, Black Power profoundly affected Sylvia during these California years.

Dramatic events touched many American lives in 1968. The April killing of Martin Luther King Jr. provoked riots in more than a hundred cities. While cities burned, the war in Vietnam and the antiwar movement continued to make headlines. Troop levels in Vietnam topped 500,000 in 1968, the year's U.S. death toll there reaching 14,592. With large racial disparities in conscription, combat assignments, and deaths, black activists increasingly opposed the war. In June, war opponent Robert Kennedy was assassinated. That August, some ten thousand antiwar protesters gathered in Chicago, where delegates to the Democratic Convention failed to nominate the antiwar winner of the party's primary. Outside, TV cameras documented a fierce police attack on demonstrators, as the crowd chanted, "The whole world is watching." But many viewers applauded the scene. Majorities of Americans strongly disapproved of protest movements. Richard Nixon won in November by harnessing that sentiment and launching the Republican Party's "Southern Strategy," a plan that tapped every region's opposition to civil rights and dread of the Black Power movement.[3]

What Black Power meant to mainstream society, negative from the start, had only grown more so by 1968. Black Power advocates did not make the news with reasonable talk such as Stokely Carmichael's "How can we begin to build institutions that will allow people to relate to each other as human beings?"[4] The media preferred sensational rhetoric, guns, and violence. In May 1967, thirty Black Panther Party representatives appeared at the California state legislature—displaying handguns, shotguns, and rifles—to "lobby" against a gun-control bill that would make their signature weaponry illegal. As intended, that spectacular move frightened whites and appealed to young blacks. Theatrics, shootouts, and rivalries among Black Power groups attracted enough attention to affect historical representations, keeping the focus on well-known leaders and groups, ideological differences, government repression, and internal weaknesses such as hierarchy, competition, sexism, and homophobia.

Historians have now made clear that the Black Power movement had a far more complicated history. The Black Power tent covered a rapid proliferation of groups, divergent schools of thought and actions. With local people working at the neighborhood level nationwide, Black Power organizations variously encouraged the development of black-identified arts, culture, and education; created community service programs; promoted black capitalism; and carried out political actions ranging from protests to electoral campaigns.[5] Interconnections and disagreements riddled relationships among groups such as the Black Panther Party and SNCC. Individuals moved from group to group. Others worked to benefit their communities through federal antipoverty programs.[6] Yet much overshadowed such subtleties in Sylvia's Black Power California.

With chapters in most large cities by 1968, the Black Panther Party had become the largest and most visible organization of radical Black Power activists in the United States. The BPP arose from Oakland's Merritt College, where readings brought students Huey Newton and Bobby Seale to view African Americans as a colonized people. Their 1966 founding statement, "What We Want, What We Believe," quoted the paragraph that begins, "We hold these truths to be self-evident, that all men are created equal," from that well-known colonial Declaration of Independence. Armed with copies of the U.S.

Constitution as well as guns, the Panthers patrolled ghetto streets and intervened in police stops. The group developed community service programs nationwide: breakfasts for children; free groceries and clothing; home repair; pest control; health services; and transportation to prisons for inmates' families. Willing to ally with white radicals, the Panthers embraced Communism and rejected African cultural nationalism, placing them at odds with a growing Los Angeles group.[7]

Sylvia arrived in a City of Angels still feeling effects of the 1965 Watts revolt that helped bring forth the words "Black Power." An interracial metropolis whose twenty-two founders included ten people of African ancestry, Los Angeles had betrayed its early promise. As their numbers grew to fifteen thousand by 1910, black Angelenos had found jobs and done well enough that a remarkable 40 percent owned their homes that year. In 1913, W. E. B. Du Bois sang the city's praises in the NAACP journal.[8] In the 1930s, however, as more whites, including one hundred thousand Dust Bowl migrants, brought their racial attitudes to the area, they increasingly used violence and racial covenants to force blacks out of residential areas.[9] Booming industries that attracted migration during World War II later collapsed or moved far from black neighborhoods. Between 1959 and 1965, the black jobless rate jumped from 12 percent to 20 percent citywide, 30 percent in Watts. Although more than half of Watts residents lived at or below the federal poverty line, the mayor made no secret of holding up the city's federal antipoverty money. Under an outspokenly prejudiced police chief, officers harassed minorities and killed an average of two individuals per month.[10] Ugly campaigning for a 1964 plebiscite that repealed California's open-housing law helped light the Watts fuse.

Out of the flames came a new Black Power organization called "Us," founded by a UCLA graduate student and Africanist, Ron Everett, who renamed himself Maulana Karenga. Convinced that African Americans could only empower themselves by unifying and reconnecting with African culture, Karenga created rituals and holidays such as Kwanzaa. Members of Us adopted African names, clothing, words, and customs. They produced a newspaper called *Harambee* ("Pull Together") and had a youth paramilitary division. Us worked with gang members as they stopped fighting each other and founded the annual Watts Summer Festival to memorialize those killed in the insurrection.

In 1967, Us joined more than twenty other Los Angeles groups—including local chapters of the NAACP and the Panthers—to form the Black Congress, an umbrella organization with its own building where member groups established headquarters. That autumn, Black Congress activists joined parents protesting conditions at the 95 percent black Manual Arts High School. The action helped inspire Los Angeles high school students, Latino and African American, who later staged their own five-day school walkout. The Black Congress collapsed, however, after a shootout between Us and the Los Angeles Black Panther Party left two dead at the UCLA campus in January 1969.[11]

By then, federal authorities were waging a covert war against black militants. FBI infiltrators spread rumors labeling real activists as undercover agents, made death threats, and produced leaflets and cartoons purportedly by one group attacking another. After the UCLA killings, the Bureau congratulated itself in internal memos. The FBI did not have to fabricate the discord. Black Power groups fought over ideas and viewed each other as rivals. Competition for control of Black Studies at UCLA precipitated the shootings there. Exploiting weaknesses, the FBI also sought to "eradicate" strengths such as the Panthers' service programs. Infiltrators set up raids such as the one where Chicago police burst in on sleeping Panther leaders Fred Hampton and Mark Clark and killed them in their beds. More than fifty Panthers lost their lives to violence in 1969.[12]

As repression and infighting decimated militant groups, Black Power continued reaching the majority of black people through popular culture. Here, too, Black Power groups disagreed. The Nation of Islam rejected black popular culture in everything from Soul food to popular music. Cultural nationalists preferred trends that could help nurture African-derived cultural forms: new strains of jazz, for example. As Marxists, the Panthers preferred the culture of the masses, but also criticized cultural expression that presented "no challenge to the existing order."[13] Most activists mistrusted commercialism as a co-opting force. Indeed, popular culture did dilute ideological purity. Consumer products look trivial alongside life-and-death struggles. Few historians of the movement emphasize the commodified Black Power popular culture so important to individuals such as Sylvia.[14]

Despite mixed feelings among activists, commercialization energized and helped spread Black Power from the start. After the assassination of Malcom X in 1965, consumers across the nation could buy T-shirts, sweatshirts, posters, buttons, and more with his image, the words, "By Any Means Necessary," even "Saint Malcom." Soon these products featured slogans such as "Black Is Beautiful," and, after the Watts riot, "Burn Baby Burn." The black fist appeared on medallions or pendants; the panther, too. Factories in Watts began producing black dolls. Soul food restaurants multiplied. Hair-straightening products lost ground as hair went "natural," with accessories such as Afro combs and wigs. African artwork and décor came into vogue, as did African names. Clothing manufacturers began producing dashikis and sandals, or the black leather jackets and berets of the Panthers. Buyers did not necessarily worry about products' ideological associations. They might hang posters of an iconic individual such as Angela Davis, for example, without thinking of her membership in particular groups. Black Power consumer products and advertising offered something more generalized: a sense of community, identity, and dignity.

Many aspects of Black Power popular culture did not require purchasing power. All African Americans could share in the Soul family idea. Every black man became a "brother," every black woman a "sister." The Black Power term "nation" entered the everyday vocabulary of individuals such as Sylvia, alongside expressions such as "right on" and "dig it." People expressed the new sense of belonging in gestures including the Black Power fist and handshake variations, as well as words. The educated middle class began reconsidering Black English as a language with its own rules, rather than a deviation from Standard English.

Black Power reached large numbers, including Sylvia, through sports. Fans kept track of sports stars such as Muhammad Ali, as he befriended Malcom X, joined the Nation of Islam, and took his African name. In 1967, Ali stunned the sports world by refusing to enter the military when drafted and commenting that, "No Viet Cong ever called me nigger." Stripped of his heavyweight boxing title, criticized and prosecuted, Ali sealed his status as an African American hero. One of the most renowned Black Power images emerged from the October 1968 Olympics in Mexico City, where, during the awards ceremony, gold medalist Tommie Smith and bronze medalist John Carlos raised black-gloved fists in the Black Power salute while the U.S. national anthem played—and the crowd booed. Banned from the Olympic Village, Carlos and Smith soon had their image on dorm-room and apartment walls nationwide.[15]

Music played a crucially important role in bringing the Black Power movement to ordinary people. Cultural nationalism valued and nurtured jazz artists such as John Coltrane, Pharoah Sanders, and Archie Shepp.[16] Selling more widely, Black Power pop music could have a profound effect on black people listening and dancing to it. Here, James Brown took the lead, in part because of his omnipresence on the radio, on jukeboxes, at home parties, and in public spaces such as roller skating rinks.[17] Everyone understood the Black Power in his song "Say It Loud, I'm Black and I'm Proud." Queen of Soul Aretha Franklin gave the point a woman's twist in her version of "Respect." Curtis Mayfield weighed in with "Keep On Pushing" and "We're a Winner." The music industry did not readily embrace this trend. Marvin Gaye had to threaten to quit Motown in order to release his concept album, *What's Going On*, with its themes of racial justice, ghetto life, the war in Vietnam, and ecology.

Black Power popular culture eluded ideological purity. Fans and consumers picked and chose amid offerings, mixing it up as they wished. Even among activists, group discipline did not prevent deviations such as individual Black Panthers wearing stylish African garb. Marvin Gaye's "What's Going On" illustrates bringing together a Black Power stance with seemingly incompatible concepts from the youth counterculture. Lyrics in the same vein as Gaye's, "only love can conquer hate," also appear in Edwin Starr's "War." As militants drew hard lines of separation, black consumers helped the Fifth Dimension take the song "Age of Aquarius" and the O'Jays their "Love Train" to the top of the charts. Strongly identified with the counterculture, Jimi Hendrix had trouble connecting with some black audiences at home, but not with black men serving in Vietnam who expressed their Black Power allegiance with wristbands, medallions, words, and gestures, as well as the music they chose.[18] However mixed, Black Power popular culture carried the message of self-worth, assertiveness, resistance, and black unity.

That message brought Sylvia into full bloom during her California years, adding an air of dignity, power, and cool to her physical beauty. Aquarian Sylvia certainly had no trouble blending her Black Power with what she calls the "magic" of "hippie times." Not mentioning militant groups, Sylvia revels in describing the annual Watts Summer Festival. Newly energized at the time, the festival featured a parade created by the black community—led in its first years by grand marshals such as Muhammad Ali—and performances by stars including Nancy Wilson, James Brown, and Stevie Wonder. Sylvia recalls meeting Tom Bradley, a ghetto-raised son of migrant sharecroppers, who nearly became the first black mayor of Los Angeles in 1969, lost in a runoff as voters fell prey to a scare campaign about Black Power, then won four years later.[19] As Sylvia bought her bus ticket in June 1968, she heard radio news and people talking of Robert Kennedy's assassination. Before she left California, the son who had mapped their way to Disneyland would enlist and go to Vietnam.

Between those historical signposts, we witness a bit more of Sylvia's unusual parenting style. Ever ready to recognize her child's intelligence and growing knowledge, she let him lead and make decisions to a remarkable extent. "That's my mama!" Douglas said later when I mentioned this particularity to him. Caring for her son, working a full-time job, cleaning homes on the side, going to school and obtaining her GED, Sylvia also never missed a beat enjoying this place where she felt "freer," and where she would have stayed but for the earthquake that ends the chapter.

Maybe five years after we bought that land, my brother Joe 'n I, we start fussin' 'n fightin'. He had lost his wife sometime before. I was tryin' to help him with the kids. But he had did a number of nasty things to me—which I'm just not gonna go into. Until I just got so angry, I figured I better get away.

I split. I say, "You can have all this land 'n everything else, 'cause I'm gone." That was the night they shot that Kennedy boy. Not the president, the other one. That night, I told Lila, I say, "Lila, my brother is just mean or evil or something is wrong with him." I said, "I'm gonna get the hell away from here, before I kill him." That's the way I told her. She said, "Oh, Sylvia, we'd miss you here at the job. We . . ." She really didn't want me to leave. 'Cause she knew I could run the machine. I could do this and I could do that. But I say, "I'm gonna hafta get outa here."

I got me a bus ticket. At the bus station, that lady say, "Where are you going?" I told her I didn't know. Honest. A friend of mines was there. He say, "Sylvia why don't you just go to Chicago and cool off." I say, "Man, I just wanta get away *so far*." California was the only place I could think of. I wanted to go to Oakland or San Francisco, 'cause I had a cousin in Oakland. But I just couldn't get it together. I couldn't say it. In the bus station they were talkin' about how they shot Kennedy in Los Angeles. It was on the radio, too. Los Angeles. Los Angeles. So I said, "That's where I wanta go."

That was the longest trip I ever saw in my life. All up through the canyons, the beautiful mountains. Wyoming. You see them big old rabbits sittin' out there lookin' like little deers. Montana. Oh, it was a beautiful scenery. There was a woman on the bus with two kids. She was about my age, probably younger, 'cause her boys was about nine, ten. Me 'n this woman, we just start talkin'.

She say, "What part of Los Angeles you goin' to?" I say, "Honey, I don't know." She say, "You mean you're goin' to a place . . . ?" I says, "I'm going to a place and I don't know *nothing*." She looked at me. So we talkin'—all the way out there. We just became very close friends.

It was almost daylight when we pulled into Los Angeles. That was quite a city. It's bigger now. But even then that was quite a city to see, to move to. Not knowin' where I was gonna stay. I mean this is it. I didn't know where I was goin'. I did this outa the clear blue sky. I didn't have no relatives there, no friends, not nothin'.

When we get to the bus station, I say, "Do they have any hotels around here?" She say, "Yeah." Then she say, "Why don't you come on home with us? We are goin' to my mother's house." I say, "Really?" She say, "Yeah, come on."

When I got to the mama's house, I looked across the street and it say, "Apartment for Rent." So I say, "I'm goin' over there." That girl say, "Oh, why don't you sit down 'n eat or somethin?'" I said, "No, I gotta go see about this apartment." I went on over there and it was plenty of 'em, nice little apartments. I got one that had the bed hangin' on the wall. Pull it down 'n go to bed. So I paid the man for a whole month's rent. This man was from Guatamaya or somewhere, the manager of the place, very nice person. I came back with my paper. I say, "Got my apartment, baby, and the key." I was ready then.

That's when I call my son. I ask him, "Can you come?" But he told me, "No, I don't wanta come right now. I'm workin'." I had ran off about when school close. And Doug had got a job for the summer with the electric company. The next year he's supposed to go into high school. He says, "When I finish my job, then I'll come out." I say, "Momma will send you your ticket." Then Doug says, "No Mama, you don't hafta send me a ticket. I'm gonna buy me a airplane ticket. I'm gonna *fly* out there." I say, "Fly?" I didn't even know where a airport was or what a airport look like. I say, "Oooo, I was gonna send you a bus ticket." He say, "No, I'm flyin'. You just pick me up at the airport."

So now I done just got to Los Angeles. I had met a friend and had found an apartment there on Vermont Street. Vermont Street run from the foot of the ghetto all the way up to Hollywood. They were tellin' me all you have to do is get on the bus and ride out to the mount 'n you can see Hollywood up there. Hollywood!

So I got on the bus that Monday, lookin' for a job. I went to Children Hospital and put down that I had worked at Children Hospital in Milwaukee. I hadn't worked there, but I put that on the application. The woman told me, she say, "You know we woulda hired you. But we checked with Milwaukee and they had no record." I said, "Oh God."

I went from there to Kaiser Hospital, the one where all the stars go. Everybody had told me, "They don't hire you at Kaiser." Kaiser was segregated they felt. So it probably was. But I went on over there and put in the application. And I told the true. I didn't lie over there. When the woman interviewed me, she say, "What do you know about nurse's aide?" So I start tellin', "120 over . . ." The blood pressure, the pulse, the respiration, the this, the that. I was a good nurse's aide. The head nurse heard me and she says, "Tell that lady to come in here." She hired me right away. 'Cause I knew what I was talkin' about.

Then I was at Kaiser Hospital, makin' pretty nice money with insurance coverage and all that kinda stuff. My son, I told him, "I got the job! When're you comin'?" He said, "Mama, I told you I'm not comin' until I finish my job here." When he finished it, he did come out.

He told me he wanted to go to Los Angeles High School. I say, "How do you know about Los Angeles High?" 'Cause it was far from where we were livin'. He say, "Well, I looked it up after I knew I was comin' out here." So that's where he went. Then, after it was so far and he had to take the bus 'n everything, I says, "I'll find me an apartment out that way." 'Cause it was movin' out closer to my job, too. We found an apartment around Santa Monica Boulevard, offa Pekoe. He could just walk to school. Now I could see that they had night school. So I went to school there myself the whole while I was out there. Douglas went to Los Angeles High. And I went to Los Angeles High.

That was the first time in my life that I had been to a town and I didn't see a white community. Where I were livin', it was every nationality in the *world*. But to get to an all-white community, you had to go way up in Big Bear. Big Bear was a resort area up in the mountains. That's where I saw a lotta white people. Or you had to go thirty or forty miles, to Riverside. That community were really *white*. Or, oh way back up in there where they have all those studios, the big ones.

Now I did work up in there. I went back to housework. Because I'm workin' at Kaiser Hospital, midnight to eight in the mornin'. I'm tired of sleepin' all day long. And Douglas wanted a new suit to graduate. So I say, "I'm goin' to the employ-ment office to see can I find some work." They would send me up in the hills. Now these are stars 'n whites. Aw, them buildin's up there, girl, I never saw homes so big in all days of my life. In California, I saw a lotta plush. No tellin' who I met out there in California 'n just didn't take interest who you are. All I wanta do is get paid 'n let me go. But I met some nice peoples out there, oh yes. They didn't slam the door in my face.

I met a lot of the black stars, too, while I was in California—like Redd Foxx 'n oh, a number of your jazz singers. And I met—what's his name? He the first black mayor for Los Angeles. He just lost that position out there. It start with a "b." He was at our black party, I mean our block party. He wasn't one of these peoples where you'd say, "Euh, that's the mayor." He was just plain ol', so plain and nice.

I really enjoyed California. I felt more freer in California than I did anyplace I ever been. I was kinda sorry I didn't go out there in the first place, instead of comin' here. But when you're a child, you just don't know how to maneuver your life. And, well, the peoples who had been there all they life, they had ran into problems—and had these riots 'n things. There was an older woman, a practical nurse there at Kaiser. She had became a very close friend of mine. She said to me, "Oh Sylvia, you and Douglas come out and I'm gonna fix dinner for you." That's in Watts. She told me about the riot in Watts—how they burn the buildin's down 'n how she had to start puttin' bars at her door. She showed me so much of that town. At that time, peoples wasn't hurtin' you or anything. There was gangs that had built up back in there—but not as bad as it is today. Me myself, I didn't try to live where riots 'n stuff was.

One reason was I had a child. He was fifteen when he came out there and he kinda led me. He told me where he wanted to live, where he wanted to go to school. I didn't knock him, 'cause I didn't know anything about school. I didn't say, "Boy, you don't know what you talkin' about. You too young to tell me where you wanta go." I did not do that to him. I don't know how he did it. But he had his program already set. And I didn't say anything.

My son helped me with maps. He was a good mapper. He would put the map down on the floor. And I would crawl right down there with him. He would say, "This is your interstate right here. You take it and you go blab, blab, blab." He say, "Oooo, here's that wax museum. And Knott's Berry Farm." We went to all these different places. We had a little car. And I had a couple friends, guys back in Watts, who knew how to work on cars. They would keep my car going. So I had a car.

Douglas came in one day and he said, "Mama, we goin' to Disneyland." I looked at him and I says, "Disneyland?" He say, "Yes. You got that ticket thing from Kaiser and I wanta go." Kaiser had gave all the employees a free card to go to Disneyland. I say, "I don't know how to get there." Right away, here comes the map on the floor.

When we got to the gate he say, "Oh Mama, I'm ready to kiss the ground." That boy knew more about Disneyland. He had all his programs laid out. We went over Disneyland in *one day*. Some people say it takes two days. I say, "Not if you have free tickets." All we had to do is show our card and we was on and off, on and off. Douglas knew where he wanted to go, where it all was, where to get on the monorail and where to get off. We went over everything there, me 'n Douglas, in one day. 'Cause he would lay all this stuff out. He were a very smart kid. He had me on all those bad rides. Oh, girl!

The most beautiful thing I saw in Disneyland, was, [*Sings.*] "It's a small world after all." You been there. Oh, you haven't? Well, always take "It's a Small World." [*Sings.*] "It's a small world after all." You go through this tunnel like. Ridin' in the boat. They singin' to you, "It's a small world after all." They got all beautiful pictures on each side. All kinda nationalities of little peoples there. The black ones, the white ones, the brown ones, the pink ones, the . . . Oh, it's just the most beautiful thing I ever saw in my *life*. That was. I haven't forgot that song yet. It's a small world after all.*

I met so many peoples in Los Angeles. I didn't know I knew anybody out there, 'til my cousin's sister found me. She say, "Oh, I wanta take you to see . . ." Kids I grew up with—right there in Los Angeles. Folks from Springfield or Hammond and Ponchatoula. One of the guys used to bring the ice to our house down there. 'Cause after we done moved up in life a little bit, we got a wooden refrigerator you put ice into. I ran into a lotta peoples from other peoples sayin', "Sylvia live in Los Angeles." Or accidental. I met Mel and he say, "Sylvia, I want you to meet this guy from Alabama." And coincident, some of the peoples from Alabama was friends of mines here in Wisconsin. Oh, it was strictly, as you say, magic. That's the way my Los Angeles thing was. Unbelievable. One guy I met there, his relative was my neighbor. When I start talkin' to him and sayin' I was from Milwaukee, these other folks overheard me. They say, "Milwaukee? I have relatives there." They start namin' they relatives. I say, "Oh I know them very well." So we all, everybody, we just start 'sociatin' with each other.

I met peoples from all kinda places workin' at Kaiser. I had a RN there from Hawaii, from one of the islands. That girl was the sweetest! She would call me Mama. Sakuta, her name was Sakuta. She would tell me about the island that she lived on and how they would erupt. When she got married, I was invited to the weddin'. Oh, we were just so close. A lotta the foreigners, we were very, very close in California. But the womens at work, they was mostly country womens from down South.

One time, we were gonna strike at Kaiser—that's later on—because of benefits. And this one woman says, "If we strike we'll be eatin' beans." I say, "Honey, we been eatin' beans all our life." Big as she was and I was, we didn't need to eat anyway. We got the strike to go and got a nice decent raise and benefits. Your teeth, your eyes. That was more important than what we were gonna eat.

That was after Douglas finished high school, graduated. For a while I had him in college, West Los Angeles College. Then one day he said to me, "Mama, I need

---

* In 1974 an archeological dig at Hadar, Ethiopia, would yield a 40 percent complete hominid skeleton dated at 3.2 million years old. Dubbed "Lucy," it was introduced to the public as the common ancestress of all human beings. Despite problems with over-simplified media presentations and Lucy's eventual eclipse by discoveries of older Ethiopian bones, such archeological evidence that we all descend from shared African ancestors, complemented later by findings of the Human Genome Project, has solidly grounded the "small world" idea that Sylvia so loved at Disneyland.

a ride down to the draft board." Or the recruitin' office. I'm not sure which. He had sign up without tellin' me. Like he wanted to go. I'm drivin' him down there and I say, "Douglas, don't do this. Do like Muhammad Ali." He say, "Mama, I ain't no Muhammad Ali." I say, "Douglas, don't do it. Don't go." He say, "It's too late now, Mama. It's done. I *got* to go now!" So he was gone by the time of the strike.

After Doug was gone, the governor of California said to all us girls who had been a nurse's aide for more than four or five years, that we could go to LPN school, nursin' school. That was right down my alley. 'Cause I really wanted to be an LPN. So I start doin' that. I would work at Kaiser 'til eight in the mornin', then have two or three hours in class. I took the classes and finished the school. But it wasn't sinkin' in good for some reason. I didn't pass state board. I went two or three times to try to get it, but I never did.

I did get that high school diploma. I had to have a high school diploma for this nursin' thing. So they were very lenient. I think they kinda just push my score up a little bit and let me get my diploma. But I feel like I still don't know anything, because I didn't learn what I wanted to learn. I admit that. I'm no false pretender. I'm for real.

I think I put myself into the books harder in Milwaukee than I did out in California. I was workin' at night and for people up in the hills a couple times a week. You just didn't have the time to really put yourself into those books. All I could do was kinda look at it 'n keep movin'. I wadn't applyin' myself to it like you could sit down 'n really study. I had to work. And then I would fish all the time on the ocean.

Ahhh, did I love fishin' on that ocean! I would keep my fishin' equipment in my car. And after work I would go fishin'. Oh, I'm surprise that ocean didn't wash me away. I didn't know there's a tidewater that comes back. So one day I was out—by myself—on some rocks somebody had told me about. Big rocks you climb up on and you fish. After a while I look back and the water had almost covered those rocks. I had to get outa there fast. I was slippin' 'n slidin', slippin' 'n slidin'. I left some of my tackles 'n everything. By time I got out, that water really wash that whole stone. That taught me not to go out on that ocean. Or be careful where you go, especially alone. But I still went fishin'. I would go out to Santa Monica. That was the pier that went for miles out into the ocean. They had a bathroom and a cafeteria 'n everything built on the pier. And Long Beach, they had a beautiful pier there also. Those waves would come up 'n jump over that sometime. I would catch beautiful fish, all kinds. Buttermouths, that's a very good tastin' fish. Bonitas, I wadn't too crazy about them. They were really wild, cut your line 'n stuff. I likeded the buttermouth and another little perch-type fish better. And the crabs. I would catch big crabs in between the rocks. Oh I went fishin' so much! That was a good part of my life out there.

One part I wanta tell was when this guy I met, he says, "Oh I'm gonna take you up to Big Bear." That's in the mountain. That man like to scared me to death. He was fast driver. Like I say, all California is fast drivers. They taught me how to be fast driver. But oh my God, to drive like that in the mountains! You lookin' down in those canyons. He look at me and he say, "You are afraid." I says, "Yes, I am—the way *you* drive." He says, "Sylvia, I didn't think I could *ever* scare you. I thought you was the type woman who wasn't afraid of anything." I was kinda boyish woman, you know, because I live with all those brothers 'n I learn to be tough. I say, "Well, I'm afraid of this." That was just torture for me. But once you got there, it was beautiful. We fished in them big lakes up there—where you can touch the sky.

So all this that happened to me in California was beautiful. That was back, as you say, in the hippie days. Hippie times. Yeah, California, it was nice. I think about this so hard now, why I left. But with the earthquakes, the rent and, oh, my health, too.

I got high blood pressure in California—not because I was under pressure, but because of my livin' standards. After my son was gone, I never cooked. My friends say, "Come on, let's go out to dinner." I would go and gobble up. My diet was richy, richy. Oh! I were puttin' on weight. The doctor told me, "Sylvia, your blood pressure is just shootin' up." And I come to my own senses. I had to get my blood pressure under control. I knew the livin' was too much. You get in certain place and you just livin' too good.

And rent was gettin' very high. I had a nice two bedroom apartment, reasonable when I took it. But the rent just went up, until it really cost too much—all my check just about. After Douglas left, I told the man, "Can't you let me have a smaller apartment?" He says, "No. I'm just fixin' to up your rent." I say, "Oh no you not. I'm movin'." I said, "Man, you have ran me all the way back to Wisconsin. 'Cause you done up this rent, look to me like it's every week or so." He did give me a smaller apartment. But that darn rent business was just too much. I had never really gotten used to payin' peoples rent. I had my own place in Milwaukee and in the country.

Then the big earthquake hit. I was workin' that night on the sixth or seventh floor at Kaiser. I wasn't on my own floor when this earthquake came. The elevators, I could hear the elevators. BOOM! They went to the bottom of the buildin'. And the buildin' was just wavin' and rockin'. The windows was crackin' and the patients was fallin' outa the bed. This woman, a patient, she ran to me. And I ran to her. She was goin', "Ilabeelaylala." And I was goin', "Oh God, oh God, what's the matter? Oh!" She was goin', "Inaboninadayga." I don't know what she were sayin', what language she was. But I were prayin', "Oh God please! Oh my God!" We were just *huggin'* each other. "Oh my God, what's the . . . ?" 'Cause she didn't know what was wrong. I didn't know what was wrong. I just knew Los Angeles had went into the ocean. You know, you're upstairs, on the seven floor. You lookin' out into Hollywood and you seein' lightnin' flashin'. It wasn't lightnin'. It was the electric light lines breakin'. You could see all the flash from this. But I thought it was lightnin' flashin'. I thought it was the end of the world.

As I started back to my floor, the buildin' was movin'. It's just movin'. How am I gonna get back to my floor, when this is movin' like that? It was just the rubber of the buildin'. That's the way they have 'em out there. Ohhh my God, honey. All the medication out of the medicine station was all on the floor, the books, the patients. The lights went out. Windows was broke. A patient—a young kid—he say, "Lady, nurse, you don't know what happen, do you?" I say, "No. What happen?" He say, "That was an earthquake." I say, "That's what it was, patient, a earthquake." Then you get a tremble. I drop everything again. It was an earthquake.

That was the one in '72, when the interstate fell down, killed people. I was there. That was the ninth of February. The next day was my birthday.*

When I left Kaiser that mornin', Bernice, one of the other women workin' there, she say, "Come on, Sylvia, aren't you gonna drive?" I say, "I don't know if I can drive home or not." All them big banks across the street there, the windows was all shattered. She say, "Oh Sylvia, look at the bank there." We were goin' home. That girl said, "Look, you could go in there and pick up all the . . ." I say, "Ooooo, I don't wanta see nothin'. I just wanta go home or *back to Wisconsin*, one or the other." I says, "Oh my God, my niece was at that house and she ain't been too long came from Wisconsin."

My niece, she was stayin' with me and goin' to East Los Angeles College at the time. When I got home, I said, "Girl, what happen?" She say, "Ooooo, that refrigerator came to the bedside and try to touch it." I had a little daybed in the kitchen. She was sleepin' on that. She said, "The refrigerator came down and it went back up, came down and went back up." That girl says, "My God, Aunt Sylvia, that was dreadful." I say, "I know."

I still think about that earthquake. That's something I never, never will forget. I was ready to come home *then*. What I did, I called Doug. He was stationed in

* Sylvia has the wrong date here. A large earthquake shook Los Angeles on February 9, 1971—not 1972.

Florida, I think, at the time. I say, "Douglas, I wanta go home." He say, "Mama, don't go home yet. Wait 'til September, 'til the Watts festival."

Me 'n Douglas, we just *love* to go to Watts festival. Every year the blacks got together down there and they would celebrate. They would have floats 'n they would parade. Some of my girlfriends, their children would be in all the parades. The parents or somebody would teach 'em to do all this acrobats or to drill and parade. It was so pretty. And a lotta black stars out of Hollywood would get on they float. This one day, Big Jim Brown was on one of the floats. I yell, "Big Jim Brown!" He heard me and turned around. And I got such a beautiful picture of him. Oh, I caught that picture just perfect. I never missed a Watts festival. They would have, oh, all the big jazz singers. When Douglas was in Vietnam, I would always tape programs from the Watts festival and send it to him. He loved that. He just thought the world goin' to Watts for that. I loved it too. So I did what Douglas said. I went to the Watts festival one last time.

That earthquake shook me up good enough to shake me outa California. Because that was the big one. They have had some worse, I think. My son was in that big one out there in San Francisco not long ago. He had *just* crossed that bridge. And I knew his route. 'Cause I had been there and he had say, "I cross this every day to go to work." When I heard about that earthquake at seven o'clock—it's two hours different—I knew. That was awful. He call me and he say, "Oh Mama, I had just got off that bridge. I had just made it." So I guess if God wants you, you can't hide. You can try, but you cannot hide. He says you never . . . the moment nor the hour. How is that? You never know the moment nor the hour. If you did you would be prepared.

19

Justice!

By the late 1970s, changes wrought by decades of civil rights activism could seem dramatic to African Americans such as Sylvia. Legislation and judicial decisions, backed by deployments of federal troops, had forced an end to the overt segregation that generations had borne with little hope of change. Signs saying "Whites Only" had come down. Black citizens had begun voting and running for office in places where law and custom had denied them those rights since the nineteenth century. When Sylvia went North in 1947, the United States had fewer than one hundred black elected officials total. That count neared fifteen hundred in 1970 and five thousand by the end of the decade.[1] Major cities, including Atlanta, Raleigh, and New Orleans, as well as Cleveland, Detroit, Newark, and Los Angeles, had elected their first black mayors by 1980. More African Americans attended colleges and universities that now offered Black Studies programs and had affirmative action plans for admissions. The decade began with increasing numbers of employers—including all federal government contractors—actively seeking to hire minority employees. It seemed, as Sylvia says, "a different world."

At the same time, however, political gamesmanship fed a growing backlash. Aiming to break the Democratic Party's traditional lock on the South, Republicans courted voters opposed to civil rights—and won votes everywhere. Democrats, too, played to emotions on issues such as court-ordered busing to remedy school segregation. Widespread opposition underlay violent outbursts such as the 1971 school bus bombings in Pontiac, Michigan. A Gallup poll that year found more than three out of four respondents opposed to busing.[2] Resentment of affirmative action emerged in sectors historically supportive of racial justice. A storm of controversy met the practice of modifying entrance requirements for black students at colleges and universities, where traditional "legacy admissions" for children of major donors had never provoked such objections.[3] Aware of reactionary sentiment building, politicians exploited the moment with code words such as "quotas" and "welfare queens."

The Republican Party gave its 1980 presidential nomination to a staunch opponent of the Civil Rights Act, the Voting Rights Act, school desegregation, and affirmative action. To kick off his campaign, candidate Ronald Reagan went first to a Mississippi town notorious for the murder of three Freedom Summer activists, where he spoke of "states' rights" and praised the Old South.[4] But all regions harbored opposition to civil rights, as well as angry reaction against antiwar activism, feminism, gay rights, and the counterculture. Such feelings spurred many working-class whites to vote for the man who would later break their labor unions and lay groundwork for the shift of U.S. manufacturing jobs overseas.[5]

As president, Reagan ushered in an era of racial retrogression. He quickly lifted the ban on tax-exempt status for private colleges and universities that practiced racial discrimination, a move overturned in court before it could take effect. More substantially, Reagan broke with precedent by firing civil rights advocates from the United States Commission on Civil Rights. Federal enforcement agencies began working against rather than for minorities' civil rights claims.[6] The War on Poverty gave way to notions of a "permanent underclass," effectively blaming poverty on the behavior and culture of the poor—and on liberals' efforts to help.[7] By the mid-1980s, blacks had reason to wonder if civil rights efforts had accomplished much at all—and if whites would ever relinquish racism.

In Milwaukee, the re-opening of the Bell case highlighted what had—and had not—changed in racial matters. The news broke in August 1979, when police arrested Thomas Grady in Colorado and brought him to Milwaukee.[8] He quickly pled guilty to reduced charges: one count of homicide by reckless conduct and one of perjury, charges that together carried a maximum sentence of ten years. District Attorney E. Michael McCann said that he could not prosecute or name other participants in the cover-up, because Wisconsin's statute of limitations protected offenders who lived in the state for six years after the offense.

That assertion would not prove as ironclad as McCann tried to make it sound. The judge in the Bell family's civil rights lawsuit later ruled that the statute did not protect a person in a case "where his own fraudulent conduct has prevented the plaintiff from filing suit within the applicable time period," a point affirmed by the Seventh Circuit Court of Appeals. As McCann declared the case closed in August 1979, Milwaukee's response made clear that the Daniel Bell story—and the racial issues it represented—were far from any such end.

Black Milwaukee took the lead in this new chapter. At the fore stood Reverend R. L. Lathan, who had tried to organize protests of the Bell killing in 1958, when few people backed the effort. Now, as a new generation marched for Daniel Bell, Lathan dramatized the problem of deadly police abuse. In a protest demonstration covered by *Jet* magazine, Lathan lay in an open casket, displayed on a slow-moving vehicle in the procession. The surrounding demonstrators' hair, clothing, and body language signaled the strength of Black Power culture.[9]

In the first weeks after the Daniel Bell story went public, other community leaders—including Sylvia's ex-husband, O.C. White—gave voice to widely shared outrage about the disclosed police misconduct, about Grady's reduced charges and the DA's refusal to name other participants in the 1958 cover-up. African American public officials now had power to pursue these issues. Fire and Police Commissioner William Gore initiated procedures aimed at forcing McCann to reveal more about officials' handling of the Bell case. Alderman Roy Nabors urged the governor to appoint a special prosecutor and demanded a federal investigation into all police killings in Milwaukee. At a Milwaukee NAACP conference in September, speakers mentioned the Bell revelations to open a larger discussion of racism in law enforcement.

Deceived and used by the police in 1958, the *Milwaukee Journal* and *Milwaukee Sentinel* covered every angle of the reopening of the Daniel Bell case, from the moment the story broke in August 1979 through all the political posturing, legal maneuvering, and such on the way to its resolution in October 1984.

Police Chief Harold Breier called the controversy raised by the Bell revelations "bull-roar." Breier represented a conservative sector that opposed changes wrought by the civil rights movement. Under his leadership since 1964, the MPD had hired few minorities and women, until a 1975 court order required improvement. As police departments in other large cities instituted programs aimed at improving police/black community relations, Breier resisted pressure from civic leaders and the police union to do so in Milwaukee. His department had a reputation for racism and brutality. When the Daniel Bell case reopened, Breier, who had worked as an MPD detective in 1958, defended that era's police department. He praised the late detectives Rudolph Glaser and Leo Woelfel, whose racial bias and role in the cover-up were beginning to emerge. When the city council passed a resolution requesting a federal investigation, Breier called it a "political sham."

Sylvia and her brothers had by then turned to Tom Jacobson for legal counsel. Black Milwaukeeans knew Jacobson as a civil rights activist and a former partner of Lloyd Barbee, who led the legal battle for school desegregation. A founding member of the city's chapter of CORE, Jacobson had represented Father Groppi and members of the NAACP Youth Council.[10] For the Bell case, he and his partner Jerome Krings enlisted two civil rights specialists from outside their firm, Curry First and, later, Walter Kelly. Citing Kelly's energy, commitment, as well as "the quality of his legal writing and his oral argument," First later insisted, despite his own role, that the only truly important contribution he had made to the case had been bringing this fourth member onto the legal team.[11] Together, the group successfully pursued a lawsuit that charged Thomas Grady, former Chief of Police Howard Johnson, and the City of Milwaukee with violating Daniel's and the Bell family's civil rights in a racially motivated traffic stop, killing, and cover-up.

The judge who heard the Bell case had a history of supporting African Americans' rights. Governor of Wisconsin from 1963 to 1965, John Reynolds ran as a stand-in candidate against segregationist George Wallace in the state's 1964 Democratic presidential primary.[12] Appointed to the federal bench by President Johnson in 1965, Judge Reynolds made the 1976 ruling that Milwaukee's public schools were unconstitutionally segregated and required immediate action—that is, the busing remedy then raising a furor throughout the nation. Although Reynolds did not always see eye to eye with the Bell family's attorneys, they considered it fortunate to have him serve as judge in this matter.[13]

When the trial began in October 1981, recent policing incidents had Milwaukee in an uproar. In July, Ernest Lacy, a twenty-two-year-old black man wrongly arrested as a rape suspect, died of strangulation—his body badly bruised—while in police custody. An inquest jury had recommended charges of homicide by reckless conduct. After the district attorney decided not to follow that recommendation, the Coalition for Justice for Ernest Lacy began holding demonstrations downtown.[14] Then, just days before the Bell trial began, a thirty-five-year-old white businessman, James Schoemperlen, suffered serious injury during a police stop and beating. Because of these circumstances, the defense asked Judge Reynolds to delay the Bell trial or declare a mistrial. The judge refused.

This kind of turbulence made it difficult to select a jury. During that process, the family's attorneys objected that the defense seemed to be striking prospective jurors solely because they were black. Declaring race-based exclusion a violation of the Constitution, Reynolds required reasons for striking any more black jurors. Only one African American woman would remain on the jury, however, after being "grilled for twenty minutes on her reactions to the word 'nigger.'"[15]

Arguments, presentation of evidence, testimony, and cross-examination continued into December. Sylvia and her eldest brother Henry chose to take the witness stand. Henry told how the killing had tormented their father's last years. Sylvia spoke of the mistreatment the family faced at the police station that night. With much of the testimony on paper, their courtroom performance helped "make it real" for jurors.[16]

Aiming to discredit Russell Vorpagel, the city's attorneys asked questions that both sides wanted answered. Why did he say nothing at the 1958 inquest about pressure to change his report or about suspecting that the knife had been planted? "I was taught to respond only to questions," he said on the stand, "and no such questions were asked of me." When the cross-examiner declared that Vorpagel had been free to say anything he wished at the inquest, the witness reiterated that, during such a proceeding, "you cannot volunteer information." Asked if he had told anyone his feelings at the time, Vorpagel recalled turning to his pastor—and being advised that, "As a police officer I should just go back and continue what I was doing." However unheroic, such play-by-the-rules answers did not hurt Vorpagel's credibility.

Beginning deliberations on Wednesday, December 10, the jurors notified the judge on Sunday that they could not agree. Reynolds called jury and attorneys into a courtroom left unheated on weekends. Walt Kelly later described exhausted jurors filing into the icy room, one of them wrapped in a blanket, all showing their intense disagreement in body language and facial expressions. The worst sticking point was the contention that Milwaukee police officers routinely carried "throwaway knives" such as Grady planted. Attorneys for the family withdrew that claim rather than risk a mistrial.

On December 16, the jury found that a racially motivated conspiracy had violated the civil rights of Daniel Bell and his family. The next day, they awarded the Bells $1,795,000. Local African American leaders and editorial writers hailed the verdict as justice for Dan and a triumph for civil rights.

It would take nearly three years to bring the case to completion. With Mayor Maier at the helm, the city appealed—and refused the family's offers to settle. When the city council finally managed to outvote conservative aldermen and pass a resolution telling City Attorney Brennan to withdraw the appeal and negotiate, Maier insisted that the appeal continue. In November

1983, Walt Kelly argued the Bell family's case in the U.S. Seventh Circuit Court of Appeals in Chicago.

Kelly later recounted that, just before going to Chicago, he met with the Bell family and asked them if there was any "particular thing" they wanted him to say to the court. The Bells "put their heads together." Then Patrick answered for the group. "We want you to tell the judges that we served our country in the war," he said, "and that there can't be two laws in this country, one for white people and one for black people like us." That, Kelly remembered, "is what I told the judges."[17]

In Sylvia's retelling, winning justice for Dan eclipses the ugliness encountered on the way. To be sure, this chapter shows us her pugnacious side. Yet it is victorious Sylvia who recounts experiences such as appearing on CBS's *60 Minutes*.[18] Her account of testifying in trial seems drawn from TV courtroom drama—and differs markedly from the adequate but dull performance recorded in the transcript. The difference seems to arise not from a failure of memory, but rather the kind of memory construction process that reshapes the past.[19] The family's deposition transcripts make clear that all would have had their say quite differently under less intimidating conditions. Deprived of the most basic education, Sylvia and her brothers found it particularly difficult to deal with moments such as giving testimony in court. Here, her narrative reveals what Sylvia—the dynamic personality Curry First had hoped to draw forth on the stand—wished she had said.

Profoundly differing notions of justice also come into view here, as Sylvia remembers the city's last-minute settlement offers and her anger toward the more pragmatic of their attorneys for urging the family to accept. Her words reveal depths of feeling behind that ire. A sense of vulnerability to manipulation. A longstanding belief that accepting such a settlement amounted to taking a bribe and betraying Dan. Inalterable on this point, the hardheadedness that helped Sylvia persevere through the ordeal had the unfortunate effect of bringing ill-will into a triumphant moment.[20] Relishing that moment all the same, Sylvia sums up by looping back—with her own twists—to Martin Luther King Jr. and the 1965 speech that capped the five-day march from Selma to Montgomery.

🌹 I was glad I came back home. California was killin' me instead of doin' any good for me. The only place did any good for me is right where I'm at now. I was the type person who had to be where you got this hard work. I was built for that. When I got back from California, I was very active in the field, in the garden, cleanin' or just usin' my muscles, usin' my limbs. I took medication, too, to get my blood pressure down. My doctor in Waterloo, I knew him from workin' at the nursin' home. He would always admire me for bein' so brave—he said—to come and work with all the white peoples. That tickle me. I say, "Why not? I live with all white peoples." I said, "I know a lotta these white womens and mens in here. I'm glad to be here." It was peoples who I wondered where they was 'n they were there. So my blood pressure went down. You know, my mother died of high blood pressure at forty-five. So I was glad when I passed forty-five.

It was kinda nice, too, to come home and not pay rent. The money that I worked for, it could go in my pocket. I had to start rebuildin' and re-doin'. But I didn't mind. I love the country.

When I came back my brother had so many vegetables growin'. That's when I started goin' to the farmer's market up there on the square in Madison. He had all these zucchini squash, green beans 'n stuff. I was puttin' 'em in pillow cases 'n bringin' 'em to Madison in this little car. Before I left California, I had bought myself a brand new Opel. That's what car you saw me in when I met you. Sellin' vegetables years 'n years 'n years ago.

Then this man from Lodi, he sold me a nice little truck—reasonable, couple hundred dollars. After that, I start goin' into Milwaukee, too, to the market on Center Street. I had so much soul food and didn't have a lotta soul food peoples up in Madison. Center Street wadn't exactly the ghetto. But it was close to the ghetto. And peoples was lookin' for that kinda food. I was the only black woman there sellin' *anything*. I were bringin' in these greens 'n things.

Then Henry he would see me sellin' all these greens. He found out that black peoples like that stuff. And he start raisin' it, too. Just about ran me outa business. 'Cause Henry 'n them, they had bigger farms and equipment, bigger trucks and all that kinda stuff. I couldn't raise enough. But I taught them. I showed 'em how to raise stuff for black people.

I kept goin' to Madison, too, goin' to both markets, until I guess '76. Then it began to be so much stuff up on the square in Madison, too much. So I start goin' just to Milwaukee. I really got off into big business with that food. I would buy corn from other peoples around by me who raised it. Oh, we would bring in a whole pickup, like three hundred dozen ears of corn to Milwaukee. Corn always was a good seller. And I had other stuff. We'd bring in two trucks. Some of my neighbors would help me.

In '76, I start workin' too, at Goodyear Tire 'n Hose in Sun Prairie. They let me in Goodyear Tire 'n Hose. Carol, Arbor's wife—you know, the little white guy who got me the job at the packin' house—his wife was the one told me to come out to Goodyear Tire 'n Hose 'n get a job. "Because they are hirin' black peoples. They gotta hire black peoples, Sylvia." This is what she were tellin' me. She says, "So many blacks is supposed to be into the plant. They want black peoples out there. So come on out 'n put your application."

The world had change—as Douglas told me. My son told me that. He was always teachin' me things. Like when he was gonna to come home from Vietnam and he called to tell me he wouldn't be at the airport the day I was supposed to meet him. He would be coming a week or so later. Because some other guy over there was havin' a nervous breakdown or somethin', just goin' crazy, and he was comin' home in Douglas's place. I said, "Is he black or white?" And Douglas say, "Mama! Does it matter? He's a human being and he needs to come home." Girl, I felt so bad about that! I really did.

It was a different world. When I start workin' at Goodyear Tire 'n Hose, I say, "Doug, they didn't even ask me what race was I black or white." I couldn't believe that they didn't have "Negro" on the application. Doug say, "Mama, they done been stopped that. That was years ago." I says, "I never notice." Because when I got a job I kept it. And I really didn't listen to the news too much. So that was a new leaf. I came through a lot of different turnin' over leaves in my lifetime. A lot.

Okay, so I'm livin' in Waterloo, workin' at Goodyear, and sellin' vegetables at the market, when the district attorney in Milwaukee called me. His name was Snyder, District Attorney Snyder. And he say, "Sylvia, I want you to get your family together and come down to the courthouse. I wanna talk to you about your brother's case." That was in 1978.

It was at Christmas time. 'Cause I can remember gettin' a phone call from the *Journal.* "Don't you know the Bell case gonna be open up again?" I say, "Ooooo, it's Christmas. The family is tryin' to get Christmas together. And now we have to listen to a buncha lies again." Or something like that. However I respond to them, I can remember 'em writin' in the paper sayin', "There is still a cloud over Sylvia Bell's house." I say, "Yes, a big cloud."

So Snyder says, "Come in, Sylvia. I wanna talk to you." I went down there with some of my brothers. This was after they took Grady to the courthouse.

Grady was the one that kill my brother. Krause was his buddy. Grady, he had moved to Colorado. 'Cause his life went boom. They fired him on the police department. They fired both of 'em. That was a year after the killin'. They were caught in different taverns boozin' it up and all that kinda stuff.

So Krause, he's down 'n out. He's a alcoholic. Well, I don't know if he's alcoholic or not. 'Cause I'm no doctor. So I take that back. But he don't have a job.

Like black peoples, I guess, no job and no way to get one. And so he goin' to Hollywood and he's gonna have a movie. He goes and tells them peoples out there that they killed this black boy for nothing. He told this in court. That's why I'm so good at tellin' you right now. So Krause goes to Hollywood. But the movie peoples told him, say, "We cannot make movies, we cannot do anything, until this is done through court."

So he came back. He went to the DA's office. The district attorney says, "If you can get Grady to say on a tape . . . We'll tape him. And if you can get him to say . . ." They taped this guy tellin' Grady, "Man, I'm havin' back flashes from this Bell thing." He says, "I can't sleep. I can't eat." Krause says all that. And Grady say, "Oh man, just let a dead dog lie. Don't bring it up. Just let it lay."

Krause kept tellin' him that he couldn't rest because of the killin' of Daniel Bell. But he really wanted to get it back in court so he could make a movie and get some money.* So he lied to his buddy on the phone, to get him to tell what happen. Grady say, "Man, if the goddamn NAACP get aholt to this— today—they would *string* us." He said, "Them days was different. But now, you can't do that." Krause say, "Oh man, statute of limitation done ran out." He lied to that man. And the man told him everything. He finally broke down and tell him. I guess the peoples was right there to put the handcuff on him, when he told this.

They had snuck. All this was undercover work. I don't know how long it was goin' on. But it had been goin' on in Milwaukee. So they brought Grady back. And when that happened, we got the chance to get back to court. Snyder, the district attorney says, "We gonna have to trial him." I couldn't believe it.

Then my brothers, they said, "Well, we gonna get an attorney." Somebody yell, "Oh, this ain't no good. You won't get nothin' outa that case. That's twenty years ago." Some of 'em said that he could not be trialed again simply because it was twenty years in between. But Grady had left Milwaukee and went to Colorado. Therefore he could be trialed again.

So we got our attorney. My brother Pat say, "Oooo, get Jacobson. He's a good attorney. So many of my friends out at A. O. Smith know him." So we got Jacobson. And Curry First came in. He were very nice. All those attorneys, those human right lawyers came in and helped us.

---

* Krause consistently asserted that a troubled conscience motivated him. Yet he admitted on the stand during the trial that he had gone to Los Angeles seeking a movie deal, signed what he believed was a $300,000 contract for book/television rights, and tried to buy an expensive home before the deal fell through.

Then, this boy, Kelly. Kelly wasn't in the picture at first. But finally Walt Kelly comes in. And when Kelly came in, ohhh, you gonna see! He's the one that said for us to get punitive damage. Those lawyers—get this—brought up the Fourteen Amendment, brought up . . . I don't even know. That Kelly, he says, "Those peoples will get paid." But that's a little later.

First, they gave Grady his trial. That's when it was all shown. Grady admit that he did kill my brother unnecessary. That he did plant the knife. They *planted* a knife in my brother's hand. He admit that. We were all sittin' there. And he turned around and looked at us. He says, "I'm sorry. I'm . . ." I say, "Keep it! 'Cause you coulda told it a long time ago. You coulda told it and the city woulda been outa this mess, too."

The judge was gonna send him up. And Snyder call me—I had a couple of my brothers with me, too—and said, "What should we do with Grady?"

I say, "Gimme a gun and let me blow his brains out like he blowed my brother's out." I guess I could've pulled the trigger to get it over with. This is it. I don't have to go through any more of this torture. 'Cause that was torture. I say, "The Bible say, an eye for an eye and a tooth for a tooth."

So when this judge sentenced Grady, he says, "Miss Bell, this court is not an eye for an eye and a tooth for a tooth." The judge, he discipline me about what I said.

They sentence Grady for no time at all, far as I'm concern. So many years in jail, like two years, with probation.* When they send a black man to jail for killin' somebody, he get *eternal life*. There is no end to his life. He gonna rot in jail. When he shoot somebody the way they did to the child. And lied.

The media, when we went hit the hallway, "Well, whadya think about it?" My brother Speedy spoke up. He say, "Yeah, I'm glad we got justice." I say, "Justice, hell! I don't think this is no damn justice." 'Cause it wadn't no justice. Givin' that man a couple years in jail? And they said, "What do you intend to do?" I say, "Take it further."

---

* Sentencing Grady in January 1980, Judge Ted Wedemeyer noted the influence of "background" on everyone in the courtroom. He lingered over his own youth on Milwaukee's conservative South Side, where people felt "tremendous respect" for the police. Overall, his remarks seemed rather apologetic for sentencing Grady to any prison time at all. Wedemeyer gave Grady seven years: five for homicide, two for perjury. He later reduced the sentence to five years, when Grady's lawyers argued that the danger their client faced in prison had increased because of the 1979 article in *Jet* magazine and the 1980 CBS *60 Minutes* segment.

I was in the camera's face. A lotta peoples told me, "Well, I don't like the way you exposed it on television about 'justice hell.'" I says, "I was serious. That's no justice." I were furious. Because it was an unnecessary killin'. Anybody could look through it. "But it was a niggah," so they say. It wasn't a nigger. It was a child, a young man who was tryin' to find his way in life. They just blew his brains out for position. I woke my own self up that night. After that, them peoples knew they had a good fight on their hands.

I'm thinkin' how did we get outa the courthouse over to the federal buildin'. We appeal I think. Because Grady didn't get enough time. Or maybe for the settlement. I don't remember how that was done. 'Cause I was very disturbed. I don't think anything was offered. Or if it was offered it was a turn down. Or we had to take it to federal court.

It took us four years later now, to get this all settled. At least four. During that time, my brother Patrick's son, Richard, said, "Let me write to *60 Minute* and tell them about it. Maybe they'll put it on television." We talked to the lawyers about it. They said, "Fine, if *60 Minutes* wanta do it." And *60 Minutes* was right back on us. They did part of the film from the courthouse. I guess everybody was involve: the police department, much as they could get to cooperate, Snyder, Krause and all of 'em. Even Grady probably had his part—in jail.

My part we did outdoors. 'Cause I ask 'em, I says, "My little house is so small. If it's a beautiful day, why can't we do it outdoors?" It was summertime. And I thought it would be real nice: the river, the trees, the bushes 'n the birds 'n everything. I'm a outdoors person. I put out the picnic tables. We sit out there with our cool lemonade and little snacks. We just had a wonderful time. It was—what is his name?—the old man. They got him on now. And there was a brother who was on the camera. He says, "Ooooo, I live in the country." He likeded the way I live, that cameraman.*

A lotta peoples knew in Waterloo that CBS was back there filmin' me. They was runnin' up 'n down the road, gazin' through the bushes. Oh, I was Miss It. I was kinda dressed up. And they did me plowing my garden with my rototiller.

---

* For *60 Minutes*, Morley Safer played excerpts of Grady's remarks on the tapped phone tapes and interviewed Sylvia, Louis Krause, Russell Vorpagel, District Attorney McCann, and Assistant DA Thomas Schneider. Grady could not appear, since the city attorney forbade interviews with defendants in the Bell family's federal lawsuit. "The Kid, the Cop and the Knife," CBS *60 Minutes*, November 16, 1980. Sylvia is not saying here that one of her siblings worked the camera for *60 Minutes*, but rather indicating that the cameraman was African American.

The whole world—not the world but the United States—saw me. 'Cause I got calls from everywhere. "I saw you on television. What were you doin' with them white shoes on?" They saw my white shoes and went on about that. I said, "Heck, my machine started and I wadn't gonna stop them guys to let me change my shoes." 'Cause it was so hard to start. When it started, I just went right behind the plow with those things on. Now, I 'magine some black peoples would say, "Girl, I never woulda got out there in that field." Too "country" or whatever. But it was a thrill for me. It wasn't a thought that, "Girl, lookit what kinda position yer in."

I was in London when they did that film on TV. My son was in the service over there and wanted me to come. It was in the fall of the year, 'cause I said, "Doug you gotta wait 'til all my vegetables are gone. Then I can stay awhile." So, I goes over there. That's when I went to Paris and, oh God, did I enjoy that! Anyway, while I was in London, somebody, I think one of the attorneys, call me and say, "You was on television on Sunday."

I was back by the time the case went to the federal building, the Supreme Court downtown there in Milwaukee. I was there. I had to be there. Some of them boys said, "Well, I can't go." I would say, "Come on, man. Let's go. The peoples want us all there." Some of my brothers said, "I'm not gonna tell them white peoples about my life." This is what they said. So I had to do it.

The day that I got up in that court to testify, my lawyer, Curry First, he say, "Sylvia, the day you went to the police department, when your brother was first killed . . ." I said, "Yes?" He says, "What happen?" And this white man was sittin' there with this big brass button on him. They made him put on the white shirt and that button. 'Cause that's what I saw that night when I walked into that police department, was this guy. So Curry First says, "Do you see that man in this court- room?" I says, "That's him." I says, "When I told him that my brother did not have his knife, he turned all red." Girl, the man turned all red. The jury looked at him. He turned as red as a beet, with the jury lookin' at him. I says, "He says, 'I can't tell you niggers nothin'. Get outa here.'" Then my attorney was done with me. And Grady's attorney got up. He says, "When he told you to get out, what did you do?" I say, "I left, 'cause I was scared to death he might kill me." They says, "Any more from this witness?" No.

Afterwards, Grady's attorney told me, he say, "Sylvia, you done won this case already." Grady's attorney. He said, "You won." He say, "The words you say will *never die*. Just like your daddy's."

And my brothers say that they could've done the things I done or said the things I said. Whew! Some of 'em wouldn't even go down there. But they wanted they money. I did all the work and they got all the gravy.

When that verdict came in, it was six o'clock. I just scream. I said, "Justice! Mama! Papa! Did you hear? *We got justice!*" I guess that's when we won the lawsuit, too. See, the lawsuit was the money business. I wadn't worried about the money part. But the justice part. I got what I had worked so hard for, justice.

I went home. I had a good night's sleep. It was so different. I don't remember no sum of money. I don't remember anything. But I remember that justice. I was in Supreme Court, one of the Supreme . . . the one downtown Milwaukee, the day I scream, "*Justice!*"

The verdict came in. But that wasn't the verdict yet. That's our third time to court. Federal. Now the city says, "No, we're not gonna pay 'em nothing." Or, "It was a justifieded homicide." The city didn't wanta pay us a certain amount of money. So they appeal. It took us years to get this all settled. Grady is sittin' jail for a couple days. A couple days, as far as I am concern. And we still goin' to court.

At that point, I was really the pusher. 'Cause my brothers, they says, "Well, we coulda took so and so amount." Or something like those words. I said, I say, "We not wrong. We not wrong." And Kelly says, "No, no no, you're not wrong. Come on. Let's go. We goin' all the way." He spoke. Kelly says, "Sylvia, if we don't win here, we goin' all the way out to *Washington* with it." So we went on to that big court in Chicago.

When we got over there, it was a different world of court. A free feelin' of court. I think it was the most comfortablest seats I ever set in—in a courtroom. You know that was the first time I ever been in this big of a Supreme Court. Oooo, that buildin' just fascinatin'. Sittin' there, I said, "My God, what are we gonna do here?"

So the court was started. All them judges, that panel sittin' there. One judge, I think he was Mr. Patrick Cudahy himself, Judge—sittin' on the bench. This one city attorney, he was tryin' to tell the judges something. But that judge interrupt. He says, "The Bells did not kill they brother. *You* did." I says, "Ohh, the judge is sayin' these words." So then the court was over. That was our fourth court.

Then it's time for you to sit and wait. We sittin' around for, honey, I don't know how long it took. A year? No, it don't take no year to get no verdict back, does it? Through the Supreme Court? You don't have no jury. It's just the judges gonna decide. Sit and wait.

Then Attorney Jacobson call me and say, "Hey Sylvia." They offered to give us three hundred and sixty thousand dollars or something like that. Jacobson call me and he say, "You know the verdict haven't came in. You wanta take that three hundred and sixty thousand dollars and settle? And be sure you get some money out of it?" No, he didn't ask me. He told me.

Peoples will sell you down the drain. You gotta keep your eyes open. But then you can't keep your eyes open because these peoples are smarter than you. You hafta do some damn good thinkin' to stay ahead of the game. Jody, Jody, Jody, Jody, Jody, Jody.

I says to Jacobson, "I'll wait for the findin' from Chicago, okay?" And hung that, oh, I threw that phone down. 'Cause I didn't wanta hear nothing like that.

When I hung up the phone on him, I walked out and here was this beautiful rainbow. I looked out to the east and there it was. I says, "Oh my God, it's beautiful!" They say you always make a wish when you see a rainbow. I say, "What should I wish for?" Somethin' say, "The case."

So I made my wish. And it came true. I think I had just hung that phone up and seen the rainbow, when Kelly calls me. He say, "Sylvia, they just called me on the phone from Chicago and told me that we won." I went back to the door. "Let me look at this rainbow again." She had disappeared. I think it happen all that day. I try to remember hard as I can but . . . Or it was within' a week or two.

Then I really became angry with Jacobson. Boy, did I get mad.

We walkin' outa the courthouse with the money in our hand. One point nine million or something like that. And Jacobson comes rubbin' me on my shoulders. I didn't want him to touch me. I says, "I wanta sue this man." One of my brothers like to faint. They almost hadda pick him up. I said, "This man woulda had us with nothing. For the killin' of my brother." I just couldn't believe what he did. I didn't like it. And he knows it.

If you do right to peoples, right will come back to you. Walt Kelly, he never tried to bribe me or say anything to me. Walt Kelly was my *savior*. He was my Martin Luther King. He really was.

It was all over. We went to court for all those years. Then we won. We won. Just like that beautiful rainbow. As Reverend Martin Luther King said, "The arc of the universe means justice."*

* On March 26, 1965, Martin Luther King spoke from the steps of the Alabama state capitol. "How long? Not long," he said. "Because the arc of the moral universe is long, but it bends towards justice."

20

Love Peoples

🖤 "I love peoples, white peoples *and* black peoples," Sylvia declares here. "I love both of 'em—when they are people." These words epitomize the way she ends her narrative. In these last moments with Sylvia, we encounter her genius for loving, her struggle against the inhumanity of racial injustice, and her sober assessment of what race means in the United States today.

In this chapter, Sylvia's words reach well into the millennium, a time frame less suited to the kind of treatment we have given other historical periods. Issues arise from what one contemporary historian calls the "political combat" of the present moment, a conflict all the more racially charged since the election of the first African American president.[1] Of course, writing about any time period engages politicized debates. The more recent the topic, however, the less time the scholarly discussion has had to judge the validity of evidence or, more importantly, to establish points of generalized agreement. We will limit ambitions here to documenting briefly some specifics in Sylvia's main concluding argument: For all the change she has seen in her life, the world has also not changed in major ways when it comes to racial injustice. African Americans still face police abuse and discrimination in housing, jobs, and education.[2]

Sylvia did not go easy on herself in this era when mainstream political culture ridiculed "political correctness" and jettisoned concern for people's feelings. She listened to the very radio talk shows with hosts and callers most likely to speak hurtfully. "I want to know what they're saying about us."

Keeping an eye on Milwaukee's black neighborhood, Sylvia came to believe that children living in today's ghettos have it worse than she did growing up in the segregated South. Life in the nation's inner cities had worsened dramatically, as middle-class black families who could get out did so. Urban employment opportunities had disappeared, as politicians facilitated industrial outsourcing by loosening regulations and changing trade laws and the tax code. Manufacturers had moved first from "Rustbelt" cities to the less-unionized, less-regulated "Sunbelt," and then shifted operations to distant countries with virtually no regulations, labor laws, or unions, where workers earned a fraction of U.S. wages. The kinds of jobs that once permitted working-class black families to make a living had grown increasingly scarce everywhere. The United States lost more than three million manufacturing jobs between 1998 and 2004.[3] In the 1990s, powerful exposés detailed the terrible everyday realities faced by ghetto children unsure whether they would grow up at all: the inadequate food, clothing, shelter, and medical care; the shocking physical conditions and learning environment of their schools; the constant threat of deadly violence.[4] Other studies, including one focused on Milwaukee, support Sylvia's remarks about the uncaring, often vilifying, politics of ending welfare and the effects of that process on nearly nine million women and their children.[5]

Sylvia expresses strong feelings about the voting discrimination that came to light after the November 2000 presidential election. The U.S. Commission on Civil Rights found that Florida black voters were nine times more likely to have their votes thrown out in that election than whites. Nor did racially discriminatory voting "irregularities" happen only in Florida. Congress heard testimony of black voter intimidation and uncounted votes from coast to coast.[6] After black and white voters elected an African American president of the United States in 2008, politicians in several states pressed for measures that discourage lower-class black participation in elections. Groups such as the NAACP question the constitutionality of measures such as I.D. laws requiring all voters to have the means to obtain identification.

Even so, Sylvia winds up her narrative with abundant positivity, fun, and love as well. She talks here about her life after the resolution of the civil rights case brought her some small measure of peace. Her remodeling of the old Bell homestead and winters in the South. Her brothers. Her "white great-grandchildren" in her rural Wisconsin home community. The Milwaukee people she continued to enjoy as a vendor at the Fond du Lac Avenue Farmers' Market. She lingers, too, on happy memories of "the play."

On January 16, 1987, *An American Journey* opened at Milwaukee's Civic Center. Almost two years earlier, the artistic director of the Milwaukee Repertory Theater, John Dillon, had encountered Walt Kelly at a social gathering. Talking with Kelly about the Daniel Bell case, Dillon resolved to turn the story into a play. Playwrights John Leicht and Kermit Frazier soon began "wading through" the eighteen boxes of documents accumulated by the Bell family's attorneys. Interviewed later, Frazier, Leicht, and Dillon all emphasized the value of Sylvia's help in developing the play, as well as the pleasure of working with her. Dillon recounted that he at first envisioned a story limited to the killing, the cover-up, and the courtroom drama. As he and the writers got to know Sylvia, however, her "powerful presence" transformed the play. The focus widened, setting the case in a larger picture of African American family life and the struggle of migrants in the urban North. The father took on more importance. Sylvia became the storyteller. Frazier recalled that Sylvia's consulting role emerged from the need for a "personal connection" to bring alive the story told by legal documents, but that her influence then expanded because of her "extraordinary" personality, as well as the importance of the larger historical tale she wanted to tell. Leicht remembered feeling proud when Sylvia referred to him and Kermit as "my writers." As the play progressed toward staging, Sylvia also worked with the actors: Tamu Gray who played Sylvia, Larry Grant Malvern in the role of Daniel Bell, Lex Monson as Dock Bell.

Milwaukee responded to the project with a display of mixed feelings. Some negative pressures intruded on the creative process. Kermit Frazier recalled tensions at Sylvia's home with Bell brothers who wished to forget the whole painful experience—and questioned the theater company's motivation. John Leicht remembered Louis Krause's attempts to interfere. Before the play opened, Krause announced to the press that he had retained an attorney and would sue if presented unfavorably. In the end, all involved in creating *An American Journey* could draw satisfaction from the effort. A two-week workshop version ran successfully in April 1986. In January and February of 1987, during the play's five-week regular run, the people of Milwaukee made this one of the best attended productions in the company's history. A *Milwaukee Journal* article reported that Sylvia, who said she was "cried out" the night the play opened, may have had "the only pair of dry eyes in the house."[7] John Dillon remembered interactive sessions after performances, where white audience members told the company that they had come expecting the play to make them feel "under attack" or somehow guilty. Instead, they felt, "This is your story, too."[8]

❧ When we got that settlement from the city, peoples thought we really had money. Ooooo, like we was all millionaires or something. But after the lawyers got they part of it, wadn't that much left—when you divide by twelve. 'Cause there were twelve of us, you know. And Milwaukee made us pay for welfare they said they paid out to the family. I think we each of us ended up with about eighty thousand dollars. Something like that. Didn't last anybody very long. But to me, the money wasn't what the case was about. It was about justice, about that verdict. And we did get that.

Me, I went back South and tried to turn it all around. I remodeled the house, Papa's house. I built an addition onto it, with a glass sliding door on one side and one of those pretty wooden doors with the oval glass on the other side. I boxed in the old porch with screens. Oh, I fixed the old place up real nice.

I used to stay down there in the wintertime—in the eighties. Me and my nephew—he was from up here, born 'n raised in Wisconsin—we would go into those swamps and woods. We didn't even have a pistol. But we had a darn good stick. A lotta snakes probably was up in the trees, watchin' us. I mean big rattlesnakes. I would just look at 'em. I didn't try to attack 'em. They wadn't gonna attack me. We saw the alligators, too. My nephew didn't care and I didn't either. Because I wanted to know what was in there. And he wanted to get this wood you can find in there, 'cause he love to carve. It's a certain kinda tree that comes up. It don't make a tree, just a stump. If you go through the woods, you'll see all these little stumps. We collected 'em and he would carve all kinda designs in 'em. My nephew the artist. I spent a great deal of time with him, even bought him a good chain saw. This is in the eighties now, when I would go back home.

It was during those years that they put on the play. I gotta backtrack and tell you about that. After the case ended in '84, Kelly met John Dillon somewhere. And John Dillon said, "I would like to make a play of this." He's the director of the Repertory Theater. Now, John Dillon wasn't a writer. So he said to Kelly, "I have just the guy, John Leicht." Then, it was . . . you had to have a black person, too. So John says, "Well, I know a black guy in New York who is a writer." Sure enough, they contact him, Kermit Frazier. And he came out.

They asked me what I thought. So I would go, whenever they were makin' this play up. We all would meet at the theater downtown. Me and all the people they picked—John found Tammy to play me and, oh, just a group of guys—to play my brothers, my dad. I would sit in and talk to them if they needed me. I would use my words that I had to use. I would tell 'em about my family—about how my dad loved us and about my brothers, how hard they had it livin' in the South. That was hard. But we had lived down South all those years and never had a death. Then this young boy come up here to make a living and they kills him just like that. My mother had passed away with a stroke. I could get over that. But Dan, I couldn't. I knew the death was wrong.

When John Dillon heard about this, he knew it was wrong, too. He wanted to show that Milwaukee wasn't the place it's supposed to be for black people. He was even scorned about it. Like, "What do you think you're tryin' to do?" But John was determined to have that play. It was a good play, a successful play. But it wasn't easy for those guys. I don't know how Milwaukee felt about it. Some of the peoples they thought it was good and some didn't because good old Milwaukee couldn't do anything wrong.

The play meant a lot to me. I was there every night. It was a full house. Sometimes I sit on the floor for other peoples, my family, to see the play. Not my brothers. I don't think I had a single brother there. I was even asked, "Where are your brothers?" I would kinda take up for my brothers. I wouldn't say they didn't wanta be here. They definitely didn't wanta be there. They had told me in the beginning. But I didn't want to explain that, didn't want the world to know that my brothers was against it. My nieces and nephews, they came. My niece Judy told the guy who played my dad, "I'm so glad you played my grandfather. I never knew him." She thought that was really great to meet her grandfather that way. My son enjoyed it, too. Did you see the picture of me and him? He did come home for that, home to Wisconsin. They did that play in Philadelphia, too. I was there. That's when I saw that bell, the Liberty Bell.

I was still going down South at the time. Kinda had two homes. But then my family let somebody set fire to my daddy's house. Or it caught afire. I just gave up then. I said, "This is enough of this." Didn't go down there for ten years.

I just went back to stayin' all year long at my place in Waterloo. I had stop livin' in that little house we built though. See, down there the water would come up from the river. I got flooded out livin' in that house a couple time. Later on in life, I moved up on the hill. I bought a mobile home, then enlarged the whole thing and made pretty nice place out of it. It'll do. I'm survivin' in it.

Right now, I'm kinda teed off that I'm not in school. I really wanta learn about computers. Everybody should know how to use a computer now. Because if you don't know how to use a computer, you are lost. If you don't know, baby, you got to pass it up. You gotta take *anything*, or accept *anything*. But the last time I was in school, I was studyin' so hard my blood pressure shot up and I wound up in the hospital. Ever since then I been kinda skeptical. Not about education now. A lotta black peoples tell me, "Well, education ain't everything." But to me, baby, education is *it*. In them days, these days . . . Because education gets so strong, so strong until it takes over the *world*. I'll maybe go back to school. But I'm kinda hesitive about it—at my age.

My doctor, he say, "Syl, you gettin' older. You gonna hafta cut back some." I still work very, very hard. But I enjoy it. Especially sellin' at the market. The market I go to now in Milwaukee is on Fond du Lac Avenue.

I meet a lotta peoples there. Saturday, I had some sweet potatoes there. And this little white kid came up. He said, "Oh, sweet potatoes." I say, "What do you know about sweet potatoes?" He say, "Oooo, I like 'em." Then me 'n him start talkin', you know. He was so friendly and so sweet. I says, "What school do you go to?" And he says, "That school right there." Garfield or something, right there in the ghetto. I looked at his dad. I say, "Wow, you must be an attorney," I say, "'cause all the attorney kids go to that school." The mom say, "Yeah, I am, too." They were nice young people. Knew all my attorneys.

I see lotta my Milwaukee peoples at the market. A couple of weeks ago, Joyce—O.C.'s third wife—comes up. The week before, I heard that O.C.'s second wife, Bernice, passed away. Me and Bernice were never that close. But when I saw Joyce, I said, "Oooo, Joyce, I'm so glad!" I grabbed her and I hugged her. I says, "Girl, I gotta talk to you." She wanted the biggest watermelon I had and couldn't carry it. Then this guy standin' there says, "I'll carry it for you." I follow her 'n him to her car. We sittin' on the front seat talkin', when a man over there says, "That's O.C.'s first wife and second wife . . ." I say, "Not second, now. This one is the third." We sittin' up there laughin', me 'n Joyce. They say, "You sure do get along well together." I say, "We always did."

You know, I love peoples, white peoples *and* black peoples. I love both of 'em—when they are people. Now when they are not peoples, I don't like either one of them.

I do have nice peoples out where I live in Waterloo. I really do. We did have more problems with this black/white stuff, when Ruth's kids was gettin' married. She would come tell me, "Oh, so and so's mama, they don't care too much for blacks." The family they were marryin' into. The words musta been spoken or she wouldna said it to me. So I didn't go to one wedding. I went to the next one, because I didn't hear that stuff. Then another one's gonna get married. And Ruth says to me, "Well, I don't know. That family, they don't sound like they too much with blacks." So I didn't go.

When Ruth's last child, Greg, got married, I went. He had his weddin' in a nice country place, great big old ballroom, good disc jockey 'n everything. That was just a family reunion. The guy talkin' about what happen to him with blacks in the service was there. But he found out that black peoples is not like he thought. He found that out through me, because he start puttin' a lotta time in with me. I told Ruth, I say, "My God, he is different!" She say, "Yeah, he's different." I say, "Well, he should be. You ain't supposed to hang that kinda stuff over your head all your life!" So he's at this reception, too. It was dancin' together, partyin' together. I was the only black there. But it didn't mean shit. The girl's mother, I met her. It was a-dancin' and a good time. The father. It was a-dancin'. They were Madison folks. A-dancin' and a good time. Oh, they played this song that night that was so touchin'. It wadn't "I Could've Danced All Night." Nothing like that. But I could've danced all night. I could've. Oh God, I had a good time.

The kids was all over me. Kids like me. Children. Well, a lotta peoples like me. But the kids all like me. See, the girl didn't have a big reception when she got married, 'cause she were pregnant. So they waited 'til after they had the babies, twin boys, Austin and Houston. Little thing come up there last week and he showed me his finger. He had mashed his finger in the car door. When I saw the finger, I said, "Ha! It got caught in the car door." He just looked at me as if, "How do you know?" That's my great-grandchildren. My white great-grandchildren, I call 'em. At the weddin', I played with 'em 'n held 'em. I was home.

My brother Eddie, he live out there by me on his little piece of land. He's in his eighties. Speedy is still in Milwaukee. I was at his fiftieth weddin' anniversary in 1998. Roosevelt, he lives in Kentucky. No contact with the family whatsoever. Jimmy's still in the institution, but Ernest died in there a couple years ago. Eight of my brothers are gone now. Joe went this year. He were livin' in Mississippi, had a bad heart. My oldest brother, Henry, died in January '98. Alfonso, the baby, he passed that year, too. My brother Pat, after he retired, he moved back South awhile, then came back up here. He passed in November '97. Dolphus, he died way back in the eighties, alcoholic. I'll never forget the last time I saw him. He was in the hospital and I went to see him with my little grandchild, Coco. So Coco, she's tryin' to get Dolphus eat his ice cream. He had his food there, but just wouldn't eat. And I'm talkin' to him about what he's gonna do when he gets outa there, tellin' him we gotta make arrangements for when he gets out. He says, "Don't worry, Sis, the arrangements have been made." I'm still worryin' about this when we leave. An hour later, he was gone. Like he knew or something. "Don't worry, Sis. The arrangements have been made." That was Dolphus. Walter, he passed away, alcoholic. I done forgot the year. And Dan.

Me, I'm still fightin'. Sometimes I feel like it was better to be dead than to try to fight with some of these peoples. That's kinda tough to say. But it's the true. I keep on fightin' though.

There's this one guy, the Waterloo drunk. One night—not too long ago—he was in the Quik-Trip where I was workin' when this policeman was in there. It was a nice policeman, too. I knew him real well. Later, he even invited me to his weddin'. So this guy said to the policeman, he says, "Oh, I know Sylvia from years 'n years ago. Me 'n her brother Dolfuss we used to work together." He say, "I used to hafta take Dolfuss back to the jailhouse." This guy, he was tellin' the cop, "I had to go over there to the jailhouse and pick Dolfuss up." My brother had passed away at the time, too.

I am in my sixties now and I felt like speakin' my piece. I said, "Now you quit talkin' about my brother. 'Cause you standin' there drunk as a skunk, right now.

Your car is sittin' out there. And I can smell you all the way over here." The cop is standin' there. I say, "My poor brother didn't know how to read or write. That's why he was in jail. He would've had a driver's license if he could," I says, "Me myself, I have *never* been in your dumb jails. How many times have you been in jail?" I'm really gettin' goin'. I say, "You criticizin' poor black peoples for not bein' able to read or write." He says, "Sylvia, I didn't mean it that way." I said, "Well, quit talkin' about Dolfuss 'n talk about yourself. 'Cause you are more an alcoholic than my poor brother. Or just as bad as my brother. You runnin' around here drunk up 'n down this road. But nobody do anything about it, 'cause you're white."

That was the true, too. 'Cause if a black man were doin' that . . . Honey, I was goin' up to the Dells—this is lately—and a police pull me to the side. He told me my November wasn't showin', you know, on my license plate. I say, "Is that all?" Of course, I realize it's his job. But all the other peoples there, all them cars speedin' up that road. "Good God Almighty, man. You missed the boat. It was a lotta peoples there that you coulda pulled over and really got something on 'em." And then I got stopped that day on my way to meet you at the library. You there wondering what happened to me, me talkin' to this police who said I was speedin'. After he checked my record—I have no record—he let me go. But we do have it shitty. The black person. I know I said it's a different world. And it is—in some ways. But in other ways . . .

I was readin' an article how the white man say, "You still a nigger. You still, I still call ya a nigger." And this is up-to-date book that I was readin'. I say, "My God! That's not fair." That "n" word, to still be . . . It's a mean world.

I think about those boys, my poor brothers and how they suffered. Not only my brothers. Girl, the world. The whole world. Don't get this book wrong. When I get to talkin' about how hard it was for my brothers, I mean all my black peoples, as a nation. This was hard for all of us. Please put it that way. You understand what I'm sayin'. All them poor peoples is sufferin'—just like my poor brothers had to suffer. Went to jail unnecessary. Was kicked off a job unnecessary. With them boys, it was then. With all my black peoples, it was then. But it's now, too. That is my point.

My son told me—this is now—he told me his ex-wife is not workin' anymore. I say, "What?" He says, "She showed a white girl"—and Douglas don't make no impression of peoples bein' white or black. He doesn't do that. But this hurted him. He says, "She showed a white girl how to do the computer." She taught this girl, 'cause her white boss told her, "Now you show this girl how to do this job like you doin' it." Then they laid her off and give the white girl the job. And this is in California! I says, "Douglas, did you tell her she could protest this or go to the labor law or go to somebody?"

247

This is now. Now we talkin' 2000. The year 2000 and you got this voting mess. That was just really . . . It was black peoples, you know, black peoples they kept from votin'. Jewish, too. But mostly black. They kept those black peoples from voting just like they used to do down there. And not just in Florida. Everywhere. Girl, it's as if . . . What upset me about this voting thing is that Martin Luther King, he wanted us to vote so bad. That man really wanted us to vote. He went through so much to get us to vote. So you vote and this is what they do. They don't count it. You black, *your* vote doesn't count. It's depressin'.

The poor children today, they worse off than when I came along. They in them ghettos. The mothers don't know anything, never did know anything. Now they bein' tossed around with this welfare mess. That's another killin'. Where are them poor peoples gonna go? These peoples need help. I see 'em down there where I sell my vegetables. Them children are hurtin'.

I have a nephew and he is depress. This is the one who's an artist. He can draw anything and carve wood. I wish I could show you a piece that he carved right now. I showed a girl. And she say, "Sylvia, that's the stick that Moses touched the water." But he still depress. He is so out of it. All he want is a bottle to drink. He is so down. That child has so much up here. Jody, I gonna bring you that wood to show you. About a black person. How *deep* it goes with those kids. Black peoples are so hurt until these children today is *still hurt*. It's a deep hurt. It's sad. I cry all the time about that. About how my peoples is so hurt. I don't know how I've made it myself.

Last night, my father came to me and touch me. They were showin' that the tornado was comin' right through Dodge County, the TV tellin' me the storm is comin'. They say Jefferson and all those places. Well, I'm right there in that area. And I know they do come through. I shut the TV off and I start readin'. I'm sittin' there into the book, the Biblical part. And my lights just went out. Said, "Well it's time for me to quit." Then my little dog comes over to me, 'cause he saw I was upset. He were just shakin', tremblin'. I say, "Buster, it is a storm out there. It's the tornado. We gonna hafta take for the basement, if it comes through here." I went to the back window and I looked out. It's dark and I can't see. I can see a tornado in the daytime. But I can't see it at night. I was afraid to open the door, because that wind was powerful. Out in the country, you don't know. All I could think about was how hard my father *prayed* when those storms would hit in Louisiana and he got us sittin' in the middle of the floor. I just thought about my father and I sent up *my* prayer. After that I went to bed. I went to sleep.

Notes

Introduction

1. *Milwaukee Sentinel*, September 7, 1979.

2. In addition to the *Milwaukee Journal* and *Milwaukee Sentinel*, sources for the case include interviews with Bell family attorneys Walter Kelly (August 1999) and Curry First (June 2001); Kelly's presentation to the Civil Rights Section of the Wisconsin Bar Association Convention, June 2000; records for: *Dock Bell v. Thomas Grady and the City of Milwaukee*, 1960 (Milw. Co. Case No. 286 538); *State of Wisconsin v. Thomas F. Grady* (Milw. Co. Case No. 79 CF 6087); and records of the Seventh Circuit Court of Appeals in Chicago for *Patrick Bell, Sr. et al. v. City of Milwaukee, et al.*, 1979, Docket No. 79-C-927.

3. *Milwaukee Sentinel*, August 30, 1979.

4. On May 15, 1980, all of Daniel's siblings except Jimmy gathered around a table at the city attorney's office to take questions from an attorney opposing their lawsuit. The whole group heard each deposition. *Patrick Bell, Sr. et al. v. City of Milwaukee, et al.*, 1979, Docket No. 79-C-927.

5. *Milwaukee Journal*, December 14, 1982.

6. Deposition of Lawrence Bell in, *Patrick Bell, Sr. et al. v. City of Milwaukee, et al.*, 1979.

7. *Milwaukee Sentinel*, August 30, 1979.

8. Louisiana sources include Gwendolyn Midlo Hall, *African Americans in Colonial Louisiana: The Development of Afro-Creole Culture in the 18th Century* (1992); Roderick A. McDonald, *The Economy and Material Culture of Slaves: Goods and Chattels on the*

Sugar Plantations of Jamaica and Louisiana (1993); and Bennet H. Wall, *Louisiana: A History* (1984).

9. Milwaukee sources include Joe William Trotter Jr., *Black Milwaukee: The Making of an Industrial Proletariat, 1915–1945* (1984); John Gurda, *The Making of Milwaukee* (1999); Patrick D. Jones, *The Selma of the North: Civil Rights Insurgency in Milwaukee* (2009).

10. The rumor campaign came to national attention in *Time*, April 2, 1956 (23). See related materials in the Frank Zeidler papers (Boxes 47 and 48), Milwaukee Public Library.

11. Milwaukee Commission on Community Relations, "The Negro in Milwaukee: Progress Report and Portent," (1963), cited in William F. Thompson, *Continuity and Change, 1940–1965*, vol. 6 of *The History of Wisconsin* (1988), 377.

12. Originally entitled "Harlem," the poem, read by Hughes himself, was interwoven with jazz in the audio recording *Montage of a Dream Deferred* (1951).

13. A historiographical essay published in 2000 characterized work on the civil rights era as not yet truly scholarly because "historians have tended to share a sympathetic attitude towards the quest for civil rights." Charles W. Eagles, "Towards New Histories of the Civil Rights Era," *Journal of Southern History* 64, 4 (November 2000): 816. Many historians would disagree with this notion of the scholarly.

14. See, for example, Gwendolyn Etter-Lewis, *My Soul Is My Own* (1993), 139. Taking the opposite view, Paul Thompson asserts that habits of "social conformity" can distort interviews between individuals too much alike. Thompson, *The Voice of the Past: Oral History*, 3d ed. (2000, orig. 1978), 140.

15. Thompson, *The Voice of the Past*, chap. 4, 118–72.

16. Discussing her grandmother's memoir, *Lemon Swamp and Other Places* (1983), Karen Fields observes that memory does not reliably fail. Fields, "What One Cannot Remember Mistakenly," in *History and Memory in African-American Culture*, ed. Geneviève Fabre and Robert O'Meally (1994), 150–63.

17. David Thelan, "Memory and American History," *Journal of American History* 75, 4 (March 1989): 1120, 1123.

18. Geneviève Fabre and Robert O'Meally discuss this turn to understanding that "history is not so much a fixed, objective rendering of 'the facts' as it is a constant rethinking and reworking in a world of chance and change." Fabre and O'Meally, *History and Memory*, 3.

19. This is a central theme in Fabre and O'Meally, *History and Memory*. See also Robin Blackburn, *The Making of New World Slavery: From the Baroque to the Modern* (1997); and Paul Gilroy, *The Black Atlantic: Modernity and Double Consciousness* (1993).

20. During slavery, abolitionists penned stories told by escaped slaves. Another large set of narratives emerged when a New Deal writers' program paid local people—almost all whites—to interview elderly former slaves in the 1930s and '40s South.

21. Darlene Clark Hine, "Rape and the Inner Lives of Black Women: Thoughts on the Culture of Dissemblance," in *Hine Sight: Black Women and the Reconstruction of American History* (1994), 37–47.

22. A central idea in The Personal Narratives Group, *Interpreting Women's Lives: Feminist Theory and Personal Narratives* (1989), 13–14, 201–3.

Chapter 1. I Thought I Was a Nigger

1. A turning point came with Kenneth M. Stampp, *The Peculiar Institution: Slavery in the Antebellum South* (1956). For a selection of slave narratives, see George Rawick, *From Sundown to Sunup: The Making of the Black Community* (1972).

2. Richard Price, *Maroon Societies: Rebel Slave Communities in the Americas* (1996, orig. 1979); Herbert G. Gutman, *The Black Family in Slavery and Freedom, 1750–1925* (1976); Janet Duitsman Cornelius, *When I Can Read My Title Clear: Literacy, Slavery and Religion in the Antebellum South* (1991); Roderick A. McDonald, *The Economy and Material Culture of Slaves: Goods and Chattels on the Sugar Plantations of Jamaica and Louisiana* (1993).

3. For a discussion of this problem, see Paul A. David et al., *Reckoning with Slavery: A Critical Study in the Quantitative History of American Negro Slavery* (1976).

4. Frank M. Snowden Jr., *Before Color Prejudice: The Ancient View of Blacks* (1983).

5. David Brion Davis, *The Problem of Slavery in the Age of Revolution, 1770–1823* (1975).

6. James A. Rawley, *The Transatlantic Slave Trade: A History* (1981), 212.

7. Michel Foucault turned historians' attention to this shift with works such as *Discipline and Punish: The Birth of the Prison*, trans. Alan Sheridan (1976). For the role played by racism, see Robin Blackburn, *The Making of New World Slavery: From the Baroque to the Modern* (1997); Paul Gilroy, *The Black Atlantic: Modernity and Double Consciousness* (1993).

8. See George M. Frederickson, *The Black Image in the White Mind: The Debate on Afro-American Characteristics and Destiny, 1817–1914* (1971).

9. Allen W. Trelease, *White Terror: The Ku Klux Klan Conspiracy and Southern Reconstruction* (1971); Eric Foner, *A Short History of Reconstruction* (1990); and Dorothy Sterling, ed., *The Trouble They Seen: Black People Tell the Story of Reconstruction* (1976).

10. David S. Cecelski and Timothy B. Tyson, eds., *Democracy Betrayed: The Wilmington Race Riot and Its Legacy* (1998). William Cohen argues that laws limiting mobility laid the groundwork for segregation in *At Freedom's Edge: Black Mobility and the Southern White Quest for Racial Control, 1861–1915* (1991).

11. C. Vann Woodward reproduces an 1898 Charleston newspaper editorial ridiculing segregation in *Strange Career of Jim Crow* (1955), 67–68.

Chapter 2. This Five Acres of Land

1. For landownership among those who obtained their freedom before Emancipation, see Loren Schweninger, *Black Property Owners in the South: 1790–1915* (1990).

2. Some historians assert that former slaves themselves initiated the sharecropping system, thereby winning a struggle with planters over work arrangements.

Counterarguments cite conditions limiting what freedpeople could assert: anti-black violence, for example, or efforts by federal and local officials to restrict black people's mobility. Other scholars see a negative compromise. Planters wanted fieldworkers in gangs under white overseers. Freedpeople objected to conditions so similar to slavery, preferring sharecropping only if they could not have their own farms. Respectively, Ronald F. Davis, *Good and Faithful Labor: From Slavery to Sharecropping in the Natches District 1860–1890* (1982); Jay R. Mandle, *The Roots of Black Poverty: The Southern Plantation Economy after the Civil War* (1978); William Cohen, *At Freedom's Edge: Black Mobility and the Southern White Quest for Racial Control, 1861–1915* (1991); Edward Royce, *The Origins of Southern Sharecropping* (1993).

3. Paul Mertz, *New Deal Policy and Southern Rural Poverty* (1978), 9–10. See also Charlene Gilbert and Quinn Eli, *Homecoming: The Story of African American Farmers* (2000).

4. For a firsthand account of sharecropping and 1930s union activity, see Nate Shaw's memoir in Theodore Rosengarten, ed., *All God's Dangers: The Life of Nate Shaw* (1974).

5. Peter Daniels, *The Shadow of Slavery: Peonage in the South, 1901–1969* (1972).

6. Evictions increased after 1933 with New Deal crop reduction incentives, but had already displaced three fifths of North Carolina's sharecroppers between 1929 and 1932, according to Mertz, *New Deal Policy*, 15. For photos of evicted families, see Arthur F. Raper, *Sharecroppers All* (1941).

7. Michael D. Bordo, Claudia Golden, and Eugene N. White, *Defining Moment: The Great Depression and the American Economy in the Twentieth Century* (1998), 7–9.

8. David Kyvig mentions estimates that 40 percent of the U.S. population was "underfed," with hunger worst in the South, in *Daily Life in the United States: 1920–1940* (2002), 102.

9. Ronald Edsforth, *The New Deal: America's Response to the Great Depression* (2000), 82.

10. Errol Lincoln Uys, *Riding the Rails: Teenagers on the Move during the Great Depression* (1999), 9–13. Kenneth Kusmer reports 40 percent of transients under the age of twenty-five and 20 percent under nineteen in *Down and Out, on the Road: The Homeless in American History* (2002), 204. The 1.5 million homeless count comes from Kusmer, 194. Edsforth estimates "at least 2 million homeless," in *The New Deal*, 83. See also James N. Gregory, *American Exodus: The Dust Bowl Migration and Okie Culture in California* (1989).

11. For an overview of the debate, see T. H. Watkins, *The Great Depression: America in the 1930s* (1993), 41–47.

12. Cited in Kyvig, *Daily Life*, 179. Most histories of the Depression mention this study commissioned by FDR and conducted by the Brookings Institution.

13. Darlene Clark Hine and Kathleen Thompson, *A Shining Thread of Hope: The History of Black Women in America* (1998), 242–43.

14. Lester Rubin and William S. Swift, "The Negro in the Longshore Industry," in

Negro Employment in the Maritime Industry: A Study of Racial Policy in Shipbuilding, Longshore and Offshore Maritime Industries, ed. Herbert R. Northrup (1974), 34.

15. John C. Howard, "The Negro in the Lumber Industry," in *Negro Employment in Southern Industry: A Study of Racial Policy in Five Industries*, vol. 4, ed. Herbert R. Northrup and Richard L. Rowan (1970), 28–36.

16. William P. Jones, *The Tribe of Black Ulysses: African American Lumber Workers in the Jim Crow South* (2005), 8–52.

17. The lawsuit had demanded that the city admit the wrong and pay $18,000, then the maximum for a wrongful death. After Dock Bell's collapse, the city offered one tenth of that sum and murky legalese that the family did not see as a real admission of wrongdoing. They refused. In the end, their own attorney convinced the judge to proceed without a signature. The check sent to the Bells came back unopened. Dock Bell's Louisiana old-age pension paid the hospital. The case went on record as settled. *Dock Bell vs. Thomas Grady and the City of Milwaukee*, 1960 (Milw. Co. Case No. 286 538).

Chapter 3. I Was a Girl

1. This term from Alice Kessler-Harris, *In Pursuit of Equity: Women, Men, and the Quest for Economic Citizenship in Twentieth Century America* (2001), 5–6.

2. Norma J. Burgess and Eurnestine Brown, eds. *African American Women: An Ecological Perspective* (2000), 4–6; Teresa Amott and Julie Mathaei, "Race, Gender and Work: A Multi-Cultural Economic History of Women in the U.S.," in *We Specialize in the Wholly Impossible: A Reader in Black Women's History*, ed. Darlene Clark Hine, Wilma King, and Linda Reed (1995), 144–45.

3. Jacqueline Jones, *Labor of Love, Labor of Sorrow: Black Women, Work and the Family, from Slavery to the Present* (1986), 241; Dolores Janiewski, "Seeking 'a New Day and a New Way': Black Women and Unions in the Southern Tobacco Industry," in *To Toil the Livelong Day: American Women at Work, 1780–1980*, ed. Carol Groneman and Mary Beth Norton (1987), 163.

4. For gender and work in slavery and after emancipation, see Jones, *Labor of Love*, 11–109.

5. Louise Michelle Neuman, *White Women's Rights: The Racial Origins of Feminism in the United States* (1999); Deborah Gray White, *Too Heavy a Load: Black Women in Defense of Themselves, 1894–1994* (1999); Darlene Clark Hine and Kathleen Thompson, *A Shining Thread of Hope: The History of Black Women in America* (1998), 177–83.

6. Darlene Clark Hine, *Hine Sight: Black Women and the Re-construction of American History* (1994), xxxii, 129–45.

7. E. Franklin Frazier, *The Negro Family in the United States* (1966, orig. 1939), 102.

8. Frazier, *The Negro Family in the United States*, 350.

9. Kathleen F. Slevin and C. Ray Wingrove, *From Stumbling Blocks to Stepping Stones: The Life Experiences of Fifty Professional African American Women* (1998), 26–31.

10. Amott and Mathaei, "Race, Gender and Work," 165–83; Leith Mullings, *On Our Own Terms: Race, Class and Gender in the Lives of African American Women* (1997), 29; Elizabeth Clark-Lewis, "This Work Had an End: African American Domestic Workers in Washington, D.C., 1910–1940," in *To Toil the Livelong Day*, ed. Groneman and Norton, 196–212; Evelyn Nakano Glenn, "From Servitude to Service Work: Historical Continuities in the Racial Division of Paid Reproductive Labor," in *Unequal Sisters: A Multicultural Reader in U.S. Women's History*, 3d ed., ed. Vicki L Ruiz and Ellen Carol DuBois (2000), 436–65.

11. For gendered labor polices and gender inequality, see Kessler-Harris, *In Pursuit of Equity*.

12. Interview with Walter Kelly, August 29, 1999.

Chapter 4. That Daddy of Mines

1. John Dollard, *Class and Caste in a Southern Town* (1937), 359.

2. Wiliam T. Green, *The Negro in Milwaukee: A Historical Survey* (1968), 8. Michael W. Fedo, *They Was Just Niggers: An Account of One of the Nation's Least Known Racial Tragedies* (1979).

3. African American NAACP investigator Walter White, who could pass for white, conducted interviews with lynching participants and published his findings in *Rope and Faggot* (1929).

4. See George C. Wright, "By the Book: The Legal Executions of Kentucky Blacks," in *Under Sentence of Death: Lynching in the South*, ed. William Fitzhugh Brundage (1997), 250–70.

5. Stewart E. Tolnay and E. M. Beck consider ten Southern states (excluding Texas) from 1882 to 1930 and reach a total of 2,805, smaller by 249 than Tuskegee's for those states. They eliminate incidents not corroborated by large newspapers. Tolnay and Beck, *A Festival of Violence: An Analysis of Southern Lynchings, 1882–1930* (1995), 259–62. Walter T. Howard counts 4,743 nationwide from 1882 to 1968 in *Lynchings: Extralegal Violence in Florida during the 1930s* (1995), 18; Robert L. Zangrando numbers 3,525 from 1880 to 1968 in *The NAACP Crusade against Lynching, 1909–1950* (1980), 4–8.

6. See James R. McGovern, *Anatomy of a Lynching: The Killing of Claude Neal* (1982), 104.

7. See James Allen, Hilton Als, John Lewis, and Leon F. Litwack, *Without Sanctuary: Lynching Photography in America* (2000).

8. Allen et al., *Without Sanctuary*, 176. Cameron told his story in *Time of Terror: A Survivor's Story* (1982).

9. For an insightful discussion of police conduct, see Jacquelyn Dowd Hall, *Revolt against Chivalry: Jesse Daniel Ames and the Women's Campaign against Lynching* (1979), 139–41.

10. William F. Brundage recaps scholarly work on Southern sexual/racial anxieties in the introduction to *Under Sentence of Death*. On control of white women, see Glenda

E. Gilmore, *Gender and Jim Crow: Women and the Politics of White Supremacy in North Carolina, 1891–1920* (1996).

11. Dowd Hall, *Revolt against Chivalry*, 154.

12. Dowd Hall, *Revolt against Chivalry*, 144.

13. For a discussion of this, see Tolnay and Beck, *Festival of Violence*, 70–72.

14. Tolnay and Beck, *Festival of Violence*, 86–118.

15. Tolnay and Beck, *Festival of Violence*, 119–65.

16. Dowd Hall, *Revolt against Chivalry*, 144; Zangrando, *NAACP Crusade against Lynching*, 9.

17. Mildred I. Thompson, *Ida B. Wells-Barnett: An Exploratory Study of an American Black Woman* (1990); Patricia A. Schechter, "Unsettled Business: Ida B. Wells against Lynching," in *Under Sentence of Death*, ed. Brundage, 292–317.

18. See Patricia Sullivan, *Lift Every Voice: The NAACP and the Making of the Civil Rights Movement* (2009); Zangrando, *NAACP Crusade against Lynching*; Charles Flint Kellogg, *NAACP: A History of the National Association for the Advancement of Colored People*, vol. 1, *1909–1920* (1967).

19. Alexander Leidholdt, *Standing Before the Shouting Mob* (1997), 31.

20. In 2005, when Congress formally apologized for this, Dr. James Cameron was present.

21. Dowd Hall, *Revolt against Chivalry*, 180.

Chapter 5. Mama

1. Milwaukee Commission on Community Relations, "The Negro in Milwaukee: Progress Report and Portent" (1963), cited in William F. Thompson, *Continuity and Change, 1940–1965*, vol. 6 of *The History of Wisconsin* (1988), 377.

2. Krause's account drawn from records of the Seventh Circuit Court of Appeals in Chicago for *Patrick Bell, Sr. et al. v. City of Milwaukee, et al., 1979*, Docket No. 79-C-927.

3. Herbert G. Gutman, *The Black Family in Slavery and Freedom, 1750–1925* (1976), 531–44.

4. E. Franklin Frazier, *The Negro Family in the United States* (1966, orig. 1939), 367–68.

5. Daniel Patrick Moynihan, *The Negro Family: The Case for National Action* (1965), 29.

6. Thelma Jennings, "'Us Colored Women Had to Go Through a Plenty': Sexual Exploitation of African American Slave Women," *Journal of Women's History* 1, no. 3 (Winter 1990): 45–74.

7. Herbert G. Gutman and Richard Sutch, "The Slave Family," in *Reckoning with Slavery: A Critical Study in the Quantitative History of America Negro Slavery*, ed. Paul A. David et al. (1976), 110.

8. See Gutman, *The Black Family in Slavery and Freedom*, 220–29; see also Wilma King, *Stolen Childhood: Slave Youth in 19th-Century America* (1995).

9. Phyllis M. Belt-Beyan, *The Emergence of African American Literacy Traditions: Family and Community Efforts in the Nineteenth Century* (2004).

10. Herbert Gutman examined records of the slavery period and statistics from a sampling of communities North and South, urban and rural, from 1865 to 1880 and from 1905 to 1925. He concluded that two-parent, father-present families constituted a norm among African Americans for half a century after slavery. Gutman, *The Black Family in Slavery and Freedom*, 464–66. For Louisiana-specific study, see Anne Patton Malone, *Sweet Chariot: Slave Family and Household Structure in 19th-Century Louisiana* (1992).

11. See Linda Gordon, *The Moral Property of Women: A History of Birth Control Politics in America* (2002).

12. Charles S. Johnson, *Growing Up in the Black Belt: Negro Youth in the Rural South* (1967, orig. 1941), 96–98, 72–76.

13. E. Franklin Frazier quotes local usage in the Yazoo-Mississippi area defining the word "patch" as four to six acres. Frazier, *The Negro Family in the United States*, 110.

14. In his study of black families, W. E. B. Du Bois listed the lack of light with no glass windows among the deprivations of country life. Du Bois, *The American Negro Family* (1908), 50–54.

Chapter 6. Jim Crow Schoolin'

1. James D. Anderson, *The Education of Blacks in the South: 1860–1935* (1988), 149–50.

2. Robert A. Margo, *Race and Schooling in the South, 1880 to 1950: An Economic History* (1990), 18, 23–24, 37; 43–44.

3. Henry Allen Bullock, *A History of Negro Education in the South, from 1619 to the Present* (1967), 180.

4. Adam Fairclough, *A Class of Their Own: Black Teachers in the Segregated South* (2007), 135–45.

5. William Rudolph West strongly disputes the widely accepted idea that Washington furthered the cause of black education in the South in *The Education of Booker T. Washington: American Democracy and the Idea of Race Relations* (2006), 12–16.

6. Anderson, *The Education of Blacks in the South*, 141.

7. See Phyllis M. Belt-Beyan, *The Emergence of African American Literacy Traditions: Family and Community Efforts in the Nineteenth Century* (2004), 1–28; and Heather Andrea Williams, *Self Taught: African American Education in Slavery and Freedom* (2005), 1–6.

8. Williams, *Self Taught*, 56. See also Belt-Beyan, *The Emergence of African American Literacy Traditions*, 23, 103–7.

9. Belt-Beyan, *The Emergence of African American Literacy Traditions*, 101; 107–9; 16, 41–90.

10. Thomas L. Webber, *Deep Like Rivers: Education in the Slave Quarters Community, 1831–1865* (1978), 131; Janet Duitsman Cornelius, *When I Can Read My Title Clear: Literacy, Slavery, and Religion in the Antebellum South* (1991), 6.

11. Williams, *Self-Taught*, 174–200.

12. Anderson, *The Education of Blacks in the South*, 152–76, 183–85, respectively.

13. For conditions in 1930s rural black schools, see Fairclough, *A Class of Their Own*, 297–302.

14. Margo, *Race and Schooling in the South*, 24–28.

15. Fairclough, *A Class of Their Own*, 344–53; 407.

16. For Milwaukee's battle over this issue, see Jack Dougherty, *More Than One Struggle: The Evolution of Black School Reform in Milwaukee* (2004); and Patrick Jones, *The Selma of the North: Civil Rights Insurgency in Milwaukee* (2009).

17. For Black Milwaukee's move away from integration, see Dougherty, *More than One Struggle*.

18. Peter Irons, *Jim Crow's Children: The Broken Promise of the Brown Decision* (2002), 289–92. See also Jonathan Kozol, *Savage Inequalities: Children in America's Schools* (1991), 236–37.

19. Thomas J. Sugrue, *Sweet Land of Liberty: The Forgotten Struggle for Civil Rights in the North* (2008), xix.

20. Irons, *Jim Crow's Children*, 6, 16–21.

21. Dougherty, *More than One Struggle*, 36–37; Sugrue, *Sweet Land of Liberty*, 183–88. Relatively integrated in the 1910s, Chicago's public school system entered the 1940s fully segregated and with black schools less well funded. Michael Homel, *Down from Equality: Black Chicagoans and the Public Schools, 1920–1941* (1984), 28.

22. Judy Jolley Mohraz, *The Separate Problem: Case Studies in Black Education in the North, 1900–1930* (1979), xii, 144–45.

23. For examples, see Vincent P. Franklin, *The Education of Black Philadelphia: The Social and Educational History of a Minority Community, 1900–1950* (1979), 137.

24. Dougherty, *More than One Struggle*, 14–32.

25. Sugrue, *Sweet Land of Liberty*, 163–81.

26. State statistics cited in Harry S. Ashmore, *The Negro and the Schools* (1954), 153.

Chapter 7. Galilee

1. John Giggie, *After Redemption: Jim Crow and the Transformation of African American Religion in the Delta, 1875–1915* (2008).

2. W. E. B. Du Bois, *The Negro Church*, with an introduction by Alton B. Pollard III (2011, Du Bois orig. 1903), vi. Du Bois also acknowledged an African/American "nexus," albeit "broken and perverted," in his book about family life, *The American Negro Family* (1969, orig. 1908), 9.

3. Curtis J. Evans vividly evokes the force of these now hard-to-appreciate ideas in *The Burden of Black Religion* (2008). This discussion drawn largely from Evans, 141–76; 179–84, and 223–63.

4. James H. Cone, *Black Theology and Black Power* (1969), 34–36, 112.

5. James H. Cone, *My Soul Looks Back* (1982), 54–55.

6. Thomas N. Ingersol, "Releese Us Out of This Cruell Bondegg: An Appeal from Virginia in 1723," *William and Mary Quarterly*, 3d series, 51, no. 4 (Oct. 1994): 776–82.

7. Frederick Douglass, *The Life and Times of Frederick Douglass* (1962), 159–60.

8. More examples in James H. Cone, *The Spirituals and the Blues: An Interpretation* (1972), 90.

9. Albert J. Raboteau, *Slave Religion: The Invisible Institution in the Antebellum South* (2004, orig. 1978), 311.

10. Raboteau, *Slave Religion*, 58. Raboteau recalls the enthusiasm of the historical moment that surrounded the first edition in an afterword to the 2004 edition.

11. Cone, *Black Theology*, 112.

12. Gayraud S. Wilmore, who trained pastors for civil rights actions, argued that, despite accommodationist periods, an "exceedingly elastic" thread of resistance ran through the entire history of African-American religion. Wilmore, *Black Religion and Black Radicalism* (1972), vii.

13. See Evelyn Brooks Higginbotham, *Righteous Discontent: The Women's Movement in the Black Baptist Church, 1880–1920* (1993). John Giggie emphasizes the poor and illiterate in *After Redemption*.

14. David D. Hall, ed. *Lived Religion in America: Towards a History of Practice* (1997), vii.

15. Giggie, *After Redemption*, 5–6; 27–58.

16. Marla F. Frederick, *Between Sundays: Black Women and Everyday Struggles of Faith* (2003), 7.

17. Womanist theology arose in response to male-centered Black Power theologies, sexist church structures, and racial insensitivities in white women's feminism. Monica A. Coleman offers an overview of major womanist theologians in *Making a Way Out of No Way: A Womanist Theology* (2008), 6–36.

18. Coleman, *Making a Way Out of No Way*, 27–31, 101–23, and 33, respectively.

Chapter 8. Teenagers

1. British teenage culture developed differently, since 70 percent there left school at the age of fourteen. See David Fowler, *The First Teenagers: The Lifestyle of Young Wage-Earners in Interwar Britain* (1995).

2. Grace Palladino, *Teenagers: An American History* (1996), 5–7.

3. This description of the mainstream teenager phenomenon drawn largely from Palladino, *Teenagers*, Parts 1 and 2. See also Kelly Schrum, *Some Wore Bobby Sox: The Emergence of Teen Girls' Culture, 1920–1945* (2004).

4. For "German Swing Kids and French Zazous," see Jon Savage, *Teenage: A Prehistory of Youth Culture, 1875–1945* (2008), 375–90. For U.S. high school enrollments, see Palladino, *Teenagers*, 66.

5. Under the direction of Charles S. Johnson, researchers from Fisk University administered questionnaires to 2,000 adolescents and interviewed 916 families. Johnson, *Growing Up in the Black Belt: Negro Youth in the Rural South* (1967, orig. 1941). E. Franklin Frazier directed a Howard University study of Washington, DC, and Louisville, KY, where interviewers spoke with 268 teens. Frazier, *Negro Youth at the Crossways: Their Personality Development in the Middle States* (1969, orig. 1940). Old methodologies make these studies somewhat problematic as sources of data—and interesting as primary sources.

6. For an overview of the significance of the ring shout, see Samuel A. Floyd Jr., *The Power of Black Music: Interpreting Its History from Africa to the United States* (1995), 6–7.

7. This oft-quoted 1819 letter by tourist Arthur Singleton cited here from Dena J. Epstein, *Sinful Tunes and Spirituals: Black Folk Music to the Civil War* (1977), 96.

8. The many sources for these Africanisms range from book-length explorations to Samuel Floyd's single page in *The Power of Black Music*, 6; and Portia K. Maultsby, "Africanisms in African American Music," in *Africanisms in American Culture*, ed. Joseph E. Holloway, 2d ed. (2005), 185–210.

9. See Daphne Duval Harrison, *Black Pearls: Blues Queens of the 1920s* (1988).

10. David Suisman, *Selling Sounds: The Commercial Revolution in American Music* (2009), 204–39.

11. These numbers from Jean Van Delinder, "Harlem Renaissance in Oklahoma," in *The Harlem Renaissance in the American West: The New Negro's Western Experience*, ed. Bruce A. Glasrud and Cary D. Wintz (2012), 118.

12. See Kathleen Blee, *Women of the Klan: Racism and Gender in the 1920s* (1991).

13. For the beginnings of the Nation of Islam, see Jeffrey O. G. Ogbar, *Black Power: Radical Politics and African American Identity* (2004), 12–18.

14. Johnson, *Growing Up in the Black Belt*, 15.

15. Floyd, *The Power of Black Music*, 106–10 and 131–35.

16. From Locke's "The New Negro" cited in Cary D. Wintz, *Black Culture and the Harlem Renaissance* (1996), 30.

17. Hughes's "The Negro Artist and the Racial Mountain," cited in Wintz, *Black Culture and the Harlem Renaissance*, 153.

18. See Glasrud and Wintz, *The Harlem Renaissance in the American West*.

19. Davarian L. Baldwin, *Chicago's New Negroes: Modernity, the Great Migration and Black Urban Life* (2007), 5–6. The rest of this description drawn from Baldwin.

Chapter 9. My Roosevelt

1. Many histories tell this story largely drawn here from Patricia Sullivan, *Days of Hope: Race and Democracy in the New Deal Era* (1996), 98–101.

2. This early work includes: Bernard Sternsher, ed., *The Negro in Depression and War: Prelude to Revolution, 1930–1945* (1969); Raymond Wolters, *Negroes and the*

Great Depression: The Problem of Economic Recovery (1970); Paul E. Mertz, *New Deal Policy and Southern Rural Poverty* (1978); Harvard Sitkoff, *A New Deal for Blacks: The Emergence of Civil Rights as a National Issue* (1978).

3. Alice Kessler-Harris cites statistics for Social Security in 1935 in *In Pursuit of Equity: Women, Men, and the Quest for Economic Citizenship in Twentieth-Century America* (2001), 146.

4. Harold Ickes, Secretary of the Interior, had headed the Chicago NAACP. His assistant, Clark Foreman, was one of a group of liberal white Southern appointees including Will Alexander, Aubrey Williams, Clifford and Virginia Durr.

5. Sullivan, *Days of Hope*, 76. These included then Harvard graduate students William Hastie, later the first black federal judge; Robert Weaver, later Secretary of Housing and Urban Development for President Lyndon Johnson; and Ralph Bunche, later awarded the Nobel Peace Prize for Middle East diplomacy.

6. Glenda Gilmore describes such a friendship arising over lunches between Robert Weaver and Will Alexander in *Defying Dixie: The Radical Roots of Civil Rights, 1919–1950* (2008), 234.

7. Lauren Rebecca Sklaroff, *Black Culture and the New Deal: The Quest for Civil Rights in the Roosevelt Era* (2009), Federal Theater Project, 33–80; photo of *Swing Mikado* audience, 77; Federal Writers' Project, 81–121.

8. Sklaroff, *Black Culture and the New Deal*: Joe Louis, 140–57; *Jubilee*, 159–92; films, 193–222.

9. Andrew E. Kersten, *Race, Jobs, and the War: The FEPC in the Midwest, 1941–46* (2007), 135, 136.

10. Slogan quoted in Sitkoff, *A New Deal*, 314–5. For more on this March on Washington Movement and the executive order, see chapter 13.

11. Charles A. Simmons, *The African American Press: A History of News Coverage during National Crises, 1827–1965* (2006), 87–88.

12. The NOI also urged members not to register for Social Security numbers. Ula Taylor, "Elijah Muhammad's Nation of Islam: Separatism, Regendering, and a Secular Approach to Black Power after Malcom X (1965–1975)," in *Freedom North: Black Freedom Struggles Outside the South, 1940–1980*, ed. Jeanne F. Theoharis and Komozi Woodard (2003), 179. See also Jeffrey O. G. Ogbar, *Black Power: Radical Politics and African American Identity* (2004), 18–19.

13. Jack D. Foner, *Blacks and the Military in American History* (1974), 149, 163–72.

14. The experiment placed black platoons totaling 2,500 men into white divisions of the U.S. Army, where they ate and slept in separate spaces, but fought alongside whites.

Chapter 10. Goin' North

1. See William. P. O'Hare et al., *Blacks on the Move: A Century of Demographic Change* (1982).

2. For an overview of this discussion, see introduction in Joe William Trotter Jr., ed., *The Great Migration in Historical Perspective: New Dimensions of Race, Class, and Gender* (1991).

3. Darlene Clark Hine and Kathleen Thompson, *A Shining Thread of Hope: The History of Black Women in America* (1998), 213–39; and Hine, *Hine Sight: Black Women and the Reconstruction of American History* (1994), 87–107.

4. Peter Gottlieb, *Making Their Own Way: Southern Blacks' Migration to Pittsburgh, 1916–30* (1987).

5. See Kimberly L. Phillips, *Alabama North: African American Migrants, Community, and Working Class Activism in Cleveland, 1915–1945* (1999); Richard W. Thomas, *Life for Us Is What We Make It: Building Black Community in Detroit, 1915–1945* (1992).

6. Carole Marks, *Farewell We're Good and Gone: The Great Black Migration* (1989), 80–99.

7. Malaika Adero, *Up South: Stories, Studies, and Letters of This Century's Black Migration* (1993).

8. E. Marvin Goodwin, *Black Migration in America from 1915 to 1960: An Uneasy Exodus* (1990), 14.

9. Richard Wright, *Later Works: Black Boy (American Hunger) and The Outsider* (1991, orig. 1945), 258.

10. This discussion of the Chicago Defender's role drawn from James R. Grossman, *Land of Hope: Chicago, Black Southerners, and the Great Migration* (1989).

11. Guichard Parris and Lester Brooks, *Blacks in the City: A History of the National Urban League* (1971).

12. Josh Sides, *L.A. City Limits: African American Los Angeles from the Great Depression to the Present* (2003), 43; Robert Self, *American Babylon: Race and the Struggle for Postwar Oakland* (2003), 147; Donna Murch, "A Campus Where Black Power Won: Merritt College and the Hidden History of Oakland's Black Panther Party," in *Neighborhood Rebels: Black Power at the Local Level*, ed. Peniel E. Joseph (2010), 94.

Chapter 11. Let Me Go Home

1. Cited in Andrew E. Kersten, *Race, Jobs, and the War: The FEPC in the Midwest, 1941–1946* (2007), 17. See chapter 13 for more on the FEPC and employment discrimination.

2. Kersten, *Race, Jobs, and the War*, 130.

3. Richard Wright, *Later Works: Black Boy (American Hunger) and The Outsider* (1991, orig. 1945), 253.

4. Roy Hamilton, "Expectations and Realities of a Migrant Group: Black Migration from the South to Milwaukee, 1946–1958" (unpublished MA thesis, University of Wisconsin–Milwaukee, 1981), 56.

5. Kevin E. McHugh. "Black Migration Reversal in the United States," *Geographical Review* 77, no. 2 (1987): 178–79.

6. Minnesota and Nevada completed the top ten. William H. Frey, "The New Great Migration: Black Americans' Return to the South, 1965–2000," *Living Cities Census Series*, Brookings Institution (May 2004), http://www.brookings.edu/reports/2004/05demographics_frey.asp

7. Jesse Carney Smith and Robert L. Johns, *Statistical Record of Black America*, 3d ed. (1994), 575. Wisconsin data from Felicia Thomas-Lynn, "Reversing the Exodus," *Milwaukee Journal Sentinel*, May 16, 1999.

8. Heather Boushey and Robert Cherry, "What Does the Current Expansion Tell Us?," in *Prosperity for All? The Economic Boom and African Americans*, ed. Robert Cherry and William M. Rodgers III (2000), 164.

9. Carol Stack explores reasons for choosing the country through narratives of returnees to rural areas in the Carolinas in *Call to Home: African Americans Reclaim the Rural South* (1996).

Chapter 12. What About My Career?

1. For the effects of discriminatory policing specifically on families, a problem that worsened after the 1950s, see Bruce Western, *Punishment and Inequality in America* (2006), 131–67.

2. Elaine Tyler May, *Homeward Bound: American Families in the Cold War Era* (1988), 11. See also, David Monteyne, *Fallout Shelter: Designing for Civil Defense in the Cold War* (2011); Kenneth D. Rose, *One Nation Underground: The Fallout Shelter and American Culture* (2001).

3. Nixon cited in Lizabeth Cohen, *A Consumer's Republic* (2003), 126; Karal Ann Marling, *As Seen on TV: The Visual Culture of Everyday Life in the 1950s* (1994), 243–83; and May, *Homeward Bound*, 16–20.

4. Stephanie Coontz, *The Way We Never Were: American Families and the Nostalgia Trap* (1992), 39; and *A Strange Stirring: The Feminine Mystique and American Women at the Dawn of the 1960s* (2011).

5. Joanne Meyerowitz, "Sex, Gender, and the Cold War Language of Reform," in *Rethinking Cold War Culture*, ed. Peter J. Kuznick and James Gilbert (2001), 106–23; Jane Sherron De Hart, "Containment at Home: Gender, Sexuality, and National Identity in Cold War America," in *Rethinking Cold War Culture*, ed. Kuznick and Gilbert, 124–55; see also Alison J. Clarke, *Tupperware: The Promise of Plastic in 1950s America* (1999).

6. Alan Petigny, *The Permissive Society: America, 1941–1965* (2009), 188. Petigny offers chapter-length discussions of each example cited here and others as well.

7. Petigny, *The Permissive Society*, 201–16.

8. According to the city's first black deejay, Nat Williams, cited in Margaret McKee and Fred Chisenhall, *Beale Black and Blue: Life and Music on Black America's Main Street* (1981), 95.

9. Guthrie P. Ramsey Jr. grounds his analysis in vivid evocation of musical and

generational continuum in his own Chicago family in *Race Music: Black Cultures from Bebop to Hip-Hop* (2003).

10. Office of Policy Planning and Research, U.S. Department of Labor/ Daniel Patrick Moynihan, *The Negro Family: The Case for National Action* (1965), preface and 5–12.

11. Robert Staples and Leonor Boulin Johnson, *Black Families at the Crossroads: Challenges and Prospects* (1993); Charles V. Willie and Richard J. Reddick, *A New Look at Black Families*, 6th ed. (2010).

12. See, for example, Niara Sudarkasa, "Interpreting the African Heritage in Afro-American Family Organization," in *Black Families*, ed. Harriette Pipes McAdoo (1981), 37–53; and Staples and Boulin Johnson, *Black Families at the Crossroads*, 202–3.

13. Jacqueline Jones, *Labor of Love, Labor of Sorrow: Black Women, Work, and the Family, from Slavery to the Present* (1985), 263–74.

14. Paul H. Geenan, *Milwaukee's Bronzeville 1900–1950* (2006); Ivory Abena Black, *Bronzeville: A Milwaukee Lifestyle* (2005).

15. Although some critics questioned O.C. White's use of federal anti-poverty funds, community leader Reuben Harpole told me that black Milwaukee remembers him as having done a lot of good for the community. Interview with Reuben Harpole, August 1999.

Chapter 13. Get a Job

1. Andrew E. Kersten, *Race, Jobs, and the War: The FEPC in the Midwest, 1941–46* (2007), 10.

2. Harvard Sitkoff, *A New Deal for Blacks: The Emergence of Civil Rights as a National Issue* (1978), 314.

3. The recalcitrant company was A. O. Smith. Kersten, *Race, Jobs, and the War*, 71–72, 141.

4. For an overview of the debate, see Kersten, *Race, Jobs, and the War*, 3–6; and William J. Collins, "Race, Roosevelt, and Wartime Production: Fair Employment in World War II Labor Markets," *American Economic Review* 91, no. 1 (March 2001): 274–75, 278–85.

5. On the role of the FEPC in galvanizing opposition to racial change in the South, see Patricia Sullivan, *Days of Hope: Race and Democracy in the New Deal Era* (1996), 157–58.

6. Robert O. Self, *American Babylon: Race and the Struggle for Postwar Oakland* (2003), 54–55.

7. Kersten, *Race, Jobs, and the War*, 2–3.

8. Robert H. Zieger, *For Jobs and Freedom: Race and Labor in America since 1865* (2007), 123–24.

9. William F. Thompson, *Continuity and Change, 1940–1965*, vol. 6 of *The History of Wisconsin* (1988), 323; Thomas J. Sugrue, *Sweet Land of Liberty: The Forgotten*

Struggle for Civil Rights in the North (2008), 77; Kersten, *Race, Jobs, and the War*, 135; Collins, "Race, Roosevelt, and Wartime," 272.

10. For Milwaukee women's struggle to get FEPC help, see Kersten, *Race, Jobs, and the War*, 72.

11. Clarence Lang, *Grassroots at the Gateway: Class Politics and Black Freedom Struggle in St. Louis, 1936–1975* (2009), 55–56 and 60–61.

12. Zieger, *For Jobs and Freedom*, 149.

13. Kersten, *Race, Jobs, and the War*, 138–39.

14. Paul Burstein, *Discrimination, Jobs, and Politics: The Struggle for Equal Employment Opportunity in the United States since the New Deal* (1998, orig. 1985), 43–47, 56–57.

15. Zieger, *For Jobs and Freedom*, 150, 142.

16. Sugrue, *Sweet Land of Liberty*, 257.

17. Self, *American Babylon*, 171.

18. Thomas J. Sugrue argues in *The Origins of the Urban Crisis: Race and Inequality in Postwar Detroit* (2005, orig. 1996) that the urban crisis of later decades began in the postwar interplay of racial attitudes, local politics, and the logic of capitalism. For more on housing and white flight, see chapter 14.

19. Roy Hamilton, "Expectations and Realities of a Migrant Group: Black Migration from the South to Milwaukee, 1946–1958" (unpublished MA thesis, University of Wisconsin–Milwaukee, 1981), 69.

20. Thompson, *Continuity and Change*, 330.

21. Milwaukee Urban League, *Labor Study of Negro Workers* (1949), 8; Annual Report (1950), 1.

22. Ruth Zubrensky, *Report on Past Discrimination against African Americans in Milwaukee* (1999), 29.

23. Thompson, *Continuity and Change*, 361–65.

24. Patrick D. Jones, *The Selma of the North: Civil Rights Insurgency in Milwaukee* (2009), 243–46.

25. Self, *American Babylon*, 173.

Chapter 14. House on Palmer Street

1. William F. Thompson's account of this event in *Continuity and Change, 1940–1965*, vol. 6 of *The History of Wisconsin* (1988), 334–36, led me to the fascinating newspaper coverage that is the focus here.

2. Christ T. Seraphim, who also opposed Joseph McCarthy in the postwar years, is best known in Milwaukee for his later behavior as an outspoken opponent of open-housing activism and a "law and order" criminal court judge with a reputation for racial bias.

3. The 1895 law forbade discrimination in public accommodations such as hotels, restaurants, places of amusement, and public transportation. It was passed after

Milwaukee African Americans organized and successfully sued an opera house for excluding a man of color. One historian calls the law "watered down," for its minimal penalties. John Buenker, *The Progressive Era, 1893–1914*, vol. 4 of *The History of Wisconsin* (1998), 199.

4. Ruth Zubrensky, *A Report on Past Discrimination against African Americans in Milwaukee, 1835–1999* (1999), 41, 44.

5. "Search for Housing Made as Test in Discrimination," *Milwaukee Journal*, May 25, 1960.

6. Stephen Grant Meyer, *As Long as They Don't Move Next Door: Segregation and Racial Conflict in American Neighborhoods* (2000), 90.

7. William J. Collins and Robert Margo call the "indictment" of FHA policies "somewhat overblown," in "Race and Home Ownership, 1900 to 1990," NBER Working Paper # 7277, National Bureau of Economic Research (August 1999), 23, http://www .nber.org/papers/w7277.

8. Thomas J. Sugrue, *Sweet Land of Liberty: The Forgotten Struggle for Civil Rights in the North* (2008), 203–4.

9. Charles M. Lamb, *Housing Segregation in Suburban America Since 1960: Presidential and Judicial Politics* (2005), 12–17.

10. Cited in Sugrue, *Sweet Land of Liberty*, 203.

11. John Yinger, *An Analysis of Discrimination by Real Estate Brokers* (1975), 29.

12. Yinger, *An Analysis of Discrimination by Real Estate Brokers*, 19–25. For a detailed version of the oft-retold Willie Mays story, see Meyer, *As Long as They Don't Move Next Door*, 30–31.

13. For a book-length chronicle of violence, see Meyer, *As Long as They Don't Move Next Door*.

14. Meyer, *As Long as They Don't Move Next Door*, 212–21.

15. Report of the Wisconsin Committee of the U.S. Commission on Civil Rights (1972) Transcript 6: 68.

Chapter 15. The Killing of Daniel

1. See David Cole, *No Equal Justice: Race and Class in the American Criminal Justice System* (1999); Bruce Western, *Punishment and Inequality in America* (2006); Janet L. Abu-Lughod, *Race, Space, and Riots in Chicago, New York, and Los Angeles* (2007). For views from inside the system, see John L. Burris, *Blue vs. Black* (1999); Ellis Cose, ed., *The Darden Dilemma: Twelve Black Writers on Justice, Race, and Conflicting Loyalties* (1997); Bruce Wright, *Black Justice in a White World* (1996).

2. Charles Ogletree Jr., et al., *Beyond the Rodney King Story: An Investigation of Police Misconduct in Minority Communities*, NAACP and Harvard Law School Criminal Justice Institute Report (1995), 8; Jerome H. Skolnick and James J. Fyfe, *Above the Law: Police and the Excessive Use of Force* (1993), 12.

3. Kenneth Meeks, *Driving While Black* (2000), 21–26.

4. United States Commission on Civil Rights Report, *Justice*, vol. 5 (1961), 13–14.

5. Parker appeared on the TV game show *What's My Line?* in the mid-fifties and reaped public relations benefits from the TV series *Dragnet*, which fictionalized the LAPD. The *Saturday Evening Post* also published a flattering article, "Portrait of a Police Chief." Dean Jennings, *Saturday Evening Post* 232 (May 7, 1960): 87–89. Asked during 1960 Civil Rights Commission hearings if he believed some racial groups more crime-prone, Parker replied with cultural stereotypes about blacks and Hispanics and added that "you can't throw genes out of the question." Hearings Before the U.S. Commission on Civil Rights, Los Angeles, Jan. 25–26, 1960, 331–32. For other racist remarks and Parker's policies against "race mixing," see Mike Davis, *City of Quartz: Excavating the Future in Los Angeles* (2006, orig. 1990), 294–95.

6. Tim Rutten, "Change Has Come to the LAPD, Too," *Los Angeles Times*, January 21, 2009; Glynn B. Martin, "LAPD Chief Parker: A Product of His Time," *Los Angeles Times*, January 28, 2009.

7. Gordon G. Brown, *Law Administration and Negro-White Relations* (1947), cited in Karl E. Johnson, "Police-Black Community Relations in Postwar Philadelphia: Race and Criminalization in Urban Social Spaces, 1945–1960," *Journal of African American History* 89 (2004): 121.

8. Report of the Wisconsin State Committee of the U.S. Commission on Civil Rights (1972), 61.

9. William M. Kephardt, *Racial Factors and Urban Law Enforcement* (1957), 90–110.

10. Kephardt, *Racial Factors and Urban Law Enforcement*, 158.

11. United States Commission on Civil Rights Report, *Justice*, vol. 5 (1961), 18–21, 5.

12. Grady's personnel file showed his supervisors had faulted him for not having enough citations.

13. Grady never admitted this particular utterance of the word "nigger," but did use racial slurs in the tapped phone conversations. Krause's and Vorpagel's accounts and the rest of the information here drawn from records of the Seventh Circuit Court of Appeals in Chicago for *Patrick Bell, Sr. et al. v. City of Milwaukee et al.*, 1979, Docket No. 79-C-927.

14. "Hand-picked" by the sheriff, as provided for in Wisconsin law governing inquests, according to the *Milwaukee Journal*, February 2, 1958.

Chapter 16. Marches, Riots, and Martin Luther King

1. This quote and condensed/paraphrased narrative, as well as most of the Milwaukee civil rights story here, are all drawn from the detailed and dramatic account in Patrick D. Jones, *Selma of the North: Civil Rights Insurgency in Milwaukee* (2009), 2.

2. Bettye K. Eidson, "The Riots and White America," in *Cities Under Siege: An Anatomy of the Ghetto Riots, 1964–1968*, ed. David Boesel and Peter H. Rossi (1971), 389–92.

3. According to their lawyer, Tom Jacobson, who later represented the Bell family. Cited in Jones, *Selma of the North*, 41.

4. For a detailed examination of the school issues see Jack Dougherty, *More Than One Struggle: The Evolution of Black School Reform in Milwaukee* (2004).

5. For a brief description and photo of this event, see Dougherty, *More Than One Struggle*, 120–21.

6. See Chuck Taylor, *Decade of Discontent, 1960–1970* (1981), Videocassette [VHS], 60 min.

7. The Kerner Commission established to study causes and solutions of 1960s ghetto riots frankly blamed "white racism" and its concrete effects on people's lives. Besides objections that that assertion did not distinguish among whites with varying racial attitudes, the report received criticism not so much for its assessment of causes as for proposing solutions that required far more spending than Congress would approve for programs to help the disadvantaged. See *The Kerner Report: The 1968 Report of the National Advisory Commission on Civil Disorders* (1968); for a discussion of the criticism, see Janet L. Abu-Lughod, *Race, Space, and Riots in Chicago, New York, and Los Angeles* (2007), 4–7.

8. A brief account of Milwaukee's movement appears in William F. Thompson, *Continuity and Change, 1940–1965*, vol. 6 of *The History of Wisconsin* (1988), 368–400; the open-housing campaign in Stephen Grant Meyer, *As Long as They Don't Move Next Door: Segregation and Racial Conflict in American Neighborhoods* (2001), 189–96.

9. David J. Garrow, *Bearing the Cross: Martin Luther King, Jr. and the Southern Christian Leadership Conference* (1986); and *The FBI and Martin Luther King, Jr.: From "Solo" to Memphis* (1981); Keith D. Miller, *Voice of Deliverance: The Language of Martin Luther King, Jr.* (1992); August Meier and Elliott Rudwick, *Core: A Study in the Civil Right Movement, 1942–1968* (1973); Doug McAdam, *Freedom Summer* (1990); Clayborne Carson, *In Struggle: SNCC and the Black Awakening of the 1960s* (1981).

10. Thomas J. Sugrue, *Sweet Land of Liberty: The Forgotten Struggle for Civil Rights in the North* (2008); Jeanne Theoharis and Komozi Woodard, *Freedom North: Black Freedom Struggles Outside the South, 1940–1980* (2003); Martha Biondi, *To Stand and Fight: The Struggle for Civil Rights in Postwar New York City* (2006); Robert Self, *American Babylon: Race and the Struggle for Postwar Oakland* (2005).

11. Glenda Gilmore, *Defying Dixie: The Radical Roots of Civil Rights, 1919–1950* (2009); Lynne Olson, *Freedom's Daughters: The Unsung Heroines of the Civil Rights Movement, 1830–1970* (2001); Danielle McGuire, *At the Dark End of the Street: Black Women, Rape and Resistance—A New History of the Civil Rights Movement* (2010); John Dittmer, *Local People: The Struggle for Civil Rights in Mississippi* (1994); Brian Ward, *Radio and the Struggle for Civil Rights in the South* (2006); Sasha Torres, *Black, White, and in Color: Television and Black Civil Rights* (2003); Gene Roberts and Hank Klibanoff, *The Race Beat: The Press, the Civil Rights Movement, and the Awakening of a Nation* (2007); Maurice Berger, *For All the World to See: Visual Culture and the Struggle for Civil Rights* (2010).

12. Timothy Tyson, *Radio Free Dixie: Robert F. Williams and the Roots of Black Power* (1999), 149; Lance E. Hill, *Deacons for Defense: Armed Resistance and the Civil Rights Movement* (2006), 2; Simon Wendt, "'We're Going to Fight Fire with Fire': Black Power in the South," in *Neighborhood Rebels: Black Power at the Local Level*, ed. Peniel E. Joseph (2010), 137.

13. Jones, *Selma of the North*, 234.

Chapter 17. Crawfish River Hill

1. Zachary Cooper, *Black Settlers in Rural Wisconsin* (1974).

2. Benjamin C. Wilson, *The Rural Black Heritage between Chicago and Detroit, 1850–1929: A Photograph Album and Random Thoughts* (1985), 79–80 and 83–89.

3. Stephen A. Vincent, *Southern Seed, Northern Soil: African-American Farm Communities in the Midwest* (1999), 114.

4. Earl Spangler, *The Negro in Minnesota* (1961), 66.

5. U.S. Census statistics from 1940 and 1960, cited in William F. Thompson, *Continuity and Change, 1940–1965*, vol. 6 of *The History of Wisconsin* (1988), 306–7 and 337.

6. Governor's Commission on Human Rights, *Negro Families in Rural Wisconsin* (1959).

7. The following discussion thanks to William F. Thompson's mention of this book in *Continuity and Change*, 391n96.

8. This quote and the description of what happened in Watertown drawn from Lynn Eden, *Crisis in Watertown: The Polarization of a Community* (1972), 134.

9. Eden, *Crisis in Watertown*, 70–71.

10. Peter Braunstein and Michael William Doyle argue against naming this countercultural outburst in any way that suggests a stable, coherent, and unified movement, in their introduction to Braunstein and Doyle, eds., *Imagine Nation: The American Counterculture of the 1960s and '70s* (2002).

11. Thomas Frank examines how advertising expressed, fueled, and used "the enthusiasm of ordinary, suburban Americans for cultural revolution" in *The Conquest of Cool: Business Culture, Counterculture, and the Rise of Hip Consumerism* (1997), 13.

12. Nick Bromell emphasizes rock music, particularly the Beatles and their fans, in the development of counterculture in *Tomorrow Never Knows: Rock and Psychedelics in the 1960s* (2000).

13. Braunstein and Doyle, *Imagine Nation*, 11–13.

Chapter 18. Freer in California

1. Founded in 1961, the Afro-American Association attracted Huey Newton and Bobby Seale of the Black Panther Party, Ron Karenga of US, as well as future U.S. Congress member Ron Dellums.

2. Josh Sides, *L.A. City Limits: African American Los Angeles from the Depression to the Present* (2003), 2.

3. For a relatively recent treatment of this well-documented phenomenon, see Robert Mason, *Richard Nixon and the Quest for a New Majority* (2004).

4. Speech at UC-Berkeley, October 1966. Stokely (Kwame Ture) Carmichael, *Stokely Speaks: From Black Power to Pan-Africanism* (2007), 45.

5. Peniel E. Joseph, ed., *Neighborhood Rebels: Black Power at the Local Level* (2010), 5–12.

6. Robert O. Self, *American Babylon: Race and the Struggle for Postwar Oakland* (2003), 233–42.

7. For the BPP, see Donna Murch, "A Campus Where Black Power Won: Merritt College and the Hidden History of Oakland's Black Panther Party," in *Neighborhood Rebels*, ed. Joseph, 91–105; Robyn Ceanne Spencer, "Inside the Panther Revolution: The Black Freedom Movement and the Black Panther Party in Oakland, California," in *Groundwork: Local Black Freedom Movements in America*, ed. Jeanne Theoharis and Komozi Woodard (2005), 300–317; Judson L. Jeffries, ed., *Comrades: A Local History of the Black Panther Party* (2007); Judson L. Jeffries, ed., *On the Ground: The Black Panther Party in Communities Across America* (2010); and Jeffrey O. G. Ogbar, *Black Power: Radical Politics and African American Identity* (2004), 69–122.

8. Sides, *L.A. City Limits*, 11. See also Lonnie G. Bunch III, "The Greatest State for the Negro: Jefferson Edmonds, Black Propagandist of the California Dream," in *Seeking El Dorado: African Americans in California*, ed. Lawrence B. de Graaf, Kevin Mulroy, and Quintard Taylor (2001), 129–48.

9. James N. Gregory, *American Exodus: The Dust Bowl Migration and Okie Culture in California* (1989), 40.

10. Mike Davis, *City of Quartz: Excavating the Future in Los Angeles* (2006, orig. 1990), 294–95; and Raphael J. Sonenshein, *Politics in Black and White: Race and Power in Los Angeles* (1994), 75–80.

11. See Scot Brown, "The Politics of Culture: The Us Organization and the Quest for Black 'Unity,'" in *Freedom North: Black Freedom Struggles Outside the South, 1940–1980*, ed. Jeanne F. Theoharis and Komozi Woodard (2003), 223–53; William L.Van DeBurg, *New Day in Babylon: The Black Power Movement and American Culture, 1965–1975* (1992), 170–77; and Jeanne Theoharis, "'W-A-L-K-O-U-T!': High School Students and the Development of Black Power in L.A.," in *Neighborhood Rebels*, ed. Joseph, 107–29. For the Los Angeles BPP, see Judson L. Jeffries and Malcom Foley, "To Live and Die in L.A.," in *Comrades*, ed. Jeffries, 255–90.

12. See Ward Churchill and Jim Vanderwall, *Agents of Repression: The FBI's Secret War against the Black Panther Party and the American Indian Movement* (1990): cartoons, 40–50; Chicago raid, 70–82.

13. Ogbar, *Black Power,* 112.

14. One exception here is William Van DeBurg's *New Day in Babylon* from which our discussion of consumer products is largely drawn.

15. For Black Power in sports, see Van Deburg, *New Day in Babylon*, 83–92; and Amy Bass, *Not the Triumph but the Struggle: The 1968 Olympics and the Making of the Black Athlete* (2002).

16. Mark Anthony Neal, *What the Music Said: Black Popular Music and Black Public Culture* (1999), 31–33; Samuel A. Floyd Jr., *The Power of Black Music: Interpreting Its History from Africa to the United States* (1995), 185–91; and Ogbar, *Black Power*, 110–13.

17. Guthrie P. Ramsey Jr., *Race Music: Black Cultures from Bebop to Hip-Hop* (2003), 149–55.

18. Van Deburg, *New Day in Babylon*, 97–106. For first-person testimony, see the classic Wallace Terry, *Bloods: An Oral History of the Vietnam War by Black Veterans* (1984).

19. For the Tom Bradley story, see Raphael J. Sonnenshein, *Politics in Black and White: Race and Power in Los Angeles* (1993).

Chapter 19. Justice!

1. Gerald David Jaynes and Robin Murphy Williams, eds., *A Common Destiny: Blacks and American Society* (1989), 238; and Emmett Devon Carson, *Black Elected Officials 1991: A National Roster* (1991), xix.

2. Cited in Peter Irons, *Jim Crow's Children: The Broken Promise of the Brown Decision* (2002), 226.

3. Charles R. Lawrence III and Mari J. Matsuda, *We Won't Go Back: Making the Case for Affirmative Action* (1992), 96–100; for an overview of the debate, see John David Skrentny, *The Ironies of Affirmative Action* (1996).

4. The role of race remains clear as newer work has nuanced the picture, by including the effects of black political mobilization after the Voting Rights Act, for example, and by recognizing the inadequacy of "top down" analysis that makes voters the object of actions by national political campaign strategists and politicians. M. V. Hood III, Quentin Kidd, and Irwin L. Morris, *The Rational Southerner: Black Mobilization, Republican Growth, and the Partisan Transformation of the American South* (2012); Earl Black and Merle Black, *The Rise of Southern Republicans* (2002); Tali Mendelberg, *The Race Card: Campaign Strategy, Implicit Messages, and the Norm of Equality* (2001). See also Alexander P. Lammis, ed., *Southern Politics in the 1990s* (1999); Earl Black and Merle Black, *The Vital South: How Presidents Are Elected* (1992).

5. Jefferson Cowie examines pop cultural backlash to suggest how working-class New Deal Democrats became Reagan Republicans to their own detriment in *Stayin' Alive: The 1970s and the Last Days of the Working Class* (2010).

6. John Hope Franklin and Alfred A. Moss Jr., *From Slavery to Freedom: A History of African Americans*, 7th ed. (1994), 533–38.

7. See Michael B. Katz, ed., *The "Underclass" Debate: Views from History* (1993); Herbert Gans, *The War against the Poor* (1995).

8. Besides the *Milwaukee Journal* and the *Milwaukee Sentinel*, sources for the case include interviews with attorneys Walter Kelly (August 1999 and March 2012) and Curry First (June 2001 and January 2012); Kelly's presentation to the Civil Rights Section of the Wisconsin Bar Association Convention, June 2000; and records of the Seventh Circuit Court of Appeals in Chicago for *Patrick Bell, Sr. et al. v. City of Milwaukee, et al.*, 1979, Docket No. 79-C-927.

9. *Jet,* September 27, 1979: 6.

10. For more on Thomas Jacobson's role in Milwaukee civil rights history, see Patrick D. Jones, *Selma of the North: Civil Rights Insurgency in Milwaukee* (2009).

11. Curry First made this assertion in our June 2001 interview and reiterated it in a phone conversation on January 27, 2012.

12. "Favorite son" candidates in several states did this to prevent the well-known segregationist from running unopposed in primaries that took place before Lyndon Johnson declared his candidacy.

13. Interview with Walter Kelly, August 1999. In his presentation to the Civil Rights Section at the Wisconsin State Bar Association convention in 2000, Kelly noted that the panel of judges at the Seventh Circuit Court of Appeals in Chicago also showed a strong commitment to civil rights.

14. For more on the Ernest Lacy case, see Laura R. Woliver, *From Outrage to Action: The Politics of Grass-Roots Dissent* (1993).

15. *Milwaukee Journal*, October 8, 1981.

16. Interview with Walter Kelly, August 1999.

17. Phone and email conversation with Walter Kelly, March 2, 2012.

18. "The Kid, the Cop and the Knife," CBS, *60 Minutes,* November 16, 1980.

19. David Thelan, "Memory and American History," *Journal of American History* 75, no. 4 (March 1989): 1120 and 1123.

20. In a phone conversation on September 9, 1999, Thomas Jacobson declined to be interviewed for this book.

Chapter 20. Love Peoples

1. Thomas J. Sugrue, *Not Even Past: Barack Obama and the Burden of Race* (2010), 8; for other scholarly work on the racial politics of our present history, see Clarence E. Walker and Gregory D. Smithers, *The Preacher and the Politician: Jeremiah Wright, Barack Obama, and Race in America* (2009); and Michael Tesler and David O. Sears, *Obama's Race: The 2008 Election and the Dream of a Post-Racial America* (2010).

2. Statistics show that black unemployment rates continued rising as white rates began decreasing in 2009 and 2010, and that, although poorer education played a role, blacks with college undergraduate and graduate degrees also had significantly higher unemployment rates and took longer to find new jobs than similarly educated whites. See David B. Grusky, Bruce Western, and Christopher Wimer, eds., *The Great Recession* (2011). On housing, the U.S. Department of Justice reached a settlement

agreement with Bank of America in December 2011 to stop pursuing racial discrimination cases against Countrywide Financial, which Bank of America bought in 2008. Evidence showed that, between 2004 and 2007, Countrywide charged higher fees for mortgages and higher interest rates to African American and Hispanic borrowers than to whites with similar incomes and credit scores. All major news outlets carried this story on December 21, 2011.

3. Robert H. Zieger, *For Jobs and Freedom: Race and Labor in America since 1865* (2007), 218.

4. Alex Kotlowitz, *There Are No Children Here* (1991); Jonathan Kozol, *Savage Inequalities: Children in America's Schools* (1991) and *Amazing Grace: The Lives of Children and the Conscience of a Nation* (1995). Aided by radio journalist David Isay, two thirteen-year-olds, LeAlan Jones and Lloyd Newman, provide a firsthand account in *Our America: Life and Death on the South Side of Chicago* (1997). Jonathan Coleman based his dismal assessment of race in post–Civil Rights America on conditions he found in Milwaukee. Jonathan Coleman, *Long Way to Go: Black and White in America* (1997).

5. Jason De Parle follows the stories of three Milwaukee women in *American Dream: Three Women, Ten Kids, and a Nation's Drive to End Welfare* (2004). See also, Gwendolyn Mink, *Welfare's End* (1998); and Sharon Hays, *Flat Broke with Children: Women in the Age of Welfare Reform* (2002).

6. United States Commission on Civil Rights and Marion Frances Berry, *Voting Irregularities in Florida during the 2000 Presidential Election: Report and Appendix* (2003, orig. 2001); Committee on Government Reform of the U.S. House of Representatives, *Election 2000: An Investigation of Voting Irregularities* (2005).

7. *Milwaukee Journal*, January 17, 1987.

8. Interviews with John Dillon, June 29, 2001; John Leicht, June 29, 2001; Kermit Frazier, July 19, 2001.

Sources

Interviews and Oral History

Bell White, Sylvia, and Jody LePage. Madison, WI. Weekly taping sessions from March 22 through May 26, 1998; additional taping on September 30, 1999, and June 24, 2001. Untaped conversations cited: October 10, 2000; September 12, 2001; November 5, 2008; July 4, 2009. Tapes and notes in possession of coauthor LePage.

Dillon, John. Interview by Jody LePage. June 29, 2001. Notes in possession of author.

First, Curry. Interview by Jody LePage. November 22, 2000. Tape in possession of author. Phone conversation. January 27, 2012.

Frazier, Kermit. Interview by Jody LePage. July 19, 2001. Tape in possession of author.

Harpole, Reuben. Interview by Jody LePage. August 28, 1999. Notes in possession of author.

Kelly, Walter. Interview by Jody LePage. August 27, 1999. Tape in possession of author. Phone conversation and email March 2, 2012.

Leicht, John. Interview by Jody LePage. June 29, 2001. Tape and notes in possession of author.

Newspapers and Magazines

Ebony
Jet
Los Angeles Times
Milwaukee Community Journal

Milwaukee Journal
Milwaukee Magazine
Milwaukee Sentinel
Milwaukee Star
Saturday Evening Post

Selected Bibliography

Abu-Lughod, Janet L. *Race, Space, and Riots in Chicago, New York, and Los Angeles*. New York: Oxford University Press, 2007.

Allen, James, Hilton Als, John Lewis, and Leon F. Litwack. *Without Sanctuary: Lynching Photography in America*. Santa Fe: Twin Palms, 2000.

Anderson, James D. *The Education of Blacks in the South: 1860–1935*. Chapel Hill: University of North Carolina Press, 1988.

Baldwin, Davarian L. *Chicago's New Negroes: Modernity, the Great Migration and Black Urban Life*. Chapel Hill: University of North Carolina Press, 2007.

Belt-Beyan, Phyllis M. *The Emergence of African American Literacy Traditions: Family and Community Efforts in the Nineteenth Century*. Westport, CT: Praeger, 2004.

Burstein, Paul. *Discrimination, Jobs and Politics: The Struggle for Equal Employment Opportunity in the United States since the New Deal*. 2d ed. Chicago: University of Chicago Press, 1998.

Cameron, James. *Time of Terror: A Survivor's Story*. Baltimore: Black Classic Press, 1982.

Carson, Clayborne. *In Struggle: SNCC and the Black Awakening of the 1960s*. Cambridge, MA: Harvard University Press, 1981.

Cecelski , David S., and Timothy B. Tyson, eds. *Democracy Betrayed: The Wilmington Race Riot and Its Legacy*. Chapel Hill: University of North Carolina Press, 1998.

Cohen, William. *At Freedom's Edge: Black Mobility and the Southern White Quest for Racial Control, 1861–1915*. Baton Rouge: Louisiana State University Press, 1991.

Cole, David. *No Equal Justice: Race and Class in the American Criminal Justice System*. New York: The New Press, 1999.

Coleman, Monica A. *Making a Way Out of No Way: A Womanist Theology*. Minneapolis: Fortress Press, 2008.

Cone, James H. *Black Theology and Black Power*. New York: Harper & Row, 1969.

Daniels, Peter. *The Shadow of Slavery: Peonage in the South, 1901–1969*. Urbana: University of Illinois Press, 1972.

De Graaf, Lawrence B., Kevin Mulroy, and Quintard Taylor, eds. *Seeking El Dorado: African Americans in California*. Seattle: University of Washington Press, 2001.

Dougherty, Jack. *More Than One Struggle: The Evolution of Black School Reform in Milwaukee*. Chapel Hill: University of North Carolina Press, 2004.

Eden, Lynn. *Crisis in Watertown: The Polarization of a Community*. Ann Arbor: University of Michigan Press, 1973.

Evans, Curtis J. *The Burden of Black Religion*. New York: Oxford University Press, 2008.

Fabre, Geneviève, and Robert O'Meally, eds. *History and Memory in African-American Culture*. New York: Oxford University Press, 1994.

Fairclough, Adam. *A Class of Their Own: Black Teachers in the Segregated South*. Cambridge, MA: Harvard University Press, 2007.

Floyd, Samuel A., Jr. *The Power of Black Music: Interpreting Its History from Africa to the United States*. New York: Oxford University Press, 1995.

Frederick, Marla F. *Between Sundays: Black Women and Everyday Struggles of Faith*. Berkeley: University of California Press, 2003.

Giggie, John. *After Redemption: Jim Crow and the Transformation of African American Religion in the Delta, 1875–1915*. New York: Oxford University Press, 2008.

Gilbert, Charlene, and Quinn Eli. *Homecoming: The Story of African American Farmers*. Boston: Beacon Press, 2000.

Gilmore, Glenda E. *Gender and Jim Crow: Women and the Politics of White Supremacy in North Carolina, 1891–1920*. Chapel Hill: University of North Carolina Press, 1996.

Gilroy, Paul. *The Black Atlantic: Modernity and Double Consciousness*. Cambridge, MA: Harvard University Press, 1993.

Glasrud, Bruce A., and Cary D. Wintz, eds. *The Harlem Renaissance in the American West: The New Negro's Western Experience*. New York: Routledge, 2012.

Grossman, James R. *Land of Hope: Chicago, Black Southerners, and the Great Migration*. Chicago: University of Chicago Press, 1989.

Gurda, John. *The Making of Milwaukee*. Milwaukee: Milwaukee County Historical Society, 1999.

Gutman, Herbert G. *The Black Family in Slavery and Freedom, 1750–1925*. New York: Pantheon, 1976.

Hall, Gwendolyn Midlo. *Africans in Colonial Louisiana: The Development of AfroCreole Culture in the Eighteenth Century*. Baton Rouge: Louisiana State University Press, 1992.

Harrison, Daphne Duval. *Black Pearls: Blues Queens of the 1920s*. New Brunswick, NJ: Rutgers University Press, 1988.

Hazzard-Gordon, Katrina. *Jookin': The Rise of Social Dance Formations in African American Culture*. Philadelphia: Temple University Press, 1990.

Hine, Darlene Clark. *Hine Sight: Black Women and the Re-construction of American History*. Bloomington: Indiana University Press, 1994.

Hine, Darlene Clark, Wilma King, and Linda Reed, eds. *We Specialize in the Wholly Impossible: A Reader in Black Women's History*. New York: New York University Press, 1995.

Hine, Darlene Clark, and Kathleen Thompson, eds. *A Shining Thread of Hope: The History of Black Women in America*. New York: Broadway Books, 1998.

Irons, Peter. *Jim Crow's Children: The Broken Promise of the Brown Decision*. New York: Penguin Books, 2002.

Jones, Jacqueline. *Labor of Love, Labor of Sorrow: Black Women, Work and the Family, from Slavery to the Present*. New York: Basic Books, 1985.

Jones, LeAlan, and Lloyd Newman with David Isay. *Our America: Life and Death on the South Side of Chicago*. New York: Washington Square Press, 1997.

Jones, Patrick D. *The Selma of the North: Civil Rights Insurgency in Milwaukee*. Cambridge, MA: Harvard University Press, 2009.

Jones, William P. *The Tribe of Black Ulysses: African American Lumber Workers in the Jim Crow South*. Urbana and Chicago: University of Illinois Press, 2005.

Joseph, Peniel E. *Waiting 'Til the Midnight Hour: A Narrative History of Black Power in America*. New York: Holt, 2006.

———, ed. *Neighborhood Rebels: Black Power at the Local Level*. New York: Palgrave Macmillan, 2010.

Kersten, Andrew E. *Race, Jobs and the War: The FEPC in the Midwest, 1941–46*. Urbana: University of Illinois Press, 2007.

King, Wilma. *Stolen Childhood: Slave Youth in 19th-Century America*. Bloomington: Indiana University Press, 1995.

Kozol, Jonathan. *Savage Inequalities: Children in America's Schools*. New York: Crown Publishers, 1991.

Margo, Robert A. *Race and Schooling in the South, 1880 to 1950: An Economic History*. Chicago: University of Chicago Press, 1990.

McDonald, Roderick A. *The Economy and Material Culture of Slaves: Goods and Chattels on the Sugar Plantations of Jamaica and Louisiana*. Baton Rouge: Louisiana State University Press, 1993.

McGuire, Danielle. *At the Dark End of the Street: Black Women, Rape and Resistance—A New History of the Civil Rights Movement*. New York: Knopf, 2010.

Meyer, Stephen Grant. *As Long as They Don't Move Next Door: Segregation and Racial Conflict in American Neighborhoods*. Lanham, MD: Rowman and Littlefield, 2000.

Miller, Keith D. *Voice of Deliverance: The Language of Martin Luther King, Jr.* Athens: University of Georgia Press, 1992.

Mullings, Leith. *On Our Own Terms: Race, Class, and Gender in the Lives of African American Women*. New York: Routledge, 1997.

Ogbar, Jeffrey O. G. *Black Power: Radical Politics and African American Identity*. Baltimore: Johns Hopkins University Press, 2004.

Olson, Lynne. *Freedom's Daughters: The Unsung Heroines of the Civil Rights Movement, 1830–1970*. New York: Scribner, 2001.

Price, Richard. *Maroon Societies: Rebel Slave Communities in the Americas*. 3d ed. Baltimore: Johns Hopkins University Press, 1996.

Raboteau, Albert J. *Slave Religion: The "Invisible Institution" in the Antebellum South*. 2d ed. New York: Oxford University Press, 2004.

Ramsey, Guthrie P., Jr. *Race Music: Black Cultures from Bebop to Hip-Hop*. Berkeley: University of California Press, 2003.

Rawick, George. *From Sundown to Sunup: The Making of the Black Community*. Westport, CT: Greenwood Press, 1972.

Rosengarten, Theodore. *All God's Dangers: The Life of Nate Shaw*. New York: Knopf, 1974.

Sides, Josh. *L.A. City Limits: African American Los Angeles from the Great Depression to the Present*. Berkeley: University of California Press, 2003.

Sklaroff, Lauren Rebecca. *Black Culture and the New Deal: The Quest for Civil Rights in the Roosevelt Era*. Chapel Hill: University of North Carolina Press, 2009.

Skrentny, John David. *The Ironies of Affirmative Action: Politics, Culture and Justice in America*. Chicago: University of Chicago Press, 1996.

Smith, Margaret Charles, and Linda Janet Holmes. *Listen to Me Good: The Life Story of an Alabama Midwife*. Columbus: Ohio State University Press, 1996.

Staples, Robert, and Leonor Boulin Johnson. *Black Families at the Crossroads: Challenges and Prospects*. San Francisco: Jossey-Bass, 1993.

Sterling, Dorothy, ed. *The Trouble They Seen: Black People Tell the Story of Reconstruction*. Garden City, NY: Doubleday, 1976.

Sugrue, Thomas J. *Not Even Past: Barack Obama and the Burden of Race*. Princeton: Princeton University Press, 2010.

———. *The Origins of the Urban Crisis: Race and Inequality in Postwar Detroit*. Princeton: Princeton University Press, 1996.

———. *Sweet Land of Liberty: The Forgotten Struggle for Civil Rights in the North*. New York: Random House, 2008.

Sullivan, Patricia. *Days of Hope: Race and Democracy in the New Deal Era*. Chapel Hill: University of North Carolina Press, 1996.

Theoharis, Jeanne F., and Komozi Woodard, eds. *Freedom North: Black Freedom Struggles Outside the South, 1940–1980*. New York: Palgrave Macmillan, 2003.

———, eds. *Groundwork: Local Black Freedom Movements in America*. New York: New York University Press, 2005.

Thompson, William F. *Continuity and Change, 1940–1965*. Vol. 6 of *The History of Wisconsin*. Madison: State Historical Society of Wisconsin, 1988.

Tolnay, Stewart E., and E. M. Beck. *A Festival of Violence: An Analysis of Southern Lynchings, 1882–1930*. Urbana: University of Illinois Press, 1995.

Trotter, Joe William, Jr. *Black Milwaukee: The Making of an Industrial Proletariat, 1915–1945*. Urbana: University of Illinois Press, 1984.

———, ed. *The Great Migration in Historical Perspective: New Dimensions of Race, Class, and Gender*. Bloomington: Indiana University Press, 1991.

Tyson, Timothy B. *Blood Done Sign My Name*. Chapel Hill: University of North Carolina Press, 2004.

———. *Radio Free Dixie: Robert F. Williams and the Roots of Black Power*. Chapel Hill: University of North Carolina Press, 1999.

Van De Burg, William L. *New Day in Babylon: The Black Power Movement and American Culture, 1965–1975*. Chicago: University of Chicago Press, 1992.

Vincent, Stephen A. *Southern Seed, Northern Soil: African-American Farm Communities in the Midwest*. Bloomington: Indiana University Press, 1999.

West, William Rudolph. *The Education of Booker T. Washington: American Democracy and the Idea of Race Relations*. New York: Columbia University Press, 2006.

Western, Bruce. *Punishment and Inequality in America.* New York: Russell Sage Foundation, 2006.

Williams, Heather Andrea. *Self Taught: African American Education in Slavery and Freedom.* Chapel Hill: University of North Carolina Press, 2005.

White, Deborah Gray. *Too Heavy a Load: Black Women in Defense of Themselves, 1894–1994.* New York: W.W. Norton, 1999.

Wintz, Cary D. *Black Culture and the Harlem Renaissance.* College Station: Texas A&M University Press, 1996.

Woliver, Laura R. *From Outrage to Action: The Politics of Grass-Roots Dissent.* Urbana: University of Illinois Press, 1993.

Yinger, John. *Closed Doors, Opportunities Lost: The Continuing Costs of Housing Discrimination.* New York: Russell Sage Foundation, 1997.

Zieger, Robert H. *For Jobs and Freedom: Race and Labor in America since 1865.* Lexington: University Press of Kentucky, 2007.

Index

Wisconsin Studies in Autobiography

William L. Andrews
General Editor

Robert F. Sayre
The Examined Self: Benjamin Franklin, Henry Adams, Henry James

Daniel B. Shea
Spiritual Autobiography in Early America

Lois Mark Stalvey
The Education of a WASP

Margaret Sams
Forbidden Family: A Wartime Memoir of the Philippines, 1941–1945
Edited with an introduction by Lynn Z. Bloom

Charlotte Perkins Gilman
The Living of Charlotte Perkins Gilman: An Autobiography
Introduction by Ann J. Lane

Mark Twain
Mark Twain's Own Autobiography: The Chapters from the "North American Review"
Edited by Michael J. Kiskis

Jim Lane
The Autobiographical Documentary in America

Sandra Pouchet Paquet
Caribbean Autobiography: Cultural Identity and Self-Representation

Mark O'Brien, with Gillian Kendall
How I Became a Human Being: A Disabled Man's Quest for Independence

Elizabeth L. Banks
Campaigns of Curiosity: Journalistic Adventures of an American Girl
    in Late Victorian London
Introduction by Mary Suzanne Schriber and Abbey L. Zink

Miriam Fuchs
The Text Is Myself: Women's Life Writing and Catastrophe

Jean M. Humez
Harriet Tubman: The Life and the Life Stories

Voices Made Flesh: Performing Women's Autobiography
Edited by Lynn C. Miller, Jacqueline Taylor, and M. Heather Carver

Loreta Janeta Velazquez
The Woman in Battle: The Civil War Narrative of Loreta Janeta Velazquez, Cuban Woman
    and Confederate Soldier
Introduction by Jesse Alemán

Cathryn Halverson
Maverick Autobiographies: Women Writers and the American West, 1900–1936

Jeffrey Brace
The Blind African Slave: Or Memoirs of Boyrereau Brinch, Nicknamed Jeffrey Brace
as told to Benjamin F. Prentiss, Esq.
Edited with an introduction by Kari J. Winter

Colette Inez
The Secret of M. Dulong: A Memoir

Before They Could Vote: American Women's Autobiographical Writing, 1819–1919
Edited by Sidonie Smith and Julia Watson

Bertram J. Cohler
Writing Desire: Sixty Years of Gay Autobiography

Philip Holden
Autobiography and Decolonization: Modernity, Masculinity, and the Nation-State

Jing M. Wang
When "I" Was Born: Women's Autobiography in Modern China

*Conjoined Twins in Black and White: The Lives of Millie-Christine McKoy and Daisy and
    Violet Hilton*
Edited by Linda Frost

Four Russian Serf Narratives
Translated, edited, and with an introduction by John MacKay

Mark Twain
Mark Twain's Own Autobiography: The Chapters from the "North American Review,"
    second edition
Edited by Michael J. Kiskis

Graphic Subjects: Critical Essays on Autobiography and Graphic Novels
Edited by Michael A. Chaney

Omar Ibn Said
A Muslim American Slave: The Life of Omar Ibn Said
Translated from the Arabic, edited, and with an introduction by Ala Alryyes

Sister: An African American Life in Search of Justice
Sylvia Bell White and Jody LePage

KISHWAUKEE COLLEGE LIBRARY

3.7943 10117 363

**Sister : an African American life in
search of justice / Sylvia Bell White
and Jody LePage.**

F589.M653 W47 2013
Gen Stx

DATE DUE

PRINTED IN U.S.A.

Kishwaukee College Library
21193 Malta Road
Malta, IL 60150-9699